RETHINKING JOURNALISM

There is no doubt, journalism faces challenging times. Since the turn of the millennium the financial health of the news industry is failing, mainstream audiences are on the decline and professional authority, credibility and autonomy are eroding. The outlook is bleak and it's understandable that many are pessimistic. But this book argues that we have to rethink journalism fundamentally.

Rather than just focus on the symptoms of the 'crisis of journalism', *Rethinking Journalism* tries to understand the structural transformation journalism is undergoing. It explores how the news media attempts to combat decreasing levels of trust, how emerging forms of news affect the established journalistic field, and how participatory culture creates new dialogues between journalists and audiences. Crucially, it does not treat these developments as distinct transformations. Instead it considers how their interrelation accounts for both the tribulations of the news media and the need for contemporary journalism to redefine itself.

Contributors: Stuart Allan, Chris Atton, Kevin Barnhurst, Jo Bogaerts, Kees Brants, Marcel Broersma, Nico Carpentier, Amira Firdaus, Todd Graham, Thomas Hanitzsch, Ansgard Heinrich, Brian McNair, Chris Peters, Colin Porlezza, Stephan Russ-Mohl, Michael Schudson, Ingrid Volkmer, Tamara Witschge.

Chris Peters is Assistant Professor at the Centre for Media and Journalism Studies, University of Groningen, the Netherlands. His most recent edited publication is *Retelling Journalism* (2012).

Marcel Broersma is Professor of Journalism Studies and Media at the University of Groningen, the Netherlands. He is currently director of the Groningen Centre for Media and Journalism Studies and acting head of the Journalism department. His recent edited publications in English include *Form and Style in Journalism, European Newspapers and the Representation of News, 1880–2005* (2007) and *Retelling Journalism* (2012).

RETHINKING JOURNALISM

Trust and participation in a transformed news landscape

Edited by
Chris Peters and Marcel Broersma

Routledge
Taylor & Francis Group

LONDON AND NEW YORK

First published 2013
by Routledge
2 Park Square, Milton Park, Abingdon, Oxon OX14 4RN

Simultaneously published in the USA and Canada
by Routledge
711 Third Avenue, New York, NY 10017

Routledge is an imprint of the Taylor & Francis Group, an informa business

British Library Cataloguing in Publication Data
A catalogue record for this book is available from the British Library

Library of Congress Cataloging in Publication Data
Rethinking journalism : trust and participation in a transformed news landscape /
edited by Chris Peters and Marcel Broersma.
p. cm.
Includes bibliographical references and index.
1. Journalism – History – 21st century. 2. Journalistic ethics. 3. Journalism –
Technological innovations. 4. Citizen journalism. 5. Online journalism. I. Peters,
Chris, 1977-II. Broersma, Marcel Jeroen, 1973-
PN4815.2.R48 2012
070.4 – dc23
2012010118

ISBN: 978-0-415-69701-9 (hbk)
ISBN: 978-0-415-69702-6 (pbk)
ISBN: 978-0-203-10268-8 (ebk)

Typeset in Bembo
by Taylor & Francis Books

CONTENTS

List of tables   viii
List of contributors   ix

Introduction: Rethinking journalism: the structural
transformation of a public good   1
Marcel Broersma and Chris Peters

PART I
Public trust in journalism   **13**

1   Trust, cynicism, and responsiveness: the uneasy situation of
    journalism in democracy   15
    Kees Brants

2   A refractured paradigm: journalism, hoaxes and the challenge
    of trust   28
    Marcel Broersma

3   Getting the facts straight in a digital era: journalistic accuracy
    and trustworthiness   45
    Colin Porlezza and Stephan Russ-Mohl

4   The postmodern challenge to journalism: strategies for
    constructing a trustworthy identity   60
    Jo Bogaerts and Nico Carpentier

PART II
Participatory forms of journalism 73

5 Trust, truth and objectivity: sustaining quality journalism
  in the era of the content-generating user 75
  Brian McNair

6 News making as an interactive practice: global news exchange
  and network journalism 89
  Ansgard Heinrich

7 Between networks and 'hierarchies of credibility': navigating
  journalistic practice in a sea of user-generated content 101
  Ingrid Volkmer and Amira Firdaus

8 Talking back, but is anyone listening? Journalism and
  comment fields 114
  Todd Graham

PART III
Emerging journalisms 129

9 Separate, supplementary or seamless? Alternative news and
  professional journalism 131
  Chris Atton

10 Journalism as interpretive performance: the case of WikiLeaks 144
  Stuart Allan

11 Transforming journalistic practice: a profession caught
  between change and tradition 160
  Tamara Witschge

12 'Even better than being informed': satirical news and
  media literacy 173
  Chris Peters

PART IV
Rethinking journalism rethought 189

13 Would journalism please hold still! 191
  Michael Schudson

14 Journalism, participative media and trust in a comparative context   200
   Thomas Hanitzsch

15 'Trust me, I'm an innovative journalist,' and other fictions   210
   Kevin G. Barnhurst

Bibliography   221
Index   245

TABLES

1.1	Responsiveness of media and journalism	23
3.1	Error types ranked by per cent of stories	51
3.2	Causes attributed to errors ranked by per cent of stories	52
3.3	Pearson correlation coefficients for accuracy measures with credibility	53
8.1	Type and frequency of claims used	119
8.2	Sources used by journalists and participants	121

CONTRIBUTORS

Stuart Allan is Professor of Journalism in the Media School, Bournemouth University, UK. His recent books include *The Routledge Companion to News and Journalism* (revised edition, 2011), *Journalism After September 11* (co-edited with Barbie Zelizer, 2nd edition, Routledge, 2011) and *Citizen Witnessing* (2012). He is currently researching and writing about photojournalism, with a particular interest in citizen contributions to war, conflict and crisis reporting.

Chris Atton is Professor of Media and Culture in the School of Arts and Creative Industries at Edinburgh Napier University, Scotland. He has made special studies of alternative media, fanzines, the media of new social movements and new media in Africa. His books include *Alternative Media* (Sage, 2002), *An Alternative Internet* (Edinburgh University Press, 2004) and *Alternative Journalism* (Sage, 2008). His current research examines how audiences make aesthetic sense of free improvisation and other 'difficult' musics.

Kevin Barnhurst is Professor of Communication at the University of Illinois, Chicago. He is the author of seven award-winning books and monographs, including *Seeing the Newspaper* (St. Martin's Press, 1994), *The Form of News,* with John Nerone (Guilford Press, 2001), and *Media Queered* (Peter Lang, 2007), as well as more than a hundred communication research articles, essays, book chapters, reviews and commentaries.

Jo Bogaerts is affiliated to the department of German Literature and the Institute of Jewish Studies at the University of Antwerp and is a member of the university's Centre for Philosophy of Culture. Currently, he is working on a dissertation on the French existentialist reception of Franz Kafka. He has published on journalistic rituals as 'performativity' and the controversy surrounding the Dutch journalist Joris Luyendijk, and has contributed to a series of articles on documentary film.

Kees Brants is Honorary Professor at the University of Amsterdam's School of Communication Research (ASCoR) and Emeritus Professor of Politics and Media at the University of Leiden. He specializes in, and has published extensively about, political communication, media policy and journalism studies. In 2011 Palgrave issued his *Political Communication in Postmodern Democracy: Challenging the Primacy of Politics*, edited with Katrin Voltmer.

Marcel Broersma is Professor of Journalism Studies at the Centre for Media and Journalism Studies, University of Groningen, the Netherlands, and heads its journalism programmes and research centre. He is the author of numerous books and articles in Dutch and English on both the history of and current developments in journalism, with a strong focus on comparative studies. He currently directs a research project that investigates the transformations in form, style and strategies of European journalism between 1880 and 2005. In 2007 he edited the volume *Form and Style in Journalism. European Newspapers and the Representation of News, 1880–2005* (Peeters).

Nico Carpentier is Associate Professor at the Communication Studies Department of the Vrije Universiteit Brussel (VUB – Free University of Brussels) and Lecturer at Charles University in Prague. He is also vice-president of the European Communication Research and Education Association (ECREA). His theoretical focus is on discourse theory, and his research interests are situated in the relationship between media, journalism, politics and culture, especially towards social domains as war and conflict, ideology, participation and democracy.

Todd Graham is a Postdoctoral Research Fellow at the Centre for Media and Journalism Studies, University of Groningen, the Netherlands. He earned his PhD from the Amsterdam School of Communication Research (ASCoR), University of Amsterdam. His main research interests include (new) media and democracy, popular culture and democracy, online participatory journalism, online deliberation and public-sphere theory. Recent articles have appeared in the *European Journal of Communication*, *Javnost – The Public* and the *Journal of Information Technology and Politics*.

Amira Firdaus is currently completing her PhD at the University of Melbourne. Her thesis deals with journalistic integration of social-media sources, and her wider academic interests include global journalism, 24-hour news channels, news agencies and journalists' lived experience. She is a member of the founding editorial team of *Platform: Journal of Media and Communication* and a tutor at the University of Malaya in Malaysia.

Thomas Hanitzsch is Professor of Communication at the University of Munich, Germany. He founded and chaired the Journalism Studies Division of the International Communication Association. A former journalist, his teaching and research focuses on global journalism cultures, war coverage, celebrity news and comparative methodology. He is the Editor-in-Chief of *Communication Theory* and has co-edited

The Handbook of Journalism Studies (Routledge, 2009) and *The Handbook of Comparative Communication Research* (Routledge, 2012).

Ansgard Heinrich is Assistant Professor at the Centre for Media and Journalism Studies, University of Groningen, the Netherlands. She specializes in global journalism studies and digital media. She gained her PhD from the University of Otago in New Zealand and was honorary research fellow at the University of Melbourne. Prior to her academic career she worked freelance as a local radio journalist in Germany. She is the author of *Network Journalism: Journalistic Practice in Interactive Spheres* (Routledge, 2011).

Brian McNair is Professor of Journalism, Media and Communication at Queensland University of Technology, Brisbane. He is the author of many books and articles on journalism, including *The Sociology of Journalism* (Arnold, 1998), *Journalism and Democracy* (Routledge, 2000), *Cultural Chaos* (Routledge, 2006) and *Journalists in Film* (Edinburgh University Press, 2010). His work has been translated into fourteen languages.

Chris Peters is Assistant Professor at the Centre for Media and Journalism Studies, University of Groningen, the Netherlands. Along with this volume and *Retelling Journalism* (co-edited with Marcel Broersma, Peeters, forthcoming) he has published articles in *Journalism Studies* and *Journalism: Theory, Practice and Criticism*. He is currently researching the changing audience experiences, patterns, and spaces of news consumption in the contemporary digital age.

Colin Porlezza is a PhD student at the Università della Svizzera Italiana in Lugano, Switzerland. He is research and teaching assistant at the Institute of Media and Journalism as well as collaborator for the European Journalism Observatory (EJO). He is working on a dissertation project about the 'Bridges over the Chinese Wall – Newsrooms in the Focus of Economic and Journalistic Interests'. His research interests are the relationship between journalism and advertising, online journalism as well as media accountability.

Stephan Russ-Mohl is Professor of Journalism and Media Management at the Institute for Media and Journalism, Università della Svizzera Italiana, in Lugano, Switzerland. His current research interests include the quality of media and media management, media journalism, economic theory of journalism, and comparative journalism research. Russ-Mohl is also director of the European Journalism Observatory, an institute designed to build bridges connecting journalism cultures across Europe and the US, facilitating collaboration between media researchers and practitioners.

Michael Schudson is Professor of Journalism at the Columbia Journalism School, Columbia University. He is also Emeritus Distinguished Professor at the University of

California, San Diego. His most recent works are *Why Democracies Need an Unlovable Press* (Polity, 2008) and a second edition of *The Sociology of News* (W. W. Norton, 2011). He also co-authored with Leonard Downie, Jr. a report on the future of news, 'The Reconstruction of American Journalism' (2009). That report can be found on the Columbia Journalism School website or in Robert McChesney and Victor Pickard's *Will the Last Reporter Please Turn Out the Lights* (New Press, 2011).

Ingrid Volkmer is Associate Professor, University of Melbourne and Senior Fellow, London School of Economics (Global Governance). She has published widely in the area of global political communication, including *News in Public Memory: An International Study of Media Memories Across Generations* (Peter Lang, 2006).

Tamara Witschge is Rosalind Franklin Fellow at the Centre for Media and Journalism Studies, University of Groningen, the Netherlands. From 2007 to 2009 Witschge was a research associate at Goldsmiths Leverhulme Media Research Centre and worked on the 'Spaces of News' project, which explored the ways in which technological, economic and social change is reconfiguring journalism. She has published widely on this topic, and while lecturing at the Cardiff School for Journalism, Media and Cultural Studies, co-authored the book *Changing Journalism* (Routledge, 2011). Tamara is the General Secretary of European Communication Research and Education Association (ECREA) and a member of the editorial board of various international journals, including *New Media & Society*.

INTRODUCTION

Rethinking journalism: the structural transformation of a public good

Marcel Broersma and Chris Peters

There is no doubt, journalism faces challenging times. Since the turn of the millennium, the financial health of the news industry is failing, mainstream audiences are on the decline, and professional authority, credibility and autonomy are eroding. While over the course of the twentieth century, mass media succeeded in unifying large communities of readers – and in some instances they still do – this seems to be disintegrating. The market for news, traditionally structured by supply through mass media, is now increasingly guided by the demands of ever-fragmenting audiences. Consumers have far more possibilities to obtain news whenever and wherever they want and they at least feel they have the capabilities to navigate the news themselves. What do they need journalism for when they can get personalized information at any time for free?

Some fear this might lead to the deterioration of the profession. Revenues from readership and advertising are shrinking, especially in the US and Europe; newspapers are merged, closed or go online-only; and journalists at traditional media companies are losing their jobs. The dire warnings about the influence of market logic on the news media seem to be coming true, which may mean that shareholders, advertisers, and the public will refuse to keep funding the 'journalism we need'. Cuts in funding beget shortcuts in production and the worry is that a lack of resources for proper reporting leads to a decline in the overall quality of news, which quickly descends in a downward spiral (Davies, 2008). 'Will the last reporter please turn out the lights?' asks a volume on the depressing state of the US news industry (McChesney and Picard, 2011). The outlook is indeed bleak, and it is understandable that many are pessimistic.

Attempts to address these recent transformations in the profession are often negative because they usually start from the perspective of what will be lost if current trends are to continue. While there is a certain level of agreement in scholarship on the importance of journalism for democracy and civil engagement, as well as over the existence of a contemporary economic and professional crisis, the scale of the decline and the harm this does to democracy are perceived differently. Most authors stop short of predicting some sort of future equivalent of a journalistic nuclear winter; an informational wasteland populated by dazed and uninformed citizens, wandering about, texting and tweeting the latest celebrity gossip on their iPhones, unaware of politics or social issues. Yet many do argue that young adults seem to be 'tuning out' from the news, a trend that they find worrisome for democracy as the next generation comes of age (Mindich, 2005). Other observers have swung in the opposite direction, and tend to preach journalism's historical resilience. They argue that journalism is a remarkably robust institution that has always been, and always will be, capable of absorbing change.

What both perspectives have in common, however, is the basic assumption that journalism primarily has to adapt to technological and economic changes in order to survive. Many point at journalism's business model as being outdated, implying that the 'crisis of journalism' is first and foremost a crisis of funding that, some suggest, could be resolved by viable alternatives like micro-financing, apps and paywalls, or government and public funding (cf. McChesney and Picard, 2011). Others believe that journalism has to do a better job anticipating the rise and impact of digitization, the internet and social media. If outlets can find innovative ways to distribute news, and if newsrooms can incorporate new technologies in journalism practice, the idea is that journalism can move – more or less undamaged – into a new era. Depending on the diagnosis, the range of possible cures is infinite.

Discussions concentrate, in sum, on the symptoms of the crisis, or the traditional conception of journalism. But the changing nature of the object itself often goes unnoticed. Moreover, since the challenges it faces are usually the analytic point of departure, it is easy to fall into the trap of quarantining the analysis of journalism from interconnected transformations in the broader media landscape. Much of this is because the focus is generally on the democratic deficit were the journalistic infrastructure to collapse, or on how journalism adapts to technological innovations. A primary thrust seems to be the idea that, with a few well-thought-out tweaks, journalism will keep itself relevant because its societal importance is self-evident. Solutions to journalism's ills are thus generally looked at in terms of modifying the pre-existing structure of the news media to adapt to the changing environment. This urge to try to address the symptoms of the crisis is understandable, and is a good first step to move beyond apocalyptic visions to tangible solutions. However, we think this still misses the point somewhat. What is regularly overlooked in these conversations is asking what the profession of journalism 'is', and how it defines itself.

Research that strives to conceptualize the dynamics of change, and to understand the structure of transformation, is scarce. The fundaments of journalism, at least in terms of its professional ideology, remain largely unquestioned by both journalists and academics. And while the *societal role* of journalism may be enshrined in many influential documents – the idea of a free press being fairly central to democracy – unfortunately, its *societal relevance* is not. Journalism tends to try to give the public what journalists think it needs or wants, so the profession tries to adapt to its current crisis by treating symptoms of its perceived ailment. Declining audiences are considered in terms of 'how do we get them back'; declining profits in terms of 'how do we increase revenues'; declining influence in terms of 'how do we make ourselves matter'? At first glance this seems reasonable. But what such thinking doesn't recognize (or perhaps, more accurately, doesn't want to recognize) is that the symptoms are part of a significant structural change which can't be undone.

This book argues that the problems journalism is facing are far more structural than is often voiced and that to prepare the profession for the next century, we have to rethink journalism fundamentally. What strikes us about current scholarly, professional and social debates is the supposed stability of the object being discussed – journalism – and the commonality of what is considered. Aspiring to the idea of a mass press, distributing information to a mass public, employing a managerial discourse of acting 'for the good of the public' may work well in constitutional documents and philosophical treatises, but it's a fairly unconnected and wishful self-definition in the current multi-media, digital environment. Basically, the point for many seems to be to hold onto this object, 'professional journalism', as tightly as possible, as though if we lose our grip on it, it is no longer journalism we have. If journalism alters its goals, practices, content and conventions too much, so the story goes, we don't know what this future journalism would look like or what we would call it, but we are quite sure we know what it wouldn't be. After over a decade's worth of debate about the chaos in the industry, many of these discussions are, by now, quite familiar, and maybe even a little bit stale.

An apt metaphor for the challenge journalism faces might be found with climate change. Climate-change scientists can point to a number of problematic indicators: rising sea levels, unstable temperature patterns, the deteriorating ozone layer, retreating glaciers, and so forth. Yet most will say that any proposed solution also demands a fundamental reconceptualization of our relationship to the environment. If we don't rethink concepts like progress, innovation, production, and sustainability we will face an increasingly polluted planet, where resources are scarce, and the quality of life is on the decline. Similarly, if we don't rethink concepts like trust, participation, and engagement – if we don't recognize that journalism itself must change in response to our relationship with information – we will face an increasingly feeble profession, alienated from the public it claims to serve, whose relevance is on the wane. The aim of this book is to rethink journalism, considering trends in a less fatalistic light, without practicing a naïve optimism that ignores its uncertainties. To reinvigorate discussion on its current situation and future cures, we will first discuss what we consider to be two intertwined trends that underlie the structural transformations of journalism: de-industrialization and de-ritualization.

The de-industrialization of information

The key to journalism's success in the past century might be that it effectively claimed to be of crucial importance for democracy and society in general, while substantiating and reconciling this rhetorical claim with an orientation on the market.

As a public good and a watchdog of the citizenry, journalism established itself parallel to the expansion of democracy and suffrage, and the rise of the industrial society. It thus succeeded in positioning itself in the heart of what Schudson (1978) has called a 'democratic market society'. By reaching out to as many people as possible and catering to their demands for various kinds of information, while simultaneously claiming to represent them politically, journalism established itself as a commodity that was not just valuable for the well-being of individual citizens but also necessary for a healthy society at large. By constructing social reality on a daily basis, it builds and connects communities. It provides the glue that binds parts of society together.

Accordingly, one can say that as an industry, journalism is first and foremost characterized by its focus on a mass audience and mass production. It is driven by and developed around an inherent industrial focus on standardized production and economies of scale. Just as the creation of the mass-market automobile was the result of industrial logic brought to transportation, the rise of the mass press was the result of industrial logic *brought to information*. Journalism disseminates a limited amount of identical information in a fixed order to a mass audience in an efficient, attractive, relatively cheap and convenient way. News consumers can, like in a department store, pick from every individual issue or broadcast whatever they consider interesting, useful or just fun to read, listen to or watch. However, contrary to shoppers, they are charged for the whole package, and usually before they even know what they will be buying or what it will look like. This 'trick' is essential to journalism's business model. In the past, consumers were prepared to pay for this because journalism was the most important tool for obtaining not just information on current events and developments, but also everyday practical information like movie programmes, weather reports and arts reviews, and – maybe just as important as these categories – advertisements that helped them to find jobs, houses, partners and bargains. Advertisers, from multinationals to local stores, were equally eager to pay for journalism because it put them in touch with a wide audience. Moreover, they did not have (many) alternatives. Key to all of this was that journalism in various ways connected people to the democratic market society. It succeeded in positioning itself as an essential commodity to navigate daily life, a rich source of knowledge to climb the social ladder, and an invaluable asset to breed an informed citizenry that fuelled democracy.

Over the course of the twentieth century, journalism successfully created an information monopoly because it controlled the distribution channels for news, advertising and other current information. This obviously has changed. The digitization of information, the innovation of home equipment to produce media content, and the rise of the internet as a free and easily accessible distribution channel has eroded journalism's position. Much of what made journalism 'journalism' in the twentieth century – basically the industrialization of information – therefore no longer works. Citizens increasingly stop consuming news and information in a linear way through one or a few mass media, but literally assemble information associatively by interacting with it online. They go on the internet for 'free' news and information from various sources that satisfy their needs and interests. They upload content on community sites, blogs or social networks. They assess information by comparing different websites and then discuss these current issues, as well as their personal affairs, in online fora. And they visit the web to consult film listings, check Craigslist or other sites for classifieds, look at real-estate aggregators for house listings, head to travel sites to book cheap plane tickets, hotels and tours, check continuously updated weather apps for up-to-the minute radar imaging and reports, find a new love on a relationship site, and so on.

A major problem for journalism is thus that it tries to tackle the technological and social transformations of today with the logic of yesterday. Every aspect of the news industry is organized according to the principles of scale, which solved the issue of how to produce and distribute knowledge to a mass audience in a profitable way. However, it simply does not work, or is not good enough anymore, in a world with cheaper, faster and more 'personalizable' options. The original industrial function of journalism no longer matches its use-function. One-to-many communication with a strong dominance of the outlet that not only determines the content but also determines its use has been replaced by networked communication in which citizens have more power. This implies that both the news industry and journalism have to transform fundamentally to anticipate the new environment. They have to de-industrialize. This is a tough challenge, however, because of the dominance of industrial logic in every thread of the industry and the profession. One could discern at least three levels on which de-industrialization should take place: journalism's business model, its production process, and the paradigm that guides journalism practice and, accordingly, its societal function.

First, as is concluded by many observers, journalism's business model seems to be outdated. Firmly rooted in the notion of mass marketing and economies of scale, it rests on two pillars: revenues from readers, listeners and viewers and, of course, advertising. These sources are mutually dependent: when circulation increases, the rates of advertisements will follow. This interplay has in the past led to an upward spiral which resulted in obtaining information monopolies – more readers meant more advertisers and revenues, which in turn allowed an outlet to invest in the quality and breadth of its reporting, which consequently (it was hoped) attracted a larger audience, and so on. However, the inverse relationship also held true. When the circulation or number of viewers dropped, the outlet would fall into a downward spiral from which it was hard, if not impossible, to escape. This is what happened in many local, regional and even national markets over the course of the twentieth century. In many cities of the world only one major catch-all outlet survived. Today many of these 'dinosaurs' – mainly newspapers that, it should be noted, not only employ most journalists but are also far more important for the informational infra-structure than radio and television stations – have gotten into trouble themselves. They try to compensate for the decline in readership and advertising revenues with cuts and raising subscription rates, but this only compensates for short-term losses. In the long run this – industrial – strategy will probably be disastrous. After eating all the other species they are now cannibalizing themselves.

New technological opportunities have also affected the position of advertisers. For them, it has become far easier to reach out to specific target groups themselves through direct marketing, websites and databases, based upon the aggregation of personal information of (potential) customers. Moreover, advertisers are increasingly dissatisfied with the logic of scale and one-to-many communication through news media. They aim less at reaching a large, singular audience, but rather want to target specific groups of consumers that are of possible commercial interest through media. Quantity, as such, is not good enough anymore: advertisers want to have a clear insight in the specifics of the people they reach with their ads. This desire for personalized marketing on the part of advertisers potentially conflicts with another law of scale that says that it is profitable to diminish production costs by acquiring as many outlets as possible, merging them or, at least, standardizing and rationalizing all processes of individual outlets. This strategy of selling 'mass' to advertisers, which many media outlets and media chains employed over the past century, resulted in a loss of organizational flexibility and a decreased ability to tailor content and distribution to specific audience demands. To turn this around, the business model has to be de-industrialized.

Second, every step in the production process – from the processing of information, to printing or broadcasting, to distribution – is organized according to industrial principles. To get the news out on time to as many people as possible, fixed deadlines are set for every department involved, and the production of both news and news outlets is to a large extent routinized. There is no time for delay and it is nearly impossible to diverge from the planned organizational patterns. As a consequence, a large degree of social control and discipline is present in news companies, even for journalists who, contrary to those involved in the technical production of news, tend to envision themselves as bohemians with much freedom. The domestication of news workers is still an ongoing project but has, according to many 'old hacks', now reached a level with which they are, to put it mildly, not comfortable (Davies, 2008). Their complaints about a lack of time and resources, and of being chained to their desks to meet ever-growing requirements to fill as many columns, seconds or pixels as possible, at least resembles the images of factory workers trying to keep pace with a fast-moving assembly line. Work patterns are even more rationalized now that many journalists have been laid off because of cuts.

This industry-like organization of news production was obviously a historical necessity for a media that targeted mass audiences with a fixed frequency. And despite the decline in readers, subscribers, and viewers over the last few decades, traditional mass media have transposed these principles even more rigorously to their online newsrooms. But these procedures go against the logic of the internet, which does not have to care about the distribution of a physical product, does not know deadlines, has infinite space to publish and archive information, and is networked so it can use knowledge and information from others. The industrial logic underlying news production could therefore be restraining innovation in the industry. Successful initiatives like the *Huffington Post* or hyperlocal sites seem to have found – or are at least looking for – new ways to deal with the overload of information on the internet.

They organize, specialize, and make use of other outlets and the wisdom of the crowd. They are less focused on publishing 'everything that's fit to print' as soon as possible and don't try to cater to an audience that is as wide as possible. Rethinking the organization of journalism might therefore involve the de-industrialization of news production.

Third, journalism itself, as both a practice and discourse, is structured by industrial logic. During the twentieth century, a political or ideologically-oriented journalism that wanted to unite distinctive political communities to obtain the power to change society gave way to a journalism that aimed at unifying the audience and constructing large, overarching communities. The pace of this development obviously differed from country to country, and to some extent one could argue that a political press has still a strong position in some parts of the world (Broersma, 2010c). But it is no secret that mainstream news outlets began to cater to the needs of as many news consumers as possible, an aim to which many organizations still hold fast nowadays. To do this, journalism became depersonalized and standardized. Therefore reporters had to follow a single news format that turned them into 'machines, without prejudice, colour, and without style' of their own, as Lincoln Steffens provocatively wrote in the early 1930s (Matheson, 2000: 565). To be attractive to news consumers, journalism presented itself as a non-biased representative of the public good and phrased the news in neutral, authoritative language. In aiming for the masses, journalism made an imagined social contract with the audience in which it promised not to take sides in its representation of social reality. This promise resembled the guarantee every other industrialized commodity offered to its customers: each product that left the assembly line was exactly the same and had the same unrivalled quality.

This stance, typically referred to as the 'objectivity norm', provided a strong rhetorical claim to persuade a mass audience of journalism's ability to cater to their needs and to be an independent Estate in democracy. But it also had a more profound function. Moral norms act as a 'stick' to establish and discipline social groups. As Michael Schudson (2001: 151–52) points out, building upon Durkheim and Weber, the objectivity norm was used to establish both 'horizontal solidarity' and 'hierarchal social control'. It united journalists through shared rituals and a shared identity, and allowed the profession to discern itself from competing professions in the information market. In this respect it also encouraged a 'pedagogical economy' in which professionals were disciplined and controlled by their (editorial) management. One might even say the objectivity regime is thus closely connected to, and could even be considered a precondition for, the industrialization of journalism. However, it is questionable if the new dynamics of a networked media system fit within this regime. Successful new informational outlets on the net often do not seem to bother with the pretence of objectivity. They connect and support, favour attachment over detachment, and are openly biased in the knowledge that their readers are exposed to multiple truths and outlets and wish to be convinced (cf. Broersma, 2010b; Peters, 2011). To be visible, valuable and to differentiate themselves from competitors in the jungle of the internet they have to demonstrate and display their convictions.

Another way to rethink journalism may thus be to reconsider if the objectivity regime still fits the new de-industrialized reality, especially when it comes to how people select and engage with media.

The de-ritualization of news consumption

Historically, or so we would like to believe, the story of everyday life for many people included regular, definitive moments of news consumption. Journalism, in fact, was distributed around these routines: papers were delivered before breakfast, television news buttressed the transitions from work to home (early evening news) and home to bed (nightly news), radio updates centred around commuting patterns, and weekend editions of newspapers contained longer feature articles to contemplate. There was a certain stability to news consumption, and although audience research has never been a strong suit of journalism studies, the notion of ritual – habitual, formalized actions which reinforce the 'symbolic power' of media institutions (Couldry, 2003) – provided a good fit to explain these practices.

Many of the archetypal moments when journalism entered our lives – watching the evening news in our living room, reading the newspaper by the breakfast table, listening to the radio on the way to work – helped shape, structure and give meaning to everyday life. However, what it seems we are witnessing now, in terms of many of these old familiar patterns, is a de-ritualization of news consumption. As journalism spreads to any potential moment and every possible location we desire, it becomes somewhat diluted and indistinguishable from other mediated forms of communication. As Livingstone (2004: 76) notes, 'The activity of viewing ... is converging with reading, shopping, voting, playing, researching, writing, chatting. Media are now used anyhow, anyplace, anytime.' When technology overcomes many of the temporal and spatial limits of news consumption, when the public is unshackled from the distributional constraints of unidirectional, programmatic, mass media, our habits have a tendency to transform. Although the pace of technology outstrips the pace at which audiences incorporate such change, there seems to be little doubt that audiences are slowly catching up to the possibilities. This is not to say that 'new' news rituals will not form, however: as we've seen with entertainment programming, many of the old patterns of consumption are becoming outdated or obsolete.

So if we want to know what journalism 'is', or what it might be in the future, a more sound empirical basis is to look at how it is actually being perceived and used. How has the structural transformation of journalism impacted what is 'done' with the news? More and more, it seems that young people – also sometimes referred to as the audience, public, citizens, consumers, users, participants and produsers, a terminological smorgasbord which indicates the danger of oversimplifying journalism's relationship to the world outside the newsroom – tune into the news for specific information, or in response to particular incidents, as opposed to as part of a daily ritual or out of a sense of civic duty to be informed. Of course specificity and personalization of the news has always been an aspect of journalism – newspaper sections are a great example of this – but more and more journalism isn't an everyday thing, even though it's increasingly available in all spaces of our everyday lives. This should have an impact on professional autonomy, and should have an impact on how journalists perceive their role. But often, as we see, it does not.

The traditional conception of journalism's role is society is resilient, surprisingly so in the face of a profession that seems to be having difficulties sustaining a consistent and stable relationship with 'the public'. The old model and perception of journalism's societal role sounded great for democracy and even better for the news industry. News audiences supposedly read, watched or listened to journalism on a regular basis, by which they familiarized themselves with social issues, so they could potentially fulfil their 'duty' as 'good citizens'. The inverse also held true. The bourgeois norms of self-improvement became widespread in the nineteenth and twentieth centuries and many groups embraced the newspaper as part of a broader strategy of developing themselves. However, the trends we have seen over the past decade indicate a widening gulf between the news industry and the public and point to a news media less and less able to connect with audiences. An attentive citizenry can no longer be assumed. This is somewhat troubling for many theorists of political communication, who look to what impact this has on civic culture – 'the factors that can enhance or impede political participation' (Dahlgren, 2005: 157) – in terms of how people come to see themselves as potentially active citizens. Being politically up to date means being informed, and journalism has historically been conceived of as a key social institution in this respect. If people turn away from journalism, it seems, there must be some impact on social cohesion, effective politics, sustainable communities, and individual self-governance.

In this sense, we seem woefully uninformed in terms of how people's view of themselves as citizens relates to contemporary reconceptualizations of journalism, and how this changes the way people 'use news' to inform their everyday lives. Media and communication technologies have been, and will continue to be, fundamental for connecting diverse members of society but it's hard to envision exactly what role journalism plays in this new media landscape. As mediated communication becomes increasingly ubiquitous in every aspect of our social life, we have progressively more possibilities and opportunities to connect. However, the mediation of everyday life has not necessarily led to increasingly stable social bonds – many authors assert that the degree of social cohesion and willingness to interact with others is being challenged or, at the very least, that the public is being fractured, fragmented, and splintered. Both perspectives have some validity. There is no doubt that connectivity may lead to action, but as the 2011 riots across Britain demonstrated, the ability to connect may not always lead to benevolent outcomes or a more stable society. The move towards sustainable, modern social relations is not linear, but is associated with conflict, disruption and negotiation processes for which media provide the stage. One thus wonders what function journalism continues to play in increasingly mediated, yet increasingly fragmented, societies?

In this sense, it is not enough to just look at the institution of journalism in isolation; it is necessary to consider it in terms of the social role it fulfils and how various changes across different aspects of society alter journalism from how we traditionally think of it. In terms of individuals, the last few decades have seen the emergence of an era where the governance of the self – what Foucault called governmentality, the conduct of conduct – no longer relies so heavily upon established social institutions, including journalism. Put another way, there is much speculation that modernity underwent a 'reflexive' transformation in the latter half of the twentieth century, a move which saw prominent 'modern' institutions that were charged with producing 'truthful information' experience a decline in authority while smaller social groups and individual experience rose in terms of their epistemological prominence (Giddens, 1994). As Rose, O'Malley and Valverde (2009: 26) note, the dominance of large institutions was mitigated by the increasing influence of the 'grey sciences, the minor professions, the accountants and insurers, the managers and psychologists, [those] in the mundane business of governing everyday economic and social life.' In other words, journalism as the principal and authoritative source for conveying knowledge became fragmented by the emergence of – more mundane – forms of authority and power.

The rise of the digital era only exacerbates this further, as people turn away from journalism to blogs, discussion boards, independent media, specialist websites, Twitter, Facebook, and infinite other sources of readily available information. People can increasingly access the material to 'think for themselves', they can navigate this information easily, and they have cheaper and customized ways to cater to their needs. In such an environment, while we could try to focus on why such social changes happen, a more sensible analytic approach may be to look at how change happens and how it differs from what came before. Using this as a jumping-off point, perhaps we should view it as problematic when, generally speaking, our inclination is to ask why the changes journalism is facing are a 'good' or 'bad' thing, rather than questioning how they came about and how they change journalism as an object of study. For example, instead of asking what can be done to 'save' journalism, it may be more fruitful to look at how the technological proliferation of video and online platforms provided alternatives for watching, learning, and being informed; how the knowledge economy and digitization shifted our modes of engagement with information; and how discourses of citizenship shifted from civic requirements (be a good citizen, be informed) to managerial requirements (know what you need to know for yourself) to then see how contemporary journalism, and how we think of it, has been fundamentally redefined by audiences compared to what came before.

This underscores moving away from the assumption that the old rituals of news consumption are the ones that matter or count, and that trying to ensure their survival is essential for journalism. In commercial terms, journalism may be at the end stage of its product life cycle, and attempts to reinvigorate demand by relying on the same old rituals of use are unlikely to halt its decline. Instead, it helps us to recognize that the young, technologically proficient, 'sped up' generation may have different needs and expectations for news. Perhaps daily rituals are no longer necessary for 'monitorial' citizens (Schudson 1998), who expect journalism to act as a 'gatewatcher' (Bruns, 2005) on their behalf, which can be tuned into during critical moments. The routinized consumption of journalism by the next generation of citizens may be less critical than the feeling that they can potentially consume when it is interesting, necessary, or convenient. In this respect, the most significant effect of the rise of internet and digital technology might be that the autonomy to decide when to 'tune in' has essentially shifted; rather than a public being led to develop certain habits of consumption based around the temporal and spatial constraints of the media, it seems that journalism increasingly needs to habituate itself to the temporal and spatial elasticity of one-and-all.

Participation, trust and the redefinition of a profession

Journalism studies scholars, students and practitioners are in need of new perspectives to tackle the numerous economic, professional, and perceptual challenges, which challenge journalism as we know it, or perhaps more appropriately, want to know it. The problems the news media faces – often referred to under the 'crisis of journalism' label – can appear insurmountable despite the fact that scholarship and industry observation on how to 'fix' the crisis is not in short supply. However, too often it's the symptoms that garner all the attention and not the idea of journalism itself. The chapters in this book address this by considering journalism on a structural level.

The last few decades demonstrate quite clearly that the authority and status of journalism are questionable, and that it bears many of the tell-tale signs of an industry in decline. It has long been said that journalism is there to serve its public; in fact, one could arguably say that this public-service element of journalism is its definitive mission. Yet measures which ask people about their faith in the news media to fulfil this function seem to indicate that public trust is waning. Much of this seems to coincide with the proliferation of media outlets and alternative media channels, emanating from the rapid technological developments of the past few decades. Economic pressures have also followed suit, forcing journalism outlets to continuously adapt. Increased competition between outlets and pressure on individual journalists have likewise brought ethical issues to the fore, evidenced by a number of prominent scandals around the world, with each country now seemingly able to tell its own story of how the press fails. Journalists' perception of their own role is in disarray, the public's view of them is questionable, and research into the historical specificity of this moment and current responses are lacking. This somewhat austere reality provides the backdrop to this book.

For journalism, this means if it wishes to 'survive', if it still aims to serve 'the public', its practitioners must understand the limits and demarcation of their role in dialogue with it. The ability of the news media to convince the public that its stories were authoritative and important increased over the course of the twentieth century as professional journalism honed its performative discourse (Broersma, 2010a; 2010b). People believed the news gave them important, factual information and many people still likely feel this way about their preferred outlet. However, much of the social status of journalism came from its rhetorical ability to position itself as a necessary public good that implemented itself in the spaces of everyday life (Peters, 2012). It is this explicit or implicit social value that has historically driven the financing of the news media, both in terms of public funding and private revenue. And yet it is this same value which now seems to be weakening in terms of the demand for regular journalistic consumption and its pre-eminence as an informational commodity. The ways that contemporary individuals attain self-knowledge and social awareness – news consumption being one such technique, long deployed in an effort to 'improve the self' – have changed. Yet it appears that journalism, as a social institution, has not come to this recognition. The industry often still seems to declare its importance by fiat, by its possible use, while ignoring that its functional use has changed.

Therefore, rather than just focus on the 'crisis' indicators, this collection tries to understand the structural transformation journalism is undergoing. It explores how the news media attempt to combat decreasing levels of trust (Part I), how participatory culture creates new dialogues between journalists and audiences (Part II), and how emerging forms of news affect the established journalistic field (Part III). In the fourth part the previous chapters and themes are discussed and related from different angles. Crucially, despite creating these somewhat artificial divisions, the various chapters within the collection do not treat these developments as distinct transformations. Instead, most consider how the interrelation of these factors accounts for both the tribulations of the news media and the need for contemporary journalism to rethink itself.

Part I
Public trust in journalism

1

TRUST, CYNICISM, AND RESPONSIVENESS

The uneasy situation of journalism in democracy

Kees Brants

There was a time when the relationship between politicians, journalists and citizens in many a liberal democracy was of a symbiotic nature. Each profited from the other: politicians had access to the media to inform the public about their plans and achievements and thus enhance their chance of re-election; journalists had access to politicians who provided them with the stock and bone of policy and politics to fill their columns and TV news with; and the thus informed public had all the cognitive tools to rationally and seriously play their role as citizens in a strong and lively democracy. Those were the days. That is, provided we are not fooled by the strainer of the past that only lets the sun shine, as the Chinese saying goes. The relationship in what could metaphorically be described as the Golden Triangle of political communication certainly looks quite different these days.

Politicians accuse journalists of stripping the serious business of politics of its substance and reducing it to mere imagery and infotainment, sensation and scandal. Moreover, they hold them responsible for what could be seen as a legitimacy crisis, in which voters look with disdain at, or turn away from, the political process, thus claiming a double doom scenario of current political communication: as journalists become increasingly negative about politics, they create or feed a similar cynical feeling among citizens. At the same time, journalists mistrust the political 'spin', the attempts to control and steer news management by politicians and their spokespersons to positively frame policy and people, and to bypass the ways and means of being controlled. The public, traditionally at the receiving end of political communication, are now not only criticizing and turning away from those who represent them, but also question the responsiveness and empathy of media that seem to listen more to each other and to the socio-political elite than to what bothers the public. In short: what was once considered a symbiotic relationship between politics, media and the public is turning from a Golden Triangle into a Bermuda Triangle.

If both politicians and journalists are caught in an amplifying spiral of mistrust in each other's reliability, capacity and performance, and if parts of the public are becoming cynical of what media and political institutions are doing for them, that is bound to influence the role and place of journalism in democracy in the twenty-first century. How do media and journalists respond to declining trust and increasing cynicism and what does that mean for their profession?

From trust to (some) cynicism

From a theoretical point of view trust can be seen as the cement and the precondi-tion of every relationship, and in general as an important basis for social capital, social order and social cohesion in a society. Cynicism, on the other hand, is the absence of a belief in the reliability of authorities, or no or limited faith in their sincerity. As such, trust and cynicism are each other's flip side, the opposites on a continuum from very positive to very negative attitudes towards specific actors or institutions. As a relational concept, trust is built on experience or, in its absence, on the expectation that the interaction with the trustee would lead to gains for the trustor (Tsfati and Cappella, 2003). We need to be able to rely upon the reputation, honesty and good intentions of the trustee to act in some sort of general interest. When there is no experiential knowledge, our trust is based upon expectations with regard to the motivations, reliability and credibility of the trustee, be it a politician or political party, a journalist or branch of the media, or any other institution or individual who enters a relationship where there is no empirical way for the trustor to verify the intentions, character or quality of the trustee (Seligman, 1997: 21, in Tsfati and Cappella, 2003).

Looking at public trust in politics, the trend that emerges from surveys is rather sombre, although more so in the USA than in the EU. A recent poll by the Pew Research Center (2010a) shows that only 22 per cent of the American population trusts its government. Compared to half a century ago (1958), that is a drop of more than 50 per cent. Even to Ronald Reagan (42 per cent) and George W. Bush (37 per cent) the Americans give more credit than to Obama. Indications of cynicism in Europe also show a declining trust in political institutions and politicians (Thomassen, 2010). However, Eurobarometer (2008 and 2010) data are slightly more positive than those in the US: 32 per cent of the population in the EU countries say they trust their government. That hardly radiates enthusiasm though; in 2001 it was 35 per cent, not much more. Trust in political parties and politicians is even lower. While there is considerable cynicism, the picture presented by these data is not uni-form and clear cut across the continent. Mediterranean Europe and the UK score systematically lower than northern European countries.

Trust in politics is considered a prerequisite for the legitimacy of representative democracy and at the same time as the remedy when things go wrong. Adriaansen (2011) distinguishes two dimensions of trust: reliability and competence of political actors. The first is related to their integrity (are they honest, do they do what they promise, do they have good intentions) and whether they act in the public interest (are they responsive to the needs of people). Competence has to do with their ability to do their job (are they skilful), the extent to which they take charge of problems (are they decisive, effective and efficient), and whether they know what is important for the people. Being sceptical of these characteristics of politicians is part of the professional attitude of journalists. But they can also lack belief in politicians for another reason: for their media salacity, their permanent campaigning and their strategic electoral motives when they say what they say (Brants et al., 2010). The combination of these three dimensions of journalistic mistrust can be seen as cynicism.

There is a relationship between trust in politics and trust in media, but there is disagreement over its direction. Some, especially in the US, say that press criticism of political officials (notably their strategic and conflict framing) breeds cynicism among the public. Robinson (1976) speaks of a 'video- or media-malaise', while Cappella and Jamieson (1997) prefer to call it a 'spiral of cynicism', accelerated by a mutual distrust of journalists and politicians. Although negative reporting is certainly not uncommon, there is as yet in Europe little support for the hypothesis of a spiral of cynicism (Norris, 2000; de Vreese, 2005; Poletti and Brants, 2010). Others (e.g. Lipset and Schneider, 1987) believe that if trust in government goes down, trust in the media rises, and vice versa. Stephen Bennett et al. (1999) assert that jaundiced views of government and of the media co-vary, hinting at a decay of something more fundamental that affects people's trust in society or a mutual destruction of government officials and the media: as they attack and criticize each other, they pull down evaluations of themselves and related institutions. As support for institutions in general has declined, media might be considered by the public as another institutional power next to the government.

Compared to politics, survey data on public trust in the media show a similar bifurcation between the US and Europe. In 2010 the average 'believability' of news media in the US was 24 per cent (down 7 per cent compared to 1998 and not much more than their trust in government). There is here a clear political divide and even polarization among the American population: generally Republicans trust Fox, while Democrats put their bet on CNN (Pew, 2010a). It seems that the populations of the EU countries have generally more trust in their media than in their politicians and political parties, with a downward trend in most (Eurobarometer, 2010). Television dropped from 58 (2001) to 49 per cent (2009), while trust in the press is down from 45 to 42 per cent. Here too, the UK and France stand out in their doubt about the media. If they are typical for Hallin and Mancini's (2004) political media systems, liberal and polarized pluralist countries respectively give media and politics less credit than democratic corporatist countries like Germany, Scandinavia and the Benelux countries.

Trust in media is seen as the lifeblood of journalism's role in and contribution to people's sense making. Most of us cannot be everywhere, account for ourselves or understand the complexities of society. We need to be able to rely – or at least think we can – upon the reputation of the journalist without permanently having to check everything that is presented to us (Coleman et al., 2009). In the same vein, as with politics, trust in media and journalists can be seen along three dimensions as well:

reliability, credibility and responsiveness. Reliability is, as with politics, related to journalistic integrity and whether we can believe in their professional honesty. Credibility has to do with the way they find and present the truth, whether we can believe their interpretation of the facts, how they separate them from opinions; in other words, whether they live up to their own professional standards. Different from politics, responsiveness of journalists has not so much to do with their acting in the public interest as with what the public is interested in, taking their agenda of urgency seriously, providing a platform for the expression and exchange of articulated wants, desires, protests.

Mistrust of journalism can be seen as a subjective feeling that the

> mainstream media are neither credible nor reliable, that journalists do not live by their professional standards, and that the news media get in the way of society rather than help society (...), are not fair and objective in their reports, that they do not always tell the whole story, and that they would sacrifice accuracy and precision for personal and commercial gains.
>
> *(Tsfati and Cappella, 2003: 506)*

Bias, poor performance, little substance, dumbing down are certainly the images portrayed by politicians when criticizing media and journalists. Whether those are the elements the public thinks of when indicating mistrust is the question. They seem to be more preoccupied with the third dimension: (the lack of) responsiveness of journalism. People's mistrust of the media is usually not heard beyond letters to the editor and certainly not articulated with the same loudness as the objections of politicians. But where in the twentieth century dissenting voices of the *vox populi* have mostly been excluded from the elite discourse that tended to dominate Western Europe's political-publicity arenas, things have changed in the twenty-first century.

A bumpy ride to uncertainty

In the last ten or twenty years, trust in media and politics and in the process of political communication in many Western countries, has been put to the test by a number of, often interrelated, developments. In the first place, the media market has changed considerably. With declining advertising revenue, the rise of the internet and free dailies, the phenomenon of *de-reading*, especially among the young, increasing competition between and commercialization of media, and decreasing loyalty and changing news-consumption patterns of their audiences, a shift can be noted from a supply to a demand market in communication (Van Cuilenburg et al., 1999). It is no longer the producer of news who decides exclusively what the public should consume, based on what the former thinks the latter need as democratic citizens. Rather, the assumed demands of the public have become more decisive for what the media provide. In a competitive media market, the freedom for the consumer to choose what they like has increased, and every medium and every TV programme is forced to take note of its market share and subsequent audience statistics.

As a consequence, in the second place, journalism has changed. The selection and presentation of news is beginning to waver between professional and market considerations, between what is important and relevant and what sells and is probably more interesting to the public as consumer than as citizen. That means an increasing focus on the sensational, on where politics has failed instead of on what it has achieved, on scoops filled with drama and conflict, on scandals small and large, framed as such or constructed, on opinion polls, on the strategies and ulterior motives of politicians and other power holders. Not only the selection of news has been influenced by this shift from a supply to a demand market; form and style have too. At the same time, these shifts from a focus on substance and content to the personal and the dramatic are as yet greeted with unease and ambivalence by both the producers and the sources of news. And although European research is not conclusive about the pervasiveness of this stylistic shift, the effect has been twofold. On the one hand, politics feels it has to adhere to the production routines of the media, to provide attractive pictures and suitable politicians who are able to speak in sound bites, deliver relevant quotes and are willing to (also) show their personal and authentic sides. On the other hand, it has resulted in a further professionalization of political news management and a fiercer debate about media power.

In the third place, internet and mobile-phone-related technological developments have created new opportunities for interaction, consultation and communication, and thus for the demand side of the media market. Social media have provided a platform to share with others, to post personal information and clips as well as political statements and exited messages, and to multiply and magnify one's feelings, anger, indignation. As such they have blurred the distinction between sender and receiver, and between private and public sphere. In fact, the private is propagated as public. Web 2.0 has, moreover, given the traditional media an opportunity structure, an incentive and a perceived coercion to connect with the public. The discussion sites of traditional 'offline' media and news blogs have clearly filled a lacuna in the arena where public opinion is formed. On some sites lively and more critical-rational debates take place on political issues of the day, where arguments are substantiated and explained. Others are filled with emotional commentary from those who feel their plight and opinions are neglected in the news or who never participated in the publicized opinion formation that one can find in the quality press.

In the fourth place, citizens and the populace, on the one hand, and politicians and members of the socio-political elite, on the other, are increasingly part of what Manin (1997) has called an audience democracy. He notes a move away from traditional party democracy – where the political party, its manifesto and the authority of its leaders were in the driver's seat – towards an audience democracy – in which personalities have become more important than the party, performance, permanent campaigns and polls more than the party programme, and authenticity more than authority. In such a democracy, charisma and empathy become preconditions for success. This trend coincides with and triggers populist tendencies, both in politics and in the media, and with the more demand-driven tendencies in media markets. Expressing anti-establishment sentiments and the emotional truths of *fact free politics*, and siding with the 'ordinary people' – characteristic of populist appeals – can have a definite media attraction, especially when packaged in strong words and extreme views. In an audience democracy, the 'truthiness' of bloggers and experience experts begins to hold equal weight with the factualness of the elected politician and expert source. For some even more.

Finally, substantial parts of the electorate are on the run. Traditional left-right dimensions and religion as characteristic of cleavages in society are overhauled by a new, cultural, dimension, characterized by postmodern hedonism on the one hand and new conservatism on the other (Kriesi et al., 2008). Where socio-economic issues used to drive electoral considerations of much of the public, increasingly protectionist views on immigration and integration begin to top their agenda of urgency. Where the winners of globalization, who enjoy the benefits of internationalization, emphasize cultural tolerance, the losers of globalization – many of them the less educated and small entrepreneurs – fortify the other side of the demarcation line, angry about and fearful of the consequences of the encroaching process of change.

At the same time, considerable parts of the public – consumption-oriented and fragmented – begin to challenge the Enlightenment ideal of rational discourse and its moral claim on civic engagement and political participation. In an Enlightenment-inspired *Rechtstaat*,[1] however, politics and political communication are usually more for than with the people, let alone by the people. A representational democracy is usually run by a rational elite, entrusted with the power to decide for, and thus rule over, the people. In such responsible democracy, politics is a serious business, where the irrationality of emotional argumentation is, or should be, kept at bay. But with the represented lacking trust in the capabilities and integrity of those who represent them, the *populus* begin to demand a voice. It is no longer satisfied with (the promise of) transparency or accountability, it wants to participate and speak its mind. And they tend to do that in a way that makes the authorities nervous. In the new public discourse of everyday life, enabled by reality TV programmes like *Big Brother*, and more recently via the likes of YouTube, Facebook, Twitter and the discussion sites of news portals, the populace have found a platform to express indignation, be angry, emotional and irrational. It looks as if these sites have transformed the traditional 'silent majority' into a large 'noisy minority', if that is what it is.

Holding journalism to account

In this changing environment, we find media and journalists torn between their sense of professional autonomy vis-à-vis the populace and the political elite, their social responsibility to and economic dependence on the public, and between their professional values and the demands of the market. At the same time, they are confronted by political demands to be more socially responsible, transparent and accountable, and by public demands to be more responsive and empathic.

The idea that media and professional journalists have a socially responsible role to fulfil in and for society follows from a normative theory of democracy in which they are expected to critically inform the public, so that as citizens they can participate fully in that democracy. The media have a responsibility to do this for the public good, in a reliable, careful and independent way. As signifiers they have the power to define and explain reality and interpret its meaning, a power entrusted to them in the expectation that they will perform well and in all honesty.

But media and journalists have to perform under increasing pressure from all sides. They have to be socially responsible to as well as attractive for the public. They have to speak and to listen, to laugh and to cry, be independent and neutral, be involved and take sides – and while doing all of that, uphold their professional values of reliable newsgathering, accurate interpretation and intelligent sense-making. On the one hand, we now see the *vox populi* taken increasingly seriously by media, government and political parties in an attempt to close the gap of legitimacy and win back the trust of a volatile public (Brants, 2008). But on the other hand, the socio-political elite, including leading journalists, are uncertain and ambivalent about the people's voice entering domains traditionally open only to them. Taking account of the public has, however, opened the eyes of many a journalist, socialized in the ivory tower of the *trustee* model, characterized by a cultural-pedagogic logic of 'what the public needs to know' (Schudson, 1999).

In his classic *On Liberty*, John Stuart Mill wrote in 1859 that only a press fully independent of government control can see to it that those elected by us do not misuse the power we have entrusted to them. The market, he wrote, is the best guarantee for an optimal free exchange of ideas. That was 150 years ago. Now politicians in many liberal democracies and from all denominations often complain that media and journalists have too much power: they try to set the political agenda, can make and break, frame and blame politicians, and tell half-truths and whole lies. And who or what can hold them to account, make them responsible for their actions in a transparent way? Where Mill saw the free market as the best guarantee for controlling the misuse of political power, the present socio-political elite sees the competitive media market as the root of most, if not all evil, as the main cause of the poor performance of many a journalist. The latter exercises power without the kind of accountability that they, as elected politicians, are used to and subjected to. Up to a point, media can be held to account by advertisers, shareholders and newspaper subscribers – who all have the power to withdraw their ads and money or change their loyalty – individual journalists can generally not be held to account by the market.

Increasingly, demands can be heard for new instruments of political accountability, tougher legal and contracted structures that set and define responsibilities through rules, laws and the institutions that control their strict application, in order to protect the rights of others and of society in general against any harm caused by media. The market model of accountability that Mill envisaged, based on the principle of supply and demand and judged by the interests of the consumer, is seen by the critics as insufficient, or even counterproductive. At best the market has led to competition and commercialization, and media content characterized by what sells.

Next to political and market accountability, McQuail (2003) distinguishes two more types: professional accountability and public accountability. Where political accountability is organized top-down, these two are more bottom-up and considered softer and safer, certainly by media and journalists. Professional accountability is based on voluntary actions by media professionals to act according to their journalistic principles and the self-regulatory structures that uphold them. It is answering to your peers for your actions, to those who are part of the profession or their organization. It can take the form of internal accountability, like a code of practice, or external accountability, as with most press councils, which are usually a combination of being accountable and a means to keep one's house clean. Public accountability is answering to the public or their organized representatives. It is intended to show media's voluntary obligation to find ways to strengthen the relationship with citizens more directly. The instruments are usually self-initiated, as in an official right-of-reply policy, the ombudsman that some newspapers and broadcasters employ, or answering readers' letters.

The attitude of media and journalists towards political and market accountability is generally defensive: independence from political and economic influence is the Achilles' heel of press freedom and a necessity when being a public watchdog. Otherwise the controllers will be controlled by those they are supposed to control. Both public and professional accountability are mostly internal reactions by media institutions and journalists to external pressures for more government steering. These are ways in which they try to counter the political demands for stricter regulation, and avoid government interference by propagating self-regulation. Probably more than about power holders, however, media and journalists these days are concerned about their readers, viewers and listeners, their growing self-assuredness and lack of loyalty.

Journalism's answer: responsiveness

The apparent gap between the media and the public as consumer, as citizen and as populace, has compelled media and journalists to reconsider their professional performance and their relationship with the public. While politicians urge media to be more accountable, media tend to resist institutionalized forms. To fill the gap and restore trust with the public, they have introduced more responsive measures and strategies to take the public's interests and needs into account.

The response that I see emerging in the ways some media and journalists begin to come to terms with the versatile public in a socio-political environment in flux, is more diverse and complex and less institutionalized than professional or public accountability, but more pressing than market accountability. Increasing awareness of and uncertainty about the public have triggered different kinds of responsiveness (see Table 1.1). Media and journalists differ as to why and how they are responsive, and what they want from interaction with their public: there is a professional response to a more demanding public, a commercial response to a volatile consumer, an emotional response reflecting a more empathic discourse, and a populist response to a

TABLE 1.1 Responsiveness of media and journalism

Type Characteristic	Civic	Strategic	Empathic	Populist
Motive	Social responsibility	Commercial	Moral crusade	Anti-establishment
Aim vis-à-vis public	Bridging	Binding	Bonding	Backing
Kind of topics covered	Socio-economic and political	Emotional/ entertaining human interest	Victims of power/ bureaucracy	Whole range
Public addressed as	Citizen	Consumer	One of us	Disaffected individual
Public's involvement via	Iterative information and discussion sites, blogs	Electronic polls, studio audience, vox pop interviews	Informative, discussion, social networking sites	Blogs, discussion sites, activism
Presentational style	Informative/ cognitive	Entertaining/ sensational	Partisan, involved, personal	Comical/cynical/ ironic

disaffected public (see Brants and De Haan, 2010, in which the first three forms are not only discussed but have been empirically put to the test too).

In what could be called *civic responsiveness*, media try to develop forms of listening to and connecting with the public. They put the latter's agenda first and thus enter the terrain of public journalism, where the focus is less on the traditional news values of negativity, conflict and scandal, and more on the possible range of solutions to perceived problems (cf. Rosen, 1991). The starting point is to get away from those sensational news values and back to the old value of being socially responsible, and so to bridge the gap with the public, particularly the politically interested public. Although topics covered are predominantly economic and political, it is not so much the socio-political elite that set the tone, but the connection and overlap between the public's agenda and that of the journalist. Members of the public are addressed as citizens, empowered by the media's now-relevant news angle and journalistic performance to hold their own in a complex and socio-economically unequal society. Ways of connecting with the public can be manifold, but are typified by their iterative character, by learning through interaction. The informative and cognitive style of journalistic presentation is reflected in internet sites that are informative, debate-oriented and function as a source of input for journalists.

In this new style of civic responsiveness, the dissatisfaction of and solutions proposed by the Hutchins Commission – which after WW2 proposed a new, more responsible journalism in the US – resonate as much as the anxieties and propositions of the American public-journalism movement in the 1990s. Both responded to commercialization of the media and its effect on news values, styles of reporting and market-driven editorial choices. It is a responsiveness based on a sense of co-responsibility for the well-being of the socio-political system and the democratic process, in which media identify more with the public good than with what would entertain the public. It is in part a return to the *trustee* model of the cultural-pedagogic logic, in which the public is informed about what they should know as citizens in order to participate rationally in a democracy. Where it differs is in its starting point, the public's social agenda, and in its less paternalistic horizontal approach: public and media should learn from each other. Examples can be found with the 'citizen channel', the 'civic reporter' and the 'democracy barometer' at some Finish newspapers, aimed at making readers co-producers of news and politics, the audience advisory councils of BBC and Irish public broadcaster RTE, the readers' councils (*Leserrat*) of some German (*Bild*) and Swiss (*Neue Luzerner Zeitung*) newspapers, and the reader representative at the Austrian *Der Standard*, who has tasks similar to those of an ombudsman (EJO, 2011). In the Netherlands some local newspapers developed so called 'village squares', where readers discuss the coverage of potential news items with journalists. Another instrument, crowdsourcing, which involves the audience in research, is popular in Poland. But with its particular marketing potential it seems to be aimed more at the next kind of responsiveness.

Listening to the demands and needs of the public can also take the form of *strategic responsiveness*. Here the motive is not so much social as commercial and market-driven, not so much bridging the gap with the public as persuading and binding them as consumers to the product on offer. No means are spared, as long as they attract and arouse the public. The commercial nature of this type of responsiveness 'invites' consumers with the kind of human-interest stories that supposedly attract them, with sensational, entertaining and life issues and topics that touch them emotionally, or amuse, excite or frighten them. Characteristic of strategic responsiveness is the range of binding styles and means: making the public part of the programme as involved bystanders or as experience experts; bringing the man on the street to the studio; vox pop interviews; electronic polls that are not so much about political topics but about celebrities, historical figures, the nation's heritage, its identity. Internet sites aim less at bringing the public together or interacting with them, but more at bringing them or their wishes to the journalists. Viewers are also invited to send in their stories and video clips. In Germany, the *Bildzeitung* has handed out digital cameras to its readers to make them 'people's correspondents' that can provide the tabloid paper with pictures.

One would expect this strategic responsiveness to be characteristic of commercial TV stations that, basically, make programmes 'to sell eyeballs to advertisers', as most of their CEOs will admit. However, in a competitive market the public media also consider the saleability of their commodities to an emotionally engaged audience. The style of BBC News, for instance, of reporting murders, war and disasters seems to have changed from factual and distanced cool to involved and emotional warmth. Journalists report as if at a funeral, with flowery language about relatives mourning *loved ones* or whole nations in *grief*, and *floral tributes* to victims who the public have taken to their heart. Increasingly, audience research, as a way of finding out what viewers, readers and listeners are interested in, is part of the marketing approach of publishing and journalism (Stanyer, 2007: 106ff). In public broadcasting and in profit-pressured newspapers, growing audience orientation can also be read positively as an indication of taking the public seriously. Generally, a shift from a supply to a demand market can be interpreted both as an incentive to base editorial decisions more on commercial research and as a power shift benefiting the informational desires of the audience (Brants, 2007).

Third, we see forms of *empathic responsiveness*, in which journalists act as moral entrepreneurs, crusaders even, siding with a public that traditionally has had no voice in the media or that finds itself in a situation against its own will. These journalists perform a role as advocates of the victims of public authorities, the downtrodden social losers. They bond with the voiceless and their sympathizers. The latter are addressed as involved members of the public, as one of us against the powerful, the establishment or the bureaucratic leviathan. The presenter of the Dutch commercial TV programme *Crowbar* (*Breekijzer*, broadcasted between 1995 and 2004), a metaphor which exemplifies his style and tone of voice, literally forced open the doors to the corridors of power. Empathic journalists speak on behalf of one group against another, or against a powerful civil servant or politician, in an often excited and angry tone and style that is involved, partisan and anti-authority. The internet is used for further bonding and social networking, but also for providing extra information as a means of empowering the powerless.

Without its anti-establishment and populist rhetoric, empathic responsiveness in principle builds on the remit of many a public broadcaster. Consumer and other service programmes that were part and parcel of the public-service output not only had a moral and pedagogical undertone but were also aimed at the victims of bureaucracy and of capitalism run wild. In the new empathic responsiveness, that traditional remit is combined with the anxieties of the risk society and the 'uprising', if you can call it that, against the elites in many European countries that seem to embody these risks. In some instances, media have fought for a specific cause and even launched campaigns against particular issues. The Murdoch Sunday tabloid *News of the World*, which came to a sudden end in 2011 following the phone-hacking scandal, campaigned for the victims of paedophiles in the UK. Following the abduction and murder of young Sarah Payne the then editor Rebekah Brooks had the newspaper naming and shaming alleged paedophiles and later campaigned for the introduction of 'Sarah's Law' to allow public access to the Sex Offenders Register. What the police called 'grossly irresponsible' journalism won them the sympathy and support of (most of) their readers, giving this empathic responsiveness a strategic undertone.

Next door to and in line with empathic responsiveness is *populist responsiveness*. Here strategic responsiveness – aiming at a young audience not interested in regular news – is combined with the more empathic responsiveness – going along with anti-establishment sentiments in the land and adding to the unease about Europeanization, globalization and multiculturalism. As caretakers-cum-trustees, media and journalists back the political cynicism of the *vox populi*, cover issues which are close to the ignored man in the street, report on the self-centredness and greed of the political elite and confirm that 'old politics' is past its sell-by date. All of this is presented in an ironic, anti-intellectual and anti-establishment tone and style; and also in an anti-professional form, so as not to side with those critical journalists who are part of the socio-political elite. Journalistic values like neutrality, check and counter-check, and separating facts from opinion are not only put aside, but openly ignored, as if to show that objectivity only favours authority in power. When taking note of professional norms, populist responsiveness investigates their borderlines and, in sometimes crossing them, blurs the distinction between amateurism and profession-alism and introduces para-journalism. On the one hand it reminds us of the stand-up comedy style of Jon Stewart's *Daily Show*, which also tends to take the mickey out of authorities in the news, but in populist responsiveness humour is combined with cynicism. On the other hand it is investigative, anti-authority and critical. It is an extreme form of what Blumler and Kavanagh (1999: 219ff) have called anti-elitist popularization and populism. It is not so much, however, tapping into the voice of the man on the street, as performing the role of caretaker of the disaffected individual, speaking for him, in a cynical and humorous tone, mixing critique and laughter.

In the Netherlands, a country inundated and marred by populist leaders and par-ties, populist responsiveness began a year after the murder of Pim Fortuyn in 2002, with the news blog *GeenStijl*. It combined spreading rumour, exposing personal scandals that traditional media wouldn't burn their fingers on, with strong, strongly worded or ironic opinions and accusations. It has since been picked up by TV shows on both the public and private stations and resulted even in a new public-broadcasting organization, PowNed, the news show of which has all the characteristics of populist responsiveness. Their reporters ambush politicians, celebrities or other people in the news with unexpected, unusual, aggressive or plain ridiculous questions meant to make a fool of the interviewee. Sometimes facts in the presentation are replaced by rumours or the 'truthiness' of an experience expert, blogger or the jour-nalist himself. Politicians from the left and the right are first caricatured as celebrities and then mowed down in a cynical, anti-celebrity style and tone. It is a sometimes hilarious, sometimes blunt form of anti-establishment watchdog journalism, where the elite is pilloried for the fun of it.

Sailing between Scylla and Charybdis

If trust is the glue of social relations and the medicine for restoring or establishing cohesion in a society in a midlife crisis, then we are slightly in trouble. Trust is a necessity for the contribution of politics and media to a well-functioning and legiti-mate democracy, but politicians and journalists also feel it as a burden that bothers them. They need the support and loyalty of publics – as voters, consumers, audience – to guarantee and legitimize their own existence and *raison d'être*, their decisions and choices. At the same time, politicians and journalists also feel uneasy about them, their inquisitive participation, their cynicism, their unpredictable disloyalty. But how bad is it?

Where declining trust and increasing cynicism in government, political parties and politicians are indicated by polled publics, complaints about the performance and power of media and journalists are more often heard in the outbursts of politicians – not least those that have just lost an election. The European public – socialized in broadcasting's public-service ethos and journalism's tradition of politicization – seem (still) less critical of their media than the American public. But, to paraphrase Thomas's well-known aphorism, if politicians define situations as real, they are real in their consequences. The political elite increasingly want more accountability of the media. But journalists are objurgatory when those they control want to control them, and uneasy about transparency, about letting the public and authorities inspect their kitchen. In avoiding political and market accountability and going for somewhat watered down versions of public and professional accountability, media and journalists can only hope to regain the trust of politicians (and the critical public) when transparency of editorial decisions and social responsibility are taken seriously. And if not, is that bad? It would and should raise more questions if politicians are happy all round with journalistic performance.

Where we see a defensive response of media to the political demand for more accountability, the public seem less bothered by this and more interested in responsiveness and empathy, in being taken seriously. Some of the public's publicized opinion – particularly in online discussion fora where the *vox populi* actively and angrily participates – wants journalists to come down out of their ivory tower and side with the people, their plight, interests and anxieties. The multiple and often overlapping styles and forms of responsiveness that media and journalists begin to engage in are hesitant ways to win back loyalty. To succeed in that it is obvious that all forms of responsive journalism always have a strategic motive too, to counter dwindling audiences; even empathic responsiveness, which at the end of the day is a form of campaign journalism.

It demands a capable steersman who can sail between the Scylla of pleasing audiences and the Charybdis of autonomy and authority, where he already has to steer between the accountability demands of politicians and the responsiveness wishes of publics. And, to complicate things, is responsiveness going to win back trust if some of these new forms of journalism are reaching the usual suspects of heavy information users, while others are ultimately commercial ploys or based not on professional values or a sense of public interest, but on the presumption of authenticity as a sort of replacement of authority and truth? Then personal experience replaces expert knowledge, and strongly voiced opinions the claim of objectivity. In such a form of populist journalism no one is responsible anymore for the rules of the game. Where responsiveness might be a start to restorative journalism, it may also be the end of journalism as we know it.

Note

1 The German term *Rechtstaat* refers to the European continental civil law concept of constitutional state and rule of law, and is untranslatable.

2

A REFRACTURED PARADIGM

Journalism, hoaxes and the challenge of trust

Marcel Broersma

Between an epic world-wide scoop and a humiliating failure there is sometimes, on first sight, scarcely any difference. The day after CBS's *60 Minutes* and the *New Yorker* published their first stories and now iconic pictures on the Abu Ghraib scandal, the *Daily Mirror* shouted on its front page 'Vile ... but this time it's a BRITISH soldier degrading an Iraqi'. A full-page picture showed a soldier urinating on a tied up, half-naked and hooded prisoner. The next pages contained more 'shocking photographs', a detailed story about the abuse and an outraged leading article (*Daily Mirror* (DM), 1–5–2004). However, while in the next days, weeks and months the Abu Ghraib story developed into a national and international scandal, the *Mirror*'s 'world exclusive' turned out to be untrue. After two weeks, in which the paper faced significant pressure, it had to admit it was betrayed. It published a shameful front page apologizing in big bold capitals 'Sorry ... we were hoaxed' (DM, 15–5–2004).

The *Mirror* was not the only European newspaper that blundered. In the aftermath of the Abu Ghraib disclosures, torture hoaxes tended to be pandemic. Five days before the general elections of 2006, the Dutch quality paper *de Volkskrant* published a front-page story that stated as a fact that Dutch soldiers had been torturing prisoners in Iraq (*de Volkskrant* (Vk), 17–11–2006). Moreover, the paper contended that these incidents were covered up by the commander-in-chief of the army. Although less obviously fraudulent than the *Mirror*, *de Volkskrant* had to admit that it too had jumped to conclusions. While tough interrogations had indeed happened, there was no actual proof of torture. *De Volkskrant* did not kowtow to pressure as the *Mirror* felt it necessary to do, but it still felt obliged to tell its readers that it regretted the use of the term torture. It also assured them that it had not intended to manipulate the national elections which were to occur in the week following publication (Vk, 19–7–2007).

I will analyze these two cases to rethink the dynamics of journalism practice, and the relationship between journalism and audiences in the digital age. Hoaxes are excellent occurrences to do this because they challenge journalism's normative and epistemological foundations and its relation to the public. In the turmoil that starts after a hoax is revealed, the profession is forced to expose itself. The stir in the journalistic field makes it possible to look behind the, normally concealed, journalistic paradigm – a shared system of values that sets out how to gather, interpret and validate information, and as such structures and legitimizes the work of journalists. When that paradigm is broken and stakeholders attempt to repair it, they have to be open about their past and future performance. The public has to be persuaded that the norms and routines that guide journalism practice and allow journalism to meaningfully make sense of social reality are still valuable and effective. In the era of the mass media's information monopoly, a shared interest in upholding this paradigm meant that journalism was quite successful in persuading the public of its value and legitimacy. However, the key question is if journalism will *continue to succeed* in concealing its inherent limitations to its (potential) audience.

When we want to rethink journalism, we should not just analyse its situation in terms of new technologies and outmoded business models. In the current age the journalistic paradigm is continuously refractured. At the same time, repairing it has become more complicated, if not impossible. First, digitization and the economic downfall have stimulated competition between mass media. In addition, new niche media have been founded that tend to subvert the 'rules of the game' journalism has developed in its long-term project of professionalization. To obtain a position in the field they openly question and challenge the established norms, for example by crossing ethical boundaries or publishing information that has not been verified. This confronts the public with the vulnerability of journalism's paradigm. Second, news consumers are more media literate and have more possibilities to challenge professional news production. They openly comment on coverage, check news 'facts' themselves and publish alternative representations. A linear flow of information from mass media to the public has been replaced by a database structure in which instantly available and manipulatable information is continuously looped on the internet.

The loss of its information monopoly has severe complications for the credibility of journalism as a producer of specific knowledge. Especially now, the profession is in a vulnerable position due to new digital possibilities, changes in news consumption and the economic consequence of that. Journalism as we knew it in the past century is currently suffering from a state of osteoporosis. When its paradigm is refractured again and again it eventually enters a state of progressive degeneration in which the damage will not be curable anymore. The societal function that journalism traditionally aims for is still valuable for people and essential for democracy, but in order to survive journalism needs to redefine itself. It has to develop a new paradigm to guide its performance in order to adapt to new demands of audiences and to cope with the fundamental transformations in the accessibility of information.

Journalism hoaxes

Controversial hoaxes violate the legitimacy of journalism and undermine trust in it more than anything else. Because of the revealing and often scandalous nature of the facts they disclose, they initially trigger a tremendous stir among the general public, and consequently among politicians and other authorities. The consequences for journalism are therefore all the worse when an amazing scoop in the midst of public discussion turns out to be a hoax. News consumers feel betrayed. The imaginary contract between journalism and citizens who trust in the veracity of information is broken and journalism's credibility is undermined. Consequently, a process of paradigm repair takes place (Bennett et al., 1985; Reese, 1990; Berkowitz, 2000). The media organization responsible apologizes and tries to rebuild a trustful relation with the audience by framing the hoax as an incident in an otherwise reliable process of professional practice. Typically, a reporter or editor is held responsible, fired and publicly expelled from the profession. Meanwhile competitive media challenge the culprit because of commercial reasons and because the legitimacy of journalism in general is violated. However, they too have an interest in repairing the paradigm. Therefore they usually point to specific journalists, practices or circumstances of their wrongdoing competitor. By doing so, they imply that these mistakes are isolated deviances and would have never been made in their newsroom.

Hoaxes can either be caused by individual journalists and media outlets themselves, or by sources that have misled reporters. First, journalists or media can purposely fool the audience. Fraud by individual journalists or photographers, with well-known examples such as Janet Cooke, Jayson Blair, Stephen Glass or Brian Walski, can have many reasons, including psychological problems, but is usually grounded in the social structure of the journalistic field. Ambitious journalists want to climb the social ladder by providing scoops, or want to maintain their position under severe (commercial) pressure. This triggers them to make things just a bit 'better' than they are (Eason, 1986; Mnookin, 2004; Carlson, 2009). Other deliberate hoaxes are 'invented' to attract attention. Stunts and practical jokes have a long history, especially in the popular press, which uses these as a means of marketing (cf. Chalaby, 2000). Other media productions, like Orson Welles' radio play *The War of the Worlds*, more or less unintentionally turn into hoaxes simply because (parts of) the audience do not get the reality play (cf. Campbell, 2010; Van Drom, 2010).

Second, and far more interesting, hoaxes occur when – in the negotiation process between journalists and their sources – the interplay between mutual interests and motives results in a fraudulent representation of reality. This can happen intentionally, as was the case with the *Daily Mirror*'s torture story. Soldiers deliberately provided fake pictures and testimonies that fitted in very well with the *Mirror*'s editorial opposition to the British involvement in the Iraq war. A hoax can also be the result of a more complicated journalist–source relation in which provided information, sayings and interests are mutually misinterpreted. The interplay between sources that frame events in a way profitable to them and reporters who are eager for a good story and all too happy to go along with these accounts, can almost inevitably lead to a story that misrepresents reality. This seems to have happened with the *Volkskrant* hoax.

Not much research has been done on hoaxes, which is both remarkable and problematic considering the harm they do to journalism. When hoaxes are studied they are usually analyzed in terms of misrepresentation and paradigm repair (Hindman, 2005; Patterson and Urbanski, 2007). Scholars usually ask why things went so terribly wrong. They reconstruct how false reporting made it into the medium, why norms were violated and the checks and balances of journalistic practice bypassed. Subsequently, they examine what has been promised to readers to prevent new 'mistakes' and what practical measures have been taken to avoid new incidents. Investigative journalists writing books about notorious hoaxes tend to ask the same questions in an attempt to uphold the journalistic paradigm retrospectively (Mnookin, 2004; Davies, 2008).

In this chapter, I will reverse the angle of research and ask instead why journalism is so remarkably *successful* in misleading its public. After all, hoaxes are often so convincing that they are, at least for a while, commonly believed and discussed, and necessitate governments taking action. By analyzing hoaxes as success stories, the gaze shifts from studying journalism as a descriptive discourse to studying journalism as a performative discourse. When journalism successfully persuades readers to believe that what it describes is real, it transforms an interpretation into truth – into a reality the public can act upon (Broersma 2010a; 2010b).

Truth and the journalistic paradigm

Journalism's claim to truth is at the core of the journalistic paradigm. As a producer of knowledge, journalism derives its authority from its presumed ability to provide a truthful representation of the social world within a limited time frame. Since their founding in the early seventeenth century, newspapers unconditionally promised their readers to present reality as it is, implying that facts exist independently of human thinking and outside the text. This discourse of truthfulness helped newspapers to position themselves in the market for information on current affairs and to distance themselves from neighbouring activities such as gossip, polemic, literature or PR. Journalism legitimizes its special position in society by its rhetoric of safeguarding society from the abuse of power that is based upon this truth-claim. While the powerful want to suppress information that threatens their social position, journalism claims to expose their true intentions and actions. By providing people with true information about the social world, they are enabled to act as citizens, the rhetoric claims (Ward, 2004: 101; Broersma, 2011).

It is exactly this discourse of working in the common good that was applied by the *Daily Mirror* and *de Volkskrant* after they published these hoaxes. 'We told the truth', the *Mirror* shouted on its front page when its initial publication was cast into doubt. The paper said it had no pleasure publishing the story but called it its 'duty to reveal this appalling behaviour'. A few days later it stated that 'it is in all our interests that the truth should come out'. When it finally had to confess it had been hoaxed, the paper again emphasized: 'Our mission is to tell the truth. That is something this newspaper has been doing for more than 100 years and will always strive to do' (DM, 3–5, 7–5 and 15–5–2004). *De Volkskrant* used a less dramatic, though similar, vocabulary. The editor said that it was the paper's duty to publish important disclosures as soon as possible. He called accusations of manipulating the elections an 'attack on our journalistic integrity'. In a critical evaluation of the use of the term 'torture' the paper's ombudsman contended that 'a journalist who knows these facts but does not bring them into the open is partially guilty of suppressing reprehensible facts' (Vk, 20–11 and 22–11–2007).

Key to journalism's authority is that it successfully conveys that it has developed reporting techniques and discursive strategies to discover truth and mirror this in a comprehensible way to a general audience. The objectivity norm that was developed in the US in the 1920s became the leading ideology of journalism in the Western part of the world during the twentieth century (Høyer and Pöttker, 2005; Broersma, 2007). As a counterbalance to reflexive styles of journalism that judge the world from a personal, partisan or moral point of view, objectivity as a procedure aims at depersonalizing journalism. As Schudson (2001: 149) has noted, the objectivity regime should be regarded as 'at once a moral ideal, a set of reporting and editing practices and an observable pattern of news writing.' While its claim to truth is the ontological foundation of journalism's paradigm, the objectivity regime has provided the epistemological tools – routines and conventions – to substantiate that claim. Objectivity is, as Tuchman (1972) argued, a strategic ritual that has to safeguard journalism from criticism. As a moral norm it functions on the level of discourse *on* journalism in which journalists rhetorically discuss and defend their profession and the norms involved. As a set of routines and conventions objectivity can be traced *in* journalistic discourse – the language in which journalism captures social reality.

Although the actual interpretation of the objectivity regime is subject to national and regional variation (Donsbach, 1993; Hanitzsch et al., 2011), there is some common understanding of its basic features and the essential procedures journalists have to follow to get to an 'objective' account of reality. Norms like impartiality and non-bias, balance and fairness, factuality and detachment are operationalized in routines like separating facts from opinions, only considering something a fact when it is confirmed by various independent sources, attributing quotes and information, hearing both sides in conflicts, and so forth. Consequently, these norms are translated into formal conventions that allow readers to recognize in the text if reporting procedures have been followed correctly. According to the paradigm, journalists will be able to reveal the truth when they follow the rules of the objectivity regime, depersonalizing and rationalizing their working methods, and comparing the (often conflicting) statements of all those involved in an event with one another, and with available documents (cf. Ettema, 2009). Journalists like to describe their work as 'truth finding', which suggests that truth is hidden somewhere out there – only to be uncovered by the reporter.

However, journalism's claim to truth and proclaimed adherence to the objectivity regime is an ambiguous one. Theodore Glasser has strikingly noted that objectivity 'requires only that journalists be accountable for *how* they report, not *what* they report' (cited in Goldstein, 2007: 67). Reporters can apply the procedures of the objectivity regime correctly but still end up with a story that is completely untrue. The paradox of journalism is that it rhetorically claims to present an ontological truth while knowing this is impossible on the epistemological level. As Epstein (1975: 5) concludes, even if 'journalists had unlimited time, space, and financial resources at their disposal, they would still lack the forensic means and authority to establish the truth about a matter in serious dispute.' In most cases journalists have no means to access an objective truth. They have to weigh various accounts of sources that have particular interests, relate these to documents and general information, frame the obtained and selected information in a coherent and compelling story that relates to the knowledge and taste of their audience, and balance the public interest of a story with their own interests and those of their medium. Journalism is a process of selection and reduction. When we evaluate journalism as a descriptive discourse that is able to create a correspondence between social reality as it is and the stories reporters write about it, it will always fail (Broersma, 2010b).

It does not make much sense to study journalism as either reflecting or distorting reality. Journalism is in the business of meaning-making. In the past centuries it has been remarkably successful in obtaining an authoritative position in society that enables it to impose its constructed truths on the public. That is why we should regard journalism as a performative discourse that strives to persuade the public of the truthfulness of its accounts. If it succeeds, it transforms an interpretation into reality upon which citizens, and by extension politicians and other elites, can act. Journalistic discourse derives its power from its ability to simultaneously *describe* and *produce* social phenomena. News is thus, to a large extent, a self-fulfilling prophecy (Broersma, 2010a; 2010b).

The performative power of journalism is located in the formal conventions it applies and not in its correspondence with reality itself. While reporters have to rely on second- and third-hand knowledge, the public itself is even more poorly equipped to assess the truthfulness of news. Readers simply tend to believe facts that come with the textual conventions they are familiar with (Ward, 2004; Jones, 2009; Broersma, 2010a). When information is published in a news medium – and looks like news – readers tend to believe it is true. As a meaning-making practice, journalism satisfies the public's need for security and stability. 'There comes a point where you have to believe something', a British news consumer who was questioned about trust in the media sighed (Coleman et al., 2009: 12). Most readers know in the backs of their minds that they should not believe everything in print, but they still tend to do so and are shocked when news turns out to be untrue.

Although almost any journalist would confess that objectivity is a myth and that truth, besides getting the mere facts straight, is an unattainable ideal, journalism's claim to truth remains its *raison d'être*. Certain practical limitations and unavoidable distortions are acknowledged and accepted in discourses on journalism, but in news discourse itself ambiguity is commonly avoided. Journalism speaks with an authoritative voice that leaves no space for doubt. Were journalism to admit its shortcomings, and were doubt to be allowed into its discourse, its paradigm would be broken. That is why pleas for transparency about choices underlying reporting and admitting that reports, at best, temporarily resemble truth, subvert journalism. Similarly, Schudson's (2009: 113) plea for a 'humble journalism' that acknowledges that truth is only provisional and particular, but at the same time sticks to factuality, would unavoidably undermine the journalistic paradigm as it currently is.

To conclude, hoaxes do not occur in spite of the journalistic paradigm but, conversely, because they fit the paradigm so incredibly well. They successfully link up to established routines for reporting and editing, and conventions for news writing. By doing so they fit into the framework of journalism and meet the expectations of the audience. The life cycle of a hoax – at least when it is recognized as such – follows three stages. In the first stage the hoax is published and causes a stir. In the second, the truthfulness of the story is challenged. In the third stage the medium has to acknowledge that it has been hoaxed and a process of paradigm repair takes place. This is also what happened in the cases of the *Daily Mirror* and *Volkskrant* torture hoaxes.

Two torture hoaxes

'Show, don't tell' is a famous motto in creative writing. When a newspaper has pictures of a scandal it's even better. The disturbing photo of the humiliated captive on the front page of the *Mirror* (1–5–2004) was accompanied by a caption that interpreted the image as a 'vile display of abuse'. It added that the Iraqi was beaten and 'hurled from a moving truck'. To give even more credence to the scoop, it stated that the British Army was investigating the case. A spread on pages 4 and 5 contained four more pictures that documented the abuse. On these the hooded prisoner is kicked in the face, stamped on his neck and gets a rifle placed at his head and in his groin. The captions spoke of an 'eight-hour nightmare' before the young man was 'dumped close to death' with a broken jaw and smashed teeth. The newspaper presented the pictures as the ultimate proof of its claims. When, after a few days, competitors were questioning the genuineness of the story, the *Mirror* (5–5–2004) referred to the pictures that 'substantiated' it. It even published a photo of a soldier taking pictures of another arrest as 'damning' proof that British soldiers genuinely took 'trophy' photos in situations like this. In the accompanying story an anonymous soldier confirmed this was a regular practice in Iraq (DM, 8–5–2004).

The initial news story used additional discursive strategies to convince the reader of its truthfulness. It closely reconstructed the abuse of the Iraqi who was suspected of stealing. Although the two soldiers who handed over the pictures remained anonymous, they were presented as reliable eyewitnesses. Their account contained many telling details about the battering and the injuries of the victim. 'You could see blood coming out early from the first digs. He was p****d on and there was spew. He could only speak a few words, saying "No, mister. No, mister".' The quotes of the soldiers, who acknowledged they had not just witnessed but also participated in the incident, underlined the authenticity of their account. Statements of army chiefs and the Armed Forces Minister, who called the photos 'deeply disturbing and unacceptable', stipulated the credibility and importance of the news story even more. A reference to the Geneva Convention briefly contextualized the incident and signified that it had been clearly wrong (DM, 1–5–2004).

The headline of the story framed it in a broader debate on the war in Iraq: 'Hearts & Minds? World Exclusive: Rogue British troops batter Iraqis in mockery of bid to win over people.' The Blair Government had 'sold' the war in public debate as an attempt to liberate the Iraqi people from dictatorship and prevent the world from terrorism. In a fierce campaign that was motivated by both genuine concern and commercial reasons, the *Mirror* had opposed that policy since 2002. It had attempted to win circulation by repositioning itself on the left wing of the tabloid market by appealing to the sentiments of working- and middle-class readers who had to pay with lives and money for a war far from home. At the same time, the anti-war *Mirror* supported the armed forces personnel who were bravely doing their duty (Tulloch, 2007; Freedman, 2009). It was 'an almost impossible position to make credible in a newspaper such as the *Mirror*', concluded editor Piers Morgan later. 'Sales fell off a cliff' (Morgan, 2008: 20).

The balancing act of the *Mirror* was visible on its editorial page. The paper stated that the British troops were 'renowned and admired for their courage, discipline and peacekeeping abilities' and that the Blair Government should immediately punish the 'sick squaddies'. Next to the news story, the outspoken statements about Abu Ghraib by an apparently deeply disgusted President Bush were printed, as well as the now iconic picture of a hooded prisoner connected to electricity wires (DM, 1–5–2004). The performative power of the pictures and the story created a reality to which the British Government, which had just strongly condemned the American mis-behaviour, had to react. Although their genuineness was immediately questioned when the pictures arrived at Number 10 Downing Street, officials realized that they could not openly challenge their authenticity. An adviser said: 'We could have stalled and said we were looking at the issue, but that could have given the wrong impression that we weren't taking it seriously. So we decided to immediately make it clear how appalled we were about the allegations' (*Observer*, 2–5–2004).

Though there were similarities, in the Dutch case, *de Volkskrant* used different discursive tools to persuade its readers of the truthfulness of its story. The identity of a paper and its relation to its audience determine which formal conventions are essential to its performative power. As a quality paper, *de Volkskrant* targets a highly educated readership, while the *Mirror* is a mid-market tabloid. To gain authority and to position itself among its competitors, *de Volkskrant* applies a rather sober design and detached writing style, whereas the *Mirror* uses many large pictures, big headlines and a style of writing that is more appealing to the hearts than to the minds of its readers. Furthermore, *de Volkskrant*, as a quality paper, considers itself a trustee of the public, and as such it presupposes that its readers have faith in its professionalism. It applies a more descriptive or argumentative style, in which reporters take responsibility for what they write. The *Mirror* is oriented towards the market and a lower-educated audience. It uses a narrative style in which pictures, telling details and quotes of eyewitnesses are foregrounded to persuade readers of the truthfulness of a story (Schudson, 1999; Broersma, 2010a). Finally, the British paper was campaigning against the war – a notorious strategy for market-driven tabloids to win readership – while its Dutch counterpart had a relatively neutral stance when it came to the Dutch participation in what was called the 'peace keeping mission' in Iraq and Afghanistan.

The article *de Volkskrant* published on its front page in advance of an extensive story on Saturday stated clearly that Dutch soldiers had been 'torturing' prisoners in Iraq. In three sentences it described what had happened: during an interrogation, prisoners had to wear black ski goggles, were exposed to light and sounds, and were doused with water. Furthermore, the article said the commander-in-chief had known of the incident but had not reported it to the public prosecutor. Both accusations were highlighted in big headlines that were stretched over the full front page: 'Dutch tortured Iraqi' and 'Former commander-in-chief did not report what he knew to the public prosecutor'. By using an omniscient narrative style and not attributing these assertions to sources, the reporter took accountability for his story. The reader had to trust that all the facts in his reconstruction were true. The story only included attributed reactions to the incident by the Ministry of Defence, the former commander-in-chief, two union leaders and the military prosecutor (Vk, 17–11–2006).

The subsequent story, which framed the news in a broader reconstruction of Dutch policy and politics regarding the peacekeeping mission, used the same authoritative style of reporting. It started with an exposé about earlier statements of Dutch ministers, who had said that Dutch soldiers would not misbehave as the Americans had in Abu Ghraib and that it would be unthinkable that they would cover up and remain in office. Subsequently, an explanation followed of the agreements that were made with the allies when the Dutch entered the mission in Iraq. The Dutch rules of engagement differed from the British and the American rules. Dutch soldiers, for example, were not allowed to interrogate prisoners, but according to the story this had still happened. The public prosecutor contended that to his knowledge the Dutch had not violated human rights, and two union leaders stated that the legal framework and the moral thinking in which soldiers had to work were outdated. A detached description of the incidents, without quotes or details and just containing of a few factual sentences, was embedded in this broader framework (Vk, 18–11–2006).

The Dutch Government, just like the British, felt obliged to respond promptly and conscientiously to the allegations. These could have severe political implications in the then tense debate on the country's involvement in Iraq, especially after the Abu Ghraib disclosure. On the evening before publication, *de Volkskrant* asked the Ministry of Defence to comment on the supposed incidents, but without indicating that it would label them as torture. After an hour of hasty information gathering, the spokesman of the Minister confirmed that tough interrogations had happened but did not go into any further details (Vk, 10–2–2007). In the early morning, just after the newspaper was distributed, the Prime Minister himself called the Minister of Defence and forced him to issue an official investigation. Two official committees were established to investigate the torture accusations.

A stir in the journalistic field

For high-impact news stories that are able to change the course of events, the odds are very high that they will be challenged. Stakeholders, such as politicians, the army, civil organizations or unions, will most probably try to alter the coverage in the direction they prefer. Triggered by professional and economic competition, other media will either try to link up with the story, publishing articles themselves, sometimes without even mentioning the original source, or will try to subvert the story by offering challenging representations of what happened. Citizens increasingly publish their doubts and comments online. All of these effects occurred in the weeks after the *Mirror* and the *Volkskrant* published their 'world exclusive' scoops.

Though the *Mirror* only published its story on Saturday, the news was already picked up by other media on Friday. The *Mirror* had sent the pictures to the Ministry of Defence so it could respond to them. It did so by releasing a public statement in which an investigation was announced. Almost all newspapers and other media covered that news on Saturday without doubting the story. According to Morgan he even got a call from BBC newsreader Fiona Bruce saying: 'That is a great story. I knew it wouldn't only be the Yanks' (Morgan, 2005: 3). When the pictures were published on Saturday, a debate about their authenticity started. Drawing upon military experts, the Sunday papers carefully cast doubts (*Observer, Independent on Sunday*, 2–5–2004). On Monday the first articles appeared in which the story was literally submitted to an exegesis. Every detail of the pictures was disputed: the rifle, the clothing, the truck, the lack of wounds on the victim, the perfect quality of the black and white photos (*Independent, Guardian, Financial Times*, 3–5–2004). Competing tabloids were most fierce in their reactions. The *Daily Star* (3–5–2004) called them 'bogus torture photos' and the *Daily Express* (4–5–2004) shouted 'liars'. The latter published 'The 20 clues that say fake', in which the *Mirror* photos were republished with numbers in the pictures that indicated which elements proved they were false (3–5–2004).

The *Mirror* (7–5–2004) responded four days later with a story that mimicked the *Express*'s without naming it. A new eyewitness, soldier C, confirmed the earlier accounts and commented on the issues raised. He refuted all arguments for the falseness of the pictures in statements like: 'I heard soldiers bragging about their assaults and these men would have something to illustrate their story with. British soldiers posing in this photo would know the consequences if they showed their faces'. A day later another soldier, labelled D, confirmed the accusations and 'produced damning proof' that taking so-called trophy pictures was common practice among British soldiers (DM, 8–5–2004). On Wednesday the 12th, soldiers E and F stepped forward and confirmed the abuse of Iraqi prisoners. They gave detailed accounts of incidents they had witnessed. In the interviews the paper once again came back to soldiers taking pictures. 'I thought the whole idea of taking trophy pictures was abhorrent. There were people done for it because they had them on their laptop – but it doesn't take a genius to hide them' (DM, 12–5–2004).

In the first week after the *Mirror* publication, most newspapers, even the tabloids, kept their options open. The *Daily Star* (5–5–2004), for example, said on Wednesday that 'if the pics are genuine, the soldiers responsible need to be tracked down and thrown out of the army. But if they're fake, it will have been unforgivable of the *Daily Mirror* to have published'. Roy Greenslade in the Tuesday *Guardian* (4–5–2004) still praised the *Mirror* for its 'strenuous checks' on their sources and its investigations on the issue in Iraq. He called the *Mirror's* response to the accusations of fraud 'impressive' and even wondered if the government had smeared the paper to distract attention from possible misbehaviour by British troops. He emphasized that 'genuine scoops are often trawled over by rivals eager to rubbish them' in 'a combination of media jealousy and media narcissism'.

There are interesting differences in the stances of the broadsheets and the competing tabloids in the weeks after the *Mirror* publication. The former were bothered mostly by the effects a false story would have on the credibility of journalism and by the ethical question of whether the benefits of revealing such a story outranked the obvious harm it could do to the British forces in Iraq. They generally emphasized the good intentions of the *Mirror* and its editor, but nonetheless claimed that he should resign if the story was false. The *Guardian* (14–5–2004), for example, wrote:

> There is an important matter of journalistic faith at stake, as well as one of the safety of people on the ground in Iraq. People should be able to believe what they read and see in newspapers. There is no newspaper on earth that does not make mistakes, big or small, in every issue. But it should be a fundamental principle (indeed it is written into the PCC code of conduct) that errors are acknowledged promptly and with due prominence.

The tabloids, on the other hand, tried to cash in on the downfall of their competitor. They focused on the threats to British soldiers. The *Daily Star* (11–5–2004) published a story on vandalized graves of British war veterans in Palestine with the headline 'And it's all the fault of the lying *Daily Mirror*'. An article on the assault and killing of two British soldiers read 'Pics got our boys killed' (20–5–2004). The *Daily Express* (4–5–2004) published a 'hall of shame' of the *Mirror's* stands on the Iraqi war. It revealed the 'shameful truth' that the paper had provoked the submission of 'phony photos that become propaganda around the world' by paying 'a fortune' for them (5–5–2004). A moving front-page story – 'So Proud: The Real Face of the British Army' – on the burial of a soldier in the regiment involved contained a range of quotes in which the *Mirror* was accused of complicity in his death. The commander of the regiment said: 'You can't print what we think about the *Mirror*. We are furious, livid and angry. It has ruined all the good work we did in Iraq' (7–5–2004). In a commentary at the end of the affair, the *Express* (14–5–2004) once again emphasized that the *Mirror* had acted immorally by recycling old allegations 'to boost its circulation and save its skin'.

The response of the Dutch papers to the *Volkskrant* story was far friendlier. On the one hand this had to do with the nature of the hoax. A story like the *Mirror's* that is supporting its claim with direct evidence such as pictures and detailed eyewitness accounts is far easier to challenge than an article that phrases general accusations in authoritative language. On the other hand, the *Volkskrant*'s story turned out to be far more solid. Initially most Dutch papers simply published the allegations of *de Volkskrant* and the response of the Government. However, when the Ministry stated that the incidents had been reported to the public prosecutor and that he would not press legal charges, competing papers started to doubt the scoop. They now put 'torture' between quotation marks (*NRC*, 18–11–2006). *De Volkskrant* itself published a commentary in which it casually admitted that the use of the word 'torture' might have been jumping to conclusions and that comparisons with Abu Ghraib were 'premature'. In a separate piece it quoted experts in international and military law who commonly condemned the incidents but were not sure if they amounted to torture. The paper therefore contended that there was enough 'hard evidence', although 'interpretations diverged'. It repeated its accusation of a cover up (Vk, 18–11–2006).

The popular right-wing daily *De Telegraaf* (19–11–2006) attacked *de Volkskrant* most severely. It accused it of using a font for its headline that it 'solely uses for announcing the Third World War' and said the average initiation at a student union was more violent than what had happened in Iraq. Furthermore, it questioned the timing of the publication, four days before the general elections, and the eagerness of the left-wing opposition to condemn the case. It quoted government officials at length who labelled the publication as negligent. A speech by the Liberal Party leader, who accused *de Volkskrant* of manipulating the elections, was reported in all newspapers. The *Volkskrant* editor-in-chief in turn qualified these accusations as 'absolute nonsense' and 'an attack on our journalistic integrity'. He said that reporters had been working on the story for months and that it was simply fit to print (*Parool*, 21–11–2006). Another line of defence was printing a full transcript of the initial interview with the public prosecutor. He had, in various newspapers, challenged the sincerity of the reporter, who had not confronted him with the specific accusation of torture. The transcript had to convince readers that reporting had been done carefully (Vk, 20–5–2006).

De Volkskrant (22–11–2006) showed itself to be reflexive and accountable by printing an article by its ombudsman. He refuted criticism about the timing of the publication but argued that the paper should not have used the word 'torture' and a seven-column headline. 'There is nothing to be said against the substance of the story, that is still sure as fate, but the form could have been better.' That same day the paper also printed an opinion piece of the Minister of Defence, who argued that the story was, if not incorrect, certainly incomplete. He wondered why he had not been given more time to respond and suggested that the paper had been manipulated by sources who had leaked information selectively. In an editorial, *de Volkskrant* denied that it had been manipulated and said its reporting had been meticulous. It again emphasized that Dutch soldiers had clearly misbehaved. The paper (Vk, 30–11–2006) also printed a letter from the expert who had labelled the incidents as torture in the initial publication. With hindsight he confirmed his prior judgement.

Paradigm repair

Exactly two weeks after the publication of the torture pictures, the *Mirror* apologized to its readers and the Army. Under the giant headline 'Sorry … We were hoaxed' it admitted to being betrayed. Its editor, Piers Morgan, who refused to apologize, was held responsible and sacked by its publisher Trinity Mirror. However, the paper emphasized that it had published the photos in good faith and after 'rigorous checks'. It stressed that, unlike the pictures, the allegations were true. It pointed to reports by Amnesty International and the Red Cross that supported its accusations and argued that the hoax should not 'allow the Ministry of Defence to avoid dealing with the real issue'. The paper might have had to say sorry, but it was 'categorically NOT SORRY for telling the truth that acts of cruelty were committed by a tiny number of British troops'. It concluded by stating that it was looking forward to 'serv[ing] our readers in truth and honesty' (DM, 15–5–2004). Two days later it continued its attack on the Government in two columns reading 'Sorry … We were hoaxed. By Blair' and 'Now Blair must apologize for war' (DM, 17–5–2004).

In the course of the second week of the affair, the *Mirror* changed its line of defence. Although at that time it still contended that the pictures were genuine, it now focused on the use of torture in general, which it claimed to have revealed.

> Yet the *Daily Mirror* had told the truth. And if we had not, this scandal would still be a secret, known only to a few high-ups in Whitehall. (…) All the *Daily Mirror* has wanted is to halt the abuses by a small number of our forces. In the interests of this country's reputation and for the sake of every decent member of our armed forces.
>
> *(DM, 10–5–2004)*

The paper contended that the Blair Government used the hoax affair to distract attention from genuine abuse of prisoners in Iraq (DM, 14–5–2004).

With the self-proclaimed confirmation of its rightfulness, and the summary dismissal of Morgan, the case was closed for the *Mirror*, though competing tabloids would refer to its 'scandalous misbehaviour' for years. Morgan also kept returning to the incident that broke his newspaper career. In interviews and in his 'private diaries', published as *The Insider*, he emphasized that the *Mirror* had done 'everything by the book' and had not violated the paradigm (Morgan, 2005: 3). In his opinion the paper 'went to every possible length' to verify the authenticity of the story, the pictures and its sources (*Observer*, 9–5–2004). The architect of the *Mirror*'s anti-war campaign raised the issue of a conspiracy over and over again. 'I don't want you to say I was set up, or even infer that I think it was a conspiracy, but it may be that someone thought they might suit the *Mirror*'s agenda on Iraq' (*Sunday Telegraph*, 13–5–2005). In June 2004, Trinity Mirror announced that the paper had lost about 40,000 readers because of the hoax. It expected them to be lost forever because they did not trust the paper anymore (*Independent*, 25–6–2004).

De Volkskrant was haunted by the affair for a year and felt forced to take multiple steps to repair the paradigm. In January 2007, the right-wing magazine *Elsevier* identified a Socialist parliamentary candidate and former military unionist as the paper's informant. It said he also had actively cooperated in investigating the story and pressured (and blackmailed) a former military commander who investigated the incidents in Iraq to cooperate with *de Volkskrant*. The latter declared a week later that he had told the reporters the opposite of what they had written: there had been an investigation, but no signs of torture or a cover-up (*Elsevier*, 27–1 and 3–2–2007). In reply, the editor of *de Volkskrant* said his paper would protect its source but that it was 'ridiculous' to suggest that it had cooperated with the Socialist Party to manipulate the elections (Vk, 26–1 and 27–1–2007).

This statement was not sufficient to control the damage. Therefore *de Volkskrant* (10–2–2007) decided to publish a lengthy reconstruction of the genesis of the story. It said it felt forced to do so because of the doubts that were cast about the meticulousness of its reporting and the sincerity of its motives. It admitted to having made mistakes but hoped to prove that it had acted conscientiously and sincerely. The article, written by the initial reporter, closely reconstructed the process of reporting over a few months. Although the reporter showed some reflexivity, his line of argument was apologetic. He justified the choices he made during his investigations and did not discuss any doubts, mistakes or alternative options. Other media spoke of putting up a smoke screen (*Elsevier*, 17–2–2007). In the same issue the ombudsman criticized the paper for protecting its sources for too long. It should have replied to their accounts of what happened and the 'mud' in other media by opening up. A week later the ombudsman raised a number of critical issues that compensated for the defensive stand of the paper (Vk, 10–2–2007; 17–2–2007).

In June 2007 two committees that were established by the Government to investigate the accusations concluded that neither torture nor a cover-up had taken place. In a statement on its front page, *de Volkskrant* (19–6–2007) apologized again for the term 'torture'. At the same time it stressed that it had done its 'journalistic duty'. Just as in the case of the *Mirror*, it emphasized that its accusations had been false but that it had put an important issue on the public agenda. Its ombudsman praised the continuing reporting on supposed misbehaviour by Dutch soldiers in Iraq but believed the coverage was out of balance. He believed the paper in the past months had dug into the topic deeper and deeper because it wanted to justify itself, and made a plea for procedures to avoid future mistakes (Vk, 23–6–2007). Soon thereafter, the editor of *de Volkskrant* asked a journalist and a lawyer to investigate the paper's policy. They concluded that reporters had been too eager to score and had tunnel vision, while there were neither internal discussions nor sufficient mechanism of control. In reply, the paper published 'five lessons learnt'. Procedures were introduced that were intended to guarantee that reporters would uphold the journalistic paradigm. The report itself, a summary of a longer piece, was made available on the paper's website (Vk, 5–12–2007).

A profession suffering from osteoporosis

Hoaxes reveal the structural weakness of the current journalistic paradigm. It is firmly rooted in the objectivity regime that contends that journalism has developed practical procedures that guarantee it the ability to both access and assess ontological truth. But in fact the paradigm derives its performative power only from the formal conventions it applies. Whether readers 'believe' a story depends on its rhetorical strength. It has to fit into existing frameworks of knowledge and the routines underlying reporting have to be made manifest in textual conventions that are familiar to the reader. However, contrary to what its paradigm contends, journalism only offers provisional 'truths'. If new accounts are more convincing they will replace older stories. Objectivity as a strategic ritual, both reflected in discourse on journalism and in journalism discourse itself, has to mask the preliminary character of meaning making. It aims to safeguard journalism from criticism. As a moral norm, set of practices and textual conventions, it underlies a social contract between journalism and the public. As such, it embodies and manifests the authority of journalism.

Journalism wants to persuade the reader that the facts it presents are true. It therefore presents the social world in authoritative language that leaves no space for doubt. The textual conventions it uses to do so are adapted to the audience that an outlet addresses. Popular papers like the *Mirror* not only appeal to moral outrage, but also support their truth-claims with factual information such as pictures and quotes from eyewitnesses that convey authenticity and speak for themselves. Conversely, quality media like *de Volkskrant* use compelling and omniscient accounts that present events, opinions and the context in which they take place as indisputable facts. Although paradigm repair frames them as deviant, hoaxes are generally accepted as 'real stories' at their outset because they fit the journalistic paradigm so incredibly well. What does this imply for journalism?

The current journalistic paradigm is the product of a specific historical situation. It was 'invented' as a strategy in journalism's struggle for autonomy from both political (partisan) and economic (market) conditions (cf. Schudson, 2001; Broersma, 2007). It proved to be tremendously successful as the industry developed, convincing the public of journalism's potential to neutrally mirror reality, which, as a result, granted the profession a certain authority and credibility. The mass-medium system made it possible to control the flow of information and to monopolize truth by naturalizing facts in authoritative discourse. Only two decades ago, news consumers could access a limited number of media and alternative views. They were also less well educated, less media literate and less capable of navigating information. Moreover, the journalistic field was more or less neatly arranged. News organizations, even when they were competing, could more easily negotiate consensus. They had a mutual interest in upholding – and if necessary repairing – the paradigm. In addition, it was far easier for the medium to keep sources and information to themselves, because politicians, PR people and other stakeholders were more dependent on the mass media to get their message across and had fewer options to manage their image.

In the past decades we have slowly moved from linear communication into the age of the database. As Lev Manovich has argued, database logic has superseded the narrative and argumentative logic of modernity. Now information is digitized and available on the internet, and 'the world appears to us as an endless and unstructured collection of images, texts, and other data records, it is only appropriate that we will be moved to model it as a database' (Manovich, 2001: 219). Through computers, and increasingly with mobile devices, we are able to continuously interact with an immense database filled with contending truth-claims: the unlimited set of media objects that form the internet. These nodes of information do not necessarily obey the cause-and-effect structure of linear communication such as journalism. News consumers are nowadays able to navigate and manipulate information online. They range from mass media to niche sites and individual bloggers, to information from former journalistic sources like politicians, companies and pressure groups, to Wikipedia and digital libraries.

Instead of being dependent on the authority of mass media, news consumers can increasingly construct their own truth-claims and representations of social reality with greater ease and individualization. They obviously do not do this on a permanent basis but mainly when a topic interests them or is important to them. This ability simultaneously fascinates and confuses news consumers. But either way it structurally undermines trust in the journalistic paradigm. As one of the participants in a focus group on declining trust in the UK media stated: 'Before, if you heard something, it was gospel absolutely true – now nothing is straight forward' (Coleman et al., 2009: 34). Coleman et al. found that news consumers tend to trust online information more than they do mainstream media. They contend that Google gives them all the information they want. 'It makes sure you don't take anything for granted', as one respondent said. The researchers concluded that the internet's 'open method of gathering information, allowing public comment and making contestation visible' explains its credibility. Citizens value the possibilities of engaging with news. 'This expanded space exposed them to more sources, opportunities to discuss and pathways to explore aspects of the news that "they" (elites/the establishment) would prefer to remain inconspicuous' (Coleman et al., 2009: 34–35).

A more sceptical and engaged public should obviously be valued from a democratic perspective. However, if citizens – metaphorically and literally – do not 'buy' journalism anymore, and if no alternative suppliers of information have taken its place to 'feed' an informed citizenry, not just the news industry but also democracy is in trouble. As follows from the analysis of these two hoaxes, journalism's claim to truth is still the fundament of its authority and credibility. However, in the age of the database it is much harder if not impossible to uphold to that claim. There is not only more information accessible to citizens, but the formal conventions journalism uses to convey news stories are increasingly challenged. Therefore, its paradigm is continuously refractured. Every mouse click reassures news consumers that news does not convey *the* truth but *a* truth. Hoaxes, and the growing contestation of (news) facts in general, confirm the impression that journalism is not reliable. The argument used by the *Mirror* and *de Volkskrant*, that facts can be untrue but still reveal – or better symbolize – the truth, contributes even more to the rise of uncertainty that subverts journalism's paradigm.

What is often labelled as 'the crisis of journalism' is not just a crisis of technology or an outmoded business model. The problem is first and foremost that journalism is struggling to survive in a new age by means of a paradigm that suited an era that is quickly turning into history. As the balance in the practice of meaning making at least partly shifts from the media organization to the consumer, journalism as a symbolic form might be losing its performative power. When its formal conventions are increasingly challenged they will become incapable of convincing news consumers that the message they carry is authoritative. Essentially, the crisis of journalism is thus one of vanishing authority and vaporizing trust because citizens have more access to information and can assess alternative representations of social reality. Currently journalism is a profession suffering from osteoporosis. Its paradigm is refractured over and over again, and might even eventually be broken. This does not mean that what journalism aims for – making sense of social reality by digging for new information, and organizing and packaging it – is redundant. On the contrary, the demand for that may only increase. However, it might be much harder, if not impossible, to unite the public under one regime of 'objective' truth. Journalism has to adapt to this new reality, and to rethink its fundamentals. Paradigm change might be not just advisable but even necessary for journalism to retain its social function.

3

GETTING THE FACTS STRAIGHT IN A DIGITAL ERA

Journalistic accuracy and trustworthiness

Colin Porlezza and Stephan Russ-Mohl

No tenet of journalism is as widely accepted as the obligation to report the facts accurately. But from the public's point of view, journalists fall short of their high-held principles. According to a survey by the Pew Research Center (2009), the public's assessment of the accuracy of news stories is currently at its lowest level in the United States. Just 29 per cent of Americans say that news organizations generally get the facts straight, while 63 per cent say that news stories are often inaccurate. The public's scepticism is well founded. Journalism is a fast-paced field and therefore vulnerable to errors. More than 70 years of accuracy research in the United States has documented that error rates have been rising. According to the largest, most recent American accuracy study, nearly half of all stories in US regional newspapers contain at least one factual error as perceived by news sources (Maier, 2005). If subjective errors are counted as well, inaccuracy rises to 61 per cent, an error rate among the highest so far reported.

This is an alarming trend that should be of concern for journalists and researchers worldwide. Committing mistakes without correcting them endangers trust and credibility – which are possibly the most precious assets of professional journalism. When the American Society of Newspapers conducted focus groups and telephone surveys, asking readers about the trustworthiness of their papers (Urban, 1999), it found that the public saw too many errors in the press, and that readers perceived these mistakes quite differently compared to journalists themselves. The report concluded: 'Even seemingly small errors feed public scepticism about a newspaper's credibility. Each misspelled word, bad apostrophe, garbled grammatical construction, weird cutline and mislabelled map erodes public confidence in a newspaper's ability to get anything right.' Without credibility and trust, journalism may be considered superfluous by audiences at times when it is needed more than ever to reinforce democracy by providing relevant information to these very audiences, and by serving as a watchdog on the powerful. According to Briggs (2008), journalism is not only slowly disconnecting with its community but more fundamentally 'journalism's brand is broken'.

Codes of ethics worldwide stress the importance of getting the facts straight. In the United States, the Society of Professional Journalists' code of ethics states: 'Test the accuracy of information from all sources and exercise care to avoid inadvertent error. Deliberate distortion is never permissible.' The International Federation of Journalists has a similar mandate, and the Swiss Press Council (2008) goes one step further, as its guidelines state: 'The search for the truth is the starting point of every journalistic activity (...) Journalists shall correct every article, whose content is proven to be false in whole or in part.' The Chamber of Professional Journalists in Italy similarly stresses the importance of accuracy and the need to correct errors (Ordine dei Giornalisti, 1993).

However, the situation for the newsrooms is getting even more complicated. The times of one-way communication have definitely come to an end as journalism grows more interactive with Web 2.0. Scott Maier (2009) notes that 'the corrections system is often flawed in print journalism, but the checks and balances needed to assure accuracy are arguably even more haphazard with the journalism that news organizations display online'. A recent study of 155 US newspapers, carried out by John Russial (2009: 12), confirms the notion that copy editing is clearly no priority for online stories: about 50 per cent of all surveyed newspapers reported that they did not always copy edit their online news stories before they were published on their websites. Some stories are corrected after publication, others are corrected without notification, while some stories simply get 'scrubbed' and disappear from the web-page. As Craig Silverman (2007: 234) notes, a clear standard on handling online errors is lacking.

Accuracy as a research topic draws attention to what may be the deepest difference between professional journalism and lay communication, as well as public relations: the commitment to provide accurate, relevant, trustworthy, balanced news. Our study on how Swiss and Italian regional newspapers relate to accuracy compared to their American counterparts reveals that inaccuracy seems to be an almost inherent, though undesirable, aspect of journalism. Journalism research could and should hold a mirror up to those working in newsrooms, while at the same time being transparent about its limits. This is increasingly important since the internet and social networks impose new challenges for accuracy in reporting and correction policies. If journalism wishes to regain its credibility and the trust of its publics – and perhaps also their willingness to pay – accuracy should remain on its agendas.

Between credibility and trust

According to Matthes and Kohring (2007: 232), 'research concerning trust in news media has emerged almost entirely under the label of media credibility'. However, if one analyses past research on credibility of the media, the lack of a clear conceptual basis for analysis with a certain level of complexity still remains a problem. Much research has been conducted, mainly in the United States, but theoretical imprecisions cause problems concerning the operationalization of the studies. The results, therefore, should be interpreted with some scepticism.

Research on credibility is rooted in psychological research on persuasion. An early, methodologically significant step was made by the so-called Yale Group led by the social psychologist Carl Hovland. Together with Walter Weiss (1951), Irving Janis and Harold Kelley (1953) he profoundly influenced later research by identifying two components of (source) credibility: expertness and trustworthiness. Expertness in this case means the communicator's ability to provide a truthful account of 'reality'. Trustworthiness is defined as the absence of persuasive or manipulative aims of the communicator and the desire to transmit all the information in a complete and accurate way. In their model, the effect of communication is closely linked to the source and his characteristics, so that credibility seems to be an objective characteristic of the communicator; the concept of credibility, however, cannot be restricted solely to the communicator, because the content of communications has to be taken into consideration, too.

Another dominant aspect of credibility research is linked to the question of how much credibility different types of media enjoy. This was Roper's (1985) research question in his comparative media-credibility approach. Regardless of the prominence of the studies, Roper's research conceals a weakness: it only takes into account the relative credibility of one medium compared to the others, although recipients apply different concepts for attributing credibility to television or newspapers. Different publication types are thus put on the same level and analysed on the basis of a one-dimensional concept (cf. Matthes and Kohring, 2007: 234).

As interest in credibility increased throughout the 1960s, the theoretical debates on the concept of credibility grew more intense. As part of another American Society of Newspaper Editors (ASNE) study, Gaziano and McGrath (1986) developed an overall credibility score through factor analysis. The analysis showed that constructs such as being fair, unbiased, trustworthy, complete, factual and accurate are central dimensions of the concept of credibility. While Gaziano and McGrath identified 12 credibility factors, Meyer (1988) found that credibility could be gauged with as few as 5 factors. In this approach, credibility is understood to be a multidimensional construct, where 'semantic differentials of adjectives and some journalism-related items were analyzed with the help of factor analysis' (Matthes and Kohring, 2007: 235).

German communication researcher Günter Bentele (1988; 1994; 1998) analysed the concept from a more theoretical perspective, distancing his research from a purely causal model of credibility as well as from a mere 'classification' of objective characteristics which make up credibility. In his theory, credibility cannot be manufactured, or created, only on the supply side, because the communicator cannot determine the choices and behaviour of the recipient: credibility becomes an attribute awarded by the recipients during the communication process. If they award credibility to a communicator, this is their construct based on certain observations, expectations and experience linked to the media in question.

Finally, Matthes and Kohring (2007: 238ff) offered a new multidimensional approach combining the concepts of trust and credibility with theories of journalism and modern society. In their 'multiple factor model of trust in news media',[1] they argue that the trust of the recipients in the news media is based on four dimensions: 'trust in the selectivity of topics', 'trust in the selectivity of facts', 'trust in journalistic assessment' and, hence, 'trust in the accuracy of depictions'. This last factor, defined as a dimension that includes trust in verifiable and approvable accuracy of depicted facts, shows that *accuracy* plays a central role in assessing trust in media. As the two authors themselves acknowledge, the observations of recipients are highly selective and their classification into 'right' or 'wrong' is not objectively assignable.

Accuracy research

Though one of the first German media researchers, Emil Dovifat (1931), described major reasons for errors in news reporting years ago, very little data has been gathered in Europe detailing the frequency with which newsrooms commit errors. In the United States, however, research done in the past seventy years estimates error rates from 40 per cent to over 60 per cent of news articles. Systematic empirical news-accuracy research started with Mitchell Charnley's seminal pioneering study in 1936.[2] He clipped a thousand articles from three local newspapers and asked the people cited as sources to examine the articles for errors. Following his method, researchers have commonly classified factual accuracy into the following error categories: incorrect quotation, spellings, names, ages, other incorrect numbers, titles, addresses, other locations, time and dates. According to Charnley, close to half of all analysed news-paper articles (46 per cent) contained errors, an error rate that surprises veteran jour-nalists even today. Almost thirty years later, Charles Brown (1965) carried out a similar study, examining 200 articles from 42 Oklahoma weeklies. Brown's sources found errors in 41 per cent of the stories examined.

Fred Berry's study (1967) introduced a new perspective on accuracy research by creating a dichotomy between *factual* and *subjective* errors, i.e. information considered misleading even if factually correct. Later William B. Blankenburg (1970) examined two US West Coast dailies, one rural and one suburban. Applying Berry's identifi-cation of objective and subjective errors, he found 60 per cent of news stories erro-neous. Using Blankenburg's sample, Gary Lawrence and David Grey (1969) conducted personal interviews on accuracy with both news sources and reporters. In an analysis exclusively of subjective errors, sources attributed errors to sensationalism and the lack of personal contact, while reporters mentioned internal organizational problems within the newsrooms and the time pressures inherent in the profession. Tillinghast (1982) found similar results: according to sources, errors occurred due to haste, while reporters cited carelessness and editors' misunderstandings.[3] While sources claim nearly half of all articles to be in error, reporters – especially younger ones – often insist their work was accurate. Examining mathematical accuracy in the press, Maier (2003) found similar evidence that news sources and reporters often disagree about what constitutes an error, in particular when there is room for interpretation. This might lead to the conclusion that Charnley's inductive and pragmatic approach of asking news sources to examine the articles in which they are cited is still a useful option.

One other reason why Charnley's model has remained so popular is its simplicity. If one is analysing huge quantities of articles for mistakes, there is simply no better instance for identifying errors than the primary sources mentioned. At first glance, one might argue that the credibility of a medium is not harmed if *only* the source identifies an error. Credibility will only be affected in cases that receive a great deal of public attention (i.e. other media inform the general public about the mistakes a competitor made, as in the current *News of The World* crisis, the Jayson Blair scandal, or the role of the media in Princess Diana's death). But does this also hold for 'isolated' cases in which only the source concerned knows that a name was misspelled or other 'facts' were wrong? First, it could be argued that it is highly probable that not only the primary source, but also other knowledgeable readers discover mistakes. Second, a multiplication factor is at hand; sources are frequently opinion leaders, influencing the opinions of others with their observations. By discussing mistakes, they may create a snowball effect, damaging the credibility of journalism. According to Urban (1999), severe errors also have a severe impact on credibility. Sources' first hand 'experience' with news media will inevitably spread by 'word of mouth'. Third, a dangerous lack of quality and mistakes may cause cumulative effects. In a wake-up call to its employees, the leading Finnish newspaper *Helsingin Sanomat* pointed out years ago the importance of caring for quality. Assuming that due to errors and mistakes 0.1 per cent of their subscribers are 'unhappy' daily, the *Helsingen Sanomat* noted that it would end up with 450 unhappy subscribers every day. Piling up over the year, 136,000 subscribers would be unhappy – which was more than a third of subscribers.

On the other hand, using the source as a determinant of accuracy leaves identification of errors open to interpretation. Therefore Kocher and Shaw (1979) suggested a so-called 'record comparison' model. 'This involves comparing what is said in newspaper accounts with an official record that has been stipulated in advance as a "verifiable certainty"' (Kocher, 1981: 172). This finally seemed to be an improvement on Charnley's method. However, only in a few cases do newspapers have such an 'official record' as counterpart, and 'official records' can, too, be very dubious sources – as most journalists knew even before President Bush went to war claiming that Saddam Hussein had command of weapons of mass destruction.

Some research on news accuracy has also been conducted in the German-speaking world. A pioneer was Bernd Wetzenbacher (1998), discussing the poor handling of errors and lack of correction policies in German newspapers. Several other studies refer to the relationship between public relations and journalism. Breiden (2002, as quoted in Baerns, 2007: 50f) studied how press releases were used by the major news agencies in Germany. According to her study, the handling of the incoming information by news agencies was, overall, 'accurate'. Sources of errors were 'distributed evenly, that is to say that (a) errors caused by adopting information from sources which contain errors, (b) errors in the processing of the information by sources and (c) errors in the agency's own research occurred in equal proportions'. Baerns (1999) studied the next step of news processing: How do errors contained in news distributed by news agencies affect the reporting of the daily press? Her work showed that approximately 90 per cent of the news provided by news agencies is correct. However, those news stories containing errors are not corrected by the newspapers; instead, they multiply and thus grow out of proportion.

Accuracy at Swiss and Italian regional newspapers

To address the gap between the US and Europe in accuracy research we conducted an accuracy audit of two hundred newspaper articles from each of five daily newspapers published in Switzerland and five more dailies in Italy. We wanted to find out how often errors occur in the analysed regional newspapers in Switzerland and Italy, what kinds of errors occur most often and how serious they are. In a second step to our research we tried to assess how these errors affect the credibility of newspapers. We did so by assessing how sources relate news accuracy to media credibility. Building upon Maier's (2005) findings about the American situation, our investigation for the first time provides a European perspective on the topic.

Based on Hallin and Mancini's (2004) differentiation of media systems, we expected different error rates in Switzerland and Italy compared to the US. We assumed that we would find the highest rate in Italy due to fewer resources in the average newsroom and the polarized pluralist journalism culture. We also supposed that the number and severity of the errors would have a negative impact on the credibility of the analysed newspapers as seen by the sources, and would have a negative effect on their willingness to act as sources again.

To generate comparable data, our study closely followed the methodology pioneered by Charnley (1936) and adapted by Maier (2005). We investigated five midsized regional newspapers in Switzerland: *Aargauer Zeitung, Basler Zeitung, Berner Zeitung, Südostschweiz* and *Tages-Anzeiger* (Zurich) and five papers of similar size and function in Italy: *L'Eco di Bergamo, Il Giornale di Brescia, Il Resto del Carlino* (Bologna), *Il Giornale di Sicilia* (Palermo) and *Il Secolo XIX* (Genoa). For each newspaper, a sample of 200 articles was collected from the front page, the local news, business and culture/lifestyle sections of the paper.[4] For each article, a primary source was identified, who received a copy of the story together with a six-page questionnaire. The surveys were conducted from May to December 2008. Each news source was asked to identify errors and to classify them according to type and perceived severity of error.

Although the response rate in the 2005 US case was 68 per cent, the European rates in our study were considerably lower. The response to the Swiss newspaper sample was 50 per cent and in Italy it was far lower. After a surprisingly low response rate from news sources in Sicily, we decided to change the sample of Italian newspapers, adding a newspaper from the highly developed North instead of a second paper from the less developed South. Even thereafter, the final response rate was a disappointing 15 per cent. Thus, the Italian results can at best be regarded as explorative, and will be presented separately later in the chapter.

Not surprisingly, the results present evidence that newspaper inaccuracy – and its corrosive effect on media credibility – transcend national borders and journalism cultures, though there are cultural differences which need to be investigated further. Politicians, government spokespersons and business representatives turned out to be the prevalent sources in all three countries. We noticed that in Switzerland so called 'experts' are consulted very often (24.5 per cent). In the other countries 'experts' are not consulted as frequently – in the US they account for 11.6 per cent, in Italy only for 7.8 per cent. The consulted news sources found factual inaccuracy in 60 per cent of Swiss newspaper stories they reviewed – one or more objective 'hard' errors such as incorrect names or dates – compared to 48 per cent of the US newspaper articles examined.[5] A higher percentage of perceived factual errors was identified in the Swiss newspapers compared to the US newspapers in every error category except 'numbers wrong' (see Table 3.1).

Despite differences in overall error rates, the rank order of error types was generally similar. The two most common factual errors cited for both countries were misquotations and inaccurate headlines; the least common was an incorrect age and an incorrect address. The most significant difference in factual accuracy concerned headlines: more than 25 per cent of them were found to be inaccurate by sources among the Swiss newspapers studied, compared to only 15 per cent of US news stories. While more factual errors were found in the Swiss press, these inaccuracies were considered somewhat less severe than those identified in US newspapers. On a Likert-like scale in which 1 is a minor error and 7 a major error, the mean rating was 2.5 by Swiss sources, compared to 2.8 by US sources.[6] An adage in American public relations only half-jokingly proclaims: 'Say anything you want about me as long as you spell my name right.' The credo apparently extends to Switzerland: the factual error held most grave among Swiss news sources was having their name wrong (earning a 3.6 severity rating). Reporting the wrong location for an event was also ranked among the most severely rated errors, earning a 3.3 rating by Swiss news sources. (See Table 3.1 for complete rankings.)

TABLE 3.1 Error types ranked by per cent of stories

Factual Errors	Swiss		US	
	%	Severity	%	Severity
Headline wrong	26.6	2.4	14.7	3.1
Misquoted	26.5	2.5	21.0	3.0
Misspelling	12.9	1.7	10.0	1.9
Numbers wrong	12.4	2.6	12.9	2.8
Job title wrong	11.6	2.7	8.5	2.6
Name wrong	8.0	3.6	3.4	3.1
Time wrong	4.3	2.7	2.2	2.6
Location wrong	3.1	3.3	2.7	2.9
Date wrong	3.1	3.0	2.2	3.1
Address wrong	2.7	3.1	1.7	3.3
Age wrong	2.6	2.2	1.4	2.6

TABLE 3.2 Causes attributed to errors ranked by per cent of stories

	Swiss %	US %
Lack of understanding	27.0	25.9
Deadline pressure	23.2	18.9
Insufficient research	17.1	17.3
Events were confusing	13.3	12.6
Didn't ask enough questions	7.5	12.7
Pressure to scoop others	7.0	6.7
Didn't ask right questions	5.8	12.1
Laziness	4.6	9.9
Source provided misinformation	1.7	0.9

Percentage total exceeds 100 per cent because multiple reasons were given for errors in some stories

News sources were also asked to identify supposed reasons why the inaccuracies occurred. The top response from both Swiss and US news sources was that the reporter didn't understand what she or he was writing about, a complaint made for more than one in four stories in which errors were found. Swiss sources attributed inaccuracies to deadline pressure in greater proportion than US sources. They were less likely than US sources to blame errors on reporter laziness or poor questioning. Other attributed causes were fairly similar, with sources from both nations mentioning – as is to be expected – source misinformation as the least likely cause of error (see Table 3.2), a phenomenon which psychologists have named 'self serving bias' (Miller and Ross, 1975).

Despite the frequency of errors, news sources remained trusting in their newspapers and willing to serve as informants again. Swiss sources gave their newspapers a 5.5 rating on a 7-point credibility scale, even higher than the 5.1 trust score attributed by US sources to their newspapers. The majority of Swiss sources also characterized themselves as 'eager' to cooperate with the newspaper again, compared to slightly more than a third of US sources. Only 1 per cent of Swiss sources said they would be 'reluctant' to serve as a source again, compared to 3 per cent of US sources. While sources from both nations seemed strikingly forbearing when finding newspaper errors, inaccuracy nonetheless has a significant negative effect on media credibility and source willingness to cooperate on future stories.

To evaluate the relationship between error and credibility, Pearson product-moment correlation coefficients were computed for story and newspaper credibility and four measures of newspaper accuracy. This measure considers the degree of linear dependence between two variables, in this case instances of inaccuracy and perceived credibility. A negative value implies that as the number and severity of factual errors increases, credibility decreases. By every measure in our study, Swiss and US media credibility among the sources significantly declined in relation to the number and severity of errors (see Table 3.3). The severity of errors had a stronger negative effect on the overall credibility of Swiss newspapers than the overall credibility of US

TABLE 3.3 Pearson correlation coefficients for accuracy measures with credibility

		Story credibility	Newspaper credibility	News source willingness
Number of factual errors	US	−.449	−.236	−.201
	Swiss	−.230	−.167	−.105
Total number of factual and subjective errors	US	−.581	−.326	−.246
	Swiss	−.310	−.237	−.146
Mean severity rating of factual errors	US	−.463	−.305	−.242
	Swiss	−.393	−.349	−.148

Each correlation is significant at the .001 level

newspapers. However, the relationship between story credibility and the number of errors in a story was not as strong with Swiss newspapers as with US newspapers, perhaps because many of the factual errors identified by Swiss sources were considered relatively insignificant.

While the Italian results were not conclusive because of the low response rate, it is still valuable to consider the initial results. Sources reported factual errors in 51.9 per cent of Italian newspaper stories (compared to 60 per cent in Swiss newspapers and 48.2 per cent in US newspapers). A larger percentage of factual errors were identified in Italian newspapers than in US newspapers in every category studied, with misquotations and inaccurate headlines leading the list for both nations. Italian sources rated the severity of factual errors somewhat higher (a mean score of 2.7 on a 7-point Likert scale) than the 2.5 rating by Swiss and slightly lower than the 2.8 rating by US sources. Italian sources gave their newspapers a 5.2 score on a 7-point credibility scale, slightly higher than the 5.1 US sources gave but lower than the 5.5 Swiss sources rating.

Inaccuracy without borders

Overall, this study underscores that accuracy is a serious quality problem. Newspaper inaccuracy transcends national borders and journalism cultures. Whether in Switzerland, in the United States or, with less validity, in Italy, the findings indicate that perceived errors are to be found in at least half of the articles printed. While overall error rates vary, the most frequent kinds of errors identified − and their perceived causes − are almost identical in the three countries examined. Inaccuracy has a corrosive effect on media credibility. News sources, while surprisingly tolerant of errors, maintain high expectations that the news media will get the story right. If in each of the analysed countries every second article contains at least one mistake, this is definitely at least one mistake too many.

In Switzerland, where regional newspapers are considered the premier source of news and newsrooms are well equipped, we did not expect error rates to exceed those found in Italy or the United States. The findings did suggest that inaccuracy is pervasive, even among newspapers with a well-trained staff and a serious purpose. But it would be over-reaching to conclude from this study that Swiss or Italian media are less accurate than the US press. The accuracy judgements of sources may also reflect differences in expectations of news sources and their willingness to attribute error. Swiss sources may be less likely to overlook errors than their Italian counterparts. This proposition is supported by the high level of trust Swiss sources attributed to the press while also holding the newspapers accountable for factual errors they considered minor. Conversely, Italian sources may have lower expectations of newspaper accuracy.

An intriguing aspect to the discussion has been contributed recently by an accuracy study of 14 Irish newspapers. Surprisingly, only 3.4 per cent of the 134 responding news sources rated the errors they found as serious or very serious. The authors summarized: 'At a time when, worldwide, journalists' reputations for honesty and integrity are falling, that may be seen – by the industry particularly – as welcome news' (Fox et al., 2009: 5). However, in a separate fact-check of 54 newspaper items, the researchers found that only 25 contained no error, thus ending up with a 46 per cent accuracy rate, perfectly in line with our research and with previous American studies.

Accuracy rates may also reflect different editing procedures in Europe, where work tends to be reviewed by other journalists, if at all, versus the United States, where stories traditionally are edited prior to publication by editors. However, the difference in perceived accuracy could also be explained differently. As Blankenburg (1970) observed, the relationship between the source and the journalist has an impact on the perception of accuracy: news sources tend to be less critical of a reporter whom they know personally than of an anonymous reporter. In a country like Italy, where communication is generally much more based on personal acquaintance, this factor may also partially explain why sources 'discover' fewer errors.

Errors in a digital age

Taking into account our findings from the old 'dinosaur' media in the three countries, even multimedia newsrooms in the age of Web 2.0 and media convergence need to devote more attention to the problem of errors and corrections management. If between 48 and 60 per cent of regional newspapers' original articles contain errors, what does this mean for journalism online with its 24/7 news dynamic and a shortage of human resources? Do online journalists have a different mentality when it comes to accuracy, as news is an evolving story, as facts are only 'temporary truths', and as online one truth may be simply exchanged for another when there is new information available? As media organizations increasingly use social networks such as Twitter and Facebook to pinpoint their users and to reach their audiences even faster, how should newsrooms react to errors distributed within such channels?

Of course, the best solution would be to avoid mistakes during the journalistic production process. To care seriously for avoidance may be the best 'unique selling proposition' for professional journalism in a news environment influenced strongly by

PR experts and spin doctors, and increasingly also by bloggers and citizen journalists. But even journalists who work meticulously are fallible human beings. Thus inevitably errors will occur. Until recently, journalists were in the comfortable position of explaining the world to their recipients based on one-way communication. Errors were rarely corrected, because it was easy and convenient to hide them. With the emerging Web 2.0, this is fundamentally changing. Competition has become more intense, and thus so has mutual observation.

With its 24/7 cycle, the web seduces journalists to publish as fast as possible unchecked news that needs further professional care (Jarvis, 2009). Traditional filters often do not work online. Breaking news items are no longer processed daily, as was and still is the case in newspapers. Dissemination has become a matter of minutes or even seconds. Timeliness nowadays has priority, as Meckel (2010: 227; see also Meckel, 2011) asserts. It outplays other quality criteria such as accuracy and relevance. Due to an online-first policy, contributions frequently get checked only after publication. The effect is aggravated as errors, once published, diffuse everywhere within minutes due to viral distribution in social networks and to cross-media production techniques of larger publishing houses.

If newsrooms want to be taken seriously in the fast, error-prone digital world, they will have to learn how to deal adequately with mistakes. There are several obvious options for remedy. Anglo Saxon media in particular have been practicing some of them for quite a while: *Correction Corners*, in which errors should be corrected continuously, reliably and voluntarily; *Editor's Notes*, in which heavier errors can be analysed and explained *ex post*; and *Ombudsmen*, serving as institutions of complaints management and as mediators who systematically investigate errors. However, a daily correction corner may not be enough to deal with the flood of mistakes, and it may not be the most adequate way to handle errors online. In newspapers, a page would be needed to ensure that mistakes are not only corrected incidentally, and that corrections do not remain mere cosmetics (Maier, 2007: 40; Nemeth and Sanders, 2009: 99). Nevertheless, the sheer existence of correction corners has helped to increase accuracy. No journalist likes to be exposed in front of his colleagues and to be subject to ridicule.

Digitization offers, however, new ways of implementing correction policies: If online articles published on the webpages of news outlets need to be corrected after publication, newsrooms should document these changes explicitly. Corrections can also be added directly to the original article to make readers aware of them, a policy that many bloggers have been using for a long time. Besides that, independent 'third parties' observing the media help them to become aware of errors as well. Blogs like *Regret the Error* or the German *BildBlog* keep track of mistakes, while others like *Media Bugs* serve as intermediaries supporting newsrooms to correct their errors faster and more reliably.[7]

One of the challenges in the digital era remains how media organizations should react to the diffusion of errors in breaking news if they are active in social networks like Twitter or Facebook. On the web it is virtually impossible to simply erase mistakes. The editorial production process no longer ends with the publication of an article. Moreover, when a story goes online, it is often a starting point for more journalistic work. 'Online errors don't disappear like yesterday's print edition. News organizations need to recognize what the new permanence means for errors and corrections, and act accordingly' (Silverman, 2008). The discussion was reopened after the shooting on 8 January 2011 in Tucson (Arizona), when US congresswoman Gabrielle Giffords was seriously injured. Several major media organizations wrongly reported and tweeted that she had died.[8] National Public Radio (NPR)'s newscast broke the story, and soon after CNN, Fox News and the *New York Times* followed with the same false news. The media organizations started to retract the information – but in different ways. While NPR left the erroneous tweets on their account, CNN, Fox News and the *New York Times* deleted them altogether. Considering how fast errors can spread online, particularly in social networks, how should media organizations handle similar cases in the future? For private users of social networks it is easier to just delete a wrong message because the consequences are not that severe. For professional journalists using these channels to distribute breaking news, the situation is more complex. Most media organizations have more followers than individuals, hence their errors spread more rapidly. Given their important role within democracy, they also need to act more transparently.

Two valid lines of argumentation have emerged: the first is committed to transparency and wants to preserve the narrative of the story, the second wants to prevent the retweeting of wrong information. Proponents of the latter argue that if a flawed message is left on a channel, it continues to spread, even if a correction is posted in the meantime. According to Steve Safran, editor of the social TV site Lost Remote, for hours after it was reported that the congresswoman was alive, 'people kept discovering the original tweet that she was dead, retweeting it to their friends without seeing the update. In several cases, the retweet of the incorrect report came three or more hours after the report first spread' (quoted in Silverman, 2011). On the other hand, deleting factually incorrect tweets without telling your audience that you have done so is not the most transparent way to handle such cases. As Rosenberg (2011) affirms, it 'always leaves open the possibility that you are trying to hide the error or pretend it never happened'. This is also risky for a media organization. Today it is quite easy to discover journalistic errors disseminated on the net, and this may severely harm the reputation of a media brand.

A more transparent way to handle such cases is to simply leave the mistakes on the Facebook or Twitter account. Andrew Phelps of WBUR, a radio station in Boston, argues that:

> We have decided not to delete the erroneous tweet, because it serves as part of the narrative of this story. Facts can change fast when news is breaking, and that leads to errors. We need to own the error, not hide from it. But we also need to rectify the error and explain ourselves to people who trust us. Deleting the tweet would do more to harm trust than preserving it would do to harm truth.

The question of trust and credibility is central to the discourse. Admitting that one was wrong can help to establish a more trustful relationship with audiences. Mensing and Oliver asked more than one hundred editors of smaller US dailies about the damage that errors cause to their newspapers' credibility. Three-quarters of them thought that errors were a very serious problem for their newspapers: 'Given the fact that 58 per cent of the respondents said they saw errors of fact either daily or more than once a week in their own papers, accuracy is clearly a significant issue for many editors at small newspapers' (Mensing and Oliver, 2005: 16). There is no reason why these insights should not apply equally to websites.

According to Maier (2009), 'setting the record straight is essential to restoring trust that is eroded by errors'. And Rosenberg (2011) affirms: 'Public tweets play an increasingly important role in our news ecosystem. They tell us stories and are part of the story, too. We should minimize tampering with them. We need better tools that might let us correct them responsibly, whether this takes the form of fixes auto-propagating to re-tweeters or correction notices or revision tracking or all of the above.' Media organizations must accept that on social-network sites errors can and should be corrected near to real time. Moreover, they know who follows them on social networks. Hence, they should at least make an effort 'to reach out to people who re-tweeted the incorrect information in order to make sure they pass along the new, correct information. We have a responsibility to follow up on our correction tweets and help give them the push and distribution they require' (Silverman, 2011).

The toll of inaccuracy

Due to the emergence of new media tools, managing corrections, at least theoretically, has become a lot easier. However, newsrooms need to overhaul their structures and news processing. They should both correct errors and develop new forms of interactive two-way communication, including the handling of feedback provided by audiences concerning mistakes. New roles should be added in the newsrooms: editors dealing with commentaries, journalists publishing, controlling and continuously correcting feeds on Twitter and Facebook, and mediators who serve as an interface between the public and the media outlet. Overall, media organizations have to set up and implement a social-media strategy – an issue that goes well beyond increasing their responsiveness, implementing correction policies and improving their quality management.

Yet these kinds of initiatives need resources newsrooms may be unable to make available in times of shrinking income from advertising and decreasing willingness of publics to pay for news. Thus, changes in the media landscape also need to be made transparent in order to help people to understand why the error rates are so high and even increasing. As stated by Maier:

> Today's newspaper reporters, though more highly educated and professional, are perhaps stretched thin by staff reductions and other pressures brought on by

> media consolidation and Wall Street profit demands. Copy editors, the last line
> of defense against newspaper errors, could be missing mistakes as production
> demands impede careful review of articles before they go to press.
>
> *(Maier, 2005: 546)*

A difficult, uncertain economic environment is, however, no strong argument against
improved corrections management. Neither corrections nor editor's notes are really
costly; they should simply be seen as part of a strategy to regain credibility and trust.
Moreover, the publics themselves should be invited to report errors directly to the
newsroom, by using innovative forms of collaborative action similar to crowd-
sourcing techniques, which, for example, the *Guardian* applied successfully in the case
of the expenses scandal of Members of Parliament in the UK. The insight that
loyal readers are also cooperative readers could facilitate more systematic readers'
involvement.[9] The *Washington Post* has just started to implement this form of out-
sourcing.[10] It may be helpful in grim economic times; however, when readers mail
the newsroom, a specialized editor will still be needed to check these mails before
correcting the indicated errors.

More research dealing with errors and corrections management would be highly
desirable – both in old and new media. One track of future research should deal with
the different expectations of the publics in different journalism cultures. More
important, however, may be to ensure that existing research which has been compiled
over so many years will finally arrive in newsrooms and inspire changes which might
help journalists to regain credibility and trust. Is there hope that newsrooms will show
more initiative in reducing the number of errors and/or improve their correction
policies? More studies won't change the behaviour in the newsrooms unless incentives
are created making it more 'attractive' to admit that the news business is and will
remain error-prone. Across cultural boundaries, accuracy matters. Credibility and trust
are at stake. As Kovach and Rosenstiel (2001: 43) observe, the accuracy of news is the
'foundation upon which everything else builds: context, interpretation, debate, and
all of public communication. If the foundation is faulty, everything else is flawed.'

Acknowledgements

We are deeply indebted to Scott Maier, who generously supported our empirical
research during his sabbatical at the European Journalism Observatory in 2008. We
would like to thank Marta Zanichelli for the gathering of data in Italy, as well as our
student assistants Rahel Aschwanden and David Oehler for their contributions to the
data-gathering and analysis. We also owe thanks to Kate Nacy for editing the English
version of the manuscript and to Marcel Broersma, Mark Eisenegger, Kurt Imhof and
Chris Peters for their inspiring comments.

Notes

1 In their article, they focused on the term trust instead of credibility because they wanted
  to directly link research in the field of communication with sociological theories of trust.

2 The part of this sub-chapter dealing with the American research record closely follows Maier's (2005) overview.

3 This somehow astonishing self-critique by journalists is unique in the history of accuracy research.

4 To exclude material from news agencies, only articles signed by name or by the initials of the author were included. To broaden the sample, no news source was surveyed more than once. Our researchers used web-based databases and telephone directories to locate sources. Questionnaires were delivered by electronic mail when possible, otherwise by ordinary mail. When the questionnaire was not returned within two weeks, another questionnaire was delivered.

5 The difference in error rates is statistically significant (Pearson chi sq (1) = 23.8, p < .001).

6 In an independent-samples t test, the difference in means is statistically significant (t(499.7) = 2.99, p = .003).

7 http://www.regrettheerror.com; http://www.bildblog.de; http://mediabugs.org.

8 A complete history of the erroneous tweets can be seen at: http://www.regrettheerror. com/2011/01/08/npr-reuters-cnn-and-other-major-news-orgs-incorrectly-declare-death- of-rep-giffords/. It is interesting how NPR handled the fact of its inaccurate tweets, calling it 're-learning the lesson of checking sources', see: http://www.npr.org/blogs/ ombudsman/2011/01/11/132812196/nprs-giffords-mistake-re-learning-the-lesson-of- checking-sources.

9 See, for instance, the advice on how to do the right thing by Media Bugs: http://mediabugs. org/pages/best-practices-in-error-reporting-and-corrections.

10 See: http://www.washingtonpost.com/wp-srv/interactivity/corrections/.

4

THE POSTMODERN CHALLENGE TO JOURNALISM

Strategies for constructing a trustworthy identity

Jo Bogaerts and Nico Carpentier

The first decades of the twentieth century led to a period of high modernism[1] in (American) journalism because of the increasing professionalization of journalists and the consolidation of a shared occupational ideology, as authors such as Hallin (1992; 2006) and Zelizer (2004a) have argued. Hallin shows that both political and economic factors contributed to the virtually uncontested status of journalism in providing what was accepted as truthful and direct access to reality. Even though journalism remained 'caught between the competing imperatives of "freedom of the press" and the "laws of the market"' (Champagne, 2009: 48), these tensions did not seem to affect the truth claims of high-modernist journalism. Indeed, characteristic of journalists' attitudes towards their work during the era of high modernism were an apparent self-confidence and an 'absence of a sense of doubt or contradiction' (Hallin, 1992: 14).

However, in subsequent decades this 'sense of wholeness and seamlessness' (ibid.) in journalists' self-image has been thoroughly shaken. By taking a cue from the field of tension between its modernist legacy and contemporary developments in journalism, this chapter wishes to address journalistic identity politics in the face of threat. Departing from the challenges that have confronted journalism in the last few decades and the dwindling trust of audiences, we will first discuss the building blocks of the mainstream professional journalistic identity, and a number of strategies that journalists deploy in order to protect their professional identity, to maintain trust in the profession, and to reaffirm themselves as 'society's truth-teller[s]' (McNair, 1998: 65). This focus on journalistic identity is aligned with a still underdeveloped 'cultural turn' within journalism studies, showing how collective identities (and their rigidities and fluidities) structure the journalistic field.

The theoretical backbone of our analysis is provided by a discourse-theoretical perspective, which allows us to focus on the discursive building blocks (or nodal points) of the modernist journalistic identity, and then to analyze how these elements have become threatened in the contemporary era of liquid modernism. This will allow us to foreground a series of discursive coping strategies, which show how journalism attempts to protect its position as a vital societal field.

Given the broadness of the journalistic field, we will focus on one specific location, namely, online journalism, as this is one of the sites where these truth claims are both maintained and contested, which in turn renders professional identities and the coping mechanisms to protect them visible. Without aiming to create a clear-cut dichotomy between online and traditional journalism, we would nevertheless argue that online journalism is a useful object of investigation, evinced by the fact that 'professional consciousness emerges at least in part round ruptures where the borders of appropriate practice need renegotiation' (Zelizer, 1993b: 223; cf. Matheson, 2004: 446).

The passing of the 'high modernism' of journalism

Since the late 1960s journalism has awaited the same fate as science, as the era of high modernism of journalism gradually shifted to what Deuze (2006a, 2006b) – following Bauman (2000) – has called 'liquid journalism'.[2] A diversity of processes lies at the root of this shift, like for instance broader contextual changes such as detraditionalization, individualization and globalization (Krotz, 2007). Others point to the end of a consensus-based politics and an increasing economic insecurity that severely undermined the public's trust in institutions and authorities. Such distrust in the core values, norms, rhetoric and practices of journalism (Deuze, 2006a; Jones, 2009) has challenged the monopoly on truth held by news institutions. Moreover, changes within the journalistic institution such as a tendency towards commercialization, cross-media mergers and concentration, and the changes triggered by the rise of new media technologies have contributed to the breakdown of journalism's monopoly status as a news institution. Such developments might have led journalism to doubt its own rationality, but instead it has remained mostly faithful to its high-modernist convictions and beliefs.

Journalism, as Zelizer (2004a: 112) puts it, is still indebted to the 'modernist bias of its official self-presentation' and has not adapted itself to changed circumstances. Despite the 'passing of the era of high modernism' (Hallin, 1992), journalism tends to hold on to its self-proclaimed authority. In order to face such severe challenges and to maintain trust in itself and generate trust in its audiences, journalism has developed a series of coping strategies that reaffirm its professional authority. Indeed, 'abandoning the objectivity norm and confessing that journalism is unable to accurately represent reality, would undermine its authority' (Broersma, 2010b: 30).

The ways in which journalism maintains this position have been a widely researched topic in journalism studies. By claiming professionalism (Tuchman, 1972; Soloski, 1990), orienting their actions towards a certain habitus (Matheson, 2003; Benson and Neveu, 2005) and sharing interpretations of the profession (Zelizer, 1993b), journalists maintain an image of competence and authority in spite of their apparent lack of self-criticism (Lule, 1992: 92; Zelizer, 1993a: 81; Zelizer, 1993b: 222;).

Strategies of self-confirmation in the face of threat and challenge have also been researched since Tuchman's introduction of the concept of news repair in her 1978 book *Making News* (see e.g. Bennett, Gressett, and Haltom, 1985; Reese, 1990). In this chapter, we want to complement the focus on institutional reactions with a theoretical reflection on identity work and politics (Hall, 1989; Reger, Myers and Einwohner, 2008) that modernist journalism and the threats towards its position produce. To support this reflection, we will turn to discourse theory, which will allow us to develop a discourse-theoretical perspective on journalism.

A discourse-theoretical perspective on journalism

Discourse theory, mainly opened up by Foucault, Žižek, Butler and Laclau and Mouffe, regards the social space as discursively constructed, which means that their meanings are the temporary and contingent result of a *process of signification* (see Carpentier and Spinoy, 2008: 5). As Ernesto Laclau (1988: 254) explains, a discourse is 'a structure in which meaning is constantly negotiated and constructed'. Any discourse consists of a number of discursive elements which are taken from a reservoir that Laclau and Mouffe call the field of discursivity and are related to each other through articulation. This process of *articulation* involves linking up discursive elements around (a number of) privileged signifiers which temporarily stabilize discourses. Such privileged signifiers act as *nodal points*, i.e. they arrest the unceasing deferral of meaning and structure the dominant discourse in a rigid, even if structurally contingent, way. Even though nodal points 'sustain the identity of a certain discourse by constructing a knot of definite meanings' (Torfing, 1999: 88–89) that does not mean they are in some way more fully saturated with meaning than any other signifier. On the contrary, nodal points are characterized by a certain emptying out of meaning, which is exactly what accounts for their structural role in the unification of discourse.

From this perspective, journalism, like any social field, is seen to gain its meanings through discursive processes. As such, discourse theory stresses that there is no inherent meaning to the concepts and practices of journalism, but that it acquires these in the process of articulation, i.e. the relations established among signifiers. Of course, in spite of this contingency, discourses aim to hegemonize their own representation by concealing their particularity and claiming universality. The more natural and self-evident a discourse appears, the stronger its claim on universality and the better it is in maintaining its hegemonic status.

Such a claim to universality is based on the articulation of a range of signifiers that together construct 'good journalism' through an 'equivalential chain of particularities' (Laclau, 2000: 304). In keeping with the literature (in particular Carpentier's (2005) and Deuze's (2005) suggested concepts) we regard the following values as the core nodal points of the journalistic ideology: public service, ethics, management, autonomy, membership of a professional elite, immediacy and objectivity. At the same time, 'good' (mainstream) journalism needs a constitutive outside; it can only be established in opposition to other possible forms of journalism whose values are systematically excluded as 'bad', 'undesirable' or 'unwanted'. This does not only (evidently) mean that hegemony always involves the rejection of alternatives, but – more importantly – that this rejection is a constitutive moment in the production of identity. These other models of journalism, as well as the particular values which constitute them, are not necessarily 'bad', but are rather considered as unacceptable in a given ideological, temporal and spatial context. Obviously, different journalistic traditions, communities and cultures will contain different articulations of these discursive elements, but it is contended here that the elements that are discussed below remain crucial building blocks for the professional identity.

The public-service ideal (not to be restricted to public-service broadcasting) points to journalism's (self-)perceived role as a cornerstone in democratic society at large. Journalists regard themselves as bringing a service to the public which mainly consists in 'working as some kind of representative watchdog of the status quo in the name of people' (Deuze, 2005: 447). Especially in the discourse of the liberal and social responsibility models of the media, journalists have been attributed such a key role in offering citizens the means to participate in democratic regimes (see Hutchins, 1947; Siebert, Peterson and Schramm, 1956; Merill, 1974; McQuail, 1994).

In order to justify this public service role, journalism points to the existence of a sense of ethics that guarantee the integrity, reliability and status of journalists. Most often this ethical consciousness is identified with a commitment to objectivity and truth (see below), but the ethical framework is broader. Belsey and Chadwick (1992: 1), for example, call journalism an 'honourable profession', while Frost (2007: 11) emphasizes the need to gather information in a 'morally justifiable way'. Because of journalism's emphasis on the nodal point of autonomy, it has often privileged the principle of self-regulation as a guarantee for ethical behaviour. Such professional-ethical principles 'replace censorship and other barriers to communication [...] with compelling reasons for journalists regarding self-limitation in democratic societies' (Pöttker, 2004: 84).

Another nodal point that is closely linked to the public-service ideal is the journalist's role perception as gatekeepers who manage the flow of information, which is inextricably linked to the journalist's main source of professional distinction: their ability to decide what is news and what is not (see Zelizer, 1993b: 220). But journalists do more than managing the news; they also manage and control a wide series of resources. In order to achieve their objectives, which originate from their 'responsibilities for the professional production of specific media products' (Carpentier, 2005: 204), journalists can make use of the production facilities that are owned (in the strictly legal sense of the word) by the media organization.

Autonomy is another nodal point that structures the mainstream journalistic identity. Journalists emphasize that in order to carry out their work in a professional manner and to be journalistically creative they must be independent, have editorial autonomy and enjoy freedom both from internal and external pressures (see McQuail, 1994). However, in this insistence on autonomy and freedom, editorial independence has been elevated to 'the status of an ideological value in that it functions to legitimize resistance to [...] change' (Deuze, 2005: 449). In avoiding interference from marketing, corporate ownership and even public criticism, journalists claim that only journalism itself can judge its news products (Singer, 2003: 145). As a result, the insistence on autonomy points to the autopoietic nature of journalism and has played an important role in its attempts to maintain hegemonic status and to legitimate increasingly aggressive styles of newsgathering (see Clayman, 2002).

This sense of autonomy, however, does not mean that the links between media professional and news institution are irrelevant. On the contrary, what constitutes a journalist as a professional is exactly his position within a hierarchically structured organization. Indeed, as Singer (2003: 153) illustrates, 'organizational affiliation has largely defined the professional journalist in the past: one qualifies as a professional precisely because of a loss of individual control over the publication or broadcast of one's work.' However, even within the constraints of this institutional organization, journalists imagine themselves to be independent truth-seekers. Such an image of 'professionalism', as Soloski (1990) has convincingly shown, has been an efficient means to discipline journalists' behaviour while at the same time conveying the idea of autonomy within the organizational structure. Within this structure, journalists are acquainted with the media organization through socialization and with peers through informal networks ('a private world', as Burns (1969) already labelled it in his article about the BBC, entitled 'Public service and private world'). Moreover, the journalistic identity is also constructed through a broader sense of belonging, which relates to the existence of a professional group and professional bodies (Zelizer, 1993b: 223; Naït-Bouda, 2008).

Linking up with journalists' self-perceptions as elite professionals that are responsible for the means of the production of news, is the nodal point of immediacy. Though the main professional trait of journalists is deciding on newsworthiness (see above), part of that ideal is also to get that news across as quickly as possible (Weaver and Wilhoit, 1996: 263), albeit within segmented time zones. Dealing with time is indeed embedded in what Schlesinger (1987: 83–105) calls a 'stop watch culture' that is organized around an efficient organization of labour according to 'beats', deadlines and cycles. Important in this regard is the value attributed to the 'scoop' and other ways of gaining prestige by covering a news item first.

However, the key element that defines the self-perception of journalists (especially, but not exclusively, those working in a more Anglo-American(ized) context, see Carpentier and Trioen, 2010) is the notion of objectivity (see Schudson, 1978; 2001; Reese, 1990; Ognianova and Endersby, 1996; Mindich, 1998; Broersma, 2010b). By insisting on the value of objectivity in their work, in varying degrees, journalists claim to have unmediated access to reality and the ability to represent it in a factual and truthful manner. Of course, objectivity is not all-encompassing, as the distinction between 'facts' and 'opinion', and the explicit toleration towards specific ideological positions, shows. Moreover, 'the concept of objectivity has been so mangled it now is usually used to describe the very problem it was conceived to correct' (Kovach and Rosenstiel, 2001: 12). This does not resolve the fact that 'the embrace, rejection as well as critical reappraisal of objectivity all help to keep it alive as an ideological cornerstone of journalism' (Deuze, 2005: 448). Related notions such as fairness, professional distance, detachment or impartiality (see among others Westerståhl, 1983) can be considered supportive elements of this nodal point, crucial for establishing the hegemonic discourse of 'good' journalism.

Objectivity and its related notions presuppose that a news event is intrinsically newsworthy rather than the result of a process of news-selection and writing procedures. 'While most news texts are the result of the processing and editing of other texts [...], they are constructed within a set of conventions that aim for "a unified text which conceals the editor's intervention"' (Bell, 1991: 51 as cited in Matheson, 2004: 455). As a result, the notion of objectivity has often become so pervasive and self-evident that it appears as if there is no other way of practicing 'good' journalism.

However, in recent decades this discourse has become increasingly incapable of symbolizing journalism work. Such a failure to accommodate to a changed reality is apparent in the problems posed to journalism in the era of liquid modernity, where its modernist discourse, centred on the representation of reality, is under constant threat. One site where such a change becomes most conspicuous is the online environment that has had an impact on journalism in a number of ways. First of all, the internet has become used as a resource for traditional journalistic practices such as source-gathering; second, and more importantly here, the internet offered non-professional journalists the opportunity to distribute their material and, third, it spawned a distinct possibility for providing news, for professionals and non-professionals alike. Such characteristics may confront mainstream journalism with non-professional online news projects that destabilize traditional journalism; '[a]s newsgathering expert systems become available to the general public the gate-keeping function of news people will diminish and as a group, they will probably experience deprofessionalization' (Broddason, 1994: 241, as cited in Singer, 2003: 147).[3] Even though the era of liquid modernity should not be equated with the breakthrough of the internet, it is clear that the technological realm, and more specifically the features of the online environment such as accessibility, hypertextuality, multimediality and interactivity (see Deuze, 2003: 205), pose a challenge to traditional and mainstream news work.

In the wider perspective of discourse theory, we regard online journalism as provoking a break in the discursive framework of mainstream journalism, bringing the particularity of its universalist claims to light.[4] In order to theorize such a break, discourse theory has invoked the concept of dislocation, which points towards the failure of a discursive structure to fully symbolize reality. Even though dislocation is seen by Laclau as an inherent aspect of any discourse, he also uses it in a more specific way to theorize a changed reality or a particular crisis event with which a discourse cannot cope. Confronted with such dislocatory events, a new 'plane of inscription' or *myth* is provided for, which 'involves forming a new objectivity by means of the rearticulation of the dislocated elements' (Laclau, 1990: 61). In the context of this chapter, the end of high modernism in journalism is a prime example of such a dislocation.

Contested journalism in the era of liquid modernity

The self-evident function of journalism in democratic society is still paramount to journalism's self-understanding, but its truth claims are strongly contested, partially because increasingly cynical audience members no longer take it for granted and do not want to be told what to think (see, among others, Capella and Jamieson, 1997; Kovach and Rosenstiel, 2001; Singer, 2003; 2007). Since neither formal training, affiliation to an association, nor licensing and agreed-upon ethics are mandatory in the exercise of journalism, it derives its authority mainly from the aforementioned modernist discourse, i.e. its self-justifying logic of public service and ethics, its self-proclaimed autonomy, a monopoly on the management of information and resources, and the ideology of objectivity. However, this is exactly what is being challenged in the era of liquid modernity. The seven nodal points that make up the discourse of mainstream journalism, namely, public service, ethics, management, autonomy, membership of a professional elite, immediacy and objectivity, all share in this dislocation triggered by the end of high modernism in journalism.

The challenge to the notion of public service, and the related gatekeeper role and elitist position in journalism may be related to the emergence of a 'redactional society' (Hartley, 2000) in which citizens are expected to possess 'journalistic' qualities that help them find their way in an increasingly complex information society rather than depend on expert systems such as journalism. Indicative of this shift in the balance between the elite professional and the passive consumer are practices of *disintermediation* or the bypassing of cultural intermediaries like advertisers and journalists, exemplified by the practices of citizen journalism. Although some prudence is warranted, the possibilities for responsiveness that are a result of the internet's interactive features have also increased, shifting away the emphasis on the medium and on content. Both processes increase audience members' agency (in different degrees), and undermine journalists' privileged position to exclusively provide a public service.

The notion of objectivity, too, becomes subject to dislocation as its indisputability is affected and the way in which it conceals its own genesis is brought to light: News articles can no longer be regarded as self-enclosed narratives that reflect reality. Internal and external contradictions become more apparent, sometimes supported by the activism of news fact-checking organizations and media-watch organizations (e.g. FAIR) and journalist weblogs that deconstruct the narrations of mainstream media, and in some cases question journalists' autonomy and their ability to resist external and internal pressures. Moreover, j-blogs offer news with different formal characteristics: news is ordered chronologically rather than formally (in descending order of importance); written in a more informal style; and can be reworked according to user's comments (Matheson, 2004: 455). Even within traditional news articles, the use of hyperlinks may break open the rigid claims on 'truth' and move towards a conception of the audience that is more in line with a 'redactional society'. Indeed, in offering a range of sources to draw from, 'the weblog moderates the traditional claim of news journalism to know, on behalf of readers, what is happening in the world' (ibid.).

In this piecemeal construction of a news event, online mainstream journalism radically breaks with the traditional notion of immediacy in journalism. Whereas traditional journalism has always been deadline-oriented and attached much prestige to covering an event as quickly as possible within the news cycles, in the online environment (and in the 24-hour news television stations) the traditional approach to immediacy has transgressed into an ever-ongoing flux. As a result, the 'scoop' logic seems less urgent online; indeed, some critics have argued that the absence of technical production deadlines for online news means 'the story's "firstness" is of minimal market value in this new media landscape' (Hume, 1999, as cited in Matheson, 2004: 458). But more importantly, the increased speed puts pressure on the verification procedures to ensure information reliability and source credibility. '[T]he speed with which information is rushed onto the Web, a medium in which deadlines are perpetual and competition is intense, has been cited repeatedly as a problem' (Singer, 2003: 152). This increases the likelihood of erroneous reporting, which (when discovered and discussed) further undermines the truth claims of traditional journalism.[5]

Coping strategies in mainstream journalism

Such dislocations that disrupt discursive unity may be regarded as traumatic events that threaten the stability of the identity of the mainstream media professional (Carpentier, 2005). Laclau notes that 'although the fullness and universality of society is unachievable, its need does not disappear [...]' (Glynos and Stavrakakis, 2004: 207). As a result, we may assume that both journalists and the journalistic institution engage in coping strategies that attempt to protect and re-establish the claims of universality, and re-establish their authority as professionals. Of course, in suggesting this, we proceed from the premise that journalists mainly identify with a professional model of work that conveys prestige, but also causes trauma. However, one may equally regard journalism as a 'mere' trade. From this perspective journalists may not be confronted with a gap between values and practices. On the other hand, journalists may identify too strongly with the value system of journalism, causing the gap to appear unbridgeable. Such may be the case for the growing number of journalists that leave the job either through dissatisfaction with the organizational structure or through serious mental issues such as burn-out and depression (Reinardy, 2011). However, in relation to the dislocation produced by online journalism, traditional journalism deploys at least three kinds of coping strategies: marginalization of rivalling media (through the logics of the constitutive outside); normalization of the mainstream online environment; and rearticulation of the nodal points embedded in the mainstream discourse.

A first set of coping strategies aims at marginalizing online media (professionals) with regard to professionalism, ethics, autonomy and objectivity/accuracy. Testifying to this attitude is the acknowledgment that 'scholars and professionals alike use the discourse of the internet's unique characteristics as a way in which to define online journalism as something different to other journalisms – as a fourth kind of journalism' and as 'a breed apart' (Deuze, 2003: 207). This stance is reminiscent of the logic of the constitutive outside since online journalism is regarded as a threat to the identity of mainstream journalism while at the same time it allows it to constitute this very identity. This is illustrated by the BBC's (initial) stance that 'Blogging is not journalism. [...] Without editors to correct syntax, tidy up the story structure or check facts, it is generally impossible to rely on anything one finds in a blog without verifying it somewhere else – often the much-maligned mainstream media' (Thompson, 2003, as cited in Berry, 2008: 15–16).

This strategy is also reminiscent of the critiques that have been launched against alternative media by mainstream media, considering them unprofessional and amateurish (Carpentier et al., 2003). And even as mainstream journalism itself engaged in practices of online journalism such as blogging, it still testified to a similar strategy of marginalization. Initially it often regarded online journalism as an easy means to generate more profit since it has 'consistently offered shoveled, repurposed and windowed content for free, cannibalizing on its core product while treating its Web presence as an advertisement for the offline product' (Deuze, 2003). But even as it gained more importance within mainstream journalism, it has remained a constitutive outside (see Jones and Himelboim, 2010: 275).

As Singer – quoting Lasica (2001) – shows,

> Perhaps the most persistent criticism of online journalism, and the clearest line traditional journalists have sought to draw between themselves and those working online, has involved [the nodal point of] ethical behavior. There seems to be 'a generalized, unspoken notion in some newsrooms that online journalism is the gangly, misfit cousin of "real" journalism, that the Internet is a breeding ground for kooks and charlatans, and that perhaps Web journalism operates at a level below the standards of traditional news media'.
>
> *(Singer, 2003: 140)*

Thus, online journalists are regarded as less professional than journalists working for print news, which disarticulates them from the professional elite (or makes them 'lesser' members). Indeed, they are chided for not possessing the same cognitive (and thus professional) skills, such as deciding on newsworthiness, information gathering and source checking, required to make news.

Likewise, online mainstream journalism has been attacked for not being autonomous and failing to assume a non-partisan attitude. In the j-blog, it is the lack of objective language and a distanced attitude towards the audience that has caused unease and actually led in some cases to journalists being fired (cf. Matheson, 2004: 452; Singer, 2005: 178). Such events also testify to the problem that 'stepping outside that set of [linguistic] conventions risks stepping outside the claim to be able to "get at the truth"' (Matheson, 2004: 446). However, in online journalism it is also the emphasis on immediacy and commercial interests that lie behind such allegations (Singer, 2003: 155). Online journalism has similarly been repudiated for the problems associated with the notion of immediacy. As noted above, online journalism's speed in getting information across challenged one of mainstream journalism's competencies to which social prestige is accorded. Rushing news on the internet (even more than before) constitutes a process of communal truth-seeking practices that dislocated traditional notions of objectivity, public service and gatekeeping.

A second set of coping strategies has been to incorporate the online environment, i.e. to provide only limited use of the internet's interactive possibilities and to domesticate alternative voices by bringing them into the logics of the mainstream media. Such coping strategies testify to efforts to maintain the ideal of the gatekeeper. As such, it has often been noted that major online news sites offer only limited hyperlinks, especially to other news websites (Hermida, 2001: 13; Deuze, 2003: 212; Matheson, 2004: 454; Oblak, 2005; Mitchelstein and Boczkowski, 2009: 567). As such, there is an ongoing process of normalization at work in which traditional notions of good journalism are being recuperated in the online world (Singer, 2005; Robinson, 2006; Vobič, 2007). The limited incorporation of online journalism also relates to non-professional online journalism, which in some cases, like for instance the 2003 war reports of the Iraqi blogger Salam Pax (Cammaerts and Carpentier, 2009), makes it into the mainstream media. Here, a strategy of containment is used, where the otherness of the contribution is emphasized by a symbolic detachment from the other (mainstream) material. Similarly, in their 'informal' and 'personal' aspects, blogs have continued an existing tradition of commentary (e.g. in editorials and opinionated journalism) rather than actually established a conversation with the public (Singer, 2005: 192).

However, practices of disintermediation have made a more complete hegemonization of traditional journalistic notions impossible. As a result, we witness a third coping strategy in which journalism tries to hold on to its authoritative claims. As indicated above, whenever a discursive structure fails to accommodate the dislocations with which it is confronted, it will rearticulate its signifiers in a structure that offers a new plane of inscription or myth. In light of the present concerns surrounding liquid journalism, journalists protect their claim on the discourse of 'good' journalism by partially shifting their competencies away from the dissemination of news. Rather, the journalist moves closer towards a new gatekeeper function which is to direct audiences toward 'valuable' information and to offer them interpretation of these resources (Steiner, 2009: 383). As a result, new mechanisms of distinction come to the fore. Not only has online journalism instituted its own mechanisms of critical acclaim, but increasing value is now attributed to other professional skills such as breadth of knowledge and the use of appropriate links (Matheson, 2004: 456). Such a shift of attention testifies to efforts 'in finding alternative modes of newswriting that do not unravel [journalism's] power to tell authoritative stories' (ibid.).

One of these alternative modes may be the increasingly subjective tone in news reporting that shows in the wealth of blogs that are written by journalists that are affiliated to either traditional print news or mainstream online journalism. Indicative as well are the large number of autobiographical writings of journalists in recent decades (Good, 1993; Matheson, 2003). Such a tendency may be said to constitute a new truth claim in journalism, turning from claims based on objectivity to those based on authenticity. As such, journalism is in tandem with the broad evolution toward a confessional society (Foucault, 1998) which is characterized by what Richard Sennett (1986) calls a 'tyranny of intimacy'. Especially in the weblog and autobiographical writings, journalists exemplify a tendency towards externalizing their innermost feelings. Linking up with the new gatekeeper role, 'this more interpretive style serves the desire of journalists to create a public persona as much as anything else' (Kovach and Rosenstiel, 2001: 55; cf. Mathiesen, 1997: 226). This personal way of engaging with the audience recuperates the journalist as a legitimate truth-speaker in society, and may at the same time allow the journalistic community to re-appropriate an estranged public that they were no longer in touch with (see Capella and Jamieson, 1997; Kovach and Rosenstiel, 2001).

Dislocatory challenges to the high modernism of journalism

During the era of liquid modernity, the modernist belief in rationality and progress has been deprived of its self-evident character. Indicative of this development is, as Lyotard (1979) has famously put it, the loss of the 'grand narratives' in which such belief was expressed. In the wake of such growing scepticism, a range of discourses, among them that of journalism, have seen their legitimacy threatened.

Our rereading of the existing literature on this 'crisis' from a discourse-theoretical perspective regards journalism as a discursive-social construction, caught in the dynamics of stability and contingency. As is the case with any discourse, modernist journalistic identity discourses are in principle reasonably stable, but can become confronted with destabilizations that challenge its very nature. These dislocatory challenges are not exclusively situated at the individual or institutional level; they are cultural phenomena that affect these levels but also transcend them. Because of their pervasiveness, they force journalism (more than usual) into practices of identity work and politics, working through these challenges, in part accepting some rearticulations, whilst fiercely rejecting and fighting others. In the specific case of the challenges presented by online journalism, we can see coping strategies that denounce the validity of the rivalling system of online journalism, or that try to incorporate and domesticate it. On the other hand, we can also see coping strategies that shift the traditional journalistic identity more towards an interpretive and subjective position.

In conclusion, we would like to argue for the importance of culturalist perspectives on journalism to provide us with more tools to counter the tendencies of normalizing modernist journalistic identities, and for black-boxing the contingencies that have characterized these identities from their insipience. In combination with many other approaches, journalism also needs to be seen as a social-discursive struggle that reaches far beyond the material dimension of individual or institutional practices. These culturalist perspectives, for instance, allow different sets of questions, transforming more traditional – but virtually unanswerable – questions about the death of journalism into questions about the coping strategies of journalism for dealing with a changing context dislocating its core identities.

Notes

1 The concept of 'high modernism' generally subsumes the thought, practices and cultural forms (thus also journalism) of modernity (the era encompassing the nineteenth and the first half of the twentieth century) that are broadly characterized by a conviction in progress, an inclination towards rationality and bureaucratization and a lack of reflexive criticism. High modernism is not to be confused with high modernity, which is used to indicate the period that starts, broadly speaking, at the second half of the twentieth century, and which radically breaks with the assumptions of modernity.

2 'Liquid modernity' is one among a number of concepts such as 'postmodernity' and 'late modernity' that designate (despite conceptual and temporal differences) the turn to 'reflexive modernization', i.e. a tendency in the process of modernity to become self-referring, testifying to a loss of the self-evident convictions of the preceding era and the growing doubts and critiques against the latter's assumptions. This goes hand in hand with a number of transformations in the economic, social and political field and reflects the disintegration of modernist institutions (one of which is journalism).

3 Even though 'technological change has long been identified as promoting professionalization in modern society' (Singer, 2003: 143), in journalism the most recent changes in technology seem to have the opposite effect.

4 Arguably, there are other dislocations within journalism. One other example is the dislocation caused by the economic-financial pressure on journalists.

5 Even though online mainstream journalism may dislocate traditional notions of journalism because of its use of time, this may at the same time challenge the hegemony of print over online journalism. After all, it may severely undermine traditional media's ability to gain prestige from 'scoop news' since online journalism may record events faster than traditional media such as news agencies and television networks (Walker, 2001), and even do so in more depth than traditional media (Hiler, 2001).

Part II
Participatory forms of journalism

5

TRUST, TRUTH AND OBJECTIVITY

Sustaining quality journalism in the era of the content-generating user

Brian McNair

This chapter explores what news organisations and those who work in them can do to secure their futures in a digitised media environment where their cultural authority and professional status are challenged as never before in the history of journalism. It argues for a response, from both institutions and individuals, on three levels. First, there needs to be an enhancement of the traditional sense-making, sorting-and-sifting, gatekeeping functions of journalism (Bardoel, 1996). Second, the performance of the information-gathering and date-management practices understood by the term *objectivity* (which I will define below as the range of 'strategic rituals' (Tuchman, 1972) underpinning the perception of truth and trust in journalism amongst audiences, readers and users) must be given greater visibility. And third, media organisations must maximise their enabling of *user participation* in professional production environments. This includes not just the facilitation of inter-activity and the innovative management of user-generated content (UGC), but the incentivisation of user access to paid-for content through secure, convenient micro-payment and subscription tools which can recruit users and maximise their retention.

In suggesting these constituents for a renewed and sustainable profession of journalism (and the institutions which support journalism) in the era of the content-generating user I argue that new communication technologies do not reduce the need for organisational and professional structures in news-making, but enhance them. While established organisational structures may break down and transform under the influence of new communication technologies, the need for organisation as such does not diminish.[1] The digitisation of journalism and the emergence of the internet, Web 2.0 and all that goes with this technology in terms of expanded information flow and user participation strengthen rather than undermine the role of and need for organisations dedicated to the sourcing, processing, dissemination and public discussion of journalism. To renew and sustain journalistic organisations capable of servicing a globalised public sphere requires in turn the reassertion and restrengthening of what have traditionally been regarded as defining journalistic practices in the spheres of information management, sense-making and interpretation – practices which, when recognised by readers and users, generate the key perception of *trust*.

The crisis of contemporary journalism

For at least a decade – and sometimes longer, depending on the sector – journalism has been going through a period of deeply destabilising transition (McNair, 2009; 2011). As many observers have noted, and as the industry itself has at last come to accept, the age of linear, analogue, top-down, elite-mass journalism has ended, as measured in declining newspaper circulations, journalistic redundancies and closures of titles, and fragmenting broadcast news audiences, with predictable consequences on employment and industrial structure.

In June 2011, for example, job losses of 90 staff were announced at the *Daily Record/Sunday Mail* newspaper in my home town of Glasgow, Scotland. This came after the loss of 70 editorial posts in 2009, and hundreds if not thousands of others in the UK print sector in recent years (McNair et al., 2010). Owned by the UK Trinity Mirror Group, the *Record* and *Mail* had once been Scotland's top-selling newspapers, dominating the popular press landscape completely. At its circulation peak the *Daily Record* was selling more than 700,000 copies every day. In 2011, sales had fallen to 286,000. One month later, Scotland's Sunday papers, the *Sunday Herald* and *Scotland On Sunday*, were recording year-on-year circulation falls of 9 per cent and 12 per cent respectively. The London-based *News Of The World*, closed by its proprietor News Corp in the wake of the phone-hacking scandal of July 2011, had seen its circulation fall from 5 million to 2.8 million in the decade before closure (McNair, 2009b).

These figures illustrate the scale of the crisis affecting what we used to call print journalism all over the advanced industrialised world. Yes, print sales remain healthy in the developing and emerging markets such as India, China, Africa and South America (OECD, 2009), because these markets are less digitised and thus still more dependent on newspapers than, say, the European or North American markets (see Standage, 2011). That will change over time, as these emerging markets continue their rapid economic growth. So we are some way away, on the planetary scale, from the long-foretold death of newspapers as a viable commercial platform for journalism. But the writing is on the wall, in Scotland and the UK, in Western Europe, in the United States, in Australia. In all of these markets circulations and advertising revenue are falling, titles are closing or merging, production efficiencies are being sought.

The scale of the crisis varies from country to country. Australian newspapers, for example, are in relative terms doing better than the press in other comparable countries. According to the latest Pew report on *The State Of the News Media*, Australian press circulation declined by 1.5 per cent in the six months to September 2009 (that of the US fell by no less than 10.6 per cent over the same period). US advertising revenues fell by 25 per cent in the year 2008–9, while Australia's fell by a less alarming, though still damaging, 7 per cent. In the US, advertising revenues for the print media fell by an astonishing 92 per cent over the decade 2000–2010, hence the run of closures and shrinkages felt by the press in that country. Pew estimates that, judged by staff employed, US newsrooms have shrunk by 30 per cent in that period.[2]

There is thus, first and foremost, an *economic* crisis of journalism – a crisis, as Phillips and Witschge put it, not of demand but of funding (2011) – which may or may not be resolved by the introduction of paywalls, micro-payments, and flexible subscriptions of the type now being introduced in the US, the UK, Australia and elsewhere, on the back of the launch of the iPad in 2010 (Graybeal and Hayes, 2011). The invention and introduction to mass consumer culture of the networked tablet offers what many in the journalism industries see as a solution to the problem of what comes after print, though the evidence to underpin optimism is far from compelling. As of June 2011, just before the onset of the phone-hacking scandal which so damaged its reputation, News International in the UK was reporting 250,000 paying subscribers to digital editions of the *Times/Sunday Times*, though how many of these were full cost was not clear.[3]

The crisis of journalism as cultural form

The crisis of journalism is also *cultural*. For many years, and since long before the rise of the internet, journalism has shared the public sphere, and especially its more popular regions, with hybrid forms of factuality such as reality TV. This trend has been reflected in the growth of a substantial academic literature on the nature of mediated reality, and a sustained debate through the 1990s and 2000s about the alleged onset of 'infotainment' (Thussu, 2007) and 'reality culture' (Van Bauwel and Carpentier, 2010). Now the formal challenge is of a different, if yet more threatening, kind.

Put simply – what *is* journalism in the era of Twitter and WikiLeaks, of user-generated content ranging from 140 character tweets to quasi-journalistic blogs and video uploads, and of the proliferation of online channels by which means non-journalists (as well as many professionals, of course) pour terabytes of content into the public sphere, share it around and spread it, highlight and comment upon it, their tweets and leaks becoming part of the raw material of the mainstream news media, but distinct from journalism as it has traditionally been practiced?

The existential crisis of the journalist

This development has provoked what I have called previously an 'existential crisis' of journalism (McNair, 2011). A group which only recently – little more than a century or so ago – acquired the status of a profession, as reflected in university degree programmes devoted to journalism, accepted codes of ethics, legal protections on confidentiality, and so on (Conboy, 2011) suddenly find themselves vulnerable to forces impacting upon their professional identity and status which are far beyond their control. *Here Comes Everybody*, observed Clay Shirky in his influential book, and when everybody is potentially a producer, potentially a contributor to the globalised public sphere, what distinguishes the activity of the professional journalist such that he or she can lay claim to the privileges and protections, the respect and trust which have been afforded the Fourth Estate in democratic societies?

Journalism in the age of dissolutions

The economic, cultural and existential crises of journalism are propelled by the dissolution of four boundaries which have hitherto structured the production, distribution and consumption of journalism (McNair, 2006; 2009a).

The first boundary is spatial-temporal, which involves the dissolution of the boundary separating time and space in the journalism production process and is driven by technological evolution which, from print through photography, film, broadcasting, satellite and now the internet, has steadily reduced the gap between events happening and their being reported to virtually zero. A century ago newsworthy events took weeks to make it onto the front pages of newspapers. Now they are reported instantaneously, while they are still happening, and often before anyone knows what on earth is actually going on. As a consequence, and notwithstanding exceptions for key stories such as the coverage of the Mumbai bombings discussed below, the production of news has been truncated, squeezed, shortened beyond what many would regard as compatible with a journalism of analysis, interpretation and commentary. Journalists are under unprecedented time pressures to deliver exclusives, scoops and fresh angles. As the news cycle has accelerated, and outlets and platforms proliferated, more has to be done with less.

The second boundary is the technological, which revolves around the dissolution of boundaries between hitherto separate platforms for journalism and has been ongoing for decades, subsumed within the broader cultural trend of technological convergence. In journalistic terms, where once there were distinct print, TV and radio outlets which produced journalism independently of each other, organisations now produce content on a multimedia mix of platforms, with journalists increasingly expected to be competent across all. Print and broadcast journalists write blogs and prepare vodcasts for online sites. Copy written for one medium is routinely used on another.

More threatening than technological convergence, to the journalist, is the erosion of the third boundary I speak of, namely the professional boundary itself. Digital technology has radically transformed the economics and social relations of cultural production, reducing the marginal cost of entry to public discourse – entry as a writer, a speaker, a voice – to near zero. This is challenging for a profession which has jealously guarded its status as a 'new priesthood' or 'fourth estate' for at least a century. Since the late 1990s, and accelerating after 9/11, we have seen the rise of the *content-generating user*: the blogger; the citizen journalist (not a term I like, because not all suppliers of the material often associated with it are citizens, and few are or would describe themselves as journalists); the *produser* (Bruns, 2011a); the accidental eyewitness at the scene of a newsworthy event who happens to be in possession of a digital camera and has access to the internet.

Such material is now routinely used as part of the professional journalist's tool kit, and that's undeniably a good thing in terms of the diversification and democratisation of news-content provision, but it has provoked anxiety and anger from those journalists who perceive that their privileged cultural role – and the trust which has traditionally been invested in journalistic truth by publics – is being undermined by amateurs and usurpers. As a result of this dissolution, the separation between the production of journalism and its consumption is eroding. User-generated content is increasingly part of the journalistic package – a source, and a resource, which, once incorporated into the 'news', is then consumed by the people who have produced it. The spheres of production and consumption are merging, overlapping.

The generic dimension of dissolution, finally, relates to the category distinctions which structure our understanding of journalism's functions, its status as knowledge, its value as democratic resource. The boundary, for example, between information and entertainment in journalism has traditionally corresponded to normative definitions of 'serious' and 'not serious', the former referring to the traditionally patriarchal worlds of politics, economics and foreign affairs, the latter to the feminine fluff of human interest, lifestyle, celebrity. These divisions have broken down. So the death of Michael Jackson in 2009 headlined not only the UK red-top tabloid newspapers, but the 'serious' *Guardian* and *Times*. All adopted more or less the same approach, with gossip, rumour, comment and souvenir pullouts substituting for what we might regard as straight reportage (a simple example – sales of Jackson's *Thriller* album were reported as having been 65 million, 105 million, 50 million, and that just in the print and online pages of one newspaper, the *Guardian*).

Driven by increasingly competitive news markets, as well as publics endowed with evermore leisure time and resources for consumer spending, news outlets have in the last couple of decades adopted content and styles which are designed with pleasure, leisure and recreation in mind, rather than the classic journalistic functions of environmental surveillance and monitoring alone. The line which is perceived to have existed between these forms of *infotainment* – which is not an unreasonable term to describe their function – and the 'straight' or 'hard' news deemed necessary for deliberative democracy to work properly, has been eroded. The line between what we used to call a tabloid news agenda and one which prioritises 'serious' or 'quality' news has all but disappeared, even if the writing styles and registers still diverge greatly.

Also dissolving – long-dissolved, in most media markets – is the notional line which used to exist between the public and the private spheres, a dissolution seen particularly in the rise of celebrity culture and its incorporation of politics. If celebrity journalism can be viewed as a genre, today it has much more in common with political journalism, sports journalism, arts journalism and so on, in both who and what subjects it covers.

Also in the category of generic evolution – the line between fact (reportage) and opinion (commentary), and thus between objectivity and subjectivity, is dissolving. The journalism of opinion and commentary goes back four centuries at least, to

Montaigne and then the English Civil War, but the line separating this content from straight reportage in the structures of news outlets has grown increasingly porous, as the former has expanded as a proportion of total content. More journalism than ever, on every platform, presents as the articulation of opinion, speculation and punditry of various kinds. As the more expensive forms of investigative journalism and foreign correspondence decline due to the economic pressures associated with the collapse of the traditional business model – a trend especially pronounced in the relatively under-resourced online-journalism sector – the subjective journalism of the 'I' fills the gap (McNair, 2008).

In addition, as already noted, there exist today in the public spheres of most countries an array of hybrid journalistic forms, which combine elements such as soap opera and game show with documentary and current affairs. We call it *factuality* or reality TV (Hill, 2007; Van Bauwel and Carpentier, 2010). In the 1990s it was called docu-soap; before that, fly-on-the-wall documentary. Many of these hybrid forms contain an additional element not present (or present to a much lesser extent) in the analogue era of journalistic hybridisation – audience participation and interaction. Through websites, text messaging, and so on, the audience is no longer passive (in the sense that it could not directly contribute to a show being viewed) but active – voting in the millions for reality contestants; blogging, tweeting or emailing commentary on programmes as they air; participating in reality programmes such as *Wife Swap* (Enli and McNair, 2010), and *Come Dine With Me*.

Even in relation to established platforms – newspaper commentary columns, for example – audiences are much more active than ever before. Every newspaper now has its online comment section, where members of the public (not professional journalists) leave their opinions on what they have read, and engage each other in debate about the articles they are reading. In July 2011, as the News International phone-hacking scandal peaked, with News Corp's withdrawal from its proposed takeover of BSkyB, the *Guardian* undertook to sift half a million Twitter posts about the affair, in a continuation of its adoption of 'computational' journalism (see below).

The death of journalism?

None of this means the death of journalism, and few commentators seriously suggest any longer that it does. On the contrary, there is more news and journalism in circulation, accessible to a global audience, then ever before in human history. Demand for news appears to be insatiable, even if the way it is produced, consumed and distributed is changing.

Nor need these trends, and the crisis underpinning them, mean the death of the journalist as a professional category. As many observers have noted, we need professional, trained journalists more than ever. On June 30, 2009, observing events in Iran and the role of non-professional sources in their communication to the outside world, the BBC's current affairs magazine *Newsnight* ran an item asking if this meant that what it called 'citizen journalists', using social-networking sites and other online tools, would eventually replace professional journalists altogether? The answer to that question is, of course, no, and becomes ever clearer as one dramatic event in the unfolding cultural chaos of our time follows another, most recently the movements and revolutions collectively dubbed the Arab Spring, in 2011.

The decentralisation of journalistic production is welcome, for all kinds of reasons. Not only does it mean that information can be sourced from locations where professionals might not be present; it democratises the news-production process, opening it up to an unprecedented range of perspectives and voices. Some observers have criticised the value of this user-generated content in the globalised public sphere (Keen, 2007), dismissing it as noise. They miss the point of enabling popular access to cultural production, it seems to me, and understate the extent to which a significant proportion of journalism has always been flawed, prone not just to ideological bias, distortion and speculative excess but plagiarism and even fabrication (see below).

But the critics are correct to argue that, on its own, user-generated content is limited in its capacity to enable our understanding of complex events. If it is to help global news audiences in that task – and by extension to develop what might be characterised as a kind of global citizenship or deliberative global democratisation – the decentralisation of information, the diversification of public speech, has to be managed, given structure and meaning. Which is where, and why, the professional journalist retains her or his cultural value.

Of what, then, is this value comprised, and how can it be maximised? What is journalism's unique selling proposition?

Keep making sense

People on the ground tweeted, emailed and mobile-phoned the news out of Mumbai when Islamic terrorists attacked that city and killed 173 people in 2008. They provided powerful images and eyewitness accounts of what was happening, hour by hour, in multiple locations – images and accounts that no news organisation could hope to match in their instantaneity and intensity. Digital, mobile communications technology made this possible. But it took time, and the work of trained journalists and editors in newsrooms all over the world, to establish an authoritative account of the event in its totality, and then to analyse its meaning in the context of broader political and historical factors. Only professional editors, correspondents, producers, had the time and the resources to reflect on and analyse the meaning of events, rather than merely report them, or pass on what others were reporting about them. Professionals in London, Washington and Berlin added value to user-generated content uploaded from Mumbai, as they do now from Tripoli or Cairo, screening, packaging and refining it.

This sense-making function, long understood as part of journalism's cultural role (Bardoel, 1996), becomes more important in the digital age, not less. More information, and faster dissemination, from more sources, most of them untrained in journalistic techniques, means the potential for more confusion, error and honest misunderstanding. More than ever, therefore, the globalised public sphere, networked and accessible to the content-generating user as it should be, needs the professional journalist's skill set and capacity to bring order and meaning to information chaos.

Journalism in participatory culture

In addition to supporting these traditional journalistic functions within an institutional context – which is a resource issue – news organisations also have to embrace, integrate and exploit the *interactive*, *participatory* qualities of the online environment, in ways which maximise the value of user-generated content as a source of news and comment and harness the expanding public appetite for participation in the news process. This requires an *enhancement* of the traditional editorial function, to incorporate not just sense-making and interpretive work but a gatekeeping, data-processing, content-moderating role.

In the age of what some have called network, or networked, journalism (Singer, 2010; Heinrich, 2011), the professional, and the organisational structure in which she is embedded, have a central role in shepherding and facilitating UGC. The editorial function of interpreting what is coming out of Mumbai or Tehran in the heat of a crisis is self-evidently necessary. But news organisations also become, in the era of proliferating UGC, hubs, or *strange attractors* of content (if I may extend the chaos metaphor a little) which has been captured by amateurs but can be used, when sufficiently processed, in the fabric of the main news product.

Stuart Allan and Einar Thorsen (2011: 21) write about the BBC's pioneering work in this respect, from the 1997 launch of BBC News Online, which 'represented a significant initiative within the Corporation's attempt to reaffirm its public service ethos in a fledgling web environment'. Public service in this context meant serving that section of the public which wished to contribute to the BBC's news content, and thus at the same time that segment of the public which wished to consume it as part of their news diet. The BBC's example has been widely influential all over the world, and the corporation continues to devote substantial resources to the management of UGC. Braun and Gillespie (2011: 383) note that for a decade and more,

> traditional news organisations have been seeking to establish a sustainable online presence and expand the news experience by incorporating interactive mechanisms, hoping to build brand loyalty amongst users by allowing them to comment on the news, talk back to journalists and editors, and potentially engage in dialogue with each other.

This implies a shift in the journalistic mindset, and the enthusiastic embrace of connectivity, as opposed to resigned acceptance. It also requires management of the user community in ways which maximise recruitment and retention.

More recently, outlets such as the *Guardian* and the *Telegraph* in the UK have enlisted readers to assist them in sifting and making sense of the huge quantities of raw data released by WikiLeaks in 2010–11, and also in the context of the UK MPs' expenses scandal of 2009. Here we see exemplary cases of established, professional media organisations combining their resources, routines and practices with the weight of a vast crowd of users prepared to sift through leaked documents in search of newsworthy stories and angles. In computational and data-based journalism of this kind, users (or readers) are often participants in the selection of what is newsworthy, and in the transformation of raw or half-cooked data into processed news and commentary. The *Guardian* undertook a similar crowd-sourcing, collective-editing exercise with the release of thousands of Sarah Palin's emails in June 2011.

Modes of managing interactivity and participation vary in their effective ness, and news organisations are constantly experimenting with what works in building and retaining user engagement. The search for cost-effective modes of interactivity and participation continues, however, and becomes more important in the long-term retention of audience share as digital competition for mainstream outlets increases.

Working with WikiLeaks

The journalistic functions of sifting and sense-making, of narrativising and interpret- ing, reveal themselves with some clarity in the context of the WikiLeaks phenom- enon. Julian Assange has described WikiLeaks as a journalistic organisation, and himself as a journalist, in the context of defending himself against legal threats in the United States. Good luck to him on that, but he knows as well as any journalist that what his organisation does – in so far as WikiLeaks leaks raw data such as the millions of classified US diplomatic cables in late 2010 – is not journalism in the traditional sense.

WikiLeaks *leaks* information, which becomes the *subject* of journalism, both in being leaked, and in what its content reveals about power. WikiLeaks has changed the world, generally for the better, and information has been its weapon. But it is not journalism, anymore than yesterday's Wall Street share prices or a list of daytime temperatures in the world's capital cities make narrative sense on their own. Only to the extent that it is mediated *by* journalism, disseminated through mainstream media channels, is WikiLeaks as an information provider – as a content-generating user platform – enabled to have visibility in the globalised public sphere, and thus political impacts.

Assange understood this, and partnered with the *Guardian* and other news organisations in 2010 to engineer the massive dump of classified military and diplomatic data which put him on the US 'Most Wanted' list. Assange combined his organisation's capacity to leak data with that of the established news media to present it to a wide public. Both sectors – the new and the old – were required to give the story impact beyond the margins. In combination – although the rela- tionship between Assange and his media partners subsequently disintegrated into recrimination and rancour – they achieved what neither could have by acting on their own.

Perform objectivity

But how do 'old' media brands maintain their privileged positions in the crowded, chaotic media environment of the twenty-first century? How can they anchor their status as 'hubs', sense-makers and licensed interpreters of what everyone out there, including the content-generating users, is saying? Three interconnected characteristics long associated with '*quality*' journalism remain key, I would argue, to building the relationship with the audience which will sustain the provision of news as a commodity (or as a public service, as in the case of the BBC), and thus the flow of resources required to sustain the news-production process.[4] These constituents of quality are *truth*, *trust* and *objectivity*.

By *objectivity* I refer to a method of gathering and processing news which requires the provision by organisations of editorial resources; which is independent of ideology in so far as it can command universal acceptance of its reliability; which thus generates *trust* in the *truth* value of its reportage, leading to a perception of *authority* in respect of the interpretations placed upon the facts reported.

Traditionally in the field of journalism studies the professional practice of objectivity has been viewed with some suspicion as a 'strategic ritual' deployed for defensive purposes such as the deflection of criticism. The concept has been viewed as inauthentic and illusory, masking a deeper ideological subjectivity ultimately linked to the maintenance of elite interests – what Vladimir Lenin from a Marxist perspective long ago dismissed as 'bourgeois objectivism'. This critical framework is sufficiently familiar to require no explanation here, and has served a useful purpose in deconstructing the exaggerated and naive claims for journalistic objectivity which used to circulate widely in the media (Schudson and Anderson, 2009). I wish to replace it here with a usage which, as in the scientific application of the term, acknowledges its epistemological limits – that is, that there is and can be no *absolute* objectivity – while stressing its value as a shorthand umbrella term for a set of processes of information management which, when applied, and when seen to be applied, may provide some level of assurance to an audience that a journalistic text is founded on at least the aspiration to and *search* for truth. The *achievement* of 'truth' will always be constrained by any number of factors, including the availability of competing, credible truth claims.

Objectivity is here conceived as a *performance* (Bogaerts, 2011) of the techniques and methods of sourcing and processing information which when present provide a guarantee of high journalistic standards. In the postmodern intellectual environment 'everybody knows' that there is no such thing as 'pure' or absolute objectivity. But in a competitive marketplace of proliferating providers, content-generating users and participating publics, an enhanced role for good old-fashioned objectivity amidst the explosion of subjectivities becomes apparent. Objective journalism does not imply neutral, value-free or impartial journalism and journalists. It signals, rather, that an honest attempt has been made to ensure that a given journalistic text can be trusted as a source of accurate information about an event or issue making the news agenda.

Objectivity, in this sense, describes the application to journalistic production of a commonly agreed set of standards, based on adherence to particular practices of information gathering and analysis, which allow us to discount or offset individual journalists' subjectivities. We know the truth is relative, of course, but adherence to practices associated with journalistic objectivity can ease our acceptance of, and negotiation with, the reality of a multiplicity of truths. In this respect I agree with An Nguyen (2011: 207) when he writes that, at a time of proliferating information sources, 'objectivity, the "strategic ritual" of the news profession is too important to be allowed to disappear.'

Why so crucial? Because the performance of objectivity – a quality with its roots in the commercialisation and profession of journalism in the nineteenth century – is central to the construction of public trust in journalism, particularly in those established sectors of journalism which ask us to bestow upon them a privileged respect, merely *because* they are established. It is especially crucial now, in this period of transition from analogue to digital platforms, and from top-down linearity to networked complexity, which comes at the end of an extended crisis of trust for the 'old media'.

Regain trust

In the digital era of proliferating providers, not just of news and journalism but content of all kinds, a key factor in attracting and retaining audiences of sufficient size to enable monetisation in some form is *trust*. Trust in the content provider, which in turn can be reduced to belief in the honesty and integrity of the provider; confidence in the accuracy and reliability of the content *as information*. For journalism especially there must be confidence in the capacity of the information provider to represent fairly a complex reality in which 'the truth' may not be readily accessible. If the performance of objectivity is a 'strategic ritual', securing the trust of users is the strategic purpose of the ritualising.

Nothing has damaged trust in journalism more in these past years, and contributed more to the crisis outlined above, let us recall, than the deliberate fabrication of facts by print and broadcast journalists of the old media – the invention of stories and sources, the presentation of lies as truth, the manipulative and deliberately misleading editing of documentaries. If the greatest ethical sin of scholarship is plagiarism, journalism's is to invent stories which are not true; to lie and deceive, and then to use the privileged cultural status of journalism to have those lies believed. The unacceptable breach of the contract between journalist and public occurs when a story which has been invented, wholly or in part, is presented to the reader as true, in a context where the audience is entitled and likely to believe the truth claim. It is, as Billy Ray's 2003 film *Shattered Glass* makes us see so poignantly (McNair, 2010), a deception not only of the audience, and thus a violation of public trust in journalism as a cultural form, but of the editors of the publication or outlet in which the piece appears, who are rarely complicit in the fabrication (except in so far as their editorial procedures have failed to spot it).

Shattered Glass is about the case of Stephen Glass and the extended hoax he played on the *New Republic*. The film focuses on the *New Republic*'s meticulous editorial process, with a key sequence portraying the checking and revising stages through which every article passes. Not only is the sequence an interesting lesson in one dimension of 'objectivity' – the importance of checking sources, and verifying claims – it raises the question: if such a rigorous process is in place, how on earth could a young novice such as Glass so abuse his employers' trust and get away with it?

Shattered Glass, I have argued elsewhere, marks the moment when authority and influence in the public sphere began to shift from print to the internet. It shows how the rise of digital journalism brought the capacity of the 'old media' for fabrication and plagiarism to light. The lies of Stephen Glass were uncovered by what was then, in 1998, the very new medium of online journalism – Forbes Digital Tool. The internet was key to the exposé, as search engines failed to show up any reference to a company referred to by Glass in one of his faked pieces, 'Hack Heaven', or to enable confirmation of any of the other details in the story. An online publication, using internet search methods, had exposed the flaw at the heart of America's old media.

The tendency for journalists to undermine trust in journalism is not new, of course, nor is it confined to a particular platform or market sector. The BBC and other UK-based TV journalism providers were caught in a wave of faking scandals in 2007 (Hibberd, 2010). In those years, nonetheless, anxiety about the level of journalistic fabrication in the media, and associated declines in recorded levels of public trust in journalism as a whole, coincided with the trauma of technology-driven transition from analogue to digital platforms. One trend fed the other, and threw up new challenges to the notions of journalistic truth, objectivity, and reliability – not least because examples of fabrication and sloppy editing in print and broadcast journalism became the subject of an expanding online sector eager to assert its rights *vis-à-vis* the 'old' media. Online newsmakers spent a great deal of their time checking up on, and then spreading the news about, errors of fact, not to mention deliberate deception on the part of the 'old media'. If the established news media had acted as a Fourth Estate watching over political power, emerging online media have acted as scrutineers of the print and broadcast watchdogs – what Bruns calls 'gatewatchers' (2011a) – harrying them and deflating their presumptions of superiority with repeated examples of fabrication and plagiarism.

Once-trusted journalistic institutions such as the *New Republic* or the *New York Times* now face an online, 24-hour, globalised news culture in which ordinary people – amateurs, in most cases, though growing numbers of trained journalists work in this sector – have unprecedented capacity to follow stories back to their source, and to communicate their own take on these stories to a global audience, at great speed and with relatively few opportunities for censorship or control. This trend has been welcomed by many, including this author, as part of the digitally driven decentralisation and democratisation of journalism, liberating it from the stultifying effect of the old, top-down, capital-intensive media organisations, as well as the authoritarian control of governments. But we still need to know who is trustworthy and who isn't, given that we cannot experience directly all the events which make the news, or have direct access to the 'facts' behind every issue.

The survival of journalistic professionalism

Dan Gillmor's 2010 book *Mediactive*[5] argues that in the era of UGC the construction of trust should be rooted in the application – by professional and amateur – of basic journalistic principles. Information-management skills, for Gillmor, required at both the production and consumption ends of the news cycle, become core not just to journalism but to everyday life in an environment characterised by what he calls 'information overload' (p. 3), and in which we need not just 'to manage the flood pouring over us each day, but also to make informed judgements about the significance of what we see'.

This is a challenge for the news consumer, and what could be the defining role of the professional news producer in the digital age – the application of critical, creative thinking to information; the demonstration of thoroughness, accuracy, fairness, independence; transparency in the information-management process; the making of time and space for checking, double sourcing, and reflection. All of these belong to the rituals of objectivity, and help build trust in the veracity and reliability of what is being reported, analysed, interpreted, commented upon. They require resources, and organisational support, which, if forthcoming, will greatly improve the chances of the survival of journalism as a professional practice in the years and decades to come.

Notes

1 Here I echo an observation made by Professor Cynthia Stohl in a keynote address to the 2011 Australia and New Zealand Communication Association conference. Identifying a 'paradox of connectivity', Stohl (2011) argued that 'the very features and the affordances of new technologies that free us from institutional structures, also make formal organisations evermore central'.

2 But in Australia too the trends are, if less alarming, unmistakeable, as is the reason for them. The rise of the internet, and the migration of readers away from print to online, where much news content is accessible free of charge, is eroding the fundamental business model which sustained the press for centuries. The global financial crisis may not have impacted so hard on Australia as it did in the UK and the USA, but that technology-driven process of structural change is every bit as evident there. In March 2011 West Australian Newspapers' A\$4.1 billion proposed purchase of the Seven Media Group to create the country's biggest listed media company was correctly viewed by industry insiders as the start of a wider consolidation of the Australian media industry. Subscription television networks Foxtel and Austar were exploring a merger, while the Australian Competition and Consumer Commission (ACCC) had just approved the merger between Southern Cross Broadcasting and Austereo, leaving only Fairfax Media and the Nine network as stand-alone media players of significance in the Australian media market, and question marks hang over the long-term future of the former. For commentary on this story see McNair, B., 'WAN Horse

Town Just the Beginning for Media Mergers', *The Conversation*, 11 March 2011. Available at http://theconversation.edu.au/wan-horse-town-just-the-beginning-for-media-mergers-266.

3 In July 2011 *The Economist* published a special report on the global news industry detailing trends in circulation, revenue and other measures (see Standage, 2011).

4 People don't buy news just for information, of course. They buy 'story', 'sensation', 'spectacle', 'drama', 'tragedy', 'scandal'. They buy a quality of narrative, wrapped in attractive packaging, in which they can believe and invest emotionally as well as financially. And quality narrative requires training, practice, talent. For those reasons it costs money to acquire.

5 *Mediactive* is available to download free of charge at http://mediactive.com.

6

NEWS MAKING AS AN INTERACTIVE PRACTICE

Global news exchange and network journalism

Ansgard Heinrich

Professional news organizations have undoubtedly faced major challenges in the first decade of the twenty-first century. With the rise of the world wide web as an interactive platform for information trade, the business of information exchange has been catapulted into a global sphere that enables connections spanning the globe in a manner unthinkable just a few decades ago. What seems most striking in this respect are the changes in the pace at which information travels and the scale of information available. These changes in pace and scale have, in effect, accelerated so much that the practice of journalistic newsgathering, production and exchange are inevitably impacted.

As digital technologies enable the transmission of messages loosened from spatial constraints, we witness a shift from 'place-based' information networks into a 'space-based' arena of information exchange and the shift towards a 'network society' (Castells, 1996) that operates fundamentally differently from previous societies. Content of whatever kind criss-crosses the globe in virtually no time and news today takes place in a 'digital space' which creates new relevance factors such as 'speed, connectivity, and flexibility' (Hassan, 2007: 49).

Much recent research in the field of journalism studies is dedicated to studying the effects of the technological changes on newsroom work (e.g. Pavlik, 2000; Deuze, 2003; Straubhaar, 2007; Avilés et al., 2008). However, it appears that we are just at the beginning of this transformational process and coming to terms with it is a struggle felt by journalists in their day-to-day work just as much as by scholars trying to catch up with the ongoing changes that are shaking up the business of journalism. We have entered a state of 'chaotic' information flows, as McNair (2006) explains. These flows do not only reach from one end of a country to the other, but span the globe via digital connections. What information to look for, how to filter it and who to choose as information sources are some of the questions journalistic organizations now readdress in light of these developments.

The ever-increasing number of information providers that roam in a global space of information exchange adds to the confusion as journalistic organizations are trying to identify where they stand now. Social-media platforms such as Twitter contribute to the erosion of traditional news production, with stories breaking at the speed of light and 'ordinary' users, independent journalists, pressure groups and many others feeding eyewitness accounts, commentary or links into today's news-exchange chains. Side by side with traditional news organizations, platforms such as the NGO-driven blogging aggregation site Global Voices Online provide news updates, commentary or background information from virtually any digitally connected corner of the world. At the same time, mapping tools such as Ushahidi enable users to collaboratively put together maps filled with information on various crisis regions in the world.

Journalistic organizations are not the sole information providers accessible any longer, no doubt, so are they also slowly losing control to have the privilege of being the *leading* information providers? While the traditional practice of journalism is rather grounded in an authoritative approach towards information provision ('We, the journalists have the power and privilege to set the news agenda'), how do journalistic organizations have to rethink their practices in order to fit into an increasingly interactive sphere of information exchange? To discuss these questions, one also has to reflect upon the notion of the 'public' that journalists serve. As digital technologies help members of the public to gain a voice and contribute viewpoints, information and their version of 'the news', the idea of a 'homogenous' public that journalism caters for is contested (Coleman and Ross, 2010). Rather, the numerous counter-publics within societies that form this rather heterogeneous group of *publics* have now become visible. Be it the Occupy movement or the people of the Arab Spring, these digital publics use digital tools to distribute their views. Yet how much of a 'public connection' (Couldry, Livingstone and Markham, 2007) is drawn through seizing the digital tools on offer by journalistic organizations?

This chapter will reflect upon these developments by demarcating some of the main characteristics of an emerging global news sphere that is shared by journalists and alternative media, i.e. digital counterpublics. Based on the paradigm of 'network journalism' (Heinrich, 2011) it argues that it is first and foremost a question of relocalizing journalistic outlets within the vast mix of voices at a time where information exchange takes place in increasingly interactive spheres. A network journalism sphere is made up of many digitally connected information nodes and allows connections to a diversity of other nodes. Seizing this diversity through collaboration with a variety of nodes – 'old' and 'new', 'traditional' and 'alternative' – might allow for more depth in coverage and that is where the potential of the sphere of network journalism lies. Relocalizing journalistic organizations within the sphere of network journalism, however, has to be met by a deeper understanding of how news flows function in a technology-driven, fast-paced and globalized sphere of information exchange.

Areas of global news exchange

In his book *What is Globalization?* (2000), sociologist Ulrich Beck explains what he identifies as a shift from national frameworks to a world society:

> The national state is a territorial state: that is, its power is grounded upon attachment to a particular place (upon control over membership, current legislation, border defense, and so on). The world society which, in the wake of globalization, has taken shape in many (not only economic) dimensions is undermining the importance of the national state, because a multiplicity of social circles, communication networks, market relations and lifestyles, none of them specific to any particular locality, now cut across the boundaries of the national state.
>
> *(Ibid.: 4)*

Inherent in this description of a 'world society' lies the idea that the exchange of information functions fundamentally differently in an increasingly borderless environment. Information flows tend not to stop at borders, and nor do the reference frameworks to contextualize meaning in news solely rely on rather inward focusing national news agendas. Following some major arguments in globalization theory, former temporal and spatial distances are increasingly vanishing (Appadurai, 1996; Hannerz, 1996; Beck, 2000).

Technology is surely an important factor here. Driven by advancements reaching from telegraph to satellite technology (Volkmer, 2003; Price, 2008) and leading to the emergence of first global news outlets such as CNN that sprung up in the 1980s, distributing information in real time across national borders has become a lot easier. Yet, with the evolution of low cost, digital technologies and particularly the internet, this development seems to be reaching another peak. What started with blogs or alternative media sites springing up in the spheres of the world wide web seems to be culminating at this point in time with the evolution of digital social-networking sites such as Twitter, Facebook, Tumblr and Instagram. Information-organization tools such as RSS feeds and platforms such as Flipboard enable users to personalize their daily digest of news from a variety of sources, be it subscribing to the feeds of the BBC or to an individual blogger. And all these platforms allow users to share content of whatever kind via digital connections.

Alternative media outlets have, of course, also started to occupy this digital space of information exchange, and they provide users with the option to not only absorb their content. It lies in the nature of the internet that information here does not flow unidirectionally. As a 'push-pull-network' (Volkmer, 2003: 12), the internet allows for more than just 'pushing' material towards audiences (Schoenbach et al., 2005: 248). Lasswell's basic model of mass communication (1948), which aligns information flows in a one-to-many direction, this famous 'stimulus-response-model' built on the premise of a 'silent' audience unable to react and condemned to absorb, seems to be overcome when viewed in this light (if it ever held true). While users can now selectively pull content and for example mix and match their personal news preferences on a portal such as Flipboard, they can also interact with the content, be it in the form of leaving a comment on a website or by commenting and distributing the material via Twitter or Facebook.

Users can, in effect, crisscross through the net, crawling deeper and deeper into a story, by following links they find on a certain topic or by typing a topic or some key words into a search engine. This is rather an active procedure on the side of the user, and it might not necessarily lead them onto the channels of mainstream news organizations. The internet allows users to dig deep into a storyline, to scroll and screen for yet another angle, to search for more background information or contextualization. Whom of my friends is posting a comment on some political issue that might be of interest to me; what information is roaming through the spheres of Twitter when I enter the hashtag #ArabSpring; what comes up if I search for a video of the latest clashes in Syria; or what do I find if I search for information about the situation in Libya on Google?

Of course, it is naïve to believe that every user goes out to explore the depth of the internet in search of news or political information, and many sceptics of political deliberation through internet technology contest the power of digital technologies (for an overview of such positions in the academic field see Couldry, Livingstone and Markham, 2007). However, the internet renders it possible to seek for information and to seek for depth, further background layers, viewpoints and perspectives. In effect, 'the internet is built on the assumption of diversity and heterogeneity' (ibid.: 35) and digital technologies at the very least have *potentially* assigned power to the masses to control how they want to access information and what sources they want to use. Shirky describes it as a 'new ecosystem' (2008: 60) of social interaction that is taking shape, as 'we now have communications tools that are flexible enough to match our social capabilities' (ibid.: 20).

What is more, it has become a lot easier to form communities within a digital, global sphere where knowledge from diverse backgrounds can be pooled. Collaborative production modes are fostered within this environment that promise collaboration and peer production as new mechanisms to 'harness human skill, ingenuity, and intelligence more efficiently and effectively than anything we have witnessed previously' (Tapscott and Williams, 2008: 18). Lévy (1995) calls it the 'collective intelligence' that now can be seized within the interactive digital spaces. Yet, how does this possibility of mass collaboration, that characteristic of the internet as a 'push-pull-medium', affect journalistic newsgathering, production and distribution?

First, the number of information disseminators has increased and it includes now many more non-traditional players that have become digitally accessible, from the blogger to the tweeter or the NGO. Second, more sources are accessible, and third, the possibility of active participation and feedback have eroded the traditional one-to-many information flow that supports a form of horizontal networking, 'offering instead one-to-one and many-to-many at once' (Bell, 2007: 78).

Social interaction patterns have thus fundamentally changed, and what lies at the heart of Castells' paradigm of the 'network society' (1996) is what matters when studying patterns of global news exchange and their impact on journalistic practice. Journalism is widely understood as a vital part of democratic societies. But what about when these societies change, when their members start to act and connect fundamentally differently? What is journalism's reaction to that? The challenge for journalistic outlets now lies in the question of how they adapt to each one of these changes outlined above. A global information sphere with more actors taking part in the news-production process, more information in circulation as well as the options of instantaneous feedback and active participation of users, demands a reaction.

Journalism used to be acted out within the borders of a fairly closed operational system, controlled by a rather limited number of news-producer elites on one side and a rather limited number of elite sources from governmental institutions to PR personnel on the other. As the 'control' or 'dominance' paradigm – premised on economic determinacy – asserts, ruling elites are presumed to be able to extend their control of economic resources to control the cultural apparatuses of the media, including the means of propaganda and public relations. This leads to planned and predictable outcomes such as pro-elite media bias, dominant ideology, even 'brainwashing' (McNair, 2006: 3; the main theorists in this respect are Hall et al., 1978 and Herman and Chomsky, 1988).

These ideas of control fit in with a rather bleak understanding of a somewhat 'homogeneous public' that journalists cater for. It is what Coleman and Ross (2010: 45ff) refer to as the 'managed public' from the viewpoint of the journalistic organization. Here, media are led by a certain perception of what this 'public' looks like that they report for. As a result, they often marginalize and exclude certain publics through source selection. The public becomes homogeneous in the eye of the journalist beholder. Publics might be invited to participate in media operations (e.g. through a letter to the editor, phone-ins, studio discussions), but at a limited, controllable level, and they are firmly kept in their place. The public thus is seen as singular and has to fit with specific programme ideas and agendas.

This notion of a public as audience that looks alike and thinks alike is increasingly being contested in a digitally connected sphere. Besides the fact that there has never really been any such thing as a 'homogenous public' (ibid.), that audiences have always been diverse and disparate as they are made up of individuals and groups that differ from each other in attitude, thought or behaviour, the advent of digitalization and globalization has rendered this diversity in the public much more visible. Take the example of counterpublics that now can form communities online to openly address users. The Indymedia movement, widely researched as one of the first alternative media platforms that sprung to global attention (Downing, 2002, 2003; Wall, 2003; Atton, 2004; Garcelon, 2006), was the first large-scale example in this respect. The already mentioned Occupy movement, the many activist groups supporting the Arab Spring or environmental pressure groups that use the internet to advocate for their causes are others.

These groups, just as well as every single user who decides to actively use Twitter, to become part of the Tumblr community or to publicly share photos via Flickr, all roam in the exact same sphere of information exchange as journalists now. They might not have as many followers as the BBC gathers viewers in front of their television, but nevertheless they do exist side by side. And they are part of a rather heterogeneous public – this time around, however, also sharing their viewpoints and stories publicly. Trying to 'control' information flows becomes somewhat impossible, then. At the same time, hanging on to an idea of a 'homogeneous public', further excluding or marginalizing viewpoints seems to be inappropriate – or at the very least it is more contestable now than it has ever been. As these publics are now active within the rather borderless spheres of the net, acknowledging the many feedback channels on offer seems rather a necessity. What these new voices bring to the information sphere is a diverse picture of viewpoints, information and background stories.

And as these counterpublics have become digitally accessible, they are capable of contributing to news. They thus are not only part of global *information* networks, but they can be part of global *news* exchanges. They represent a fragmented 'public' that is to be met in 'real' life as well as on various online platforms. And for journalistic organizations, here lies a major opportunity to tap into these diverse publics that they cater for and that they – at least if one follows the ideals of journalism as fourth estate – might want to represent. This sphere of global news exchange, in which journalistic organizations now operate side by side with alternative news providers, carries some central characteristics and signals a paradigm shift in the organization of news and information flows. The concept of network journalism might be helpful in this respect to understand the dynamics at play in an increasingly complex and digitally connected world.

Information nodes in the sphere of network journalism

The paradigm of network journalism is informed by previous studies and assumptions about the changes in journalism. These works either concentrate on describing the evolving intersections between citizen journalists and professional journalism and use the term network*ed* journalism (Jarvis, 2006; Cohn, 2007; Beckett, 2008; Beckett and Mansell, 2008) or focus on existing forms of online journalism and their specifics (Bardoel and Deuze, 2001). Yet, the paradigm of network journalism as understood here (Heinrich, 2011) reaches further. It takes on board the above-mentioned ideas from globalization theory to attest a fundamental paradigm shift in societies that in turn impacts the interaction patterns in global news exchange.

What Castells (1996) refers to as the new organizational framework of societies in the digital age is here adapted to the journalistic sphere. As societies move towards rather open, borderless and dynamic networks of interaction within the 'network society', the paradigm of network journalism asserts a similar development for journalistic work. Network journalism, then, can be understood as the paradigm for a dynamic structure of the global news-exchange sphere that has superseded the traditional media system. And as the 'network' has become the overarching form of societal organization, digital networks are now paving the way for journalistic news-gathering, production and dissemination. To use the words of Benkler, news exchange is now 'organized in a radically more decentralized pattern than was true of this sector in the twentieth century' (Benkler, 2006: 3). Digital networks, here, are understood as Castells defines them for the evolving societal space: the network structure suits 'the increasing complexity of interaction' (2000: 70). It is a flexible structure that allows non-linear information flows. These networks are made up of an immeasurable number of nodes that connect to other nodes.

Applied to the journalistic sphere, such nodes are, for example, traditional news organizations such as CNN, the BBC or any news agency. Such nodes are, however, also the various alternative media outlets that roam online. And these nodes can represent counterpublics that have formed their communities within the space of the world wide web. A node is a tweeter who informs his or her followers about recent developments in Bahrain or the blogger who comments on upcoming elections in the US. And the person who films at the Occupy protests and uploads a video to YouTube can be considered a node. All of these nodes taken together roam through the same, shared, information sphere. Some of them can be considered big nodes (e.g. the BBC), some can be considered small nodes (e.g. the individual tweeter). Yet, however big or small, journalistic outlets here are just one part of a complex, dynamic and rather horizontally organized global information network. Each node is capable of bundling information from various corners; and all these nodes, in effect, can be connected via information strings crisscrossing through digital spheres. They all can potentially intersect, no matter what size they are or what kind of information they provide.

The challenge for journalistic organizations now lies in the question of what kind of node they want to represent. To recall Castells once more,

> The key issue is that these nodes may reconfigure themselves according to new tasks and goals, and that they may grow or diminish in importance depending on the knowledge and information that they win or lose.
>
> *(Castells and Ince, 2003: 24)*

In accordance with this, as new opportunities for connectivity emerge in this digitally networked sphere, the 'tasks and goals' for journalistic organizations now might be reformulated. Who to connect to, who to dismiss, or who to allow into one's own information networks might win them knowledge and information – or it might make them lose it. As the elite-controlled information-exchange system is being replaced by this dynamic and open structure of network journalism, news organizations thus have to decide how much of that openness they want to allow, while this dense net of nodes offers multiple connection points and non-linear news flows.

The network journalism structure thus reflects a sphere of global news exchange that allows new connection opportunities to journalistic organizations. And it is a sphere that fosters interactivity and thus carries 'participation' as one of its main characteristics. The sphere of network journalism thus lays the perfect grounds to connect to the many publics journalism might cater for. Instead of traditional one-way structures of information flow, it supports these many-to-many flows outlined previously. In line with this, one of the 'tasks and goals' of a journalistic organization – or a journalistic node – now could be to seize these paths on offer. With reference to the role of media and political participation, Couldry, Livingstone and Markham (2007: 24), for example, state that media have an important job to fulfil in 'facilitating, shaping or impeding' such participation. Yet how can journalistic organizations achieve this? What do these alternative information nodes offer that might contribute to journalistic work today? What might be the 'alternative' these new information nodes could add to coverage?

Embracing network journalism: between shallowness and depth

One of the central tasks for journalistic organizations in the sphere of network journalism is, in my view, to represent in their coverage the many voices and viewpoints that have become digitally accessible. As these voices can now be heard by journalists much more clearly – and just as journalism hears the powerful voices of governmental institutions or PR professionals – the responsibility of news organizations might now lie in embedding these voices of the many publics in favour of increasing the depth of journalistic coverage. Depth, then, can be defined as giving further contextualization and background information that reflects the viewpoints of a heterogeneous public – and this depth can be achieved through connecting to an increased number of information nodes, including non-traditional sources.

Yet to date it seems that Coleman and Ross (2010: 74) are right when they state: 'Mainstream media are extremely reluctant to give much visibility to organizations which challenge or even threaten the political frames of the media agenda'. Whereas this statement is aimed at the counterpublics that find their outlets in arms of alternative media and their relation to journalistic organizations, one might also add here: journalistic organizations might also be very reluctant to give visibility to active social-media users who might not be part of any alternative media platform, yet still represent a valuable information node. Rather, it seems that it is still a task favoured by alternative media to 'provide the means by which counterpublics can come to voice and engage a public sphere in which the traditional media's gatekeeping proclivities are curtailed or ignored' (ibid.: 77). This is in line with Atton's (2005: 15ff) understanding of alternative media, when he characterizes them as being concerned with social change, seeking to involve citizens and aiming to innovate media forms and/or content.

However, within the spheres of network journalism, where the many information nodes large and small, traditional and alternative, roam side by side, this reluctance to give voice to sources other than the 'official' ones is problematic. To point out the markers that Couldry, Livingstone and Markham (2007: 8) set: they underline the importance of a 'public connection' which is 'to understand democracy as a structure of participation, not a façade for elite control', and it is a 'public connection' that can very well be 'mediated'. Such 'public connection', as viewed here, could be ascribed as one of these tasks news organizations have to fulfil in today's sphere of network journalism. What is represented in the alternative media sphere, as well as on social-media platforms, are some of the voices of these many publics – and they deserve to be heard in the traditional media realm. One could view the digital age as an opportunity to connect with these many publics if one was to seize the many nodes on offer and to embrace that idea of collaboration that the aforementioned scholars such as Shirky, Tapscott and Williams or Lévy make out.

In the sphere of network journalism, the opportunity is there for new organizational frameworks of journalistic operations to dig deep into these digital networks, to search for background and contextualization of stories. Yet the challenge lies in tapping into these opportunities. First steps at traditional news organizations are under way to allow some influx from alternative information nodes. When witnessing the coverage of the big news events of 2011, for example, audiences were confronted with the occasional YouTube video screened on television. References were made to Twitter and Facebook when reporting about the Arab Spring, and news organizations started asking questions such as: Did the world see its first 'Facebook revolution' (Hauslohner, 2011; Taylor, 2011)? References were also made to the blogosphere in reporting. And many traditional journalistic organizations now run their own Facebook pages and Twitter accounts. So, are we there, yet? Can these moves be characterized as embracing the sphere of network journalism and seizing the tools on offer?

Yes and no, one might answer. Yes, in the respect that traditional organizations are starting to experiment with the digital tools. No, in the respect that one could also argue: what we are witnessing in terms of changing relationships between alternative media, social networks and traditional news organizations is rather a shallow and shy approach towards tapping into interactive spheres. Further research is needed here to explore how much of a network journalism we really see already at journalistic organizations. However, observations so far support Coleman and Ross's idea of the 'managed public' rather than collaboration with the public: journalistic organizations might stick one toe into experimenting with social media, yet collaboration and continuous information exchange with the many non-traditional information nodes is rather an exception.

Mentioning social media, opening an account for one's own journalistic organization on Twitter, Facebook or YouTube is one thing. But it is not so much a question of whether these outlets are present online and with an own account in the social media sphere, but more a question of *how* they are present. Do they use these tools to embrace interactive formats and collaboration? Network journalism – viewed in this light – then might be more of a future possibility than the reality in daily newsroom practice. So far, many journalistic outlets, it seems, use their Twitter accounts as another 'push-outlet' to promote articles published in their newspaper, their website or to advertise their upcoming show on television. But how are comments and replies by users dealt with? And how far do journalistic organizations dig into the option of sourcing alternative media for viewpoints and perspectives on stories? A medium such as Twitter does allow us to dig deeper by crawling through the many connections among tweeters who link to each other, tweet and retweet.

Twitter is, in a way, a mirror of the world wide web, as one can follow hashtags to crisscross through the numerous viewpoints and story angles on offer. Journalistic organizations, however, have to first acknowledge that crawling and scraping through these spheres for background information and contextualization now makes up part of a journalist's job, as it is a tool that assists in deepening coverage and representing the many publics journalism can serve. And second, journalists will need time to do so. Many of them might be willing and able to give more attention to alternative and social media; however, their busy schedules, common work practices in the newsroom and standard news packages do not leave the space for interactive and collaborative undertakings.

The work practices of some alternative media platforms might lead the way in this respect. To review Coleman and Ross (2010: 78) once more:

> One of the key differences between alternative and mainstream media lies in the determination of what constitutes news and which voices should be represented in describing, explaining, and commenting upon the social events of the day. Alternative media politicize the hidden stories which lie beneath the surface of news items covered by the mainstream.

News aggregation sites such as AlterNet provide a platform online for some of these hidden stories. Global Voices Online aggregates stories from bloggers across the world to provide regular coverage from countries that often stay outside the radar of traditional news organizations. These are just two nodes that have proven over the past years how collaboration with citizens could work in favour of more depth in coverage as they foster 'public connection' and implement regular collaboration. To use a rare example that plays out in the realm of traditional media: starting with the Arab Spring movements, NPR strategist Andy Carvin was the first to curate messages from traditional as well as alternative media via Twitter (Heinrich, 2012). The BBC created a user-generated-content hub (UGC) to allow their viewers to comment on topics or make story suggestions (Wardle and Williams, 2008; Heinrich, 2011). And the *Guardian*, proving that it can be considered one of the forerunners on the side of traditional news organizations to seize the potentials of an interactive sphere of news exchange, has begun to provide gripping liveblogs in which Twitter is a regular source of information alongside traditional large-scale news agencies. But what the BBC or the *Guardian* do are exceptions rather than common news practice today.

What sets these examples apart from the shallowness that can be identified in many of the approaches towards alternative and social media by other traditional journalistic organizations is that, here, alternative media platforms and social media have been acknowledged as information nodes and have become part of day-to-day practices in the newsroom. These organizations allow time, staff and space within their coverage to bring in alternate perspectives and voices. What is more, the *Guardian* or NPR's Carvin do not shy away from setting links in Twitter feeds or liveblogs that might take users (temporarily) off their own sites and into the depths of the world wide web. This is not common practice at many traditional news outlets, as they are afraid that such linking practices might ultimately lead to losing these users to other platforms. Instead, common linking practice often only allows users to discover the depth of an outlet's own website, as links refer back to one's own older articles or videos. Here, one might want to point to Jeff Jarvis' recommendation, which suggests: 'Do what you do best and link to the rest' (2009).

This linking is, then, another practice that embraces the opportunities of the sphere of network journalism. Stating UGC hubs are a start means that they seize the many new connections that a network journalism sphere has on offer in order to add additional layers to stories. Tapping into alternative media, continuously connecting to alternative information nodes such as Global Voices Online, might be another step to further 'public connection' and to serve the many publics. These are approaches to seize the tools on offer in favour of fostering global news exchange in a sphere of network journalism – and moving from shallow connections to depth through collaboration and contextualization.

Taking steps towards collaboration

The analysis presented above was dedicated to demarcating the structural patterns of a network journalism sphere. It pointed out some of the connection and collaboration opportunities between alternative media, social media and traditional journalistic organizations. Viewed in this light, the concept of network journalism can prove helpful to understand the dynamics of the paradigmatic shift societies have taken at the beginning of the twenty-first century. It points to some of the factors that journalists are confronted with when manoeuvring through a digital, interactive, global and horizontally organized information sphere.

The concept of network journalism, however, is only a start that can assist us to analyze the realities of newsroom work today, and it might be an inspiration for further empirical research in this area. One task for future research could now be to empirically validate how much depth or shallowness we see in the coverage provided by traditional news organizations. Such research could take place on many levels: it might include studies that look at the intersections between traditional news media and alternative news providers. This could be research on how social-media tools such as Twitter are being seized as sourcing tools in mainstream news reporting (see Broersma and Graham, 2012). And it might include content-focused studies that compare the coverage provided by alternative news providers and mainstream news organizations. This kind of research could take on board Atton's (2009) proposal to monitor the alternative media sphere and use it as a reflection tool when dissecting operation modes of traditional journalism. Comparative analyses that, for example, monitor both the coverage of events in mainstream and alternative media, might then assist reflection upon journalistic practice today. What is more, further research on user behaviour will help us to better understand how publics connect online and how they perceive the news. As users are ultimately going to make the decision on what content to read, which outlet to turn to or what news to pay for, this area deserves much more scholarly attention. Do they make use of the many information choices, and to what extent and how do they live Negroponte's vision of the 'Daily Me' (1995) when they consume news?

These are just some of the future areas of research that are embedded in a broader reflection about what the changes described mean for the profession of journalism going forward, and what professional journalism looks like under the network paradigm. The network journalism sphere here has been characterized as a complex system of information nodes. As journalists serve a diverse 'public', they might have to now make room within their organizational frameworks for continuous collaborations that reach beyond traditional journalistic networks. As pointed out here, these new ways of collaborating, of connecting with a variety of nodes large and small, traditional and alternative, can potentially add depth in coverage. And adding such depth might also assist us to replace local and national reporting frames with frames that embrace more 'global' perspectives. With globalization in full swing, linking, connecting and collaborating with information nodes from different world corners could contribute to reviewing local issues within a global context. And while the sceptic might argue that even though we are clearly connected virtually, we are still thinking – especially when it comes to news – in quite a place-based manner, the optimist might then reply: use the tools at hand in the network journalism sphere to allow for a greater level of openness and a 'truly' global news exchange.

7

BETWEEN NETWORKS AND 'HIERARCHIES OF CREDIBILITY'

Navigating journalistic practice in a sea of user-generated content

Ingrid Volkmer and Amira Firdaus

From the uprising of Tibetan monks in 2008, through to Iran's Twitter Revolution in 2009 and the 2010 Arab Spring, the journalistic coverage of transnational conflicts is often not only driven but – increasingly – framed by 'authentic' reports, uploaded to interactive media platforms such as Twitter, Facebook, and YouTube. Online sites appear to be affecting both the widening of the thematic scope through 'authentic' news of otherwise geographically distant events and also a refining of 'co-orientation', i.e. the emerging collaborative space among news outlets. From a journalism-studies perspective, these developments reveal not only new forms of digital journalism but rather a severe transformation of the journalistic professional environment to a networked 'ecology', in which the intersection between national professional journalism and user-driven media platforms merge within an increasingly complex professional transnational space. The particular form of negotiating of this emerging spatial parallelism of the journalistic professional 'ecology', between national 'place-based' organizational structures and transnational authentic news narratives and other sources, is one of the key areas of transformation, not only of journalism but of the professional identity of a news organization.

Digital news spheres are debated mainly within four contexts which, however – and this angle becomes increasingly important in such a transnational 'parallel' ecology – rarely address transcultural differences of networked spheres. One set of discourses identifies news models, such as citizen journalism (e.g. Paulussen, et al., 2007; Allan and Thorsen, 2009), blogs (e.g. Lowrey, 2006; Perlmutter, 2008), new forms of participatory online news production and dissemination (e.g. Bruns, 2005; Beckett and Mansell, 2008) and online news sites of newspapers and news broadcasters. These research foci contribute to inquiry mainly by problematizing the online modes and models of traditional print or broadcast news channels (e.g. Althaus and Tewksbury, 2002; Groshek, 2008), and by elucidating the processes of technological transformation in news production (e.g. Greer and Mensing, 2004; Boczkowski, 2005; Quandt et al., 2006; Singer, 2006; Domingo, 2008a; Phillips, 2010).

Beyond identifying these new formations of digital journalism, a second debate highlights what we might call a 'macro-level' perspective, i.e. reconstructing large-scale transformation of journalism and implications on democracy (e.g. Beckett and Mansell, 2008; Hamdy, 2009; Steele, 2009; Banda, 2010). In addition, a 'meso-level' perspective debates the implications on news organizations which are premised upon the idea of an interactive online sphere (e.g. Beckett, 2008; Heinrich, 2011). A third discourse builds upon media 'convergence' and multimedia journalism and converged newsrooms emerging in the 1990s and early 2000s, which are now evolving into a resurgence of newsroom ethnographies, focusing on online news and participatory forms of journalism (e.g. Huang et al., 2004; Deuze, Bruns and Neuberger, 2007; Domingo et al., 2008; Paterson and Domingo, 2008). A 'techno-pessimist' perspective, which seems to constitute a fourth discourse through a critique of neoliberal globalized digital news sphere, reconceptualizes media platforms either as being absorbed by powerful media corporations (e.g. Stanton, 2007) and, in consequence, contributing to the deepening of an already wide digital divide (e.g. Kovacic and Erjavec, 2008; Reich, 2008), or even as a failed tool of democratic change (e.g. Hafez, 2007).

Although these four discourses illuminate crucial conceptual frameworks which help to critically assess the increasingly fine-grained transformative parameter of journalism within network spheres, it is striking that many of these approaches relate to a 'Western' model of journalism culture. Transnational comparative conceptions of globalized news networks, as negotiative journalistic spaces between the parallel complexities of place-based 'local' organizations and spatial spheres of digital sources, are increasingly important in order to identify not only the particularities of the relevance of the network 'ecology' on journalistic professionalism in non-Western countries but also to identify the role of the networked news sphere for journalistic routines in diverse societies and public cultures. Over the last few years a small number of studies have identified parameters of such a transnational journalistic sphere, including non-Western countries, mainly relating to mainstream national media. Examples are Shoemaker and Cohen's (2006) work on a globalized news culture, which compares news values of national radio, television and newspapers in ten countries, including India, Russia and Chile. Another example is the study by Pan, Chan and Lo (2008), who identify diverse societal spheres of journalism in China, Hong Kong and Taiwan. A more recent study (Hanitzsch et al., 2011) compares institutional roles of news outlets, journalistic epistemologies and 'ethical ideologies' in eighteen countries. The study identifies, for example, quite diverse conceptions of relevance of the 'watchdog' role of journalism and of 'interventionism' in developed and developing countries (Hanitzsch et al., 2011).

Although these are important findings, little is known so far about the relevance and perception of user-driven media in professional journalistic routines of 'traditional' channels (i.e. *not* their websites) of 'mainstream' outlets in non-European and non-US news cultures. In this sense, the aim of 'rethinking' journalism also relates to an understanding of the relevance of a transnational spatial news ecology in the 'local' perception of 'place-based' journalists of national news outlets, particularly in non-Western countries, and the role of these interactive sources for the daily news routine. More specifically, it is of relevance to address the professional reality of journalists (as opposed to citizen journalists or bloggers) working at 'traditional' television channels (as opposed to online media) of 'mainstream' news outlets (as opposed to 'alternative' media outlets).

A non-Western perspective on networked media ecologies

Malaysian journalism offers an excellent biotope for examining the complexity of the journalistic network 'ecology'. To fully understand journalism in Malaysia one has to realize that journalists need to survey multiple online and offline platforms, and to monitor diverse networked and non-networked news sources, to get a grip on Malaysian politics and current affairs. We therefore conducted a study of mainstream, professional journalists, based in Malaysia, a country which is rarely included in comparative journalism studies. Furthermore, as typical of 'democracies' in many non-Western 'developing' countries, Malaysia's 'press-as-government-partner' development-journalism ethos (see Ali, 1990; Anuar, 2005) contrasts with the liberal democratic ethos of Western media. Thus the selection of Malaysia redresses the focus on Western liberal-democratic contexts in many journalism studies and contributes to an emerging 'global-comparative' turn in journalism research (Wahl-Jorgensen and Hanitzsch, 2008). Much national political contestation and public discourse in Malaysia occurs online via alternative media. The migration of Malaysian politics from physical to virtual spaces is, in this sense, a manifestation of the country's expanding networked media ecology, driven by a combination of: a global surge of digital networking; a burgeoning of networked young voters alongside the rise of a new breed of internet-savvy politicians; and also the government's 'soft-authoritarian' commitment to a free and uncensored internet (see Hafez, 2005, on democratic elements in 'soft-authoritarian' countries).

Although Malaysia is a relatively minor player in the global sphere, compared to power centres like Washington DC, London or Beijing, its capital city, Kuala Lumpur, is nevertheless a well-known 'node' and in many respects a 'global city' (Sassen, 1994) in the network 'geography' of global information flows. These flows include not only what Arjun Appadurai (1990) might call 'mediascapes' and 'technoscapes', but also 'ethnoscapes', in so far as Kuala Lumpur constitutes a media 'world city' (Globalization and World Cities Research Network, 2008) and hosts journalists from international media organizations, producing news for different global, international and national news spheres.

Our case study is based on interviews with professional journalists based in Malaysia who work in diverse national and international news outlets. Nine are expatriate 'global' journalists at Al Jazeera English's Kuala Lumpur News Centre, the channel's Asia-Pacific hub reporting regional news for its global audiences. The channel's critical coverage of global conflict and its propensity for challenging governments (Powers and el-Nawawy, 2008) belies a liberal-democratic ethos (see Samuel-Azran, 2010) that is similar to that purportedly embraced by Western news organizations like

CNN or the BBC, where many of its journalists formerly worked. Eleven participants are 'local' journalists from Malaysia's state-affiliated national news channel, Bernama TV, whose coverage of national news aimed at national polity is shaped by a development-journalism 'press-as-government-partner' ethos. Two participants are Malaysians working as 'foreign correspondents' for the Kuala Lumpur bureau of Singapore-owned Channel News Asia. These journalists cover Malaysian news for transnational regional audiences. Channel News Asia subscribes to 'development journalism' in its 'soft-authoritarian' home country of Singapore (Latif, 1998), but embraces liberal-democratic journalism elsewhere, including Malaysia.

These news-sphere differences notwithstanding, user-driven Web 2.0 media is gradually edging into the daily news-production routines of all interviewed 'professional' journalists. And this 'diffusion' of user-driven media as new 'journalistic tools' is manifest in strikingly similarly ways across these global, regional and national news channels, all based in Kuala Lumpur. Both journalistic adoption and journalistic evaluation of user-driven new media are structured by professional journalistic routines and norms.

One common aspect of journalistic adoption of user-driven media sources is in the use of blogs, social media, and alternative news sites at the initial phases of newswork. Journalists use these tools to survey the social world for potentially newsworthy events and issues. However, where user-generated content and Web 2.0 platforms have been most visible is in the coverage of emergency or crises events in locations where journalists are unable to be physically present. User-generated content allows media to overcome time constraints and physical distances, and is particularly useful in facilitating news coverage of spot news such as natural disasters, or unanticipated eruptions of conflict. For global reporters who must constantly survey the world for signs of major conflict, social-media platforms are essential, according to one Al Jazeera English presenter, as 'the first sort of flagging up' of newsworthy events, while another global journalist signed up to Twitter for this very purpose:

> I personally don't have a Twitter account. But I made one just because for certain stories like an earthquake. When the earthquake in Chile happened, telephones weren't working, nothing was working. So we were getting our updates from Twitter. And then the Gaza flotilla raid, we were also getting updates from some NGOs which had people on the boat.
>
> *(Interview producer/output producer, Al Jazeera English)*

For journalists covering Malaysian news, user-driven news media are also considered as 'some kind of alert system', alerting mainstream media editors to salient issues on the (networked) public agenda, issues that the mainstream media might otherwise miss due to its overly heavy focus on government and status-quo news sources (Assistant producer/news reader, Bernama TV).

For mainstream Malaysian journalists, in addition to serving as news leads, user-driven media also provide journalists with relevant background information. There is an important distinction where the parallelism of the news ecology we have pointed out earlier becomes apparent in a culturally specific way: laws governing publication licenses and broadcast ownership ensure that virtually all 'offline' print and broadcast media reflect 'mainstream' values and voices. Online, this 'mainstream' media sphere includes not only these 'offline' media's online ventures, but also the networked presence of mainstream institutions and their representatives, including government ministers and politicians from the ruling coalition. Alongside state-controlled mainstream media is an alternative media sphere that exists wholly online. With little access to print and broadcast media, political parties of the opposition coalition make their presence felt through networked online media, giving rise to a highly critical – and highly popular – alternative media sphere (see Tong, 2004; Steele, 2009). A journalist from the Malaysian Bernama TV expresses these distinctive spheres in a practical context:

> There are news that are being broken by these medias that are not carried by [mainstream media] … But at least I equip myself with this background […] News portals and blogs are basically just information. It could be useful, it could be not useful at this moment. But as long as you read a lot, you gather this information in your mind. You never know, one of these days you can use it.
>
> *(Assistant producer/newsreader, Bernama TV)*

In addition to keeping abreast of political issues, user-driven media platforms are perceived as useful barometers of (online) public sentiment. Journalists sometimes draw upon layperson comments to measure the climate of public opinion. As the Channel News Asia bureau chief notes, 'You read through them, you get an idea. That's good enough, you know what people are feeling on the ground.'

Countering constraints to newsgathering

Although journalists routinely monitor and survey user-driven media, they remain conservative in their mode of evaluating the newsworthiness of user-generated content. First, journalists are only willing to incorporate user-generated content into their news reports when faced with constraints to normal newsgathering. Second, despite the availability of diverse networked sources, 'professional' journalists tend to privilege traditional 'authority' news sources.

In reporting global conflict, apart from security and safety concerns, there are often restrictions placed upon international journalists by governments wishing to control the flow of information coming out of their countries. In such situations, Web 2.0 platforms are highly useful for linking newsrooms to locales where their journalists are prevented from entering. A case in point is Iran's ban on foreign journalists during its Green Revolution political protests in 2009:

> In countries like Iran obviously when there was the post election violence in Iran, our team was not allowed to operate there … We obviously had to

follow Twitter and Facebook, and the campaigns on Facebook, rather a lot. Because that was the way [information was disseminated]. And obviously any video posted on YouTube we would use because our own team could not go out and film. So yes, we do use them when are obviously very, very restricted in our news gathering ... [Otherwise] we would do our own journalism. So, if for example, we were working in Iran ... and assuming there are no restrictions whatsoever, you would have gone to the protest yourself with a cameraman, with a reporter, and you would have covered the story yourself. But unfortunately in Iran, we wouldn't have been able to do that. We would have been arrested straight away, or even worse! We didn't have the permission to newsgather there.

(Planning editor, Al Jazeera English)

Within newsroom settings, news production is a team effort in which multiple journalists collaborate to produce news programmes and bulletins, as well as pursue, package and produce individual news stories. With enough manpower to deploy to news locales and to contact and interview news sources, journalists based at the headquarters of their respective organizations have the luxury of 'doing their own reporting', to borrow from the journalist above.

Correspondents at small bureaus, however, do not have the kind of organizational support that their newsroom counterparts have (see Hannerz, 2004), and often find it necessary to turn to user-driven media platforms as a means of overcoming the constraints that being a lone reporter inevitably places upon their ability to simultaneously cover multiple news events.

... say some by-election where three by-elections are happening at the same time – I can't be at three places at one point! So I stay put in the office ... I'll be video conferencing [live with the news presenter in Singapore] and I'll be following Twitter for the latest election results. The opposition, a lot of them are very fast. Faster than the blogs. Faster than the online media ... There are a lot of them helping us out there with the latest information if you know where to look ... You'd probably know the latest result, even though you are not physically there at the counting centre, somewhere in some [remote town]. You are not there, but you know how many boxes have been counted, how many not tallied yet.

(Bureau chief, Channel News Asia Kuala Lumpur bureau)

Notwithstanding this innovative way of making social media work for professional journalistic newsgathering, long-institutionalized and apparently globalized 'professional' norms of reporting exert considerable influence over the ways in which journalists make use of user-generated content and networked news sources. Journalistic adoption of user-driven new media is not so much 'innovation' as it is 'incorporation' into existing journalistic practices.

One example of this is in cultivating reporter–source relations:

> ... Facebook is a good social web site for networking with other people [...] like economists, analysts via Facebook. Or even ministers. You can send them a personal message and then they will reply [...] I used to be in contact with [a professor and expert on managing innovation] when I was doing news on innovation [...] Of course I introduced myself [as a journalist]. And then he gave me cooperation.
>
> *(Broadcast journalist, Bernama TV)*

Another form of 'incorporation' of social media is as a supplement or complement to journalistic news reporting, for example in contributing to aesthetic television production values, or filling 'airtime'.

> If there were some really good pictures that people have taken of an earthquake for example, then we might put them at the end of the show to say, these are some pictures from Twitter and there's music to go with these pictures. And if there's comments, we'll only really follow people's comments if it's a huge story. In January [2009] when Israel invaded Gaza, we were going so big on that story, for about two or three weeks we were only covering Gaza stories. So you run out of things to put on air. And in those cases, then Twitter and Facebook comes in handy because you can just put people's comments on.
>
> *(Interview producer/output producer, Al Jazeera English)*

Professional journalistic norms dictate that user-generated information requires professional journalistic legitimation and verification before it can be incorporated into news reports:

> Number one, we have to maintain our credibility, and we need to verify our source. And even if watched it on the internet, or we see their comments, we would still want to talk to them and verify them, to ensure that it's not somebody else posting their comments.
>
> *(Executive producer, Bernama TV)*

When they do turn to user-driven media, journalists retain a heightened sense of scepticism regarding the credibility of networked sources, and go to greater lengths to verify their source:

> [Social media] is not reliable. So we need to always confirm the stuff that's posted on Twitter by calling our staff on the ground. Or calling a newspaper in the country that's being affected. Or a radio station. Just calling another source of conventional media ... Sometimes it's a matter of tracking down who posted that Twitter comment and getting their phone number and calling them. And you know 'Where are you? What are you seeing?' ... It's just trying

to get to the source. Because you know, *anybody* [participant's emphasis] can post anything on Twitter.

(Assistant programme editor, Al Jazeera English)

In cases where it is not possible to verify information from user-driven media platforms, professional routines dictate the use of attribution, even if only to attribute quotes to 'unconfirmed sources': 'Until the official [election] results are out … I just say "unconfirmed sources reported." Because there's no way that you can verify every single information that's coming in [on social media]' (Bureau chief, Channel News Asia). In addition, user-generated content and online comment posts are also sometimes used in news coverage of emergency events or lengthy follow-up coverage of major issues.

However, public comment posts would not normally be used in other types of news stories: 'If it's just a normal bulletin we won't really put any Twitter or Facebook comments' (Interview producer/output producer, Al Jazeera English). One Bernama TV assistant producer echoes this view of the non-mass layperson as possessing lower levels of news value:

> We do take text from [political] blogs to use as material in our news … I can't really recall using any non-politician's blog. But it's suffice to say that we do monitor very closely the internet. So whenever there is very heated issue we would quote blogs or new media. But that media has to be a very popular one. Or some kind of blog that is very well recognized by the audience. I can't simply just quote a Siti or an Ah Beng [i.e. any Tom, Dick or Harry] that's not familiar to [the audience] … We won't use sources that we cannot verify, because we cannot verify who are making those comments [on reader comment threads].

(Assistant producer, Bernama TV)

This reluctance to quote laypersons lies in journalists' conservative attitude towards networked news sources and their online truth-claims. There is a perception amongst professional journalists that user-generated content do not meet journalistic standards of credibility. Thus journalists rarely quote from public comments posted online as they are perceived to be incompatible with institutional and professional notions regarding what constitutes a credible source. For example, one experienced Malaysian editor explains: 'We don't use blogs as a source of news. Why? Because we cannot distinguish the source of information [in the blogs]. Is it credible? Is it hearsay? Or is it just rumors?' (Assignment editor, Bernama TV). Thus a major theme in journalistic incorporation of user-generated content is credibility, or the perceived difficulty of establishing credibility of layperson sources when compared to 'authority' sources. For 'professional' journalists, the establishment of source credibility lies at the heart of journalistic 'professionalism', a notion that allows 'professional' journalists to differentiate themselves from non-journalist 'produsers' (Bruns, 2003) or 'writer-gatherers' (Couldry, 2010).

As one Al Jazeera English reporter-producer puts it, 'A lot of these citizen journalism are one-source stories. And that is a big taboo in journalism':

> Simply because we are trained to tell stories in a way where, I think, you have to respect certain nuances, you have to get access. You have access to different points of view because you are from an established media. If someone wants to criticize the government because of an issue, it may be a valid criticism, but they cannot get the government's point of view. Because the government might not spend [or] have time of the day for them. But if you posed it, as somebody from established media, then you can get all sides of the story. That makes it a better story. More well rounded story.
>
> *(Reporter-producer, Al Jazeera English)*

While this taboo may not extend to journalism that operates under a 'press-as-government-partner' ethos, Malaysian journalists similarly draw upon 'professionalism' and access to 'authority' as distinguishing between professional journalists and bloggers:

> The main role is giving correct, accurate information to people ... Because sometimes we don't give people what they like. They like sensational stuff like what bloggers write [...] Say A says something about B, I'd have to clarify with B before reporting it. We give a balanced report. And it takes time. And sometimes it's not as entertaining as what people read on blogs ... If you have a blog, you sit in front of your PC and write whatever comes to your head. [...] Bloggers can say this and that. But we can't [if it's not accurate]. The young browse the internet a lot, but they don't know if the information they read is true ... They don't know if bloggers were there when the Prime Minister made the announcement. Were the bloggers in Parliament? Do they have a copy of the Prime Minister's speech?
>
> *(Ibid.)*

These findings show that regardless of the journalistic context within which 'professional' journalists produce news, whether the national news sphere of an 'authoritarian' developing country, or a liberal-democratic global news sphere reflective of Western forms of journalism, professional journalistic norms and routines tend to structure journalistic adoption of user-driven material and networked news sources. 'Professional' journalists only incorporate user-generated content under special circumstances when 'professional' journalistic news material is not available, and when they do turn to networked news sources, they evaluate these sources' newsworthiness according to traditional offline professional journalistic values of 'credibility'.

'Hierarchy of credibility'

Although there are no specific measures that journalists refer to in evaluating the credibility of sources from user-driven platforms, 'quantitative' influences upon the perceived credibility of such sources seem to parallel a 'hierarchy of credibility' proposed by cultural theorist Stuart Hall and his colleagues (1978) in their analysis of crime reports in the United Kingdom. In the contemporary journalistic networked media ecology, there appear to be three tiers of networked credibility. At the top of the new media 'hierarchy of credibility' are well known and *established figures of authority* with hefty official portfolios, such as government ministers, political leaders or heads of non-governmental organizations. Information posted on the blogs, Facebook pages and Twitter feeds of such key sources are perceived to be credible and require little or no verification. These allow journalists to routinely use 'screenshots' and lift text 'word for word' from these official blogs to incorporate into their news reports (Broadcast journalist, Bernama TV).

Next on the hierarchy of credibility are alternative news sites, citizen journalism, and bloggers with *sizable* followings. Journalists perceive these sources as both a form of credible, independent media, and as online opinion leaders, and routinely follow their websites or their blog posts to keep informed. Whereas the tweet of a government minister or influential activist derives credibility from the particular source's real-world authority, alternative news sites and independent bloggers derive credibility from the size of their followings, which are determined by both the hits/page views/followers they regularly enjoy, as well as the less quantifiable but equally real impact they have upon public discourse (measured by the online comments they generate and the frequent references to these sites made in mainstream media reports and in speeches and conversations of established tier-one 'authority' figures).

Finally, unknown and layperson social-media posters are perceived as credible news sources only when the following criteria are met: when massive numbers of posts regarding the same event (issue orientation) emerge at the same time (temporal coordinate), giving rise to what Tuchman (1978) might call a 'mutually verifiable web of facticity'. Herein a third tier of networked credibility emerges. Here, journalist perceptions of credibility are influenced by the *mass*-ive numbers of mutually verifiable posts, as during crises such as large-scale democratic uprisings where Twitter updates and YouTube videos of non-elite laypersons – the masses – are incorporated into news reports of these incidents.

These tiers of networked credibility suggest a gradual diffusion of user-driven media into what agenda-setting theorist Maxwell McCombs (2004) describes as 'layers' of influence upon a news outlet's news agenda. The layer closest to this core is professional journalistic norms, followed by intermedia agenda setting, where media practice of inter-outlet 'co-orientation' inevitably produce homogenized news agendas, and finally is the 'key sources' layer consisting of 'authority' news sources like the ones described in the first tier of the hierarchy of credibility.

Networked sources and 'hierarchy of credibility'

However, the emergence of user-driven media forms as elements that are slowly being incorporated into various journalistic phases suggest the emergence of an overlapping layer of influence on the news agenda. In so far as user-driven citizen news sites and political blogs function as alternative news media that have become routinized into journalists' initial 'monitoring' phase of newswork (as is the case in Malaysia), these user-driven media forms overlap with McCombs' (2004) 'intermedia agenda-setting' layer. And in so far as journalists privilege the Twitter feeds and Facebook pages of government ministers, political leaders, or well-known activists, these user-driven media platforms thus overlap with McCombs' 'key sources' layer. A conspicuously missing layer here is what we may call a 'layperson layer'. What this means for the journalistic networked media ecology is that these 'key sources' remain as the 'primary definer' of news, and laypersons remain irrelevant in journalistic processes of newsgathering.

These practices are consistent with social theorists' Galtung and Ruge's (1965) findings regarding one criteria for news inclusion of quotes from news sources: that 'top leaders' or 'elite people' are much more often quoted than 'common people'. Preference for sourcing social-media posts of key news sources over random user posts are further explained by Hall and colleagues' (1978) contentions regarding media's tendency to 'over-access' authority and official 'accredited news sources' and their versions of reality, over those of laypersons. Prior to Hall and colleagues (1978), sociologist Howard Becker (1967) coined the term 'hierarchy of credibility' to refer to sociologists' framing of 'social problems' according to the views of 'superordinate parties', those in society 'who represent the forces of approved and official morality'. Contrasted against 'superordinate parties' were 'subordinate parties', who 'it is alleged, have violated that morality' (Becker, 1967: 240). Sociologists' preference for 'superordinates' over 'subordinates' in defining morality, parallel the 'hierarchy of credibility' that latter-day journalists use to evaluate newsworthiness and the veracity of truth-claims of networked sources and online user-generated content.

As described above, in a networked journalistic ecology, journalists, long socialized to privilege what Hall and colleagues (1978) termed 'accredited sources' representing social institutions, tend to bestow the right of 'primary definition' to networked news sources advancing 'superordinate' truth-claims. As one might expect, priority is generally bestowed in the following rank order: social institutions such as government agencies, major political parties, large corporations, or major NGOs and their representatives; popular blogs or well-known alternative media sites; and mass social or political movements as manifested by a web of 'mutually verifying' online posts by massive numbers of laypersons. Within this digitally networked 'hierarchy of influence', 'subordinate parties' are those who violate the digital online logic of this networked media ecology simply by virtue of being on the wrong side of the digital divide, and *not* being connected to means of digital, online participation.

As suggested in early studies, for example by Gaye Tuchman (1978) and Mark Fishman (1980), the sources that journalists avail themselves of will determine the information that fills a news outlet's 'news net', and ultimately influence the events and truth-claims that are selected to become news stories. A 'multiperspective' approach to news, where the news agenda is determined by a diverse variety of actors including citizens (see Gans, 1980), is a very real possibility, *if* professional journalists are willing to widen their 'news nets' to include non-'official' and non-'authority' (networked) laypersons as news sources. Thus herein emerges a problematic question with regard to truth-claims: when mainstream journalists incorporate user-generated material into news stories – even when it is only as information leads or unpublished background information – whose perspectives do they expose themselves (and their audiences) to? Ideological diversity notwithstanding, ultimately it is the truth-claims of networked, digital media users, or a digital bourgeoisie, that are advanced via user-driven media platforms such as Twitter, Facebook, or YouTube. The digital bourgeoisie profile is largely that of digitally literate, middle- to high-income, urban, and younger members of middle- and higher-income countries. Given the perennial digital divide, questions must thus be raised regarding remote disasters and alternative political narratives that either: don't make the 'critical mass' needed for journalistic legitimation of user-driven online narratives; or never enter into networked public discourses because the human subjects of these narratives are not connected to – and are thus 'shut off' from – online and mobile networks that drive online public discourse.

The gradually routinized practice of incorporating user-driven media forms into mainstream news reports introduces a duality to truth-bearing in mainstream, professional journalism. On the one hand, by giving airtime and bandwidth to digitally connected groups, mainstream journalism ends up promoting as 'truth' the perspectives of networked elites. On the other hand, by not seeking and not reporting the grievances and issues of non-networked, digitally illiterate groups, news media structurally excludes them from the news agenda. This contributes to a global politics of exclusions, whereby the interests and agendas of the digitally networked are sought by time-pressed journalists, while the voices of digital illiterates are inadvertently muted. Where media organizations are willing to commit resources to cover stories from remote locations, digital illiterates in these places have at least a semblance of an advocate in the form of media coverage (though the extent to which such media coverage is accurate, and not prone to orientalist tendencies, is another matter, as is the extent that media coverage actually affects change).

However, current economic conditions, coupled with budget cuts in many media organizations, suggest that such coverage may one day be deemed not cost-effective by many news outlets. This brings us to questions of the ethics of journalistic legitimation of networked truth-claims. If, as Tuchman (1978) suggests, occurrences most accessible to journalists are more likely to be selected in the news-selection phase of news-work, this would mean that non-digitally networked truth-claims originating from regions and communities in which no journalists are present would rarely make the news agenda. In the coming years, as news outlets struggle to cover world events under tight budgets, it is possible that user-driven media forms may be further incorporated into news-work. Recent work on networked journalism (e.g. Beckett and Mansell, 2008), network journalism (Heinrich, 2011), gatewatching (e.g. Bruns, 2003; 2005) and citizen journalism (e.g. Allan and Thorsen, 2009) suggest shifts in news-work and news production that increasingly privilege user-generated content and user-driven media forms. If these shifts occur in parallel with the journalistic privileging of a 'hierarchy of credibility' found in this chapter, what then becomes of the truth-claims, concerns and needs of the world's digital poor?

Reconceptualizing the role of journalism

The answer is self-evident. As indicated by global and local professional journalists in Malaysia, the professional journalistic network ecology may at times facilitate 'multiplatformed' newsgathering, but it has certainly not affected any true kind of 'multiperspective' journalism. If even networked laypersons are perceived to be not credible or newsworthy enough to be quoted in news coverage, then laypersons on the other side of the digital divide have much less chance of having their voices heard. Given the duality of today's networked media ecology – the breaking down of communicative barriers alongside a deepening digital divide – perhaps it is time to reconsider the role of journalism. Blogger Jeff Jarvis' (2006) idea of 'networked journalism', expounded by former journalist and scholar Charlie Beckett (2006) in his book sub-titled *Saving Journalism So it Can Save the World*, seems to be a new normative ideal promising 'a kind of journalism where the rigid distinctions of the past, between professional and amateur, producer and product, audience and participation, are deliberately broken down' (Jarvis 2006).

'Networked journalism' thus embraces the ideal of journalism as a 'public service' in the same spirit as former journalist and former politician Martin Bell's (1998) call for a 'journalism of attachment' that requires a sense of commitment to the subjects of a news story, and scholar Hemant Shah's (1996) suggestion for an 'emancipatory journalism' where journalists adopt an 'activist' rather than a 'press-as-government-partner' role in promoting national development.

While there are indications that journalists are increasingly chained to their computers due to the tighter deadlines of a rolling 24/7 news culture (see Baisnée and Marchetti, 2006 on sedentary, or sit-down, journalism), it seems that both global and local journalists interviewed here remain committed to 'doing their own journalism'. A 'rethink' of 'doing journalism' requires professional journalists to go beyond the professional routine considerations of newsworthiness, to consider the truth-claims of those who are 'switched off from the network society' (on the notion of network society, see Castells, 2000). Only then can the networked media ecology achieve the kind of journalism that not only serves the agendas of 'authority' and 'magnifies' the already massive voices of networked pro-democracy protestors, but also addresses the needs of the digitally poor.

8

TALKING BACK, BUT IS ANYONE LISTENING?

Journalism and comment fields

Todd Graham

With the recent rise of the new digital media culture, mainstream news media across Western democracies have been increasingly adopting new forms of online participatory journalism. One of the most popular forms has been comment sections attached to news articles (i.e. comment fields). Such spaces are unique because they not only allow audiences the opportunity to react and comment on journalistic content, but also provide a space where audiences can debate and discuss the news with each other and journalists. Moreover, they offer the audience an opportunity to bring new and alternative ideas, opinions, arguments and sources to journalistic content, potentially allowing such content to evolve in a public and more deliberative manner. In this chapter, I argue that such a connection between public and journalistic content may have significant implications for journalism, thus requiring a reconceptualization of the role of journalism in the context of Web 2.0 technologies. Comment fields have typically been dismissed by journalists and academics alike as fostering flaming, fringe opinions and misinformation. Yet, there has been little systematic, empirical research conducted on comment fields. Thus, the aim of this chapter is to begin unravelling the potential of such spaces by exploring and assessing how audiences are engaging and participating in them.

One fruitful way of beginning to reconceptualize journalism's role in the context of comment fields specifically, and social media in general, is through Habermas's (1989; 1996; 2006) evolving theory of the public sphere. His theory, which is situated within a broader theory of deliberative democracy, is fruitful because it provides one of the most systematically developed critical theories of the public sphere to date, and more importantly, the media's role within it. He envisions the public sphere as the realm of social life where the exchange of information, positions and opinions on the discovery and questions of common concern take place, ultimately forming public opinion, which in term guides the political system. The public sphere 'springs into being' when private citizens come together freely to debate openly the political and social issues of the day. Deliberation represents the key communicative form of the public sphere as it is through deliberation that citizens achieve mutual understanding about the self and each other. Thus, journalism's role within the public sphere is not only to fuel this debate by providing information and keeping a critical eye on government and corporate affairs, but to encourage, facilitate and act as a platform for it; this is one of the core functions of journalism. Moreover, journalism should foster public debate and commentary which is characterized by rationality, sincerity, inclusiveness and discursive equality among positions/participants (i.e. it should foster *deliberative* public debate).

Given that social media is in some ways about active citizens, about facilitating social interaction and discussion and about inclusiveness, Habermas's theory provides a relevant and valuable conceptual framework for rethinking the role of journalism and assessing the potential of these new online forms. For example, as mentioned above, comment fields potentially allow for more inclusive news coverage and amplify the rational-critical debate of private people in the context of journalistic content. However, if we don't recognize or take seriously journalism's role as a platform and facilitator of public debate, then we are likely to miss out on tapping into the potential social media has to offer.

The rise of user-generated content

Over the past decade, we have seen an increase in the popularity of social media such as discussion forums, weblogs and wikis, and social-media applications such as Facebook, Twitter and YouTube, along with the proliferation of open-publishing initiatives and social news websites. Today, it seems that citizens are increasingly publishing and sharing their stories, comments, news, photos, videos and podcasts, while chatting, debating, tagging, blogging and tweeting in online communities. This vibrant upsurge of participatory values and practices has led some commentators to suggest the emergence of a new digital media culture (Deuze, 2006c; Jenkins, 2006). The rise of social media can be understood here as a sign of a general cultural trend whereby audiences are turning into active media producers, leading some to herald a new era of participatory journalism (Bruns, 2005; Gillmor, 2006).

This participatory culture challenges the top-down model of journalism by allowing anyone to post and upload content without formal, editorial moderation or filtering processes. Citizens are no longer passive receivers but rather are actively engaged in (re)creating, challenging, questioning, correcting and personalizing news media. Indeed, a recent report by the Pew Research Center (2010b: 2) suggests that people's relationship with news is changing: it is becoming portable, personalized and participatory. Regarding the latter, 37 per cent of American internet users have contributed to the creation of news, commented on it or disseminated it via social-media sites. As Deuze and Fortunati (2011: 167) have argued, this can be seen 'as a democratization of media access, as an opening up of the conversation society has with itself, as a way to get more voices heard in an otherwise rather hierarchical and exclusive public sphere.'

At the same time, we have also witnessed across Western democracies a growing rift between social and political institutions and those they serve. This has been a particular problem for mainstream news media. There seems to be an increasing disconnect between journalists and their audiences (Kovach and Rosenstiel, 2001) as more citizens question their core values and morality (particularly true in the USA, see Pew Research Center, 2005). Moreover, newspaper readership and television news viewership has been in decline, placing serious economic pressures on news-media organizations and their journalists. In such a climate, mainstream news media have recently begun tapping into the digital media culture, as a means of both combating a loss in revenue and reconnecting with their audiences, by increasingly adopting more participatory forms of online journalism. Deuze, Bruns and Neuberger (2007: 325) describe this phenomenon as a process of convergence and hybridization: 'A professional media organization (top-down) partners with or deliberately taps into the emerging participatory media culture online (bottom-up) in order to produce some kind of co-creative, commons-based news platform.' Whether such hybrid forms of news are just attempts by mainstream media to 'hop on the bandwagon' in search of economic benefits or genuine attempts driven partly by a civic-orientated rationale, the adaption of participatory forms of journalism is on the rise.

However, this adaptation has tended to be slow and messy, as editors and journalists come to terms with the changing news-media environment. It seems that the participatory ideals of the new media culture that have underpinned the rise of citizen participation in the news do not mesh well with the traditional journalistic culture. For example, despite the participatory turn in online journalism, it seems that journalists still think about their role in terms of a traditional top-down, gatekeeper model (Paulussen et al., 2007; Domingo et al., 2008; Hermida and Thurman, 2008; Harrison, 2009; Hermida, 2009; Singer and Ashman 2009). This is also reflected in the fact that most participatory forms of journalism adopted thus far only allow audience participation at the interpretation stage of the news-making process, particularly when it comes to hard news (Deuze, Bruns and Neuberger, 2007; Domingo, 2008b; Domingo et al., 2008; Pantti and Bakker, 2009; Jönsson and Örnebring, 2011). Jönsson and Örnebring's (2011: 140) study of British and Swedish newspapers found that users were mostly empowered to create popular-culture and soft-news content rather than hard-news and informational content. They concluded, 'UGC in mainstream news media so far has only limited implications for the role of the citizen in the political public sphere'.

Journalistic practices and norms also seem to be subduing the participatory nature of UGC (Domingo, 2008b; Hermida, 2009; Wardle and Williams, 2010). As Domingo's (2008b: 691) ethnography of online newsrooms revealed, in their daily routines, journalists typically regarded the user as a passive audience (a consumer of stories) rather than an active contributor to the news-making process. Similarly, Wardle and Williams's (2010: 790) ethnographic study of BBC newsrooms found that journalists perceived UGC to be just another news-gathering source. As they concluded,

Audience content is seen by most news journalists working 'at the coal face' as material to be processed, rather than as an opportunity for the public to retain creative control over their output, or a chance to [sic] for journalists to truly collaborate with the public in jointly producing content.

Journalists and editors have also been nervous about the merging of journalistic content with audience content. Research suggests that they are uncomfortable and cautious, particularly with more participatory forms of UGC, when managing them (Chung, 2007; Hermida and Thurman, 2008; Thurman, 2008; Harrison, 2009; Singer and Ashman 2009). This fear stems from their concerns over the quality, newsworthiness, credibility and decency of UGC. When it comes to comments to articles specifically, similar fears and opinions have been expressed. Comments to articles have been labelled as typically being offensive, poor in quality (e.g. inaccurate, not based in fact, and so on), untrustworthy and unrepresentative of the audience (Harrison, 2009; Singer and Ashman, 2009; Phillips, 2010). Such impressions are not unique to comments to articles. Indeed, journalists in the past have expressed similar concerns over letters to the editors (Wahl-Jorgensen, 2001)

However, do these impressions provide us with an accurate account of what comment fields have to offer? Are comment fields really just about flaming, fringe opinions and misinformation? Leaving the commentary and impressions aside, to date, studies have not explicitly investigated comment fields.[1] Consequently, questions still remain over how citizens are engaging and participating in such spaces and what sort of content they are producing. It is only through examining the functionality and nature of comment fields that we will begin to understand the potential they offer to online journalism and to the public sphere. Are citizens bringing new ideas, perspectives, facts and sources to journalistic content? Are comment fields opening up spaces for public debate? That is, to what extent are such spaces facilitating deliberative communicative practices crucial to the public sphere?

Studying guardian.co.uk

In order to address these questions, comment fields from the British online newspaper guardian.co.uk, which represents the online version for both the *Guardian* and the *Observer*, were analysed. It was selected because it is one of the leading online newspapers in the UK (in terms of traffic) and, as Jönsson and Örnebring (2011) reveal, provides one of the most extensive uses of comment fields among British newspapers.

In order to make the study more manageable while maintaining the meaningfulness of the data, several sampling criteria were adopted. First, only articles/blogs written by *Guardian* journalists or a press agency were included in the analysis. Second, a particular issue was selected. In this case, only articles/blogs on the United Nations Climate Change Summit in Copenhagen published within the environment domain of the website (http://www.guardian.co.uk/environment) were included. Finally, to narrow the sample further, the time frame of the conference was used.

Articles/blog posts which received two or more comments published on the odd days of the conference were selected for analysis. This included six days from 7 to 17 December 2009. After applying these criteria, the sample consisted of 66 articles (19 of which were blog posts) containing 2,762 comments/postings.[2]

A qualitative content analysis (Mayring, 2000), which utilized both deductive and inductive coding techniques, was employed as the primary instrument for examination.[3] The coding scheme focused on three characteristics of the use of comment fields. First, it gauged the type and level of interaction. Were participants interacting with the content, journalist or fellow participants? Second, it identified the purpose and function of the postings; i.e. did participants for example post an opinion/argument, pose a question or provide information? Finally, it examined the level to which comments to articles brought forward new and alternative opinions, arguments, facts and sources.

The use of comment fields at the *Guardian*

The analysis discussed above identified four trends in the use of comment fields at the *Guardian*: comment fields were used as a platform for public debate; a platform for Q&A and the gathering of additional information; a platform for adversarial journalism; and a platform for degrading and complimenting. In this section, I will discuss these findings and the potential they hold for online journalism and the public sphere.

A platform for public debate

The findings suggest that comment fields acted as a platform for public debate, thereby offering readers/citizens a new means by which to participate in the public sphere within the context of journalism. The exchange of claims, which represented 64 per cent of the postings, was the dominant communicative form. Participants would read an article and then debate it, either by offering new/alternative opinions and arguments or by challenging/supporting the information, positions and arguments put forth by the journalist, the sources in the article or fellow participants. When taking a closer look at the deliberativeness of these debates (i.e. rationality, critical reflection, the use of supporting evidence, reciprocity and distribution of participation), the potential of such spaces for enhancing and extending journalism and the public sphere in a more deliberative manner becomes clear.

Regarding the level of rationality, one of the criticisms of comment fields has been that they tend to foster irrational debate. However, as Table 8.1 indicates, 46 per cent of the postings provided reasoning with their clams, while only 18 per cent used assertions, indicating that being rational was the norm. When participants did post arguments they typically came in the form of critical reflection; 70 per cent of the comments containing reasoned claims provided critical arguments, which represented 32 per cent of the total postings. In terms of the use of supporting evidence, nearly a quarter of arguments used (cited) facts/sources to support their claims. In total, there

TABLE 8.1 Type and frequency of claims used

Claim type	Posting total	Percentage of postings
Reasoned claims	1265	46
Critical arguments	882	32
Alternative arguments	274	10
Supporting arguments	151	6
Assertions (non-reasoned claims)	509	18

Please note: these categories are not mutually exclusive, i.e. a single post may contain multiple claim types. This accounts for the percentages equalling more than 100 per cent.

were 340 sources/facts used (the type of sources used will be discussed later in this chapter). Participants would typically introduce (new) facts to an argument, discuss those facts and discuss how they related to the article.

Another key condition of deliberation is reciprocity. It requires that participants read and respond to each other's questions, opinions and arguments. Another criticism of comment fields has been that they tend to facilitate a many-to-one type of communication, as opposed to the many-to-many type of discussion (a web of reciprocal exchange) crucial to deliberation, to the public sphere. Slightly more than half of the postings were coded as replies to fellow participants. When taking a closer look at these exchanges, we find that 63 per cent of these postings were engaged in rational-critical debate. However, the idea that comment fields open up a space for readers to debate with journalists, in this case, was an illusion. Though 17 per cent of the postings were directed at the journalists specifically, there were only five responses, posted by three *Guardian* journalists. On these occasions, journalists did not engage in the debate but rather provided additional information, requested information and thanked participants for identifying broken links and providing new sources.

Finally, most studies that have analysed news-media discussion forums have found substantial inequalities in the distribution of participation. Graham's (2009) and Winkler's (2002) analyses of the *Guardian's* discussion forums showed that the debates were dominated by a small group of frequent posters, the so-called 'super participants' or 'regulars'. However, this was not the case for the comment fields under investigation. Though the level of one-timers was high, representing 65 per cent of the participants, the most frequent posters, posting ten or more comments, were responsible for only slightly more than a quarter of the postings.

Overall, comment fields are a unique form of UGC. They not only unite and join together journalistic content with content produced by the audience, they also allow the articles to move on, evolve and develop in a (sometimes) deliberative manner, producing a new type of journalism product for readers. They also merge together within a single public environment two dimensions of the public sphere, what Dahlgren (2005) calls the representational – media output – and the interactional dimensions – micro-level interaction between citizens. Regarding the latter, as the findings above illustrate, the potential of comment fields lies in their ability to open up and foster new communicative spaces for (deliberative) political talk (the basic ingredient of the public sphere) within the context of journalism. If one is to embrace the ideas put forward by Habermas (1989; 1996; 2006) and other deliberative democratic theorists, that a core function of journalism is to act as both a platform and facilitator of public debate, then comment fields potentially have a significant role to play in the future of online journalism (as will be discussed in the final section of this chapter).

A platform for Q& a and the gathering of additional information

Another common trend was that participants used comment fields as a platform for posing questions, requesting and providing information, and gathering background information on a particular issue, namely on the science behind climate change. Nearly a quarter of the comments served this purpose. In particular, 9 per cent of the postings requested information or posed a question, typically as a means of deepening knowledge and understanding on the issue, as the comments by two participants below illustrate:

> Participant 1: Can anyone here explain to me the case for increased temperatures causing droughts? I can't see how increased temperatures will remove water from the water cycles. I [sic] appears to me they will simply cause the water cycle of evaporation and cloud forming to increase in speed.
>
> I haven't read any peer reviewed literature on this topic, perhaps their [sic] is a climatology expert amongst the guardian faithful readership?
>
> Participant 2: Anyone have any information on how much CO_2 (atmospheric concentration) that was present in the earth's atmosphere before (a seriously long time ago) it started to be sequestered into coal, natural gas, oil etc? and what the average (which is bunk math) atmospheric temperature was?

Participants here used comment fields to gather information as a means of understanding the (complex) science behind climate change. Participants seemed to want to move beyond the information provided in the articles and used comment fields to gather this information.

Such requests for information were typically met by fellow participants; 14 per cent of the postings provided information. In addition to providing solicited information, participants also posted links to sources and/or provided information from sources by cutting and pasting it to a posting. Participants took it upon themselves to introduce a considerable amount of (new) information and sources; 234 cited sources were introduced in this manner. As will be discussed below (see Table 8.2), much of this information came from the news media, academic peer-reviewed journals and research institutions. However, providing solicited or unsolicited information did not go unchallenged. On occasions, participants would contest the information being posted (e.g. its relevance, bias, validity, and so on), which in turn sparked further

TABLE 8.2 Sources used by journalists and participants

	Journalists		Participants	
Source	Frequency	%	Frequency	%
Politician and government official	109	39	38	7
Activist/activist group	32	11	21	4
NGO, civil society organization and charity	31	11	28	5
News media	24	9	88	15
Research body, association and institute	15	5	52	9
Academic researcher/scholarship	14	5	72	13
Industry	12	4	14	2
Intergovernmental organization	11	4	16	3
Notable activist or celebrity	8	3	21	4
Police	8	3	0	0
Government agency	6	2	20	3
Other expert	6	2	11	2
Alternative media	2	1	9	2
Participant	0	0	70	12
Science blog/website	0	0	48	8
Blog (non-science)	0	0	19	3
Wikipedia	0	0	18	3
Film or TV program (science)	0	0	8	1
Other	4	1	21	4
Total	282	100	574	100

debate. Finally, in addition to cited sources, participants frequently drew on their own experiences by posting first-hand accounts and personal experiences via the use of narratives and storytelling or by posting experiences and information as an 'expert' (e.g. as a scientist, police officer, business executive, and so on).

As this case illustrates, the potential of comment fields lies in their ability to pool the knowledge and experiences of the audience/participants. In the case of comment fields on the UN Climate Change Summit at the *Guardian*, participants were ready to use that information as a means of gaining a deeper understanding of the issues being presented by journalists in the articles, as one of the participants maintained: 'Sometimes there's more to be learned from the comments section than the articles.' Thus, comment fields in some ways extended and deepened these articles by functioning as a platform for Q&A and a provider of additional information and (re)sources for participants, readers and, on occasions (as noted above) journalists.

A platform for adversarial journalism

Comment fields also functioned as a form of adversarial journalism. Namely, audiences used them to directly challenge and contradict news coverage and/or offer new/alternative arguments, positions and sources to the debate. As discussed earlier, nearly a third of the postings contained critical arguments, many of which were directed at journalists or journalistic content. Participants here frequently contradicted and challenged the accounts, interpretations, arguments, inherent assumptions, facts and sources presented in the articles. Regarding the latter, for example, participants would challenge unexplained sources, the relevance of sources and the credibility of sources, thus acting as fact checkers. Participants also challenged the type of coverage and frames used by *Guardian* journalists, as the posting below illustrates:

> Participant 3: 'But last night, violence broke out when tens of thousands of people – some dressed as penguins and polar bears, carrying signs saying: "Save the humans" – took to the streets.'
>
> This is completely incorrect. The march was largely peaceful yet (as usual …) a small number of indivudals [sic] representing their constituency of one, took matters in to their own hands and isolated incidents of violence took place.
>
> Just another example of the 'shock and awe' media which has become associated with the issue of climate change.
>
> I expect it from many media outlets but I thought the Guardian would be above associating all activism with noisy protests. There are plenty of NGOs/ activists at the COP conference who are trying to combat climate change through effective, pragmatic and peaceful means (and which are often woefully underfunded). However the media insists on reporting only those who dress up as penguins, noisily invade private events and take off their clothes to 'fight for climate justice'.
>
> Please remember there is more to activism than a flashmob.

One of the most established findings of framing research is that mainstream news media typically portray protestors as threats to authority and stability (see, for example, Bennett et al., 2004). The *Guardian* article in question used such a frame to report on the protests taking place at the summit. As the posting above shows, participants used comment fields to challenge such frames. This was commonly done by providing first-hand accounts (or personal experiences) that contradicted the article's account and interpretation of events.

Participants also used comment fields to challenge elite information and perspectives by offering alternative arguments and positions. As Table 8.1 indicates, ten per cent of the postings provided alternative perspectives to the articles. Participants also introduced a substantial number of new facts and sources. When comparing the types of sources used between journalists and participants in comment fields, this becomes clear. First, as Table 8.2 shows, the dominant type of source cited by journalists was politicians and government officials, accounting for more than a third of the sources used. Journalists too did not cite a diversity of source types. Indeed, the top four types cited accounted for 70 per cent of the sources used. However, this was not the case when participants cited sources. The first noticeable difference is the lack of a dominant type of source cited; participants drew from a multiplicity of sources.

When taking a closer look at the individual types used, we find clear distinctions between journalists and participants.

One interesting difference was the use of scientific research. Unlike journalists, participants fairly often posted references and/or links to academic peer-reviewed journals and research reports by government agencies or research bodies. Academic scholarship, research institutes and government agencies represented a quarter of the sources cited by participants, while this only accounted for 12 per cent for journalists. Participants also introduced new types of sources to the articles. For example, participants drew from the blogosphere, which represented 11 per cent of the sources cited. Finally, participants also cited themselves as sources, which accounted for 12 per cent of the sources used. Participants here typically provided first-hand accounts (like the posting above), offered their expertise as an expert or provided personal experiences. Regarding the latter, given the complexity of the science and issues surrounding climate change, the use of narratives and storytelling seemed to make these issues agreeable to human understanding by placing the complexities of these issues within the context of participants' everyday lives.

As this case has illustrated, participants used comment fields to publicly criticize news coverage and hold journalists accountable for their work, thus enhancing the quality of journalistic content. Participants, too, used comment fields to challenge media discourses by offering alternative perspectives and sources, thereby exposing participants, readers and journalists to new ideas and arguments. Thus, comment fields here created a more inclusive news product by allowing alternative and competing perspectives a voice. At the same time, these competing voices were set within the context of public debate, producing a more deliberative type of information than one would typically receive from reading the news article alone. It is this type of deliberative information which is crucial to the public sphere.

A platform for degrading and complimenting

Finally, comment fields were also used as a platform for degrading and complimenting, which accounted for nearly a quarter of the postings. Regarding the former, as mentioned earlier in this chapter, one of the common criticisms of comment fields has been (the opinion) that they tend to foster degrading exchanges (flaming). To some degree, this was the case with comment fields at the *Guardian*. In particular, 14 per cent of the postings were coded as degrading comments.[4]

Who were participants degrading? Nearly half these comments were directed at fellow participants, while 35 and 18 per cent were directed at the content (typically the opinions and arguments of the sources presented in the articles) and journalists respectively. Interestingly, when a participant degraded a journalist or fellow participant, it was typically directed at their position and/or argument; they degraded, for example, the supporting evidence used. However, when participants degraded the content, it was typically directed at another's person: a personal attack (e.g. an attack on one's character, motives, and so on). In particular, articles on Tony Blair, Gordon

Brown, Ed Miliband and activists/protestors tended to foster rant sessions. For example, a participant would make fun of Tony Blair, and this in turn would spark a string of personal attacks against him, contributing little constructively to journalistic content and public debate.

Comment fields also acted as a platform for praising. In particular, 7 per cent of the postings were coded as acknowledgements, which typically came in the form of complimenting, as the three postings below illustrate:

> Participant 5: Some good and well informed comments on here [comments by participants]. Interesting to read the various views.

> Participant 6: I must say that I am impressed that the UK should have such a responsible environment minister [Ed Miliband]. If Canada could have somebody just half as effective and straight!

> Participant 7: Excellent piece, George [Monbiot, *Guardian* journalist]. It's hard to get a hold of information like this and there is a huge tendency in many of the arguments you see and hear to just say 'this is' or 'so and so says' without any context. Stuff like this along with the met Office's release of Hadcut3 data is just what's needed when you're trying to argue a case.

As these examples show, complimenting was typically directed at the information, actions or arguments put forth by participants, sources in the articles and journalists, which represented 47, 27, and 26 per cent of these postings, respectively. In addition to this, participants can use a function to 'recommend' a specific comment, a frequent practice in the *Guardian*'s comment fields.

Unlike the other three findings above, comment fields as a platform for degrading and complimenting holds less potential for enhancing online journalism. Though acknowledgements (compliments in particular) tend to facilitate a civil communicative environment, degrading offers little constructively to journalistic content and creates an atmosphere of disrespect, thereby impeding public debate. That said, degrading and complimenting may function potentially as sort of a barometer on the popularity of a particular issue or argument, which journalists could use to develop future articles. For example, one issue reported on several times that elicited a substantial portion of degrading comments was Gordon Brown's pledge of £1.5 billion to poor countries for combating climate change. Degrading comments here stemmed mostly from participants' concerns over whether Britain could afford to contribute such an amount given the economic crises at the time. Journalists could have used these concerns to develop follow-up articles. Thus, comment fields in this sense potentially function as a means of sensitizing journalists to citizens' concerns.

Participatory journalism as a platform for public debate

Throughout much of the literature on UGC within mainstream news media, there seems to be this implicit view that those participatory forms of journalism that tap into the earlier stages of the news-making process are somehow more 'participatory' than those occurring at the latter stages. One of the consequences of this has been to interpret many of the findings discussed earlier in this chapter in a sombre manner with regard to their potential for enhancing online journalism and the public sphere. This can be partly explained by the fact that within journalism studies (and among journalists) the core function of journalism is making the news (Tuchman, 1978; Golding and Elliot, 1979; Schlesinger 1987). Thus, those participatory forms of journalism that occur at the production stage of the news-making process tend to be valorized.

However, such valorization is problematic for two reasons. First, as the case presented above has shown, participants used comment fields to 'make news', though a different kind of news. Comment fields here functioned as a provider of new and alternative information and as a form of adversarial journalism. However, I am not suggesting that comment fields constitute news in their own right. What I am arguing is that when published alongside the article in question, they create a new kind of news product, one that potentially is more reflexive, inclusive and deliberative. Second, such an implicit view of journalism in some ways neglects one of the defining characteristics of the new digital culture – namely, the interactive nature of UGC and social media. Many of the popular forms of social media are about facilitating everyday social interaction between citizens. Thus, if we are truly to tap into the potential of UGC, there is an apparent need for theoretical renewal and a reconceptualization of journalism within this context.

Given this interactive nature, one fruitful way forward is to reconceptualize one of journalism's core functions as being a facilitator of and platform for public debate. As Habermas (1989: 188) has argued, journalism should view itself as an extension of public debate by transferring and amplifying the rational-critical debate of private people. Deliberative democrats alike have criticized the media for neglecting this role. That said, Habermas's (1989; 1996; 2006) theory of the public sphere and journalism's role within it has had a considerable impact on research within journalism studies (see Dahlgren, 1995; Bennett et al., 2004; Haas, 2007; Ettema, 2007); for example, it has been one of the dominant conceptual frameworks for assessing the media in the public sphere. Much of the literature here discusses the role of journalism as a facilitator of and platform for *mass mediated* deliberation, thereby focusing on, for example, the deliberativeness of news coverage.

However, social media are partly about micro deliberation, interaction between everyday citizens. Thus, in order to truly harness the potential of UGC, we need to begin to conceptualize one of the core functions of journalism as a facilitator of and platform for what Habermas (1996: 374) calls 'episodic public spheres'. These are micro public spheres that 'spring into being' when private citizens come together freely to debate a particular political/social issue of the day, fostering the basic element of the public sphere: everyday political talk. By offering the opportunity for citizens to contribute their perspectives, opinions and/or expertise to journalistic content, news media are opening up an opportunity for promoting this basic ingredient. Moreover, as discussed above, comment fields within mainstream news media are unique because they combine two dimensions of the public sphere (the representational and interactional) on a specific issue within a single public communicative space. By taking this function seriously, news-media organizations can not only begin to enhance the deliberativeness and quality of such spaces, but they can also begin to experiment with new ways of feeding what transpires in them to the production side of the news-making process.

Regarding the former, one practical way forward is for news media to introduce facilitators. As research in online deliberation has suggested, facilitation often leads to more deliberative debate. I am not suggesting that news organizations start hiring facilitators, but rather, they can take advantage of the 'regulars' who frequent such communicative spaces by having them act as facilitators; a system whereby participants appoint other participants (based on their behaviour) as facilitators. Such systems are already quite common (and successful) in many of the other genres of online discussion forums. I am not suggesting here that journalists themselves need to be involved in such debates in any extensive manner. As this case study has shown, journalists do not typically engage in the discussions taking place in comment fields. Given the time constraints of journalists today, it would be a bit naïve to expect them to do so. However, the lack of active participation by journalists in the public debates taking place in comment fields takes nothing away from their potential for enhancing online journalism and the public sphere. There are other ways that journalists can use comment fields to reduce the gap between themselves and their audience.

One practical way forward is for journalists to report on comment fields. I am not suggesting that journalists should begin reading every comment section and report on them; journalists do not have the time for this. But during an election campaign, for example, journalists could select an important issue. During the course of that campaign, they could pick out a series of articles on that particular issue, which sparked popular debate in their comment sections. They could then publish an article for each of the comment sections selected (alongside the original article and comments) that focuses on: highlighting and summarizing the alternative and new positions; reporting on the new facts and sources introduced; addressing the concerns and worries expressed; answering questions and providing additional information; returning to the original sources in the article and posing participants' questions and concerns (and reporting back on this); and responding to critiques of their news coverage. Such an approach might not only make comment fields more accessible to readers, but also, among other things, create feedback loops between journalists and citizens.

Notes

1 I am only aware of two conference papers, both of which draw from deliberative democratic theory as a means of assessing the deliberativeness of comment fields (Manosevitch and Walker, 2009; Trice, 2010).
2 Throughout the text I use 'comment(s)' and 'posting(s)' interchangeably. Given that there was no significant difference between the way participants used comment fields attached to articles and blog posts, I refer to both as articles in the remainder of this chapter.

3 Additional qualitative textual analyses were also carried out as a means of identifying particular patterns.
4 There were 319 postings removed by moderators from the sample, which were not included in the analysis; access to these postings was not possible. Postings are typically removed for two reasons: being offensive or being off topic. Thus, the total number of degrading comments could have been higher.

Part III
Emerging journalisms

9

SEPARATE, SUPPLEMENTARY OR SEAMLESS?

Alternative news and professional journalism

Chris Atton

From pessimism

This chapter begins from pessimism. It begins by arguing that the history of alternative media is predominantly one of failure: failure to reach any but the most specialist of audiences and a consequent failure to effect the political and social transformations that represent the ambition of so many of its projects. However, I do not wish simply to reproduce past arguments here. Emerging forms of journalism and user-generated content have begun to engage with traditional media. This chapter will examine how newer ways of doing journalism are interacting with established forms. Recent developments in journalism have emphasized the role of citizens as sources, as content providers and as reporters. Some of the most conspicuous of these developments have taken place within professionalized media. Is this perhaps a more fruitful location for alternative media practices than we might think?

This chapter will explore three dominant models for understanding the contribution of alternative journalism to mainstream practices and how the two practices are interacting: user-generated content in professional news organizations; hybrid practices brought together on citizen journalism websites; and the 'pure' or 'separatist' ideologies and practices of activist journalism. First, though, we need to address a more general problem, that of the location and nature of counter-hegemonic practices. Some alternative media – such as the publications of separatist feminism or the anti-technology writings of primitivist anarchists – will, by their self-determined ideological location, lie beyond the mainstream. Their limited reach and radical content lends them a 'purity' that offers ideological protection, but it also weakens their influence. They might be oppositional in intent, but their praxis limits their reach. Raymond Williams (1983) recognized the impotence of what he termed an alternative culture that would forever be condemned to attempt to coexist with the dominant culture, but never be able to challenge it. Even alternative media that seek broader audiences have historically been constrained if not by ideology, then by the near-impossibility of breaking into distribution and retail networks beyond their immediate constituency. In the 1980s it was argued that the only route to success for alternative media was to adopt commercial imperatives of capitalization through the maximizing of audiences (Comedia, 1984). Of course, Comedia were writing at a time where the dominant alternative medium was print (cheaper and less regulated than broadcast media, requiring less technical expertise); today the dominant medium is electronic – the internet – and is able to combine print and broadcast. Comedia also recognized another commercial aspect to alternative media: only rarely were its producers paid a living wage for their journalism. Instead, alternative media tended to be generated by activists for whom commitment to a project was more important than financial reward. It is the case, though, that many such projects were short-lived, unable to be sustained by a volunteer workforce that ran on self-exploited labour. Contemporary alternative media projects suffer from the same limit; there is no evidence that this situation is about to change (Atton and Hamilton, 2008). Whilst media audiences might be attracted to alternative journalism practices out of commitment to a cause or to a community, it is just as likely that a combination of economic necessity and a lack of time will inevitably reduce their capacity to contribute.

As a technology, the internet has 'been responsible in large part for the massive increase and visibility of alternative forms of journalism' (Atton and Hamilton, 2008: 136). This is not to say that the problems of access, reach and audience have been solved, but we cannot doubt the very high levels of participation in media production and dissemination brought about by access to the internet (again, though, we must acknowledge the limits on that participation when there is little or no financial remuneration). Yet, whether in terms of resistance or democratic participation, we need to question the significance of alternative journalism projects to the degree that they demonstrate 'active citizenship'. In other words, does participation in a highly mediatized world enable the efficacy of sociopolitical activity in the lived world? Does it perhaps do no more than diminish lived experience, and with that diminish the possibility of social and political change sought by so many activist amateur journalists?

These questions are best addressed by an examination of the contexts and purposes to which various forms of alternative journalism are put. The activities of amateur, citizen journalists (whether acting alone, in groups or communities, or with professional assistance) are capable of raising many challenges. These can range from the hyperlocal benefits of community identity and cohesion (Kim and Hamilton, 2006; Bruns, 2011b) to projects that might challenge an entire state (Xin, 2010). They might entail challenges to the dominant ontological and epistemological claims for journalism, where the key questions are: What does it mean to be a journalist? What is the status of the amateur reporter as authority and expert (for example, Bruns, 2006; Lowrey, 2006; Carlson, 2007; Matheson and Allan, 2007)?

Graeme Turner's (2009) notion of the 'demotic turn' in media production is useful here. It not only captures an argument about the media's increasingly powerful role in the construction of cultural identities, but also draws attention to a set of emerging crises in corporate news organizations: crises of capital, credibility and authority. Turner argues that 'mainstream news media have lost their connection to the community' (p. 8) and have taken advantage of the high levels of audience interest in the amateur reporter and blogger. In some cases this has seen the emergence of the professional journalist as blogger, eschewing the routines of news in its objective setting to present personal (yet 'expert') opinion beyond the limits of the op-ed pages. Elsewhere we see audiences at work, most conspicuously in the setting of user-generated content. The uses to which this content is put, together with the responsibilities such content is made to bear, provide insights into how non-professional journalism is construed and deployed in contemporary settings. The first model we shall examine is developed from the practice of embedding user-generated content in professional news organizations, a practice that vividly demonstrates the tensions between two approaches to the creation of news.

User-generated content as demotic turn?

A study of the deployment of user-generated content (UGC) by the UK national broadcaster the BBC (Wardle and Williams, 2010) identifies five types of audience contributions. These comprise news content provided by audiences; audiences' commentaries on news; content created collaboratively by audiences and professional journalists (for example, video diaries); professional journalists working with online communities to produce networked journalism; and non-news content provided by audiences.

The first of these has widespread use across all platforms of the BBC (television, radio, websites, local, national and global). For the BBC, audience news content includes leads for stories, eyewitness images (caught on mobile phones or camcorders) and eyewitness accounts. Moreover, this type of content has come to define UGC at the BBC. The study goes on to find that this type of UGC is considered as only 'one source of information to be processed among many' (Wardle and Williams, 2010: 791); it is not privileged as 'citizen journalism'. Importantly, it does not sit alongside or challenge the dominant values of professional journalism. Instead of offering an alternative to the BBC's public-service tenet of impartiality (along with the broader journalistic norms such as accuracy, fact-checking and objectivity), this type of UGC is incorporated into the standard practices of the BBC journalists. However much reporting and editorial content might be enriched by the addition of 'ordinary people' as sources, practices at the BBC reinforce the professional location of journalism and its attendant epistemological claims – we will not find here a demotic turn that has any qualitative impact on journalism as discursive construction of the world. Indeed, it might be argued that even the quantitative significance (potentially a massive increase in the availability of sources) is obscure, given that UGC is transformed by professional journalists, leaving little trace of its origin. In this model, the amateur recorders (I hesitate to term them reporters under these conditions) are subsumed by the professional interpreters.

This is not the same as saying that any attempts to revolutionize or democratize the practices of professional journalism are being thwarted only by media organizations such as the BBC, zealously defending their strongholds from a mob of citizen journalists. While we have little detailed knowledge of the amount and nature of UGC, the few studies we do have (such as Sampedro Blanco, 2005, along with anecdotal accounts) suggest that audiences themselves tend to align with the professional imperatives of framing and newsworthiness. Natural and man-made disasters, major national and international political and cultural events – these are where the mobile-phone camera tends to be trained. Even a programme such as BBC Radio 4's *iPM* ('the programme that starts with its listeners') finds listeners reacting to stories already in the news, accompanied (framed) during their investigation by a professional reporter (Atton and Hamilton, 2008). More interestingly, perhaps, audience contributions to news agendas are far outweighed by amateur contributions to other areas of the media, especially non-news contributions and comment. The former is best exemplified by Wardle and Williams (2010: 788) as 'photographs of wildlife, scenic weather or community events' – images (and they usually are images) that offer no insight into affairs of state or developments in society, culture and economics. Innocuous and trivial, they present no threat at all to professional journalism. They do appear to be very popular, however, amongst audiences, and seem to represent a shared cultural identity similar to the impulse Turner finds in the 'demotic turn'.

When we consider audience comment it seems as if the traditional locus of comment has expanded from the expert elite (the anonymous editorial written on behalf of the newspaper and the senior reporters and editors of news desks) to include the 'crowd'. Inevitably comment will be reactive, whatever its sources (professional or amateur), through its direct engagement with professional news content. Importantly, though, while professional editorial comment might well go on to affect the dynamics of news reporting and representation, the practices of media organizations suggest that audience content does not interfere with these dynamics. For some journalists, this lack of interference is deliberately sought, lest journalistic values are weakened (Singer, 2009). Furthermore, if audience content is allowed to encroach on professional content, gatekeeping becomes crucial, which is expensive and time-consuming. It becomes better to build a wall in place of the gate.

An assessment of an internet journalism panel held at the 2006 World Congress of the International Press Institute (Atton and Hamilton, 2008: 66) identified a dominant theme of 'helping people form communities around content'. In practice, this suggests a familiar model: a professional news provider provides a basic social-networking site through which its audiences comment on the news. But are they 'communities' in any meaningful way? Given the reactive and 'instant' necessity of responding, and given the diverse range of topics, the likelihood is that these communities will be little more than aggregates of individuals with shifting membership. Further, the minimization of dialogue between professional creators of news and audience commentaries on that news suggests a reinforcement of audiences as consumers: 'the wall between the "comment room" and the newsroom in this view remains high indeed' (ibid.). An approach such as this construes audience comment as a publicly articulated discourse that has more in common with domestic comment or café discussions. This is not to say that the publicness of such discussion might not engender a broader impact (through citizen commentators working together, meeting in other fora – online or offline), but the ephemerality and anonymity of commenting – together with the speed of comment as it tracks the rolling news agenda – suggests that this would happen only rarely. The mediatization of audience comment prefers reaction over reflection.

If the ideology and practices examined here do not appear to directly address the crises of credibility and authority in modern media organizations identified by Turner, they have much to say about the economic crisis. Audiences seem to prefer contributing comment over producing journalism, even in its attenuated form as UGC (Bakker and Pantti, 2009; Bergstrom, 2010). By increasing the opportunities for audience comment, media organizations are able to build traffic on their websites, with the expectation of increasing opportunities for advertisers. By maintaining 'separation within a shared space' (Singer, 2009), the media organization can encourage an audience to create its own content that does not need to be monitored (at least in terms of professional encroachment). Audiences appear attracted to fora where they are able to present their own views to each other. Audience-generated content is not only attractive, it is a cheap route to the maintenance and growth of website traffic. In a fascinating self-reflexive move, members of the audience become responsible for generating loyalty to the media organization not through their championing of professional journalists, but through their affinity with each other. In this assessment, UGC, as a species of citizen journalism, whilst valuable to the profit margin and the continued viability of commercial media organizations, is hardly part of any wider political project. It has nothing to do with providing different ways of representing the world, let alone enriching or altering how news is produced (Meikle and Redden, 2011).

The BBC is presented here as representative of the approach taken by many large media organizations towards the work of audiences. In these cases the demotic turn may be understood as a strategy for developing brand loyalty and for positioning the organization favourably in the increasingly competitive environment for advertising revenue. This is achieved through the appearance of the building of a community of consumers. We should not, however, assume that professional media organizations only seek audience content to repair a deficiency in authority and a financial shortfall. While such imperatives might be important across the spectrum of journalism, local journalism in particular appears to value audience contributions beyond economic expediency. For some local editors, even the highly restrictive space afforded to readers' letters can be considered a 'key democratic responsibility' (Wahl-Jorgensen, 2006: 229). In a study that displays none of the cynicism that the preceding analysis might expect us to find, one editor goes so far as to claim that the letters page is the site where there is a 'duty to defend free speech' (p. 222). Arguments like this are reminiscent of the mixed results of projects of the public (or civic) journalism movement in the US, projects alloyed by the tension between maintaining commercial success and engaging audiences in an activist style of journalism that often threatened the commercial organizations and local-government departments on whom the media relied for their funding (see Davis, 2000; Glasser, 2000; Woodstock, 2002; Haas, 2007).

Citizen journalism: competition or poor relation?

We might consider the public-journalism movement as an attempt to consolidate the practices and limited achievements of the radical local community initiatives that were especially prominent in the US and the UK during the 1970s and 1980s. However, the limits and tensions in contemporary user-generated content projects need not mean that there will be an inevitable disjuncture between the professional and the amateur journalist. In the UK at least, some of the most successful examples (in terms of audience reach, impact and longevity) appear to be titles that were jointly run by community activists and professional journalists (Whitaker, 1981; Dickinson, 1997). Professional journalists would provide training in reporting, investigation and writing, as well as playing a major part in the editing process. This approach acknowledged the complementary strengths of activist community member and professional reporter. It emphasized both the local knowledge and networks of the former, and the communication and organizational skills of the latter. There was an understanding (often tacit) that, however radical the content might be – perhaps even as a result of its radical nature – the community newspaper needed to reach out to as wide an audience as possible. Presenting the radical in familiar form required complementarity (Comedia, 1984).

Our second model emphasizes the productive capacity of hybrid media practices, where professionals work with audiences to produce a journalism that has relevance to an audience's community. The complementarity of knowledge and skills appears to recognize crucial ontological and epistemological differences between activist (amateur, demotic) journalists and professional reporters and editors. These differences encompass questions of status, authority, ability and communication. For some, though, it appears as if these differences have been erased, particularly in light of the movement of so much citizen journalism to the internet. The ubiquity of the blog has prompted claims that 'anyone and everyone can be a journalist' (Gerlis, 2008: 126). It is not only access to communication tools to enable distribution that makes journalism a 'porous' occupation (Lowrey, 2006: 485), one that is easily learned. The professional journalist's reliance on a restricted range of sources means that non-professionals are able to create competing narratives sourced from less conventional sources (such as using 'ordinary' people as expert witnesses, beyond their dominant, superficial deployment in vox pop interviews). Lowrey also argues that the very routinization of reporting opens it up to 'jurisdictional encroachment' by non-professionals (p. 492). This runs counter to most critiques of traditional (Western) journalistic practices, where studies argue that it is this very routinization that limits access to sources and results in largely static techniques of framing and representations (the news coverage of protests and demonstrations provides some vivid examples, such as Halloran et al., 1970; Gitlin, 1980; Ashley and Olson, 1998; and Robinson et al., 2006). By contrast, Lowrey seems to argue that – because the reporting process can be reduced to an unchanging (and ideologically neutral) sequence of data collection, analysis, organization and presentation – journalism requires little training; it is therefore an especially accessible profession.

The last argument says nothing about how citizen journalism becomes capable of transforming professional journalism when it merely reproduces its discursive techniques. More broadly, arguments about the vulnerabilities of professional journalism ignore the vulnerabilities of citizen journalism itself. Perhaps this is because in a mediatized world where political economy scholars still find the major players as dominating news agendas, framing and representation, it is reassuring to identify in the mass of amateur journalism if not a revolution, then at least a powerful democratic challenge to dominant ideologies of news (a similar uncritical celebration has coloured studies of alternative media for at least 30 years).

A rare, sustained challenge to what seems something of an orthodoxy in the field comes from Reich (2008), who argues that the practices of citizen journalists online reveal limits in their capacity to function as reporters. These limits are different from those found in the studies of Dickinson and Whitaker, who argue that any shortcomings in investigative skills and writing techniques are compensated for by the amateur reporters' connections with the local communities, thereby enabling access to sources that might otherwise not trust a professional journalist. For Reich these reporting limits are part of a wider problem of news access; they show how practices of production and representation are constrained by the routinization of dominant sourcing practices (as shown in Cottle, 2000; and Manning, 2001).

Unlike Lowrey, Reich does not consider that journalism may be easily learned. The routines of the 'inference process' of reporting, which Lowrey (2006: 492) suggests is as easily available to non-professionals as it is to professional journalists, is for Reich an obstacle to participation. His argument seems to turn on industry norms and audience expectations (though this is not made explicit) – that is, non-professional (citizen) journalists are seeking to engage with journalistic norms on the same terms as their professional journalists. Far from this being a straightforward engagement, it is one fraught with hazard.

When the contributions of citizen journalists are incorporated into the content of professional news reporting as UGC, citizens will tend to be marginalized from the actual production processes. This is uncontroversial. However, Reich argues, when citizen journalists attempt to work outside the framing of professional news production, their work is still limited to the degree that it is unable to compete with professional values and discourses. Reich's argument is generated by the focus of his study, a citizen journalism website whose 'editors repeatedly expressed their desire for news that caters to wider audiences, especially in the midst of major events … This objective requires not only more mainstream topics, but more mainstream sources' (Reich, 2008: 743). Consequently, his departure point is to consider citizen journalism not as a species of alternative journalism (which he considers as explicitly political in its thrust), but as a hybrid of alternative and mainstream practices – there is a strong sense in Reich of construing citizen journalists as aspirational in their attempts to secure large audiences, in which regard 'alternative' and 'mainstream' become little more than positions along a continuum that has more to do with audience maximization than specialist content.

We might cavil at what seems a rather reductionist presentation of citizen journalism (though it is similar to the philosophy and practices of, for example, the South Korean citizen journalism project OhmyNews). Reich's findings draw attention to citizen journalism as a complementary activity with its own strengths. Some of these strengths are familiar to us from previous studies: the importance of lived experience in eyewitness reporting; the use of sources identified through, for example, workplace communities; the opportunities for the co-operative development of skills with professional local journalists. Others are surprising, since they seem to diminish the ideological power that is ascribed to various forms of citizen journalism (for example in Downing et al., 2001; Rodriguez, 2001; and Gillmor, 2006). Interviews with professional journalists and the editors of the Israeli citizen journalism website Scoop show that citizen journalists are at their best when working on stories that 'are not overly dependent on human agents' and that are based on 'technical or textual sources', 'personal experience' or 'personal acquaintances' (Reich 2008: 751). The stories examined by Reich emphasize simplicity; that is, they do not require complex discursive structures involving multiple viewpoints and do not rely on building a relationship of trust with sources.

Scoop is seeking to compete with, rather than complement, professional news organizations. However, its editors do not expect its citizen journalists to produce news to the same standards as their professional counterparts. To do so would require such a degree of 'upskilling' – and thereby conformity – with professional norms as to make the two types of journalism indistinguishable. Why hire amateurs who need training when you can hire professionals? This position argues for the ontological singularity of the professional journalist, one whose work with high-level sources – with whom trust has been developed over time and as a result of the professionalized status of the journalist – maintains the epistemological status quo of reporting that is conventionally authoritative and 'balanced'. This accounts for Reich's findings that citizen journalists are less able to produce reports that rely on trust with (we assume elite) sources and, more generally, that require regularized contact with a range of sources.

What are less clear are the reasons for arguing the inability of citizen journalists to produce stories that require 'complex discursive structures'. On the one hand this finding suggests a limit to the reproduction of Lowrey's inference process, on the other hand does it suggest that citizen journalists will always be incapable of such practices? If complexity of storytelling is unavailable to amateur journalists (and we only have limited evidence for that claim) for reasons of education, then why can that education not be provided? Moreover, claims have been made elsewhere (as we shall see in the following section) to suggest that multiple-viewpoint reporting is already taking place within alternative media, albeit not in settings always familiar to us from professional models. Neither is this practice necessarily limited in its reach by its location within a more or less 'pure' form of resistance, and therefore, as Raymond Williams would have argued, more or less impotent in its capacity to effect any professional transformation of journalism, let alone any broader social change.

Alternative journalism and complementarity

Our final model focuses on activist journalism, a practice of amateur media production that has long been considered as a separate – some might say separatist – practice, one that rejects the tenets of all professionalized journalism. Nevertheless, as we shall see, such a radical stance might well produce journalism that can sit alongside more traditional forms, enhancing and complementing them through its proximity.

In her study of an alternative journalism project (Indymedia's Athens website), Milioni (2009) argues that the project displays a counter-hegemonic strategy that challenges the dominant paradigm of professionalized media power. It does so in three ways. First, it shows that it is possible to produce journalism that sits outside the professional norms of organization, that enables participation in a non-hierarchical structure and is not answerable to the demands of commerce. Second, it sets a competitive news agenda that implicitly challenges the norms of knowledge construction in professional news reporting. Both of these methods are hardly unknown to us from the history of alternative media – indeed for some commentators they are hardly advantages at all, to the extent that they evince the very separatism that maintains the marginalization of so many alternative media projects (Landry et al., 1985). Milioni's arguments here are further weakened by the hyperbolic claim (though she is not the first to suggest this) that Indymedia and similar projects enable the 'building of an autonomous channel of unmediated communication with the lifeworld' (Milioni, 2009: 419).

Her third claim, however, is the most useful, offering as it does a way of thinking about citizen journalists that neither reduces them to pawns in a commercial enterprise governed by an abiding professional ideology, nor pushes them to the margins of society. Milioni's analysis of the Indymedia Athens site shows that, while its news stories rely predominantly on personal sources, mainstream media are used more frequently than any other source. Given the scepticism that Indymedia displays to mainstream media organizations (a scepticism common amongst radical, activist media) this seems a surprising finding. What we need to know is the use to which these sources are being put. Milioni shows that mainstream sources are positioned alongside personal, activist accounts and information supplied from protest groups and other organizations to present multi-perspectival accounts of events and their contexts that function supplementarily to dominant news reporting. In so doing, Indymedia reporting not only presents an alternative agenda, it also presents different ways of thinking about the world. To explore the construction of news is to ask questions about how reality is constructed; the professional norms of sourcing, framing and storytelling establish expectations for journalists and audiences about how to represent the world. While it is not necessarily difficult to critique the practices that derive from those norms, their dominance might make it difficult to conceive of other forms of representation. By placing apparently competing representations of the world alongside each other, Indymedia offers the possibility of a comparative critique.

I suggest that we consider what Milioni calls the supplementary function of Indymedia, as complementarity: it is not merely adding to the available accounts of the world, it is attempting to enhance or complete those accounts by offering the potential of a powerful reflexivity in media production – it is 'actively monitoring media content, checking on media processes and criticizing their own logic' (Milioni, 2009: 426). This reflexivity need not be limited to a critique of the mainstream media that results in nothing more than a debilitating scepticism; it can also be seen as a form of auto-critique, where forms of journalism are developed from the bringing together of apparently competing ideologies and practices. Rather than expecting alternative journalism to transform itself solely by adopting professional practices or being satisfied with the exploitation of citizen journalism by professional media organizations for reasons of commercial expediency, Milioni's study suggests that it is possible to produce a plurality of journalisms that can act complementarily. The implicit enacting of representational critiques by those journalisms might encourage critical media literacy amongst their audiences, as well as showing how new forms of journalism might be practised.

The practices that Milioni discusses present a clear epistemological challenge to the professional norms of journalism. In the relatively brief history of scholarship of alternative media in the modern age, such a challenge can still be considered a threat to professionalism, to 'proper' journalism. Even Reich, sympathetic though he is to the role of the non-professional (albeit in a limited sphere of activity), believes that, in order to act 'as a complement to mainstream news', citizen reporters would benefit from some professional training (2008: 753). Yet the Indymedia practices of resituating professional news by connecting to narratives of self-representation are hardly unique in the history of representation. James Hamilton has argued convincingly that accounts of authority and self in sixteenth-century England suggest that practices of premodern media participation (if we might call it that) 'can best be understood as those of gathering and framing, rather than of conceiving and creating' (Hamilton, 2003: 301). This assessment has obvious echoes of Hartley's (2000) arguments about redactional journalism in a digital age, where '[t]here is an emphasis on reduction, revision, preparation, editing and publishing' (Atton and Hamilton, 2008: 83). Rather than consider redactional journalism as proto-journalism, or as a simplistic form of participation, we might instead view it as a strategy to overcome what is becoming a perennial tension in journalism studies, the divide between the professional and the amateur, their ideologies and their practices.

This is to consider a practice of reporting that is concerned with 'informed, embodied self-representation' (Hartley, 2009: 317), where lived experience and the ability to convey that experience in writing are inseparable. This would be part of, but not the whole of, a critical redactional journalism, a practice that derives equally from lived experience and the authority of self, and from the critical 'gathering and reframing' of news from professional sources. Redactional journalism that embodies critique goes some way to enable thinking not only beyond the binary divide of alternative and mainstream, but also to take us beyond the tripartite question posed by Neuberger and Nuernbergk (2010) which reflects the structure of the present chapter: 'competition, complementarity or integration?'. We have seen how, when citizen content is incorporated into professional media organizations, it tends to be marginalized as news or other authoritative content, and generally used as opinion or colour to attract and retain audiences. The history of alternative media shows us that we cannot expect citizen-journalism projects to provide serious competition to established, corporate media – their resources and reach are insufficient, their ideologies often too specialist to appeal to broad audiences. Further, whilst the limits of citizen journalism presented by Reich might be too stark, it seems unlikely that amateur reporting practices will become routinized alongside professional practices. There is a strong sense that the profession of journalism would be unsympathetic to such a project, unless 'citizen content adheres to professional journalistic standards' (Reich, 2008: 753).

Complementarity is not merely additionality. It is not enough to vaunt citizen journalism as the provider of news from 'other' perspectives – after all, given what we know about the choices audiences make about where they obtain their news, where is the evidence to suggest that audiences will make use of these perspectives to supplement their preferred news providers? A small, sympathetic audience might seek out – and have the wherewithal to seek out – a journalism that already accords with their beliefs about how journalism might be reimagined. Most people will not – they might not even pause to consider the possibility. If alternative journalism 'belongs to the public' (Hartley, 2009: 322) in a way that dominant journalism does not, this has to do with its social basis, with its connectedness between writer and audience. How, though, to encourage that connectedness, how might it be brought to the attention of audiences? In other words, where might such embodied, redactional accounts be most usefully located? If the recent history of citizen content is one of incorporation and neutralization by professionalized media organizations, then how might we guard against a similar dilution of critical amateur journalism?

Towards optimism

We began this chapter with a pessimistic assessment of the limited reach of alternative media practices that choose to locate themselves separately from the mainstream. We have seen how this position might be justified, given the incorporation and dilution of alternative journalism by professional news organizations. In contemporary society, however, where corporate culture is quite at home dealing in subversive rhetoric, oppositional practices that lie outside the dominant practices of corporate culture no longer seem to offer a powerful enough response. The public can appear marginalized as a cultural force, only able to offer piecemeal and ultimately ineffectual resistance to those markets. (We have also noted the economic limits on public participation in the media, when there is little or no financial reward for producing journalism that can be as time-consuming as that of the professional journalist.)

Christine Harold (2007) has shown how oppositional rhetoric is easily incorporated into the discourse of the market. Many countercultural strategies of opposition, such as the detournement of popular-cultural images employed by the situationists of the 1960s and the 'subvertising' of the Canadian *Adbusters* magazine, have been incorporated into the logic of commercialization. If the institutions of advertising are already subverting radical notions of truth and authenticity, and employing pastiche and irony in their campaigns, is not possible that professional news organizations might use techniques of alternative journalism simply as an intensification of their use of user-generated content, to generate brand loyalty?

If this chapter began from pessimism, it may end with some optimism. Kunelius and Renvall (2010) offer hope in their account of experiments with reporting that took place in two Finnish newspapers in 2000, where professional journalists invited readers to contribute accounts of their own experiences of care homes for the elderly. These accounts were then brought together to produce a series of feature articles. Unusually, the features did not also rely on the expert assessments of professionals in the field; the readers were considered as experts by virtue of their direct experience, capable of converting their witnessing into narratives. Kunelius and Renvall argue that this process of 'evocative communication' (p. 518) goes beyond mere description; it enables an audience to experience a story through an aesthetics of journalism that is less to do with representativeness, and more to do with the impossibility of the deniability of experience. The authority of the readers' accounts derives from their particular experiences; by contrast, the authority of the professional expert derives from the generalizability of their claims. The journalism thus produced was redactional – it brought together multiple narrative experiences that were organized and re-presented by professional journalists. Crucially, however, the narratives were not directed through interview questions; readers were able to develop their stories in any way they felt appropriate. In one paper, the 'commissioning' journalist began her request for stories by telling the story of her own parents' experiences of nursing homes. There is a subtle challenge here to the abiding norms of journalism that guard against personal involvement in reporting – in this case, the journalist moves 'from indifference to engagement' (p. 522) in order to demonstrate a commitment both to a topic and to a representational strategy. This is neither an act of weakness nor a failure to meet professional standards; it is a transparent means of gaining the trust of readers and an implicit demonstration of respect – readers' accounts will be taken seriously.

The Finnish experiment is important for four reasons. First, it accords experiential significance to the narratives of ordinary people (Turner's demotic turn in action). Second, it does not require citizens to reproduce the reporting norms of professional journalism. Third, it offers storytelling that supplements existing journalism without presenting a threat to those norms. There is constructive symbiosis – this is important if we hope to expand our notion of what journalism does and what it is for. Fourth, the complementarity of citizen narratives provides a concrete example of a self-reflexive critique of professional journalism that shows Hartley's embodied self-representation in action.

We do not know how widespread this type of approach is, but we can expect it to be rare. How might journalists be encouraged to try further experiments with what Kunelius and Renvall call a 'language of small pictures', to counterbalance the dominance of professionalized expertise and its 'language of the big picture' (p. 523)? In large part the answer must lie in professional education. The long-standing debate – at times hostile – between the teaching of journalism as a craft and its embedding in wider critical contexts of culture, society and power is still far from being resolved. The antagonism seems to lie in the epistemological threat that critical theory poses for journalism practice (Skinner, Gasher and Compton, 2001). Alternative forms of representation suggest that authority does not need to be located institutionally or professionally; that credibility and trustworthiness can be derived from accounts of lived experience, not only from objectively detached reporting; and that there need be no imperative to separate facts from values. Kunelius and Renvall, however, suggest that these radical claims might be incorporated into practice without the fear of Lowrey's jurisdictional encroachment. The evidence from Finland suggests that it is possible to practice journalism that brings together traditional craft skills with other forms of storytelling to ask questions about power, ideology and representation. Embodied, experiential discourse need not be condemned to lie beyond the purview of professional news organizations and their audiences. It seems possible, after all, to conceive of a praxis of journalism that engages critical theory with craft-based skills. Perhaps our schools of journalism might be open to the possibilities offered by professional journalists who are themselves open to experiment.

10

JOURNALISM AS INTERPRETIVE PERFORMANCE

The case of WikiLeaks

Stuart Allan

Listening to music one evening, I found myself reading the liner notes jazz pianist Bill Evans wrote for the album *Soulmates*, released in 1963. Evans, interested in exploring questions of technique in what was being described at the time as modal jazz, decided to use this occasion to share his philosophical musings about the influence of sound recording on interpretative style. One passage, in particular, struck me as rather intriguing in relation to the themes to be examined in this chapter:

> [T]he emergence and evolution of jazz has paralleled the invention and con-
> tinued improvement of sound recording. It is not difficult to see that although
> musical notation is a device sufficient to preserve, record, and propagate music
> as traditionally composed in Western culture, there could be no conceivable
> system of notation that would allow a true and faithful recreation of the music
> of interpretive performers. The great composers as we know them may have
> been forced to many compromises in style because of the necessity of notating
> in such a way that the interpretive link could be used to preserve their music
> for future generations.
>
> *(Evans, 1963)*

This observation may be extended to encompass much earlier points in a broader history of music, of course, let alone the development of jazz in the twentieth century.[1] Here I would suggest it assumes a particular relevance for our purposes, though, because of its recognition of the impetus to uphold this 'interpretive link' in the interplay of performance. To the extent that jazz is a 'craft couched in simplicity,' as Evans proceeded to argue, the apparent spontaneity of improvisation will be nonetheless shaped by the 'disciplined work' at the heart of its claim to be 'a constant document of a social situation' – an important quality it shares, I believe, with journalism.

Evans's reflections chimed with my initial thoughts about the ways in which today's digital technologies are often credited with – as well as criticized for – influencing the scope of journalistic innovation. Inspired to formulate a line of inquiry along these lines, it seemed to me that we might consider how the *emergence and evolution* of journalism has *paralleled the invention and continued improvement* of various technologies of *recording* called upon to inscribe its materiality. This type of inscription in form and practice, once again paraphrasing Evans, will *preserve, record and propagate* journalism, but at what cost to a *true and faithful* – or impartial – *recreation* of the reporting of *interpretive performers*? While not wishing to overstate matters, I would suggest that a conception of the journalist as interpretive performer may be shown to be richly suggestive in heuristic terms. Precisely what counts as journalism in a given context is a matter of performance (albeit not necessarily consciously so on the part of the individual in question), where certain normalized, even ritualized conventions are reaffirmed as appropriate or desirable. The word *notation* similarly resonates – most literally with respect to taking notes in shorthand, but also with regard to the ordinary technical devices employed to document events – in a manner that signals its habitual imbrication in every effort to narrativize the social world with reportorial integrity. Journalists, in my experience at least, tend to express strong views about how technology shapes what they do, with some prepared to concede *compromises in style* arise due to the importance of establishing and sustaining an *interpretive link* with distant audiences over time, space and place. Where such tensions come to the fore, however, they tend to be expressed within broader discourses of professionalism, which help to engender the wider normative limits within which journalists perform their craft.

Further points of connection with Evans's ruminations come to mind, but already an interesting, if inchoate, perspective encourages us to look at familiar questions afresh for this chapter's purposes. More specifically, informing this discussion is a commitment to thinking anew about news reporting as a performative process, one that recognizes that it is much more improvisatory than is typically acknowledged in academic scholarship focusing on the perceived impact or influence of new media technologies on journalistic practice. All too frequently, I would suggest, such studies treat journalists as subscribing to – or being socialized into upholding as self-evidently legitimate – certain shared norms, values and beliefs with almost formulaic precision. My aim is to render problematic the language of causation that tends to creep into this type of research, which I shall pursue by focusing on dimensions of this performative ethos typically overlooked in more technology-centred analyses. Beginning in the next section, we turn to examine WikiLeaks, the 'world's most dangerous website' as one of its former members called it (Domscheit-Berg, 2011), and the controversy it sparked over who may claim the right to be a journalist in the digital age. In the course of examining several of its reportorial interventions, with particular attention given to the Afghanistan war logs posted in 2010, a number of questions will be raised regarding its perceived potential to reinvent journalism in the public interest. WikiLeaks' alternative conception of 'scientific' journalism – where readers are afforded access to original source material so as determine for themselves its relative significance – is shown to challenge the proscribed ideals of professionalism, revealing them to be fraught with ideological fissures and contingencies that severely curtail the impartial journalist's capacity to speak truth to power.

Rewriting rules

WikiLeaks eludes straightforward definition. While commentators are inclined to characterize it as a singular institution, closer scrutiny shows that the website's provision is underpinned by a multiplicity of convergent networks reliant on dozens of servers dispersed around the globe. Since its launch in December 2006 by The Sunshine Press (WikiLeaks.org having been registered two months earlier), the site has undergone a series of changes in its strategic rationale and objectives. A careful reading of its 'About' and FAQ pages as they have been rewritten over the years helps to document this gradual evolution, and one can frequently discern subtle re-inflections of self-definition in light of changing circumstances. One recurrent point is the acknowledgment that the 'wiki' in its name was introduced due to the initial intention to adopt an operational model similar to that of Wikipedia, the free-content online encyclopaedia created in 2001. This model – envisaged as enabling the website's users to edit or comment on the posted data – was quickly abandoned by WikiLeaks' organizers, however, in favour of a safer, more restrictive approach reliant upon volunteers to select and research submissions.

'A Wiki for Whistle-Blowers' was the title of a January 2007 *Time* magazine article by Tracy Samantha Schmidt (2007) about the fledgling website, one of the very first blips on the mainstream media's radar. Described as a 'bold new collective experiment in whistle-blowing,' WikiLeaks' organizers ('Chinese dissidents, mathematicians and start-up company technologists, from the US, Taiwan, Europe, Australia and South Africa') were credited with putting into motion – 'in theory' at least – a system that would 'protect leakers' identities while exposing government and corporate corruption worldwide.' With the prospect of more than one million leaked documents being posted online by March, when it was anticipated the website would go live, *Time* enthused about its potential as a global forum for examining otherwise confidential materials, despite the 'suspicion building around it' (namely 'conspiracy theories' that it was a 'front for the CIA or some other intelligence agency'). While conceding that it is not possible to determine 'what shadowy organization is behind WikiLeaks,' Schmidt's (2007) assessment of the site's relative merits led her to maintain:

> Savvy web users, of course, know that public wikis are never trusted for their authenticity for the simple reason that anyone can post or edit them. Instead they're viewed as a first step in the research process. And if WikiLeaks is used with a healthy dose of skepticism, it could become as important a journalistic tool as the Freedom of Information Act.

Little did she know that this qualified suggestion that WikiLeaks 'could become as important a journalistic tool as the Freedom of Information Act' would be promptly placed on the site's homepage for publicity purposes, where it has remained ever since. In addition to ostensibly affording it a major news organization's endorsement, however, WikiLeaks' decision to use the quotation was arguably indicative of a desire to cast its remit in journalistic terms from the outset.

Tensions regarding the precise nature of the journalistic underpinnings of WikiLeaks' operational rationale continued to mount throughout 2007. For most news organizations it was less a question of how best to describe the website's role in providing access to sensitive information than an issue of whether to acknowledge it at all.[2] Journalistic attention would seldom be directed at WikiLeaks in the months ahead, even though the number of news stories based on documents it put into public circulation steadily enhanced its reputation for whistle-blowing amongst hackers, activists, campaigners – and investigative reporters. Documents the site released helped to generate and sustain a number of news reports, including stories focusing on the treatment of prisoners at the detention centre in Guantánamo Bay, Cuba; allegations of corruption in a Swiss-based bank; secret information about the internal organization of the Church of Scientology; Republican Vice Presidential candidate Sarah Palin's use of private email to sidestep public record laws; and details about the far-Right British National Party (BNP) membership.

If largely ignored by the mainstream media, however, WikiLeaks' growing reputation within internet circles was increasingly subject to polarized debate in the blogosphere. Advocates enthused about its 'fourth estate' role as a vital 'check against tyranny' in the fight for a 'more open and transparent society.' Detractors, in sharp contrast, pounced on what they perceived to be the site's reckless violation of secrecy for its own sake, issuing grave warnings about detrimental implications for national security. Meanwhile several news outlets, somewhat begrudgingly, began to acknowledge the site as a 'journalistic tool' (*Time*'s initial definition) to pry loose stories otherwise being concealed. This status was reinforced, in turn, by related forms of public recognition for the site's activities, such as the *Economist*'s 2008 New Media Award as well as credit from Index on Censorship for being 'an invaluable resource for anonymous whistleblowers and investigative journalists.' In June of 2009, WikiLeaks earned a second new-media award, this time from Amnesty International for exposing 'extra judicial killings and disappearances' in Kenya. 'The material was important,' the site's co-founder Julian Assange (2009) told Journalism.co.uk in an interview at the time. 'It was difficult to get Western press attention to it. We ran it on our front page for a week. Most journalists didn't care about it. Even regular [WikiLeaks] readers didn't care about it' (cited in Townend, 2009).

Further examples of 'censorship attacks,' to use WikiLeaks' turn of phrase, continued to surface throughout 2009. Scandals included a multinational oil trading company's efforts to impose a gagging order on news organizations, not least the *Guardian*, striving to report on a health crisis associated with toxic waste dumped in Côte d'Ivoire, Africa; 'Climategate', when more than 1,000 emails and 2,000 documents from the University of East Anglia's Climate Research Unit were posted online by WikiLeaks, some of which appeared to suggest that statistical information inconsistent with scientific assumptions about climate change was being suppressed;

and the posting of more than 500,000 pager messages sent in the immediate aftermath of the September 11, 2001 attacks. In light of these and related initiatives, by early 2010 it was fast becoming apparent that WikiLeaks warranted regular monitoring from journalists anxious to scoop rivals with breaking news of leaked disclosures.

This attention threshold was finally crossed when WikiLeaks became front-page news in its own right in early April 2010, following its posting of a video documenting US military action in Iraq. Shot in black and white from an Apache helicopter gunship hovering over a Baghdad neighbourhood on 12 July 2007, the 39 minutes of classified footage shows a group of men, including two employees of Reuters, being slaughtered – and in a manner that seemed to many of those watching as jocular as it was arbitrary. Minutes later, a second airstrike is shown, this time targeting a van arriving on the scene, with the effect of killing the civilian driver and wounding his two children passengers. 'Collateral Murder,' as the video was titled, garnered media coverage around the globe (the 17-minute version having gone viral via YouTube), and ignited a bitterly acrimonious debate – not least in the blogosphere – about the ethics of WikiLeaks' decision to release it on its website. Voices weighed into the controversy from across the political spectrum. Some expressed outrage at what they perceived to be a war crime, contending that Geneva Conventions for the humanitarian treatment of casualties had been violated. Others debated the nature of 'murder' in WikiLeaks' choice of title, calling into question the legal complexities associated with the US military's 'rules of engagement.' Still others blamed the 'fog of war,' insisting that the incident was little more than a regrettable example of what can happen in the heat of battle.

As the controversy unfolded, WikiLeaks became the subject of intense media interest for the first time. In observing how the video had raised the profile for a 'once-fringe Web site,' the *New York Times* suggested that this 'clearinghouse for sensitive documents' was 'edging closer toward a form of investigative journalism and to advocacy' in a manner certain to be a thorn in the side of authorities. 'That's arguably what spy agencies do – high-tech investigative journalism,' Assange is quoted as stating in an interview with the paper. 'It's time that the media upgraded its capabilities along those lines' (cited in Cohen and Stelter, 2010). WikiLeaks itself appeared to have adopted enhanced capabilities, furthering its claim to be evolving beyond source status to embrace a journalistic role, most notably with regard to the steps taken to first decrypt and then verify the authenticity of the Apache video footage. The latter entailed Icelandic journalist Kristinn Hrafnsson and cameraperson Ingi Ragnar Ingason travelling to Baghdad to find the two children injured in the attack (the interview was later broadcast on Icelandic television), while Assange himself, working out of a 'bunker' in Iceland, endeavoured to help supply context and analysis. 'This week marked the international coming-out party for a new media organization that could upend the sacred cows of traditional journalism,' Jonathan Stray (2010) of *Foreign Policy* observed. In describing WikiLeaks as 'an Internet-savvy investigative journalism outfit,' he suggested it represented the type of 'accountability journalism' made famous by Carl Bernstein and Bob Woodward of Watergate fame.

If praise for the website was rare, in public at least, due to its controversial tactics, Stray commented that 'no journalist I've spoken to will speak ill of WikiLeaks in private: Every reporter understands that WikiLeaks is the thin end of the wedge. If they can't run a dangerous story, no one can.'

Reporting the Afghanistan war logs

This commitment, typically expressed as a 'publish and be damned' declaration in journalistic folklore, was tested almost to breaking point when WikiLeaks released over 91,000 pages of US military documents in July, 2010. The compendium, promptly labelled the Afghanistan war logs by the press, consisted primarily of classified memos and reports written by soldiers and intelligence officers, typically describing lethal military actions, over the period between January 2004 and December 2009. Some 15,000 items were held back from the archive for further review, the site explained, 'as part of a harm minimization process demanded by our source.' In a significant departure from previous form, the co-operation of major news organizations – namely, the *Guardian*, *The New York Times* and *Der Spiegel* (in its German and English online editions) – had been negotiated beforehand. Each was given the opportunity to examine the items several weeks in advance, subject to agreeing to withhold publication of their news reports until 25 July. The public interest in the material was so significant, the three ascertained, that the agreed embargo was a price worth paying.[3] The *Guardian* characterized the 'huge cache of secret US military files' as offering a 'devastating portrait of the failing war in Afghanistan, revealing how coalition forces have killed hundreds of civilians in unreported incidents, Taliban attacks have soared and NATO commanders fear neighbouring Pakistan and Iran are fuelling the insurgency' (Davies and Leigh, 2010). *The New York Times* concurred that the documents presented 'an unvarnished, ground-level picture of the war in Afghanistan that is in many respects more grim than the official portrayal' (Chivers et al., 2010; see also Allan, 2012). *Der Spiegel* maintained: 'Never before has it been possible to compare the reality on the battlefield in such a detailed manner with what the US Army propaganda machinery is propagating' (Gebauer et al., 2010).

This capacity to afford documentation of the lived experiences of soldiers reporting from the ground in a warzone was the most significant feature of the logs. The members of the 'strong journalistic team,' to use Assange's phrase, each prioritized different aspects of the material in relation to their respective judgements about relative news value. Whether or not WikiLeaks itself was part of the team, or simply the source of the material for the others to process, proved a contentious point. *Guardian* journalist Nick Davies (2010), in a personal account headlined 'Story behind biggest leak in intelligence history,' revealed several details regarding how the 'huge trove of data' amounting to a 'secret record of the world's most powerful nation at war' came to light via WikiLeaks and a 'unique collaboration' between the three news outlets. The original source of the material is identified as 'Bradass87,' who initiated a series of instant messages with a Californian computer hacker, Adrian Lamo, including one which asked: 'hi … how are you? … im an army intelligence analyst, deployed to eastern bagdad … if you had unprecedented access to classified networks, 14 hours a day, 7 days a week for 8+ months, what would you do?' In the days that followed, 'Bradass87' explained that someone he knew (presumably 'Bradass87' himself, later alleged to be a 22-year-old intelligence analyst named Bradley Manning) had been downloading, compressing and encrypting the data on to blank CDs, labelled as Lady Gaga's music, before uploading it to Assange of WikiLeaks. 'i want people to see the truth,' he is quoted as stating. 'its open diplomacy … its Climategate with a global scope and breathtaking depth … its beautiful and horrifying … It's public data, it belongs in the public domain.' Evidently Lamo, two days into their exchange of messages, had contacted the US military, who sent officers from its criminal investigations department to meet him at a Starbucks. Lamo provided them with a printout of Bradass87's online chat, Davies maintains, which led to Manning's arrest the next day at the operating base where he was stationed, 25 miles outside of Baghdad. 'I wouldn't have done this if lives weren't in danger,' Lamo told Wired.com following Manning's arrest. 'He was in a war zone and basically trying to vacuum up as much classified information as he could, and just throwing it up into the air' (cited in Poulsen and Zetter, 2010).

Assange, fearful of his own arrest, went to ground. The *Guardian*, drawing on a series of intermediaries, made contact with him in a Brussels café. There a plan began to form whereby a small team of its specialist reporters would sift through and decode the logs with a view to publishing key insights. The decision to share the database with the *New York Times* and *Der Spiegel* was taken as a strategy intended to reduce the risk of the authorities imposing a gagging order, not least because it ensured publication would occur in three different jurisdictions. 'Under the arrangement,' Davies (2010) noted, 'Assange would have no influence on the stories we wrote, but would have a voice in the timing of publication.' WikiLeaks, meanwhile, prepared to simultaneously publish much of the raw data itself (some material having been withheld to protect human sources), thereby facilitating efforts to compare and contrast the actual logs with claims made about them in the ensuing news reports.

This strategy was a useful check on newspapers' selection and interpretation, and as such indicative of tensions in the relationship. Bill Keller, executive editor at the *New York Times*, explained to readers in a 'Talk to the Newsroom' Q and A forum that the paper 'has no control over WikiLeaks – where it gets its material, what it releases and in what form. To say that it is an independent organization is a monumental understatement.' He proceeded to point out that the decision to post the military archive on the web was taken by WikiLeaks, and was going to happen regardless of whether or not *The Times* elected to be involved. Recognizing the fact that the site had obtained secret material in the first place was 'newsworthy in itself,' Keller's (2010) comments positioned the site strictly as a source, with the paper performing the journalistic work of studying the material, assessing its value and credibility, weighing it against *Times'* reporters experience of the war, and determining its larger significance. 'In doing so,' he added, 'we took great care both to put the information in context and to excise anything that would put lives at risk or jeopardize ongoing military missions.' While carefully vetting the material for disclosures, patterns and, of course, scoops was of primary importance, it was the effort made to process raw details into more personal narratives that enabled the paper, in his view, to 'give readers an intimate sense of what this war looks like and feels like to the soldiers in the field.'

The response from the Obama administration was swift. National Security Advisor General James Jones (2010) condemned the leak as 'irresponsible,' issuing a statement the same day declaring: 'The United States strongly condemns the disclosure of classified information by individuals and organizations which could put the lives of Americans and our partners at risk, and threaten our national security.' White House frustration over the leak, not surprisingly, meant the motives of the leaker were called in question, with Jones contending: 'WikiLeaks made no effort to contact us about these documents – the United States government learned from news organizations that these documents would be posted.' An administration official, this time in an email to journalists (subject line: 'Thoughts on WikiLeaks'), underscored the point in sharper language: 'As you report on this issue, it's worth noting that wikileaks is not an objective news outlet but rather an organization that opposes US policy in Afghanistan.'

The unnamed official also used the opportunity to outline a defensive posture, stressing that the events occurred before the President had announced his new strategy, and that the information revealed was of little significance in any case. Herein lay the definitional problem for the government, evidently determined to characterize WikiLeaks' actions as a harmful threat ('a breach of federal law') while, at the same time, insisting the leaked material was of little value (documents consisting of 'unvarnished, unvetted, uncorroborated reporting' from people in the region who may have 'agendas'). Meanwhile those weighing into the growing controversy included Senator Joe Lieberman (2010), who echoed the White House line by stating that 'WikiLeaks is not an objective news organization' before going even further, arguing that it was 'an organization with an ideological agenda that is implacably hostile to our military and the most basic requirements of our national security.' It was important, he warned, to be 'wary of drawing conclusions based on materials selectively leaked by WikiLeaks, as it seeks to sap support for the Afghan war among the American people and our European allies.' Time and again, critics levelled the charge that WikiLeaks had put the lives of US soldiers at serious risk. 'Somebody ought to be wearing an orange jumpsuit,' Missouri Senator Kit Bond, ranking Republican on the Senate Intelligence Committee, told Fox News (2010).

Several commentators assumed a decidedly more upbeat stance, however, perceiving in WikiLeaks' actions grounds for cautious optimism. '[T]he truth is that we don't really know what WikiLeaks *is*, or what the organization's ethics are, or why they've become such a stunningly good conduit of classified information,' Alexis Madrigal (2010) of *The Atlantic* observed. 'In the new asymmetrical journalism, it's not clear who is on what side or what the rules of engagement actually are,' he added. 'But the reason WikiLeaks may have just changed the media is that we found out that it doesn't really matter. Their data is good, and that's what counts.' This conception of a 'new asymmetrical journalism' resonated with several other assessments on offer. Roy Greenslade (2010), in his *Guardian* blog, suggested that the WikiLeaks revelations were rightly hailed as a triumph of 'data journalism,' and as such the site deserved credit – along with the news organizations involved – for performing a public service. 'We journalists should be delighted because our central task has always been one of disclosure, of revealing public-interest material that others believe wish to be kept secret,' he wrote. 'The emerging form of disclosure through the internet, pioneered so successfully in the past couple of years by WikiLeaks, deserves our praise and needs to be defended against the reactionary forces that seek to avoid exposure.'

It was this strategy to elude control from any government or legal system that academic Jay Rosen, in his blog Pressthink, sought to highlight by proposing that WikiLeaks be regarded as 'the world's first stateless news organization.' In his words:

> Appealing to national traditions of fair play in the conduct of news reporting misunderstands what WikiLeaks is about: the release of information without regard for national interest. In media history up to now, the press is free to report on what the powerful wish to keep secret because the laws of a given nation protect it. But WikiLeaks is able to report on what the powerful wish to keep secret because the logic of the Internet permits it. This is new. Just as the Internet has no terrestrial address or central office, neither does WikiLeaks.
>
> *(Rosen, 2010)*

For Rosen, government confusion over how to engage with WikiLeaks ('we're gonna hunt you down/hey, you didn't contact us!') is symptomatic of the 'new balance of power' being established. 'In the revised picture,' he wrote, 'we find the state, which holds the secrets but is powerless to prevent their release; the stateless news organization, deciding how to release them; and the national newspaper in the middle, negotiating the terms of legitimacy between these two actors.' For the prospective whistle-blower with explosive documents, he continues, WikiLeaks is a much more attractive proposition (it 'has no address, answers no subpoenas and promises to run the full cache if they can be verified as real') compared to a newspaper subject to the laws of a nation, which may or may restrict its capacity to protect sources.

Pasts justifying futures

A recurrent feature of the more positive appraisals of WikiLeaks appearing at this time was the effort made to situate it within a broader journalistic tradition of investigative reporting. Much was made of perceived connections with the *Washington Post*'s reliance on a secret informant to break open the Watergate scandal that toppled the Nixon administration. Even stronger parallels were drawn with the 'Pentagon Papers' case in 1971, when Daniel Ellsberg, an analyst at the RAND Corporation, handed over to Neil Sheehan, a *New York Times* correspondent, several sets of photocopies he had painstakingly prepared of classified documents pertaining to a top-secret Pentagon study of official decision-making concerning the lead-up to the Vietnam War and its conduct. The scale of deception revealed in the US government's secret escalation of the conflict while it made public assurances to the contrary was aston- ishing, with the Johnson administration, in particular, being shown to have system- atically lied to Congress. Shortly after the *Times* had taken the brave decision to publish excerpts of the 7,000 page document on 13 June (outside legal counsel having advised against publication), the Nixon administration succeeded in obtaining a federal court injunction prohibiting the newspaper from publishing further articles. While the *Times* appealed against the temporary injunction – only three days of instalments having being published at that point – other newspapers began publishing their own reports, before they too were restrained. On 30 June, the Supreme Court ruled in a 6–3 decision against the government's case for censorship based on prior restraint. 'Only a free and unrestrained press can effectively expose deception in government,' Justice Hugo Black stated. 'And paramount among the responsibilities of a free press is the duty to prevent any part of the government from deceiving the people and sending them off to distant lands to die of foreign fevers and foreign shot and shell.'

Differing opinions regarding whether or not WikiLeaks' disclosure of the Afghan war logs amounted to a landmark case for press freedom akin to the Pentagon Papers frequently revolved around diverging assessments of its journalistic importance. Ellsberg (2011) himself remarked: 'The WikiLeaks' unauthorised disclosures of the last year are the first in 40 years to approach the scale of the Pentagon Papers (and even surpass them in quantity and timeliness).' His one regret was that 'the coura- geous source of these secret, field-level reports [...] did not have access to top secret, high-level recommendations, estimates and decisions.' Further points of con- nection were identified by Michael Wolff (2010), who observed that '[o]ne of the burdens and wonders of the Pentagon Papers leak was the sheer logistics of copying, storing, and delivering all that material. The WikiLeak makes leaking – leaking on a historical level – just a digital transfer.' In light of this development, Wolff maintains that a new model is emerging, one which holds the promise to effectively 'save' journalism. 'As Daniel Ellsberg, and then Woodward and Bernstein, remade jour- nalism into a transaction of reporters and sources,' he contended, 'now it will be a hackers function.'

Telling in this regard, at least in my reading, is the decision taken by Assange, dubbed 'the Robin Hood of hacking' in some reports, to describe himself as 'a journalist and publisher and inventor' in an interview published at the time. 'There is a bit of a desire to romanticize what I do,' he told *Time* magazine. 'But like war correspondents who go to various countries, I do the same thing. I travel to different countries where we have supports and where I need to follow stories.' Evidently, most of his attention is focused on 'logistics', drawing on a long-standing interest in cryptography and a steadfast commitment to free speech. This 'combination of skills has proved coincidentally extremely effective in what WikiLeaks does in terms of protecting people,' he added, 'using encryption technology and being engaged in political and policy debate and producing information that will push reforms' (Assange, 2010a). Possible reasons for Assange's inclination to assume the mantle of either 'journalist' or 'publisher' invited scrutiny from commentators, especially in light of his remarks during an interview with *Der Spiegel* when asked about his personal motivations. 'I enjoy creating systems on a grand scale, and I enjoy helping people who are vulnerable,' he commented. 'And I enjoy crushing bastards. So it is enjoyable work' (Assange, 2010b).

Several critics incensed by this stance – the phrase 'crushing bastards' proving remarkably tweet-worthy – sought to transform Assange into a figure of hate. Others condemned him for disguising malicious intent in the language of 'whistle-blowing.' Jamie McIntyre, a former Pentagon correspondent for CNN, expressed his deep misgivings on this point:

> As a professional journalist I have been on the receiving end of hundreds of leaks, and they have been invaluable in helping me sort out unvarnished fact from official fiction, which after all is at the core of my job. [...] I bristled a bit Sunday night when the story first broke and I heard several news organizations shorthand WikiLeaks as a 'whistleblower' group. A whistleblower is someone who exposes wrongdoing. To apply the label to WikiLeaks is not only imprecise but unfair, in that it creates a preconceived perception that the released material 'blows the whistle' on illicit activity.
>
> *(McIntyre, 2010)*

McIntyre continued, stating:

> Let's be clear: WikiLeaks is an anti-privacy, anti-secrecy group, whose primary tenet is that nothing should be kept from the world, not military secrets, not sources or methods of intelligence gathering, not even the secret rituals of fraternities and sororities. Governments, Corporations, Private citizens all have some right, even responsibility to keep some secrets. WikiLeaks only allegiance seems to be to the source of its leaks. By remaining agnostic on the consequences of its actions, WikiLeaks seems to me to be functioning less in the tradition of good old-fashioned muckrakers, and more like anti-privacy terrorists. If I were *the New York Times*, I would not be happy about being described as one of WikiLeaks 'media partners' on the organization's website.
>
> *(Ibid.)*

Meanwhile others celebrated the boldness of Assange's personal audacity, employing terms such as 'maverick,' 'crusader' or 'info-hacker' to suggest that WikiLeaks' efforts should be recognized as a modern-day continuation of a long, proud tradition of journalistic muckraking. Several accounts called forth details of achievements secured by reform-dedicated reporters in early twentieth-century US history, perceiving in the website's mission a welcome return to 'digging dirt' at a time when investigative journalism is all too often reduced to celebrity tittle-tattle. 'WikiLeaks founder Julian Assange has publicly eschewed the role of impartial journalist, embracing instead the role of a muckraker – using modern technology to do what he says the mainstream media are not doing enough of,' Noam N. Levey and Jennifer Martinez (2010) suggested in the *Pittsburgh Post-Gazette*. Their observation echoed a number of similar accounts already circulating in the months leading up to the Afghanistan war logs story, including a *New York Times* article headlined 'Pentagon Sees a Threat From Online Muckrakers' (see Strom, 2010).

Differing views over whether WikiLeaks was aptly regarded as a 'whistle-blower' or 'muckraker' website frequently hinged on presumptions made about where it belonged on the journalist–source continuum. Steve Myers (2010), managing editor of Poynter.org, offered an alternative view, however, contending that WikiLeaks had effectively situated itself between source and publisher. The site, he argued, 'has shifted power away from the monoliths that once determined what is news and toward the people who, before the Web, would have been stopped in the newspaper lobby before they could see a reporter.' The three news organizations, in agreeing to WikiLeaks' terms in 'striking a bargain' to gain access to the logs, 'found themselves not as gatekeepers of information, but as guests with VIP access.' At the same time, however, 'WikiLeaks needed these titans of old media. It needed their reporting, their reach, their distribution networks, their reputation.'

WikiLeaks' determination to 'play both sides' suggests to Myers an emergent advocacy role intended to influence traditional media, but not replace them. 'The power of self-publication isn't quite enough,' he argued. 'To achieve the most impact, to get people to pay attention to this story, WikiLeaks needed to broker a deal with traditional media.' In striving to enhance its credibility via its relationships with major news outlets, WikiLeaks took a significant step toward garnering public trust for its actions. Far from being a neutral player, its priorities were readily apparent. 'Deep Throat had an agenda. Ellsberg had an agenda,' Keller of the *New York Times* told Myers in an e-mail. 'That doesn't invalidate the information they provide us. If we refused to work with sources whose motivations we didn't share, a lot of important stories would go untold.' For Keller, the 'critical thing is what we do with the material – check its authenticity, draw our own conclusions from it, put it in context, and lay it all out for readers on our terms, not the source's terms.'

This insistence that WikiLeaks was a source, and not a 'media partner' as the site itself claimed, was reinforced by Keller's colleague at the *Times*, reporter Eric Schmitt, when recalling his experiences in 'the bunker' preparing the materials for publication. 'I've seen Julian Assange in the last couple of days kind of flouncing around talking about this collaboration like the four of us were working all this together,' he maintained. 'But we were not in any kind of partnership or collaboration with him. This was a source relationship. He's making it sound like this was some sort of journalistic enterprise between WikiLeaks, *The New York Times*, *The Guardian*, and *Der Spiegel*, and that's not what it was' (cited in Hendler, 2010). Davies of the *Guardian* concurred that Assange's involvement was limited to that of a source, stressing that collaboration was limited to the three news organizations involved.[4] Assange himself countered this position, however, stating in a London press conference that WikiLeaks decided to work with the three publications because they 'were the best newspapers in the world for investigative research,' and because each was willing to co-operate with the website in its media strategy intended to achieve the maximum impact for the benefit of its secret source. 'We can't have a journalistic coalition which is too large [...] for logistical reasons. With three or four we could get into a room and agree on all the conditions,' he stated. 'The task of good journalism is to turn this material; who, when, where, how, how many, into something which emotionally engages people' (cited in McAthy and Gunter, 2010).

In a follow-up interview with Amy Goodman on her *Democracy Now!* programme, Assange (2010c) described what he termed the 'journalistic coalition' WikiLeaks mobilized to process the material, highlighting the role of the site's own 'journalistic teams' in extracting the data before noting, in turn, how this 'unusual collaboration' revolved around a sense of partnership. This was not to deny, however, that certain tensions existed. He conceded that WikiLeaks was not 'totally happy' about the way *The New York Times* had characterized its relationship with the website in 'defensive' terms, suggesting it seemed 'a little bit unprofessional.' He added:

> So, as an example, the *New York Times* stated that it chose not to link to our website. I mean, it is just ridiculous. The public can see that and Google it, if they want. If the *New York Times*, for whatever reason, wants to not link to WikiLeaks for its own defensive politics, then it can do that, and it's perfectly entitled to. But to deliberately say that that is being avoided smacks of unprofessional conduct, to me. Now, that doesn't mean it's been approved by the editor to do that, but it does seem to be quite pusillanimous to be engaging in that kind of defensive conduct, instead of pursuing the real meat of the story.
>
> *(Assange, 2010c)*

Assange was similarly concerned about the coalition's decision, evidently at the insistence of the *Times*, to show the White House the documents prior to publication in order to help redact sensitive information of possible harm to people on the ground. '[T]here is a bit of a difference between [...] how the American press tends to deal with government agencies prior to publication and the standards that we have and the standards the European press has,' he stated.

> We don't see that [...] in the case of a story where an organization has engaged in some kind of abusive conduct and that story is being revealed, that it has a right to know the story before the public, a right to know the story before the victims, because we know that what happens in practice is that that is just extra lead time to spin the story.

Independent, 'scientific' journalism, he suggested, demanded something different. 'It seems to us that a journalist's relationship should be with the public, on the one hand, and with their sources, on the other hand, who are providing them with information to give to the public' (Assange, 2010c). 'Scientific journalism,' it follows, aspires to a higher standard, effectively enabling members of the public to corroborate for themselves what they are being told.

Alerted to Assange's criticisms, Keller responded in an email to *The Daily Beast* website. 'Obviously our decision not to link to the WikiLeaks archive would not deter anyone who wanted to find it,' he acknowledged. 'All we could do was make this gesture to show we were not endorsing or encouraging the release of information that could cause harm.' In his view, the public interest was served by work of the three news organizations to 'mine the data for news and analysis' for a 'large audience that would take this seriously.' That said, he promptly levelled criticism of his own against Assange. 'His decision to release the data to everyone, however, had potential consequences that I think anyone, regardless of how he [or she] views the war, would find regrettable' (cited in Jacobs, 2010). No explanation was forthcoming concerning the reason why he considered the public release of the data 'regrettable,' particularly when the site had gone to such lengths to involve its 'media partners' to help ensure the documents were carefully scrutinized (and withheld those deemed to be too risky) before releasing them in the name of openness and transparency.

In any case, some commentators wondered aloud whether a more important point wasn't being missed. Assange should 'bite his tongue,' was the view of Craig Silverman (2010), commenting for the *Columbia Journalism Review*. 'The *Times*'s decision to check with the White House was of great service to WikiLeaks, because it was one of several processes that served to remove any doubts about the authenticity of the Afghanistan documents,' he argued. In this way, he reasoned, the ensuing controversy focused on matters other than the origin of the documents themselves. Assange was to be credited, he believed, for having 'expertly removed accuracy and verification from the conversation by placing the burden for these elements on the shoulders of *The New York Times*, *The Guardian* and *Der Spiegel*.' The *Times*, he added, placed some of that burden on the White House, as did the other two news organizations, albeit to a lesser extent.[5] The end result of this 'unprecedented verification challenge' was a 'big win' for WikiLeaks, Silverman concluded, recognizing 'a certain brilliance in the way Assange shifted the burden of verification and analysis away from WikiLeaks, while at the same time ensuring he was able to call out mistakes made by the very news organizations that supplied the all-important credibility to his data.'

Improvising journalism

In rounding out this chapter's discussion, I return once again to the thoughts of Bill Evans (1959; 1963), namely his conception of the jazz musician as 'interpretive performer' discussed at the outset of this chapter. His suggestion that improvisation defines the character of what is expressed resonates, in my reading, with an approach to journalism alert to the lived materiality of its performative ethos.

In considering the journalist as an interpretive performer, this sense of improvisation is pivotal. Such a view, I have endeavoured to show, strikes something of a discordant note with customary projections of journalists' collective identity, particularly where they prove unduly mechanistic in their rendering of certain mythologized images of journalists' affinity. While I hesitate to suggest that it is possible to discern a general set of principles from WikiLeaks' creative use of 'internet technologies in new ways to report the truth' (Assange, 2010d), it seems to me that there is little doubt that the website's insistent transgression of journalistic boundaries puts paid to conventional assumptions about how power is – and should be – distributed within new media ecosystems. In daring to occupy ground claimed by mainstream, corporate news organizations, WikiLeaks calls into question their discursive authority, helping to render transparent their vested interests in preserving the status quo. To pause and consider Assange as an improvising journalist of sorts, deliberately eschewing 'objective' reporting in order to expose social injustice through tactics lawful and otherwise, is to recognize the precarious nature of this authority. ('To be completely impartial is to be an idiot,' he told one interviewer; see Khatchadourian, 2010.) Perceived threats to its legitimacy become all the more acute when set in the context of the wider crisis confronting these organizations as they struggle to renegotiate the terms of their relationship with distrustful audiences, many of whom increasingly inclined to regard them as compromised or, even worse, irrelevant. To the extent that it is appropriate to characterize journalism as an interpretive performance, it follows, it is necessary to attend to the ways in which certain values associated with professionalism risk reinforcing a normative order that excludes those committed to journalism as a public service.

In seeking to lay claim to a citizen-centred conception of journalism, WikiLeaks has thrown into sharp relief the ways in which this normative order is maintained, repaired and, when necessary, policed. 'WikiLeaks is not a news organization, it is a cell of activists that is releasing information designed to embarrass people in power,' George Packer of *The New Yorker* insisted. 'They simply believe that the State Department is an illegitimate organization that needs to be exposed, which is not really journalism' (cited in Carr, 2010). Marc Thiessen (2010) went further in a *Washington Post* op-ed column, castigating the website for being a 'criminal enterprise.' One may presume that his call for the site to be shut down, 'and its leadership brought to justice,' met with the approval of those accustomed to believing that journalism's formulation of the public interest should correspond with corporate priorities. WikiLeaks, in its ad hoc fashioning of an alternative news culture, threatens to unravel this relationship of equivalence, not least by providing the opportunity for citizens to actively rewrite the rules of membership for journalism as an imagined, interpretive community.[6]

Reforming journalism that taps into the passion, innovation and expertise of ordinary people is certain to disrupt traditional hierarchies of power and privilege in its advocacy of reporting aligned with the public right to know. No one should be under any illusion about the formidable nature of this challenge, however, nor the reluctance of news organizations to confront it. 'One day, the WikiLeaks uproar was sparking a once-in-a-generation debate about the disclosure of classified information, the audacious role of a stateless organization beyond the reach of sovereign nations, and the old media's complicity in packaging the 91,000 pages of Afghanistan war documents,' observed press commentator Howard Kurtz (2010). 'The next day, the media establishment seemed to yawn: Old news. Recycled stuff. Kinda knew that. See ya. Hey, is Lindsay Lohan still in jail?'

Notes

1 Similarly worthy of attention in this regard are Bill Evans's (1959) liner notes, titled 'Improvisation in Jazz,' written for the Miles Davis recording *Kind of Blue*, released four years earlier.

2 On 31 August 2007, the *Guardian* become the first major news outlet to formally credit WikiLeaks by name. A news account written by Xan Rice (2007), headlined 'The looting of Kenya,' presented the findings of a 110-page 'secret report' commissioned by the Kenyan government. In the latter half of the *Guardian* account, Rice states that the report 'was obtained by the website WikiLeaks, which aims to help expose corruption'. Despite its central role, no further mention is made of WikiLeaks in the item, nor did it figure in the related coverage of other Western media (beyond passing references from the AP and UPI news agencies).

3 The embargo period is a crucial element in the strategy, with Assange's remarks in an earlier interview explaining the rationale. 'It's counterintuitive,' he said. 'You'd think the bigger and more important the document is, the more likely it will be reported on but that's absolutely not true.' In his view, it is all about supply and demand. 'Zero supply equals high demand, it has value. As soon as we release the material, the supply goes to infinity, so the perceived value goes to zero' (cited in Nystedt, 2009; see also Sreedharan, et al., 2012). For further discussions of related strategies, see Assange (2011), Beckett with Ball (2012), Domscheit-Berg (2011), Leigh and Harding (2011), Sifry (2011), and *The New York Times* (2011). As one would expect, these accounts differ in places, revealing contradictions and inconsistencies, but together offer an array of invaluable insights.

4 'I remember one of the things [Assange] said was that there was a problem when you put raw material on a Web site – each individual news organization says "Well we're not going to invest weeks trying to make sense of that, because for all we know, another media organization over the hill is already doing that. And two days before we're ready to go, they'll go, and all our effort will be wasted,"' Davies added. 'He isn't just putting it out there for the sake of it. He's putting it out there because he wants the world to understand whatever the subject of the information is. And our operation has hugely increased that possibility' (cited in Hendler, 2010).

5 Silverman (2010) notes that Ben Smith of Politico.com offered further details about how the three news organizations approached the White House prior to publication: 'White House officials I talked to feel the *Times* was conscientious [...] The administration was considerably less impressed with the *Guardian*'s outreach efforts – administration officials described their attempts to verify the reports through the White House and Pentagon as minimal. *Der Speigel* reporters did a little better, requesting comments on a few of the reports, the person added.'

6 See Anderson (1983) on the role of the press – or 'print-capitalism' – in the creation of the nation as an 'imagined community'; and Zelizer (1993b, 2010) on 'journalists as interpretive communities.'

11

TRANSFORMING JOURNALISTIC PRACTICE

A profession caught between change and tradition

Tamara Witschge

Institutional journalists are under pressure and the field of journalism is in flux. If twentieth-century journalism was characterized by 'a trained professional delivering objectively validated content to a reader (or viewer, or listener)', where there was room 'for a journalism of analysis and opinion delivered by an authoritative public voice' (McNair, 2009a: 347), and we agree that journalism is changing, we can wonder where journalism in the twenty-first century is heading. Even if we challenge the depiction of twentieth-century journalism as a stable and fixed profession, which it was not (see Witschge, 2011a), we can acknowledge that major changes have featured in the field of journalism.

These recent transformations have been attributed to a great extent to the introduction of new media technologies. For better or for worse, they are said to change the nature of news and the way in which it is produced. Some feel that the world of news is turned on its head as 'new technologies re-engineer the relationship between how views and information are exchanged, judged and assigned significance, and how public opinion is formed' (Lloyd and Seaton, 2006: 1). Some commentators suggest that the three major constituencies in the world of news – journalists, news-makers, and the audience – blur into each other, with audiences becoming part of the process of journalism (Gillmor, 2004: xxiv–xxv). Others suggest that the professional culture of journalism is becoming more diverse, open and dynamic when journalists turn to be identified as 'media workers' with a 'portfolio worklife' based on flexibility and multi-skilling (Deuze, 2007). This line of reasoning contends that the consensus over the qualities and skills belonging to the world of journalism changes as 'technologies of news relay broaden the field of who might be considered a journalist and what might be considered journalism' (Zelizer, 2004b: 23).

Critics object that not everything can simply converge, even though the 'inter-textual merging of journalism with other formats and discourses is maybe its most pressing present challenge' (Conboy, 2004: 224). If journalism is to survive, it has to 'assert a specific location within this media sphere, demonstrate that it can deliver a particular form of service to the public, however fragmented and commoditized that public might become' (ibid.).

This chapter examines the tensions in newsrooms as journalists are caught between, on the one hand, change in and challenges to their profession, and, on the other, their strong commitment to traditional values. The ways in which journalists discuss the challenges that they are faced with – changing work environment, amateur contributions, and increased economic pressures – tell us much about the way in which they consider the profession to be transforming, what journalism is, and what they would like it to be. Critically examining these questions allows us to take stock of the changes, and to reflect on what aspects of journalism we would like to remain intact, if we consider journalism to provide a function of public service.

The main tension that is lived out each day between change and tradition in current journalism is that of high standards versus low journalistic practices. Journalists define their profession by referring to their traditional values; this is what sets them apart, they argue, from amateurs now entering the field of news media. At the same time, however, they are unable to practise to these high standards, as their everyday practices are limited by the commercial pressures they operate under. A close examination of how the loyalty to traditional media is upheld in a time of multimedia, converged newsrooms; how the commercial and public interests that journalists seek to serve at the same time conflict; and how journalists are 'embracing' amateur contributions while upholding professional standards, confronts us with the nexus of the pressures on journalism. In this chapter, building upon interviews and ethnographic research conducted in various newsrooms across the UK between 2007 and 2010, I will address both the change in working environment and practices, and the changes in the mindset of journalists. Within these transformations, can we observe a fundamental shift in the definition of what it means to be a journalist, according to those working in the industry? Is the idea of what constitutes journalism significantly transformed?

Journalism: a changing profession?

A considerable number of studies have been conducted to study how new media technologies impact the field. These have considered the content of online journalism, the journalistic practices of production, and the organization of newsrooms (for example, Gillmor, 2004; Singer, 2004; Domingo et al., 2008; Zelizer, 2009). However, there is still a need to analyse and reflect on the implications of these changes for the profession of journalism. What is the future role of news journalism in society and democracy? This chapter examines the views that those working in the field hold with regard to the changes in and future of journalism.[1]

For those working in newsrooms, new media technologies – such as the internet, mobile phones, and digital cameras – have become ubiquitous. Their ubiquity in news production and consumption makes it difficult for journalists to perceive technology's impact on their daily work. The different functions of inquiry, observation, research, editing, and writing have had to adapt to the vast array of information available online, digital video footage, wire photos, amateur pictures taken with camera-enabled cell phones or digital cameras, the blogosphere, as well as the speed of 24/7 cable news (Fenton and Witschge, 2010). The majority of journalists make use of a number of different technologies on a daily basis, and the demand for so-called multi-skilled or multimedia (or multi-platform) journalists is growing (Lee-Wright and Phillips, 2011). New media technologies are often simultaneously increasing efficiency (with the tools they provide), and workload; there is an increased input due to email and the internet, and at the same time an increased output, with production for multiple platforms.

The technological changes in newsrooms have contributed to an alteration in the professional identity of journalist: there are changes both on the basic level of daily work and on the level of routines, implicit norms and rules (see Witschge and Nygren, 2009). On the basic level of daily work there is a change in the daily practices of journalistic production. Also, newsrooms are organized differently, as I will discuss below, and there is a change in the relations to other groups in the organization (such as design, technology, and finance). Journalists today handle more parts of the production, deal with more technical tools, and the emphasis has moved from 'research' and 'content' towards production and form – from 'input' to 'output'. So-called multi-skilled journalists have to produce much more, with less time to do the basic work of research and verification (see Phillips, 2009).

On the level of routines, implicit norms and rules, the changes are more difficult to pinpoint as there is a certain conservatism in the media: old ways of doing the work are preserved in the daily routines even with the introduction of new technological solutions. As I will develop below, newspaper journalists, for example, for the most part keep thinking in terms of the needs of the newspaper, even if the company also has an online service that needs news 24/7. In radio the work is focused on the newscasts, and the web is mostly another way of listening to the same programmes. But new ways of working have been established in the new newsrooms of the online media. The routines, norms and rules are changing but at varying paces – slowly in some newsrooms and less slowly in others.

The changing working environment

One of the most obvious recent areas of change in the field of journalism is in the way in which newsrooms are organized. The past years have seen a move towards the 'multimedia' newsroom, with a focus on integrating the different media outlets, and stimulating, or in many cases enforcing, cooperation between different departments and journalists. Newspapers developed into 'media companies' incorporating different types of media. For example, in 2009, the MEN Group consisted of a daily newspaper (*Manchester Evening News*), a TV channel (Channel M), the website MEN-online, a radio channel (Century), and several regional weeklies. Up until they merged, these different media outlets considered each other as competitors, and were located in different places. Now they are expected to cooperate:

In the time that I've been here, it's changed a lot towards being one company, [towards] 'let's all get on with it'. At various periods, we've been based in different buildings, had different bosses, belonged to different companies, and so the competition element creeps in at that point, but now we're all here in one room with one boss.

(Senior Editor, MEN)

The organizational and spatial redesign that many newsrooms have seen can be viewed as a deliberate attempt to break down barriers and protective loyalties that journalists have towards their original outlet and bring about 'multi-platform thinking'. In these multimedia newsrooms there are very few (and if any, they are low) dividers between the different sections, which are all operating from one open floor. At the centre is often something called the 'news hub' or similar, which is meant to be the heart of the news operation. In the example of the MEN, this news hub has no dividers at all, so the different section representatives are seated at attached desks that make up the news hub, making it virtually impossible for the different sections to keep news stories from one another. In a similar manner, the BBC has created a news hub, which has been designed for radio, TV and online to work together much more closely. What is more, the reporters on the ground have to be multi-skilled, so that they can provide input for the three different outlets. Throughout the organization it is expected that people think 'multi-platform'.

These types of changes that are introduced into newsrooms affect not only the working environment of journalists. The practices of journalism are also very much affected. The introduction of new media technologies in the newsrooms has had profound consequences for the way in which journalists operate as they work in different settings, with different managers, different equipment, and different expectations. However, it is more than a technological and spatial reorganization that is needed for journalists to change their working habits and attitudes. Journalists working on the ground more often than not focus on the limitations of the so-called convergence of newsrooms, and editors and online journalists talk of a change of mindset that is needed. Particularly in the early phases convergence was problematic, with considerable reluctance to embrace it among journalists affected by it.

Naturally, these misgivings and misunderstandings, or, as a regional web editor refers to it, the 'obvious competition problems and rivalries of little groups', do not disappear overnight with a converged newsroom. One of the inhibiting factors is the clear hierarchy in the newsroom still existing, most commonly among newspaper journalists, where many continue to deem the original publication as the more valuable platform.

Particularly among newspaper journalists there is the sense of history and tradition of the medium that comes to the fore when discussing new media. There is a strong affinity, or even loyalty, for it, which is influencing their position in this as well as the likelihood of success of multimedia thinking, as becomes clear in the following quotation by a regional section editor:

Oh I adore it, it will be my first love until I die, but I'm not sentimental. I love it, I love the smell of it, I love the feel of it, I love everything else. I can talk to you about the print and the feeling and I'll just you bore you death.

The idea that all of the staff should now cooperate, and work for all different media platforms, does not always get embraced by all. Resistance is, in particular, apparent among those who originally worked for the newspaper, as is stressed by web editors and managing editors who focus on the need for a cultural change in the newsroom. Particularly at the early stages, the prevailing idea was that the move online involved 'dumping journalism' rather than 'enhancing journalism'. There was a general feeling that those reading the news for free online were 'dreadful' and a 'waste of time' (web editor, regional newspaper).

Of course, there are some good reasons for this reluctance to embrace convergence as advocated by managers and editors. More often than not it involves an increase in work for journalists. Arguing that it is simply a change in mindset that is required, as many editors and newsroom managers do, fails to acknowledge the actual implications it has on newsroom practices. As one of the journalists at the BBC noted: 'basically the job spec, the description of the job has become wider and wider and wider'.[2]

Naturally one would expect resistance to major cultural shifts, but it is too easy to discard the qualms of journalists as Luddite, as is often done (see Lee-Wright and Phillips, 2011; Witschge, 2011b). There may be more fundamental issues at the heart of journalists' hesitations to embrace all the changes brought about by new media technology. If journalists are protective of their ways of working, let us address the question of what is journalism, according to journalists? One of the main themes when discussing the value of journalism and the current changes in the field is that now the saying goes that 'everyone can be a journalist' with new media. How do journalists view this, and what do they perceive journalism to be? It is in these debates about amateur contributions to the news process that journalists refer to the traditional values of journalism.

What is journalism (for)?

For journalists, the purpose of journalism has not changed much with the introduction of new media technology: it is a profession, undertaken by knowledgeable people working with certain standards. For journalists, these professional standards are what sets journalism apart from other spaces in which news might be produced, and it will be due to these values that quality is guaranteed and that the profession will survive. On this view it will be a great loss for democracy when the day comes that journalism will not be able to perform its function of providing quality information and expert commentary.

This public relevance comes to the fore when journalists reflect on their role: 'My idea of a proper function of a newspaper is something that is working for the community with the community to provide them the news that they need to know about' (feature editor, regional newspaper). Thus even though journalists are in tune with the commercial aspect of their work and acknowledge that they have an entertainment role, they focus on the 'public service' role when discussing what journalism is for. Journalism is viewed as something that is about 'questioning what's happening, representing the rights and opinions of its readers, airing the views of people and providing a record of what's happening' (specialist reporter, regional newspaper). Reflecting on the value of journalism, journalists point to the need for journalism in democracies. More often than not, they do not specify why it is important, but they do consider it to be important for democracy to have a 'rigorous professional' (reporter, regional newspaper).

Thus the interviewees refer continually to the public service that is served by journalism. In this sense there is no difference between online and offline journalism for journalists. Online, like offline, the role of journalism is to provide a public service. Online, or so the online journalists argue, they can even better serve the public interest, with the possibility to inform the public swiftly and extensively. In practice, however, the potential of the internet of allowing for diverse and extensive information is only rarely used fully and most mainstream media content is homogenous (Fenton, 2010; Redden and Witschge, 2010).

In a time where there is growing concern about the quality and role of journalism in society and democracy, we see that for the journalists it is very clear that they have a key role to play. They view it as their duty to get active in the community, to use their influence to change things, or as a specialist correspondent for a regional newspaper puts it: it is their duty 'to kick ass'. A broadcast journalist at MEN explains that Channel M's role is to report on stories that tick the 'the activism box and the citizenship box'. Thus, however much the journalistic practice is changing, journalists argue that this one value remains the same: there is still the 'view that we have to go out there and help people' (Section editor, MEN).

Of course, we can question to what extent this is really still in the remit of commercial journalism. When arguably there is less and less funding to *inform* the public (House of Lords, 2008), should we then expect, and even desire, journalists to push public agendas, to *campaign* for the public? We could argue that a requirement for having political media is maybe to have *diverse* media. But all the evidence points to the conclusion that we have this less and less, in particular at the local level (Witschge, Fenton, and Freedman, 2010).

The professional versus the amateur: what sets journalism apart?

One of the ways in which the journalistic field can be opened up, and norms and values challenged, is through the introduction of new voices to the field (Bourdieu, 2005). Amateur voices in this way would challenge the traditional practices and make journalism more inclusive (Muthukumaraswamy, 2010). A lot of academic work has assumed that because the technology is there, this new state of 'participatory journalism' (Domingo et al., 2008) will transpire. To what extent do journalists consider themselves to be affected by these new voices? Do they reflect critically on their values?

For journalists there is a clear distinction between the 'amateur' and 'professional' contributions. For them it is very clear that their values are what set them apart from other spaces of news. The professional values make journalism a distinct activity:

> We're not the same as what everybody does, you know, the kind of journalism we make is expensive, it needs to be checked, you need to be sure it's accurate and, you know, it's very difficult to see how you could avoid having professional funded journalists with experience, legal training, etcetera, making those checks so that when you actually watch it, it's got some credibility attached to it.
>
> *(Deputy editor, national broadcaster)*

New spaces of news are not able to provide this type of information and analysis, according to mainstream journalists. In discussing the value of journalism in relation to those new spaces, journalists return to the notion of journalism as a profession. When reflecting on what sets journalism apart from other sources of news, such as citizen journalism and blogs, for instance, journalists go back to the idea of journalism as a profession, sometimes even without any further indication of what that entails, as shown below. What sets journalism apart?

> Well, that's like saying what sets lawyers apart from someone who can just do all their own legal operations, whether you assume it's a trade or a profession it's something that has training and laws and ethics and practice which is different from another job. (...) Blogs are not written by journalists, you know, a blog is written by somebody else.
>
> *(Online journalist, national broadcaster)*

And yet, of course, amateur production gets more and more integrated into news practices, in particular online. The reasons for such inclusion are more often than not commercial (Witschge, 2011a), rather than satisfying a public service. Even at public broadcasters such as the BBC, where the argument is that it is part of their remit to air and listen to voices of the public, one can wonder about the cost–benefit ratio when so many trained journalists – at the BBC User Generated Content Hub, teams of journalists wade through user contributions 24/7 – spend their time going through hundreds and thousands of messages before finding one they deem of value. More importantly, perhaps, the regular practices of journalists do not meet the high standards which journalists maintain set them apart from amateur contributions.

High standards, low practices?

The standards of those working in journalism are high. What they consider good journalism is what academics have argued to be important for democracy. The public interest is one of the foremost themes that recur when discussing journalism with journalists. However, at the same time, it is clear that they cannot live up to these standards.

For journalists the long-form journalism and original stories are still the ideal. As one of the MEN reporters states: 'The "investigative stuff" is core.' But this is not what everyday journalism is about: journalists miss exercising their journalistic functions. And journalists are quite fierce in condemning a practice that does not live up to the highest journalistic standards (even though they may not practice it so much):

> Obviously, the temptation is there when there's so much material which is just out there in a written form. I guess there's always going to be a temptation to try and cut corners with it and make assumptions. (...) Professional journalists increasingly realise one of the few things that they have that for example bloggers don't is that they are working to standards, and I think there's an acceptance that if we are going to have a role in the future, a big role in the future where people have a multiplicity of choice of news sources, we have to offer something different, and one of those things has to be higher standards basically of accuracy, you know, of fairness. The basics, the journalistic basics.
>
> *(Online journalist, national broadcaster)*

There is a strong idea in newsrooms, even with the changes brought about by new media, of what journalism is, and a strong notion of journalism as a profession. We can connect this to the idea of craftsmanship as put forward by Richard Sennett (2008: 9): 'an enduring, basic human impulse, the desire to do a job well for its own sake.' This desire is very much apparent in journalism. Journalists have a certain drive that is not easily traced back to their status, money or anything particularly material. Their notion of quality in journalism suggests a particular pride that they take in their work. They will easily point you to stories that they consider examples of true journalism (see Phillips, 2010).

Craftsmanship 'focuses on objective standards, on the thing in itself', Sennett explains, like we see in these discourses on ideal journalistic practices. However, he continues to argue that 'social and economic conditions (...) often stand in the way of the craftsman's discipline and commitment' (p. 9). This is apparent in journalistic practices. The internal pressures in the newsroom, and the economic pressures that journalists are under, mean that journalists are not able to live up to their standards, and they are very much aware of this.

News media are businesses and at the same time fulfil a public service: they provide valuable information to citizens in a democratic society. These two roles, as Picard points out, 'create tensions within media companies and among media policy-makers that require careful balancing if society is to gain the benefits of a free and independent media system' (2005: 337). This is not new, but with the current challenges facing news businesses these tensions are intensified as both the business side of media and their capability (and inclination) to cater to the public interest of citizens are put to the test. Particularly now that media companies 'are struggling to adjust to wide-ranging changes that are increasing competition and eroding their audience and advertising bases' (Picard, 2005: 344), we need to consider the economic pressures that may jeopardize the public-sphere function of news media.

Even though the current mediascape, including the field of news journalism, changes rapidly, it is important to identify the challenges that make it difficult for news media to deliver the public service that journalists regard so highly:

> In the early years of the 21st century, general trends in the media businesses are   complex but relatively clear. Ownership consolidation continues (...). Technology advances, with satellite and broadband promising more media outlets, faster access, and more interaction – all at lower prices. Convergence accelerates, as digitization erases the lines between different media. Commercialism expands.
>
> *(Croteau and Hoynes, 2006: 223)*

It goes beyond the scope of this chapter to discuss all the different ways in which the economic pressures have affected journalistic practices (for an overview see Phillips and Witschge, 2011), but I want to highlight one that is particularly pressing for journalists themselves: the increased productivity which provides them with little time per story, and which goes hand in hand with increased reliance on existing material.

In many newsrooms it becomes clear that the role of press releases and particularly the Press Association (PA), for instance, is considerable.[3] At the time of the observations, the MEN Media group had four daily editions of the newspaper, and one of the main deadlines of the day was the 10.30am deadline. The journalists on the early and day shift would normally work on rewriting press releases until 10.30 and a few reporters would then spend parts of the rest of the day working on stories from 'scratch'. The press releases are rewritten in an extremely short time (five minutes), copied and pasted and tweaked only a bit, as one of the reporters explains: 'the press releases [from the Manchester police] are quite good in itself. They are a bit "police-y", so a little bit of tweaking is necessary.'

At the BBC online newsroom it is mainly the PA releases that are dealt with in this way. The PA is an important institution in this organization, and, as became apparent in my newsroom ethnography, the rule that is normally upheld here of 'two sources before publishing' does not apply to PA releases. They are considered trustworthy and do not need to be checked. Here, too, a lot of time is spent on rewriting (or 'repurposing' as it is often called) these or other BBC stories.

This repurposing of material, whether it is from the wires, press releases or from user-generated content (UGC), means that there is a very administrative news culture throughout different sections in journalism. Only a very small part of the actual work involves investigative journalism, or what journalists themselves refer to as the 'real stuff'. As an online broadcast journalist explains:

A lot of it is rewriting. (...) but the thing is a lot of newspapers do that as well. A lot of newspapers. You know, I mean it's a bit strange, if you read any newspaper, any news outlet, the main stories of the day will all be the same usually, and most of that will have been rewritten PA copy.

The extent to which the job currently involves this type of work is illustrated by a joke that is popular in newsrooms: 'If this process goes too far there will only be one reporter left in the world. He or she will be in Afghanistan and the rest of the world is using their recycling list up' (senior manager, the *Guardian*).

Justin Lewis et al. (2008: 28) have conducted a large-scale study into the use of PR in journalism, and summarize their findings as follows:

> Taken together, these data portray a picture of the journalistic processes of news gathering and news reporting in which any meaningful independent journalistic activity by the press is the exception rather than the rule. We are not talking about investigative journalism here, but the everyday practices of news judgement, fact checking, balance, criticising and interrogating sources etc., that are, in theory, central to routine, day to day journalism practice. News, especially in print, is routinely recycled from elsewhere, and yet the widespread use of other material is rarely attributed to its source.

The Cardiff report says it would be:

> grossly unfair to blame journalists for relying on pre-packaged information. (...) it is clear that most journalists are restrained by economic and organisational factors and thereby required to draft and process too many stories for publication to be able to operate with the freedom and independence necessary to work effectively. The danger signalled here is that the best values of journalistic integrity will become a luxury.
>
> *(Ibid.)*

They explain that there has been a significant increase in workload, where the number of editorial and news pages have tripled in just 20 years (p. 11). If we, in addition, consider the recent increase for demand for output with online pages, as well as the job losses throughout the industry, this paints a picture where there is little time for journalists to do what they themselves call 'proper' journalism.

The infinite space to fill online, the constant pressure of breaking news, and the general pressure of timeliness (see Fenton, 2010), mean that online these practices are even more common. When asked, an online planner states that he is not able to estimate the amount of articles that repurpose material, but he thinks it is the bulk of the material produced online. He refers to the nature of the online job as an explanation: 'I think that's the nature of what we do, who we are, covering an awful lot of news every single day.' When more and more people get their stories from mainstream news media online (Ofcom, 2007), we can see the importance of having diversity of content rather than the homogeneity now present as a result of these practices.[4]

It is important to acknowledge that it is not simply the introduction of technology causing these changes. The economic pressures have an important part to play in the cultural shift of working practices in newsrooms, even if technology may have allowed for these major changes to be made without much active resistance (see Witschge, 2011b). With convergence (if seen as a move to bi- or tri-media) a dis-embedded work culture comes into being where people do not feel comfortable with what they are doing, where they lose their expertise. One of the senior broadcast journalists at BBC online considers this as the main threat of convergence:

> [The people working in the multimedia newsroom] have no real relationship with just the tools of news gathering and just the thought processes of getting a story together other than effectively plug some holes. And the danger is of course that the site will go into that culture and lose that original journalism thing. But the thing is you need the original journalism to make the website work. It's the original journalism which makes the site distinctive, which is why you've got to protect this.
>
> *(Online journalist, national broadcaster)*

Journalists have to produce more and different types of output (text, video, radio interviews, etcetera), and this focus on news production results in less time for the actual newsgathering, so the interviewees argue. What is more, there is a different type of output online:

> What I do now is very different from what I trained in and what I did before which was long form journalism, which is you could spend three months reporting on something and write three thousand words and spend a lot of time kind of building trust with people out in their environment, their neigh-bourhoods, you know, kind of investigative journalism, which is just, that's really, you don't do that at all here. You're lucky if you get three days to write a story, you know. So I think that's a very, I think that's a negative impact of online journalism basically. It changes how many words you can actually put down because people's reading span is much, much shorter online.
>
> *(Online journalist, national broadcaster)*

Moreover, there are an increasing number of channels to monitor in the new media environment. A lot of time is spent monitoring other media to check that nothing is missed (in newsrooms the TV is on all the time, the wires are open on the computer screen, and every so often the journalists conduct a trawl through other news web-sites, blogs and user-generated content), and emails further add to the incoming stream of input. This constant monitoring of data has become an important part of the everyday practice of journalism. There is so much input of stories through all these different media, that it becomes a daily task of dealing with that for journalists, which leaves little time to actually 'go out' and look for original stories. Add to this the current job insecurities that many journalists face, with reorganizations of newsrooms frequent, and journalists are left to work in a volatile environment where optimal practices may not be expected.

Escaping the negative cycle

Journalists are understandably eager to define and defend their profession, and their focus on core values regarding journalistic practices resemble what Sennett (2008) has identified as the pride that comes with 'craftsmanship'. But what does it mean to focus on 'core values' in a time when the journalistic practices change considerably? What do these core values constitute? As Servaes points out in his article 'We are all journalists now!', the core journalistic values 'have shifted quite a bit' with the 'corporate colonization' of newsrooms (2009: 372).

Summarizing the most pressing issues in journalism at the moment, Servaes lists 'the need to focus on *service to the public*' as the first item (2009: 371). In this chapter, I have argued that journalists in their discourse on the future and definition of journalism already do so: they continually address the public service that journalism provides, or better: that it *should provide*. They indicate that at present they are not able to live up to their own high standards in everyday journalistic practice: they are under pressure to produce a lot of output in little time, relying heavily on existing material, not being able to check sources to the extent that they should, or to add the depth that they think a story requires. This practice undermines the value and future of journalism, and if we believe professional journalism delivering a public service matters, we need to consider ways of providing journalists with the possibility to deliver content that meets their standards.

New media may have allowed new voices to be heard in the public domain, but to maintain everyday as well as investigative reporting on issues of public relevance, investments need to be made: even if everyone is 'able to do journalism now', quality journalism still costs money, and still requires structural funding (see Ettema, 2009b: 320; Curran and Witschge, 2010). The continued pressure on newsroom staffing in a time of decreasing revenues (Freedman, 2010) is what forms the real challenge to journalism, not the introduction of amateur voices that journalists may choose to focus on. Indeed, the most imminent 'threat facing journalism is de-professionalization, which means that everyone can be a journalist and nobody actually is one' (Nossek, 2009: 358).

If we agree that 'a profession of journalism without journalists cannot bode well for the necessary checks and balances on a future global capitalist democracy' (Deuze, 2009b: 317), we need to ensure that we move towards a journalistic field with enough quality suppliers of news. This will involve creating an environment where different types of business models exist, not just the commercially dominated, shareholder models. We need to be creative and think of how we can inject new life into public-service journalism, acknowledging the value this has for democracy. It goes beyond the scope of this chapter to discuss the variety of possibilities there are in this respect,[5] but if we take journalism seriously, we need to not only critique it, but also support and make possible good practices.

Notes

1 Much of the material in this chapter comes from the Leverhulme Trust-funded 'Spaces of News' project conducted at Goldsmiths, University of London (2007–10). This project examined the way in which economic, social and technological changes have reconfigured news journalism (Fenton, 2010). In addition to the author of this chapter, the research team included Natalie Fenton, James Curran, Nick Couldry, Aeron Davis, Des Freedman, Peter Lee-Wright, Angela Phillips and Joanna Redden. The project featured 170 interviews with a variety of actors from the field, including national and regional journalists (broadcast and press), editors and commercial directors, as well as sources of news, complemented with newsroom visits. All interviews included in this chapter were conducted between 2007 and 2010.
2 For results of a Swedish survey on the widening of tasks involved in journalism, see Witschge and Nygren (2009).
3 Of course there is a difference between the two, press releases and agency material, and even stark differences within these two categories, but if we view it from the point of view of diversity of news content, the use of both have important ramifications (Redden and Witschge, 2010).
4 For a large-scale content analysis of mainstream media online, see Redden and Witschge (2010).
5 For a discussion of different business models, see Witschge et al. (2010) and Phillips and Witschge (2011).

12

'EVEN BETTER THAN BEING INFORMED'

Satirical news and media literacy

Chris Peters

On October 30, 2010 approximately 215,000 people assembled at the National Mall in Washington D.C. Many appeared in fancy dress, and held signs with such playful slogans as: 'Don't hate me because I'm rational', 'Stark raving reasonable', and 'I'm using my inside voice.'[1] This motley assortment had coalesced neither around a defined political movement nor to protest a substantive social policy issue.

Instead, they came to Washington at the behest of two satirical comedians, Jon Stewart and Stephen Colbert, at the 'Rally to Restore Sanity', which centred on the theme of returning respectful dialogue to both the political and journalistic spheres. Focusing on heated political rhetoric and its amplification by the cable news media – much like he did in a widely viewed 2004 critique of the CNN debate show, *Crossfire* – Stewart, host of *The Daily Show*, promoted the rally as 'looking for the people who think shouting is annoying, counterproductive, and terrible for your throat; who feel that the loudest voices shouldn't be the only ones that get heard' (Rally, 2010a). While politics may have been his focus, Stewart frequently reproached cable news, what he called 'the country's 24-hour, politico-pundit perpetual panic "conflictinator"' (Rally, 2010b), both during the rally and throughout its promotional lead-in. He unambiguously laid blame on cable news for perpetuating an intolerant, inconsistent, and at times, injurious approach to discussing social issues. In essence, he charged this sphere of journalism with failing its democratic function.

If we take this as a starting point – over 200,000 people showing up, being mobilized, attending a rally that imparts lessons on the state of journalism in the United States – it provokes the question: how are audiences' expectations and perceptions of journalism currently being shaped? If we listen to the cheers which accompanied each instance of Stewart echoing the oft-heard criticisms of contemporary journalism – sensational, polarizing, trivial, irresponsible, and so forth – it stimulates us to speculate about journalism's ongoing ability to, in marketing terms, 'capture' its audience.

This chapter attempts to engage with these questions by considering three pertinent and interrelated changes in concert: the shifting experiences of public trust in the media; increasing audience involvement in journalism; and a growing public understanding of media techniques. I propose we try to understand the shifting nature of the news landscape not by taking journalism as a starting point, but by looking at journalism through the changing lens of its audience(s). More specifically, the idea of *media literacy* is a helpful concept we can use to begin deciphering the changing audience–journalism relationship.

Contemporary audiences have certain moral or ethical evaluations of journalism (trust), but increasingly they also have certain participatory expectations (involvement). Media literacy influences both. It shapes how audiences learn to decode journalistic texts, sets the expectations upon which levels of trust are based, and helps define the parameters upon which audiences engage. For audiences to proclaim that particular journalistic products are politicized or biased (cable news), or that certain news practices are unethical (hoaxes, phone tapping), they need some degree of media literacy. If one wants to augment the journalistic product (user-generated content) or if one wants to create journalistic alternatives (citizen journalism), media literacy is essential. It is, accordingly, a foundational concept for understanding the future of journalism.

The Daily Show (*TDS*) provides an interesting counterweight in this regard. Its popular reception over the past decade demonstrates the possibilities stimulated by an alternative form of journalism that performs multiple functions for its audience, oftentimes simultaneously: it acts as a news substitute; it engages in media criticism; and it promotes media literacy. *TDS* treats its audience as a constituency which should be aware that 'something is rotten in the state of journalism' and instructs them accordingly. As Stewart notes of the media,

> The role of a free press is to be the people's eyes and ears, providing not just information but access, insight, and most importantly context. It must devote its time and resources to monitoring the government, permeating the halls of power to determine who is doing the people's work, who is corrupting the process, and who will promise to be a mole in the State Department if their homosexuality is kept secret. Only after that – and only with time permitting – should it move on to high-speed freeway chases.
>
> *(Stewart, 2005: 133)*

In these sorts of critiques, Stewart harnesses and promotes a familiar, classically modernist interpretation of the proper civic role and function of journalism.

Yet this is also where *TDS* departs from the modernist journalistic paradigm. Stewart delivers his acerbic criticism of the news media by crafting an innovative 'experience of involvement' for his audience, employing active forms of emotionality (humour, anger, shock, dismay) as opposed to relying on the types of passive emotional postures (control, gravitas, calmness) more typically associated with journalism (Peters, 2011). Broadly speaking, *TDS* can be conceptualized as one example of a nascent *public pedagogy* (cf. Giroux, 2000) that aims to educate citizens about journalism. Aspects of this pedagogy include formal education, popular culture, and emerging forms of news and news commentary. The result is an ever-increasing public emphasis on media (journalistic) literacy which leads to progressively more sophisticated *metanarratives of journalism*.

If part of journalism's future is dependent on how audience perceptions and expectations of the news are being shaped, considering the journalism industry in isolation is evidently insufficient. Media literacy has been promoted through various acts of public pedagogy over the past few decades, from the introduction of curricula at the primary and secondary school levels (see UNESCO, 2011; Network, 2011), to encounters with representations of journalism through entertainment media (e.g. *The Wire*, Stieg Larsson's *Millennium* trilogy), dedicated media commentary online (e.g. PressThink, mediaguaridan.co.uk, Media Matters for America), and the rapid institutional rise of departments of media and journalism studies in universities around the globe (Josephi, 2009; Zelizer, 2009). The news industry is not the exclusive arbiter of its future and related fields such as education and popular culture are concomitant shapers that warrant greater attention. Within the United States, *The Daily Show* is a key player in this regard.

TDS promotes media literacy for a young audience that has not yet formalized nor ritualized its relationship with journalism. Accordingly, this chapter examines the shifting dynamics amongst public trust, media literacy, public pedagogy, and popular culture (in the form of *The Daily Show*). It looks at the broader educational and popular context in which journalism now finds itself and sees what lessons are being taught to journalism's future audiences/consumers. If the educational system is the site for the future foundations of media literacy, popular culture may be the vanguard of this change. Whether it is Charlie Brooker's *Newswipe*, or critically acclaimed films such as *Good Night, and Good Luck*, we must be cognizant of incorporating popular influences into the broader equation of how to rethink the ways that audiences evaluate journalism in a media-saturated age. What *Sesame Street* did for young children's educational urge to learn arithmetic over the past 40 years, *The Daily Show* appears to be doing for young (primarily American) adults' education about journalism.

Public trust and media literacy

Public scepticism of journalism, generally measured by data which demonstrates decreasing levels of public trust in the news industry as a whole (see Barnett, 2008; Pew, 2009), is often viewed as an alarming development. However, I contend that one cannot look at the notion of trust in isolation to judge the current state of audience–journalism relations; public trust must be considered alongside audience involvement and levels of media literacy as well. While I would by no means claim that we have witnessed a universal epistemological shift, I think one can argue that many contemporary public(s) no longer view journalism just as an institutional provider of informational content, but as an epistemological performance or process of knowledge production as well (though probably not in these terms). As such, they increasingly learn to become critical consumers of the news they are provided. Audiences have learned to be sceptical – perhaps, at times, even cynical – but such an approach simply mirrors what journalism expects of itself with respect to active distrust of officialdom.[2]

Contemporary trends appear to indicate that we are witnessing an ill-fated paradox, wherein higher levels of media literacy amongst the public seem to parallel lower degrees of trust in journalism. This is accompanied by a second paradox, whereby the level of trust the public has in institutions that make the news erodes at the same time that these same institutions encourage them to become more engaged or better involved in the process of news-making (cf. Giddens, 1994). Journalism has moved past *Nineteen Eighty-Four*: ignorance is (no longer) strength.

Yet I contend that these developments are potentially beneficial, forcing greater transparency on the part of newsmakers and demanding greater efficacy on behalf of their audiences. Nowhere was the former more evident than in the *News of the World* phone-hacking scandal, while the rise of Indymedia and citizen journalism in recent years would seem to corroborate the second part of this claim. Accordingly, we can say that the trends of decreasing trust and declining audiences discussed above are subject to a few critical caveats. First, as the generic 'mass audience' turns away from mainstream media that it apparently trusts less and less, this corresponds to specific audiences seeking out media alternatives that are more in line with what they want from journalism (Jones, 2010; PEJ, 2010; Peters, 2010). So perhaps it is more accurate to say that trust has not so much decreased as fragmented. Second, even as the proliferation of 'soft' news and infotainment programming continues unabated, from vox-pop current-affairs programming, to breakfast television, personality-based cable magazines, and so forth, these more emotionally overt, journalistically involved products continue to trumpet certain modernist credentials – factuality, balance, and accuracy, to name a few – to accentuate their news and informational value (Peters, 2011). Much of the myth of objective journalism, in terms of the rhetoric outlining proper techniques and appropriate ethics, is alive and well.

The challenge facing those who want to reinforce the bedrock of 'responsible journalism' is, accordingly, to figure out how to ensure that audiences demand its fulfilment. One way is through pedagogy; just as audiences rarely flock to a 'bad movie' there needs to be some mechanism whereby they will support – attitudinally and economically – instances of critically acclaimed journalistic output. Demanding 'good' journalism necessitates first being able to recognize it, and in terms of these lessons, they seem to be increasingly, not decreasingly, widespread.

Pedagogy and global media literacy

Many of the developments discussed in relation to the contemporary shifts in journalism, especially in terms of its content, are often highly pessimistic. The industry, and not just in the United States, has evidently become more commercial, more fragmented, more beholden to technology, and more impacted by temporality over the past few decades. And for many, journalism is the worse for it.

But the significance of these developments may be more ambiguous than appears at first blush. Despite the oft-echoed critique that the news media is turning to tabloid methods, debasing itself as it capitulates to commercial interests, the irony is that, as a workforce, the industry is increasingly demanding that journalists have post-secondary education in order to be admitted into its ranks (Weaver et al., 2007). So even if we accept contentions of tabloidization and dumbing down at face value, it would seem erroneous to claim that 'unintelligent' journalism is resulting from more 'uninformed' journalists. Similarly, the promotion of media awareness is on the rise, with media literacy being promoted at the primary- and secondary-school levels and media and journalism studies programmes appearing around the globe. So if the public is increasingly being subject to a sort of journalistic Pablum, it is unlikely this is because they are now less aware of what they're being fed. As Bird (1992) notes in her studies of tabloid news audiences, and Hill in her study of factual television (2007), audiences are readily able to distinguish 'serious' reportage from diversionary 'newzak' (cf. Franklin, 1997). And programs which promote such a critical awareness are currently on the rise.

Livingstone et al. (2008) note that initiatives on media literacy generally aim to serve three purposes: to promote democratic participation and active citizenship; to facilitate technological competency in an increasingly wired world; and to develop creative and expressive awareness by ensuring audiences can navigate the everyday media landscape. These thrusts drive debate and the direction of public policy. For instance, in Canada the Media Awareness Network was established in 1996 to promote curriculum change at the primary- and secondary-school levels. This nonprofit organization is funded by the national and provincial governments, journalism and telecommunications industries, and educational and community organizations. Working alongside ministries of education, the organization has managed to get a commitment to learning about media texts included on all Canadian provincial curricula. It notes:

> Traditional media education topics—stereotyping, bias, gender and minority portrayal; objectivity and point of view; fashion, advertising and self-image; questions of ownership and content; the globalization of media; the relationship between audience and content; are as pertinent as ever in the new industrial education/entertainment complex. [...] in an environment with millions of publishers and few gatekeepers, the skills to decode online marketing and to determine the differences between fact and opinion have become essential.
>
> *(Media Awareness, 2011)*

While still in its relative infancy, the learning resources provided by the Network to teachers reflect a level of media sophistication unavailable to previous generations.

As these lessons are gradually incorporated into curricula, young adults come to possess greater critical faculties to analyze journalism. Whereas the titles of some of journalism studies' hallmark texts – *Making News* (Tuchman, 1978), *Making the News* (Golding and Elliott, 1979), and *Manufacturing the News* (Fishman, 1980) – reflect the relative novelty of critical media literacy in the academic sphere three decades ago, ideas, which in the 1970s and 1980s were only discussed at academic conferences, are now trickling down to younger and younger audiences. While the impacts of such epistemological shifts happen slowly, they are in evidence.[3]

Of course, such lessons are not restricted to Canada. The Grunwald Declaration on Media Education was passed by 19 UNESCO countries in 1982. The impetus behind the Declaration was that media literacy was essential for informed citizenship, and the first resolution of the document reads as a surprisingly poignant and prescient encapsulation of the issues with which contemporary journalism now grapples:

> We therefore call upon the competent authorities to:
>
> initiate and support comprehensive media education programs – from pre-school to university level, and in adult education – the purpose of which is to develop the knowledge, skills and attitudes which will encourage the growth of critical awareness and, consequently, of greater competence among the users of electronic and print media. Ideally, such programs should include the analysis of media products, the use of media as means of creative expression, and effective use of and participation in available media channels.
>
> *(UNESCO, 1982)*

This focus on media literacy has expanded ever since, from 1990 when UNESCO held its first inaugural media literacy conference, to 2009, when the United Nations, UNESCO, the Alliance of Civilizations, the European Commission and Grupo Comunicar published a joint report on *Mapping Media Education Policies in the World: Visions, Programs and Challenges*. The recommendations in this report were taken up by UNESCO in 2011, when it published its first international curriculum on media literacy for teachers. It opens by noting:

> We live in a world where the quality of information we receive largely determines our choices and ensuing actions, including our capacity to enjoy fundamental freedoms and the ability for self-determination and development. Driven by technological improvements in telecommunications, there is also a proliferation of media and other information providers through which vast amounts of information and knowledge are accessed and shared by citizens. Adding to and emanating from this phenomenon is the challenge to assess the relevance and the reliability of the information without any obstacles to citizens' making full use of their rights to freedom of expression and the right to information.
>
> *(UNESCO, 2011: 11)*

Somewhat unsurprisingly, analysis of journalism is a component of six of the nine core modules they propose. The second module, 'Understanding the News, Media and Information Ethics', focuses specifically on journalism and its four units – 'journalism and society'; 'freedom, ethics and responsibility'; 'what makes news: exploring the criteria'; and 'the news development process: going beyond the 4 Ws and 1H' – bode well for journalistic literacy gradually becoming a mainstream aspect of education. This is part of a broader global trend which has seen journalism and media studies departments become enmeshed in universities over the past couple of decades.

The study of journalism, originally a US-based phenomenon, has seen a rapid rise in its birthplace over the past few decades. Indeed, the number of American colleges and universities offering degrees in journalism and mass communication increased 52 per cent between 1982 and 2002, from 304 programmes with 91,016 students enrolled to 463 programs and 194,500 students (Weaver et al., 2007: 33). While some of these programmes do little more than institutionalize the apprenticeship function, providing a basic skill set to aspiring journalists, others provide grounding in mass communication theory. From would-be journalists, to communications majors, and bachelor students taking minors in media studies and related disciplines, each generation of university graduates is being increasingly exposed to various strands of critical, interpretive, postmodern and poststructuralist thought on journalism, not only within the US, but globally, as teaching and research spreads worldwide (Josephi, 2009).

It seems as though a call for an increased emphasis on global media literacy (Meyrowtiz, 1998) is being answered at a number of different institutional and supra-national levels, which implies that the global level of media literacy is on the rise. However, the implementation of media literacy often focuses upon the formal educational level, something which takes time and must overcome the bureaucracy and retraining necessary for substantial shifts in curricula. It would probably be naïvely optimistic to overestimate the current degree of news literacy on a global scale, however, within certain pockets of young adults, exposure has certainly led to a greater awareness. Yet education is not the only sphere we need to consider.

Public pedagogy and the rise of *The Daily Show*

The attention received by *The Daily Show* over the past decade serves as colloquial evidence for the assertion that the boundaries between news and entertainment have fundamentally shifted in the contemporary age, even if the historical distinction between the two is undoubtedly a false dichotomy (see Delli Carpini and Williams, 2001). From a *Rolling Stone* cover of Stewart and Stephen Colbert ('America's Anchors'), to articles in the *New York Times* ('Is Jon Stewart the Most Trusted Man in America?'), or tributes by journalistic stalwarts like Tom Brokaw, who dubbed Stewart the 'citizen's surrogate' – a role usually reserved for the media ('Jon Stewart: Wickedly Insightful') – in *Time*, there are numerous examples of *TDS* and Jon

Stewart being held up as synonymous with, or sometimes superior to, conventional journalism. What is interesting is how such articles call upon 'ideal types' of hard news, or utilize exemplars from the pantheon of trusted, traditional American journalists.

It seems that in an age of hybridized media formats, *The Daily Show* has become enmeshed for many people as indistinguishable from, in terms of the validity of its truth-claims, the traditional benchmark for 'factual television', namely professional, network journalism (cf. Hill, 2007). What is striking when one considers audience surveys is the exceptionally rapid incorporation of *The Daily Show* (a satirical news program) amidst more established alternatives of 'news' (Pew, 2004; 2008). In an age of vast media proliferation and audience fragmentation, audiences consistently renegotiate their conceptual schemas to stabilize increasingly volatile genre definitions of factual programming on television. In this regard, *TDS* has elevated its status quite quickly.

It is hard to point to a specific moment when Stewart established his imprint on *The Daily Show*, and equally difficult trying to assess its transformation from cult to critically acclaimed status. However, the win of a Peabody award for its 2000 US Presidential coverage could certainly be considered one of the stepping stones. Popular acceptance was soon to follow. By 2003, the audience for *TDS* had nearly doubled under Stewart,[4] from 427,000 in 1999, to 788,000 (Bauer, 2003). That same year the Television Critics Association named *The Daily Show* its winner for 'Outstanding Achievement in News and Information', beating such notable shows as *60 Minutes* and *Nightline* (TCA, 2007). The two previous and following years, the award was given to PBS's *Frontline*. During the Iowa and New Hampshire primaries of 2004, *The Daily Show* drew more viewers among the 18–34 male age bracket than any of the nightly network broadcasts (AP, 2004). By 2005, Stewart was averaging 1.4 million viewers per evening (Goetz, 2005) while winning another Peabody for the show's 'Indecision 2004' election coverage. As an increasingly popular source of election coverage, mid-term reporting by *The Daily Show* in 2006 drew just shy of 2 million viewers per evening (Fitzgerald, 2006). As the stature and status of the program rose and rose, a slogan on its website became less and less ironic: '*The Daily Show* with Jon Stewart – it's even better than being informed' (Comedy Central, 2007).

Yet such popularity is only one part of the calculus that warrants its study. Noteworthy to many of the academics who began to study the influence of *The Daily Show* in the mid-2000s was the suggestion, highlighted by a Pew Research poll of news consumption in 2004, that it was being viewed not just as entertainment but as a valid source of news. While the ability of the show to inform and instruct is belittled on its official website, which states: 'If you're tired of the stodginess of the evening newscasts, if you can't bear to sit through the spinmeisters and shills on the 24-hour cable news networks, don't miss *The Daily Show* with Jon Stewart, a nightly half-hour series unburdened by objectivity, journalistic integrity or even accuracy' (Comedy Central, 2007), this contention of frivolousness is significantly undermined by the critical and academic acclaim for the programme, the perception of its audience, and the eagerness with which Stewart enters into public debate about the appropriate role of journalism. Since Stewart took over the show in 1999, an increasing number of prominent politicians and public intellectuals have begun to traverse the interview desk, critical acclaim has continued to build, audiences have started to classify it as news, and academics have begun to interrogate the effect of *The Daily Show* as journalism (see Baym, 2005; Baumgartner and Morris, 2006; Young and Tisinger, 2006; Fox et al., 2007).

It is curious what, if anything, we can make of this ascendancy in terms of the increasing impetus among journalists and journalism studies scholars to regularly evaluate the 'State of the News Media'.[5] Satirical news, and *The Daily Show* in particular, may not quite be a cause célèbre in the midst of this debate, but it does raise questions about the purpose of news, the shifting media environment, the changing demographics of journalistic consumption, and the efficacy of conventional news styles in generating audience interest and involvement. What it seems safe to say is that *TDS* is not only an emerging form of journalism, often acting as a substitute or augment of traditional news for its viewers, but a forum where the metanarratives of journalism are frequently discussed, providing young adults with an unexpected avenue for media literacy.

In 2004, the aforementioned – and oft-cited – Pew Research Center poll on preferences of news audiences was released. It found that 21 per cent of 18–29 year olds cited comedy television as the resource through which they 'regularly learned' about the US presidential campaign. Only 23 per cent mentioned the traditional network newscasts, a shift from 9 and 39 per cent, respectively, in 2000 (Pew, 2004). In particular, *The Daily Show* was noted by many respondents as a primary example of this move away from traditional sources. Media outlets quickly picked up on the results and ran articles questioning what this meant for journalism, an impetus to self-reflection. This study also foretold the rise of academic investigation into the programme.[6]

The commonality between the journalistic and academic fields was that in both, the 21 per cent statistic from the Pew poll was ubiquitous. That interpretation of the results was a bit misleading did not stop a popular myth forming around young viewers and their preference for consuming 'fake' news (Jones, 2010). The survey provided a rationale for media observers to ask a fundamental question about the programme, a question which has been re-asked and re-adapted in many guises since. Simply put, people wanted to know: Is this news? This became the principle emphasis in academic discussions of *TDS*, which tended to focus on its news value or its degree of similarity with journalism.

From a political standpoint, *The Daily Show* stands firmly at the crossroads of debates over the politicization of entertainment and the stylization of news and politics (e.g. Corner and Pels, 2003; Van Zoonen, 2005; Riegert, 2007). Much academic work which focuses specifically on *The Daily Show* investigates the programme in this light, discussing its impact on political engagement and attitudes towards the political process. One such case was a forum held during the National Communication Association's annual conference in 2006, which interrogated the claim by Hart and

Hartelius (2007) that Stewart's cynical approach to discuss politics was a threat to democracy, resulting in mistrust and antipathy. Similar arguments have been made by Bennett (2007) and Baumgartner and Morris (2006), though Bennett argues that the context and the intended audience of the programme may mitigate this effect. The opposite position is pursued by authors such as Hariman (2007), who asserts that Stewart's comedic yet cynical take illustrates the equivalency between the average citizen and politicians, promoting re-engagement.

Another prominent academic thrust is to consider *The Daily Show* vis-à-vis traditional news sources and, through content analysis, to attempt to judge whether its coverage is comparable. Authors such as Fox et al. (2007) and Brewer and Marquardt (2007) conduct such studies, finding a reasonably similar level of 'serious' content. To sum, the majority of content-based studies are focused on answering the question: does this do as traditional news does?

The other primary thrust of academic work is to consider the media criticism aspect of the programme. For instance, Feldman (2007: 407) takes a look at the broader popularization of *The Daily Show* and considers how industry discourse about the programme's media criticism allows the journalism community to examine its own practices. Borden and Tew (2007) make an argument that parallels this, noting that Stewart and Stephen Colbert are better viewed as media critics rather than journalists.

Of course, *The Daily Show* is both news substitute and news criticism. It can be conceptualized as 'faux' news (Peters, 2009: 216); *faux*, in this usage, having a different sense than its direct English translation of 'false', as we see in terms such as *faux* fur or *faux* leather (an imitation based on a dissatisfaction with the killing of animals); or in the sense of a painting in the trompe l'oeil style (a *faux* front which blurs the real and its representation); or in the sense of *faux amis* in foreign languages (words which look similar but have very different meanings). The rise of *TDS* as a mainstay of television comedy must accordingly be evaluated in terms of this critical component. The show acts as a discursive point of resistance to mainstream rationales of knowledge and power (cf. Foucault, 1980), specifically, its gaze seems focused upon deconstructing the 'staged' aspects of political and journalistic performance (see Corner and Pels, 2003). Jones and Baym (2010: 281f) push this analysis in a slightly different direction, conceptualizing *TDS* not just as the zenith of news and entertainment blurring, but as a 'neo-modern approach to public affairs' that pursues modernist questions of truth and accountability in a postmodern format; a form of contemporary political talk with greater 'authenticity' than its cable-news equivalents. The remainder of this chapter adopts a similar logic to interrogate how *TDS* goes beyond being just 'newsy' content for its audience. By looking to its function with reference to the news media, what becomes apparent is that *TDS* acts as a form of public pedagogy at a time when core news values appear tenuous and hard to sustain (see Henry, 2008; McChesney and Nichols, 2010). The idea of pedagogy implies an underlying premise that it is not enough to just look at the content of *TDS*; one needs to infer what epistemological 'work' its viewers – or perhaps more appropriately fans – are expected do with its lessons.

Media literacy and *The Daily Show*

At a time when news organizations are fretting about declining consumption and the disappearance of young viewers, *TDS* seems to provide evidence that there is still implicit value, status, and appetite amongst younger generations for news values that dovetail with the modernist goals of twentieth-century objectivity. Costera Meijer (2007) notes that young people still hold the promise of professional journalism sacrosanct, use its conventions to readily distinguish between quality and trivial coverage, and report that watching 'real' news (if only occasionally) gives them a feeling of doing something productive. They may find themselves more engaged by alternative forms of news, but they don't want this to come at the expense of journalism's core ideals. Although journalism in the twenty-first century appears subject to a trend in reflexive modernity whereby institutions begin to encourage an appearance of involvement with their audiences/clients (see Giddens, 1994), studies like these, or the response to *The Daily Show*'s popular indictment of cable news, seem to indicate that there is a 'tipping point' whereby excessive interaction or dramatization comes to be seen as violating the journalism industry's fundamental mandate.

Of course, this is not a challenge exclusive to journalism. In law, taking a victim's mental anguish into account has become standard practice in recent years, but it is assumed this should not come at the expense of justice. In medicine, allowing patient involvement in selecting treatment is de rigueur, but it is assumed this should not come at the expense of health. In journalism, involvement on behalf of the journalist may have become commonplace, but not at the expense of truth. Put otherwise, much of what passes for communication on cable news is concerned with generating affect and response, rather than engaging in the pursuit of 'truthful' communication, which is a misplaced embrace of subjectivity. What is witnessed on *The Daily Show* is an apparent attempt to redress the imbalance between involvement and truth-claims that is evident on cable news. As Stewart noted in his closing address at the Rally to Restore Sanity (2010b),

> We live now in hard times, not end times. And we can have animus, and not be enemies. But unfortunately, one of our main tools in delineating the two broke. The country's 24-hour, poltico-pundit perpetual panic 'conflictinator' did not cause our problems, but its existence makes solving them that much harder. The press can hold its magnifying glass up to our problems, bringing them into focus, illuminating issues heretofore unseen. Or they can use that magnifying glass to light ants on fire, and then perhaps host a week of shows on the 'dangerous, unexpected flaming-ants epidemic!' If we amplify everything, we hear nothing.

As Stewart deconstructs the techniques of Fox News, CNN, MSNBC, and CNBC on a nightly basis, what is surprising is that by displaying cable news' foibles and faux pas, *TDS* finds a receptive audience who appear to yearn for 'authentic' displays of truth in a more 'reflexive' age (Jones, 2010). The ascendency of cable news and *TDS* dovetails, and much of the latter is based upon a critique of the former.

Learning about cable news

When one browses the top video clips of *The Daily Show* in its online library, what immediately strikes one is how often these are tagged with keywords such as 'cable news', 'media', 'pundits', and so forth. Of those clips viewed more than 1,000,000 times (15 clips in total), 13 take cable news as their primary focus.[7] The other two emphasize politics, more in the vein of 'traditional' satire.[8] If one expands the search to consider all clips with 100,000 or more views, Fox News and various Fox News personalities are, unsurprisingly, the most prominent target, although CNN, CNBC (especially a much-watched interview with Jim Cramer), and MSNBC also figure prominently. Of the 340 clips tagged as 'Fox News' in the *TDS* video archive, 101 of these have been viewed 100,000 times or more.[9]

The primary techniques to establish discourses on cable news on *TDS* are redaction (combining and juxtaposing various clips to demonstrate inconsistency, change of position, and so forth), host-based parody (impersonating the mannerisms or interpreting the thoughts of various hosts), reportage-based parody (field pieces that imitate cable-news techniques), and interview (direct questioning and engagement with cable-news personalities). With these approaches, Stewart crafts three overlapping discourses that serve as lessons about the practices and ethos of cable news.

A *discourse of hypocrisy* is the dominant formulation that *TDS* crafts surrounding Fox News, and is rarely formed around the other major networks. Simply put, hypocrisy points out those instances when the positions of various hosts – who take avowed positions in their programming about social issues – are suddenly reversed, or demonstrate inconsistency. Typically, this is done through redaction, counterpoising the previous declarations of hosts against their current stances, something which has become increasingly commonplace since the change in Presidential administrations in 2008. *TDS*'s redactions point to coverage that is based not around finding truth from facts, but about shaping facts to fit one's truth. Accordingly it reinforces lessons on foundational aspects of the journalistic mandate: neutrality, factuality, honesty, and integrity.

A *discourse of disingenuousness* is a second clear articulation crafted by Stewart in his treatment of cable news, and encompasses all major cable networks in its critique. Disingenuousness points to the disconnect between the stated journalistic aims of the networks and their actual performance. From seemingly manufactured, faux outrage on Fox, to fawning, rather than hard-hitting, financial journalism on CNBC, to CNN's soft-news techniques despite its hard-news posture, Stewart demonstrates for *Daily Show* audiences that the stated promises of cable news are not being delivered. In essence, a discourse of disingenuousness makes the claim that cable-news networks are treating audiences condescendingly. In terms of the current debates on the news industry, these lessons impart to audiences what the rightful expectations of journalistic conduct should be in a commercial landscape.

One last discourse worth mentioning is that of *superficiality*. Much like disingenuousness, superficiality points to a patronising treatment of audiences on behalf of journalists. By showing explicit cases of infotainment, inane 'happy talk' and banter, token implementation of audience interaction and similar actions, Stewart points out the lack of serious content or lack of serious engagement on behalf of the cable networks. While only a small subset of the video clips on *TDS*, these redactions make visible many of the criticisms often formed under the rubric of infotainment.

Reaffirming the core goals of journalism

For some time, there has been speculation that presentation is beginning to outstrip content in the so-called 'serious' press; the result being a merging of the supposed bifurcation of the serious from the popular within journalism (see Franklin, 1997; Kovach and Rosenstiel, 1999; Delli Carpini and Williams, 2001). The irony of this, with respect to *The Daily Show*, is that despite ostensibly exemplifying this trend, the show appears quite cynical towards such a development vis-à-vis professional journalism. The target of its discontent, cable news, is a sphere where the 'blurring' of news with entertainment is often unmistakable. And when we take a closer look at *The Daily Show*, and its treatment of cable news, what becomes strikingly evident is its promotion of a classically modernist stance on the purpose of the press. As audiences become savvier to media techniques, what stands out about *TDS* is how it tries to (re)assert ethical norms into the public discourse on the purpose of the journalism. Stewart not only critiques cable news, he attempts to teach his audience how to think about journalism.

Based upon their ubiquity and audience response, it is reasonable to say that the deconstruction of cable news is the signature dish of *The Daily Show*. Yet the recipe borrows from a set of ingredients passed down from the modernist hallmarks of 'traditional' journalism (Hallin, 1992). Stewart does not directly compare and contrast cable news to the hallmarks of professionalism, such as the *CBS Evening News* under Cronkite, nor does he contrast their reports to the most robust examples of investigative journalism, such as Watergate. Instead he relies upon the strength, stability and resilience of fourth-estate-type discourses on the purpose of news, and utilizes this invisible – but not absent – formation to put forth a coherent critique. There are possible ancillary effects, beyond entertainment, that come from *TDS* relentlessly underscoring the tension between cable news' claims to integrity and its everyday performance. While it is perhaps unsurprising that journalistic outlets and news blogs take great interest in Stewart's deconstructions of the cable-news industry (journalism has long been, as Zelizer (1993b) notes, its own interpretive community) the fact that online clips of these redactions can draw millions of views after their original broadcast means that many young people are devoting significant time, perhaps unwittingly, to developing a critical lens to view this sector of the news industry.

Amidst a shifting journalistic field, a critical form of news satire – as we get with 'faux' newscaster Stewart on *The Daily Show* or the 'truthy' news pundit Stephen Colbert on *The Colbert Report* – is not just an alternative avenue for reasoning with the facts of the day. It is also a form of media pedagogy that outlines the inappropriateness of much current journalism. These programmes, which appeal to a young demographic apparently disaffected with the news (Minditch, 2005), implicitly assert how press coverage *should be*. In effect, what the redactions, parodies, and interviews on *TDS* create is a fairly clear articulation about cable news; an avowedly normative discourse which characterizes these outlets through their opposition to 'proper' journalism. More specifically, the redactions on *TDS* have the effect of summarizing the dispersion of techniques, statements, and perspectives which appear on Fox News, CNN, CNBC, and MSNBC to craft a discursive formation that situates the performative discourse of cable news within the broader journalistic field.

Moments when the actions of Stewart transcend his typical audience to engender a broader discussion on journalistic policy and performance, as when he went on *Crossfire* to criticize the format of political 'debate' on CNN;[10] or when he critiqued CNBC for their sycophantic reporting on the financial industry;[11] or when he held the Rally to Restore Sanity,[12] spread and potentially stabilize this discourse. When this is paired with the growing distrust many people have with journalism, what we witness is a concerted effort on *TDS* to (re)articulate the bifurcation between 'serious' and 'populist' news styles.

In effect, by clarifying the place of cable news within the journalistic register, *TDS* instructs its viewers on the democratic purpose of journalism in an age of fragmentation, proliferating styles, and waning public trust. Though faux news, *TDS*'s critique of cable news (re)confirms twentieth-century discourses that valorize gravitas, accountability, proportionality, consistency and journalistic rigour for a generation that was not alive when this 'objectivity regime' was at its zenith (Schudson, 2001; Ward, 2004). Through the enduring strength of this established myth of serious journalism, Stewart positions cable news as serious journalism's 'other'. If we expand upon the contentions of Jones and Baym (2010) above, that *TDS* is a neo-modern approach to public affairs, we could say that *The Daily Show* is programme that promotes modernist values, using a postmodern format, to act as both watchdog and educator on the 'amodern' practices of contemporary cable news.

What do news audiences want?

Journalists are taught to distrust what they are told, and think it's a good thing, yet seem deeply troubled when the public begins to distrust them. When this supposed loss of trust is amplified by economic cutbacks and uncertainty, the outlook by many is understandably bleak. As debate swirls around what journalism can do to staunch its 'crisis', media outlets have responded by experimenting with style, increasing access and involvement with audiences, and altering content. Many of these changes, at least in terms of their implementation by cable news, are often viewed with scepticism to outright scorn on *The Daily Show*.

Many journalistic organizations are quite muddled in the world they now find themselves in; a world where experience and expertise become synonymous, fact and opinion are muddied, and truthiness (validity determined by personal feelings of truth) comes to the fore. Van Zoonen (2012) summarizes these trends in public discourse under the notion of the rise of 'I'pistemology, wherein personal experience is offered up as incontrovertible justification of knowledge. When one considers this in conjunction with the financial pressures facing journalism, it seems quite reasonable cause for pessimism. This chapter has resisted this urge, arguing that *The Daily Show* can be viewed as a popular instance of a broader trend towards educating audiences (or citizens or consumers, depending on one's perspective) into the practices and conventions of mass media. The lessons it imparts re-emphasize laudable goals such as accuracy, proportionate coverage, and critical reportage at a time of 'crisis' in the industry.

The Daily Show is simultaneously an alternative source of news, a form of media criticism, and a populist 'module' on media literacy that promotes a modernist perspective on media awareness to a young audience that does not yet have a fixed relationship with journalism. It is an audience that, in all likelihood, experiences disillusionment with what Stewart shows them. However, it is an audience that is also being given information on much of the 'news' of the day while being taught how to 'read' media and how to 'know' journalism in parallel. In essence, *TDS* is an emerging form of news, but it's more than that; it represents a critical, cultural pedagogy about the fundamental ethics of journalism.

As Giroux (2000) notes, many acts of cultural work should be viewed as anchoring themselves on the premise of justice. In the case of *TDS*, the site of debate is over what a 'just' journalism should look like. Of course, it is not only Stewart who marshals this rhetoric, implicitly or explicitly, about what journalism should be. The cultural work which underlies the cable magazines that dominate Fox News and MSNBC also involves proffering claims of journalistic superiority (Peters, 2010). So how can audiences be expected to separate the wheat from the chaff if every outlet claims to be wheat? One hopes that as rates of media literacy improve in general, perhaps fewer news consumers will face a sort of 'anosognosic's dilemma' (Morris, 2010), wherein their unawareness of what constitutes 'quality' journalism – or, in this chapter's terms, news illiteracy – is so pronounced that they cannot even recognize that they are unaware.

This is not exactly a revolutionary pronouncement; growing audience awareness of the processes and conventions in other media industries, from entertainment to advertising, have resulted in more creative, transparent, interactive, and hypertextual media products appearing over the past few decades. And although hype and promotion can still give 'poorly' made products a chance, audiences seem remarkably savvy in terms of denigrating and dismissing the poorly reviewed film or television series while elevating and supporting the critically received. In this sense, much of the future of 'quality' journalism lies in the hands of audiences to not only recognize but to desire and demand thoroughly researched, civically relevant, critically acclaimed, news.

This probably means the news industry needs to adopt a bimodal strategy. The first aspect is to figure out some way to clearly distinguish high quality (not to be confused with elite), journalism products for different audiences. Every news organization marshals the discourse of quality under one guise or another nowadays – news you can trust, news you need, fair and balanced, and so forth – so it is the duty of reputable news organizations and journalists, probably as a collective, to promote actions or standards that make such 'superiority' visible; perhaps this means institutionalizing distinction in some manner so as to make it more perceptible for audiences. The second approach is to encourage support through indirect funding or complimentary financing. Journalism is already recognized as a public good in many countries – a foundation it would be wise to reinforce – but it could do a better job of promoting itself as a necessary public service like medicine, education, or academic research. If the industry could forge stronger partnerships and lobby more effectively for government and trust-based funding (say by applying for framework grants to produce children's news for use in schools), it might not be quite so exposed to the invisible but unforgiving hand of the market.

Notes

1 Photographic compilations can be found on various internet sites. These were selected from the *Huffington Post* at: http://www.huffingtonpost.com/2010/10/30/the-funniest-signs-at-the_n_776490.html.
2 An old maxim to aspiring journalists states: 'if your mother says she loves you, check it out.'
3 This understanding, borrowed from Bauman (2000: 123), is that 'the way learning is structured determines how individuals learn to think' (see also Deuze 2006d).
4 Jon Stewart replaced the former host of *The Daily Show*, Craig Kilborn, in 1999.
5 Foremost among these, at least in the United States, is the annual Project for Excellence in Journalism report of the same name. Within academia, international conferences with titles such as 'Future of Journalism' or 'Journalism Research in the Public Interest' are increasingly held.
6 In 2004, when the Pew survey was released, there were no peer-reviewed articles on the programme. A standard academic database search would only uncover a five-page political communication opinion article that mentioned *The Daily Show* in passing. At the end of 2006, when the *Daily Show* was incorporated into a research project I was conducting on emerging forms of broadcast news (Peters, 2009), three peer-review articles had appeared which took it as a primary focus. By 2011, this number had climbed to 41. (Figures confirmed by an EBSOhost search of peer-reviewed articles, with 'Daily Show' as keyword or in abstract, March 1, 2011.)
7 Search conducted at http://www.thedailyshow.com/videos on September 2, 2011.
8 It is fairly evident that we can speak of 'fake' news being or quickly becoming a recognized broadcast genre. A quick Wikipedia search indicates its international scope, with programmes being launched in Australia, Belgium, Canada, Chile, France, Germany, Israel, the Philippines, Portugal, Russia, Slovenia, Spain, Sweden, Turkey, the UK and US in recent years. While this is mere speculation, I assume that, unlike *The Daily Show* and *The Colbert Report*, many programmes take as their primary point of departure the satirizing of current events and politics, as opposed to satirizing the *news media's coverage of these events*. However, the performative style of traditional newscasts is often utilized in such programmes for comedic effect (e.g. mock gravitas).
9 Survey conducted on March 1, 2011.
10 A clip of the exchange can be found at: http://www.youtube.com/watch?v=aFQFB5YpDZE. As of July 3, 2011, this clip had been viewed 3,842,507 times.
11 This clip, available at: http://www.thedailyshow.com/watch/wed-march-4-2009/cnbc-financial-advice, is the second-most viewed clip ever on the official *TDS* website, with 2,097,143 views as of July 3, 2011.
12 A Google search for 'Rally to Restore Sanity' returns 4,390,000 hits, as of July 3, 2011.

Part IV
Rethinking journalism rethought

13

WOULD JOURNALISM PLEASE HOLD STILL!

Michael Schudson

Why did we ever imagine that we knew what journalism is? Why do so many people speak as if there was this Thing called Journalism that has only recently been called into question? A volume of papers devoted to 'rethinking journalism' understandably assumes that this is an especially appropriate moment for reconsideration, that journalism stands at a time of epochal change, and that there are grounds for concern that some of the elements of change do not bode well for journalism or for some valued features of society and politics that journalism is said to support – notably, democracy. I agree with these premises, but I worry that they may seem to imply that we know what journalism was, at least up until yesterday or the day before yesterday.

It was as recently as 2005 that Svennik Hoyer and Horst Pottker put together their useful book, *The Diffusion of the News Paradigm*. Their contributors (including me) wrote about the establishment, first in the United States, of 'the news paradigm' that during the past century spread to Europe and has been accepted as the leading model of how professional journalists should report the news. The diffusion of this news paradigm is what Marcel Broersma calls in his paper for this volume the 'long-term project of professionalization', and he borrows from Hoyer and Pottker the notion of a journalistic 'paradigm.' For Hoyer, that paradigm consists of the central use of interviewing as a news-gathering technique, the use of an inverted-pyramid presentational structure in news stories, and the premise of 'objectivity' as the reporter's moral and literary stance. (Hoyer and Nonseid, 2005: 124) The acceptance of this model in European journalism was slow and uneven: 'Gradual developments over several decades seem to be the normal conditions in news journalism' Hoyer and Nonseid (2005: 11, 134) concluded in their chapter on Norway. Slow, uneven, but in the end triumphant.

Hoyer and Nonseid report on a Swedish study by Inger Lindstedt in which she examines Swedish news textbooks from 1917 to 1996 and finds the texts rejecting this news paradigm before the Second World War. They referred to the inverted-pyramid presentation of news as 'American' as late as 1953. By 1981 it was called either 'international' or even, by then, 'traditional.' In less than thirty years, 'American' had become 'traditional' and 'the news paradigm' had taken on the air of inevitability that 'traditional' signifies (Hoyer and Nonseid, 2005: 135).

In an important paper, 'Visual Strategies: Dutch Newspaper Design Between Text and Image 1900–2000,' Marcel Broersma focuses on the changing visual look of the Dutch newspaper front page from 1900 to 2000. In the beginning, the leading Dutch newspapers were arranged in what Broersma calls a 'vertical' format. The pages were nothing but grey – no illustrations, no photographs, nothing one could really call a headline. The first story began at the top of the left-hand column. If it finished mid-column, a short line would separate it from the next story that followed in the same column. Perhaps that story ran about two columns. It would go from the lower half of column one up to the top of column two, down to the bottom, up to the top of column three and finish somewhere in the middle of that column. The next story, after a short line, would then begin in the lower portion of column three. And so forth.

What's missing from this? Nothing much – just editors and readers! No one was exercising any sort of editorial judgment and no one was making any effort to market the news to readers. The front page that became familiar to American readers in the last decades of the nineteenth century and British readers by about 1920 was unknown to Dutch newspaper consumers for decades thereafter. The Anglo-American front-page distinguishes more important from less important stories by page place-ment, headline font size, number of columns the headline spans, sidebars, and so forth. This marks the significance of the item, in the eyes of the editors, and offers guideposts to readers about what they are likely to find most important, interesting and gripping to read. It is a visual mapping of journalistic news values.

The Dutch newspapers increasingly adopted these Anglo-American conventions only after 1945. And then Broersma offers a riveting sentence: 'Journalists were no longer expected merely to record happenings but to extract the news from an event.' He adds, 'Readers were no longer left to draw their own conclusions; the journalist now told them what the most important information was' (Broersma, 2007b: 187). The Dutch can be said to have invented journalism in the West. The Dutch 'coranto' was the root form of journalism in the 1600s. Dutch newspapers were by no means isolated or provincial. But Dutch journalists did not presume to tell readers what the most important information was; until at least 1945 they typically offered a chronicle of events without extracting the news from it. In the original home of newspaper journalism, not until after 1945 was there anything that *looked* like what we have come to accept as modern journalism.

The recency of recognizably contemporary journalism can be seen also in Britain, where there was nothing that *read* like modern journalism until about 1920. This is the persuasive argument of Donald Matheson's study of British news discourse – as he puts it, the birth of news discourse in Britain, between 1880 and 1930. It is not, in his view, that there was no such thing as news in newspapers in 1880. There were newspapers. There were even reporters. But the model of what a newspaper did in

1880 was that it served as 'a collection of raw information' and what it typically had become by 1930 is 'a form of knowledge in itself, not dependent on other discourses to be able to make statements about the world' (Matheson, 2000: 559). The Victorian newspaper was 'a medley of various public styles, voices and types of text' in the late nineteenth century. It is not until around 1920 that one can recognize that 'a journalistic discourse has emerged, which allows the news to subsume these various voices under a universal, standard voice' (Matheson, 2000: 564).

Both Broersma on the visuality of the front page (in the Netherlands) and Matheson on the verbal discourse of the front page (in Britain) locate the emergence of our contemporary sort of journalism in the twentieth century and not before. And this is not, it seems to me, just a matter of changing fashion in artistic or literary presentation. We can see vast changes in formal style in, say, the novel over the past several centuries, but one has little doubt that Charles Dickens in the 1850s and F. Scott Fitzgerald in the 1920s and John Updike in 2000, or Jane Austen in the 1820s and Virginia Woolf in the early 1900s and Margaret Atwood today could all plausibly, in one's imagination, have sat together on the same television talk show to discuss 'the novel' and they would have understood one another as engaged in essentially the same project. This seems much less likely – basically impossible – with journalists of 1820 and 1850 and journalists of 1920 and 1950 and today. The journalism that we know – despite its many variations and the sometimes radical changes it is undergoing today online – understands that it is offering some sort of knowledge in itself, however vaguely defined it may be.

Somewhere between roughly 1920 and roughly 1950 the voice of contemporary journalism took hold. The Americans may claim credit for having got there a touch earlier with the technique of interviewing giving shape to US journalism by the 1880s and 1890s and the summary lead and inverted pyramid form offering a common vantage for asserting the authority of journalistic discourse by around 1910. But nineteenth-century American journalism, until the last two decades of the nineteenth century, was frequently quite a lot like the 'Victorian' journalism that Matheson describes as dominating the entire Victorian era in Britain.

Much is changing today, and changing quickly, but it is not changing from a settled, static set of practices. That already happened, inside the news paradigm, particularly in the 1970s. In the United States, this was provoked by the Vietnam war and capped by Watergate, but it was also encouraged by a huge expansion of higher education and the centrality there of a 'critical' or even 'adversary' culture, and a broad rebellion – around the world – against 'the Establishment.' Journalism became less comfortable with its role as part of the Establishment and began to identify less with a political insider status that had begun to be embarrassing, and more with its outsider 'watchdog' role. When media scholar Daniel Hallin coined the phrase 'high modernism' to name the period of American journalism ascendant from the Second World War to the early years of the Vietnam war, what caught his eye, in an interview with the well-known war correspondent Peter Arnett – who staunchly defended an unbending allegiance to objective reporting – was 'the absence of a sense of doubt or contradiction' (Hallin, 1994: 170).

That self-assurance has never entirely disappeared. Professionalism as a set of values is still more often sworn by than sworn at in leading news organizations and certainly in the halls of journalism schools. But it nonetheless now incorporates assumptions about a dividing line between politicians and journalists that was much less true in the 1950s and 1960s. Meg Greenfield, editorial page editor of the *Washington Post* in the 1970s, put this well in her memoir:

> We, especially some of us in the journalism business, were much too gullible and complaisant in the old days. Just as a matter of republican principle, the hushed, reverential behavior (Quiet! Policy is being made here!) had gotten out of hand. It encouraged public servants to believe that they could get away with anything – and they did.
>
> *(Greenfield, 2001: 89)*

Journalism at the national level became substantially more critical from the 1970s on, and while there are ebbs and flows of complacency still, the journalistic insouciance of the 1950s is irretrievable. The American case is not by any means unique, as a striking historical study of Swedish public broadcasting indicates (Djerf-Pierre and Weibull, 2008).

All this suggests that the recent radical changes in journalism, thanks to the new technologies of satellite and cable television and online news forms and converged multi-media newsrooms and the vast upheavals in 'business models' that have sustained most influential news organizations for most of the past century, is not a shift from a settled brand of journalism. At any rate, if it was settled, it was a settled practice, as the Swedish textbooks suggest, that came to be thought of as 'traditional' even though it was a mode of journalism established within living memory, and borrowed from American and British models.

Whether the current moment of transformation should be welcomed or deplored is something on which people may differ. Some authors in this volume display some pleasure in new departures in news while others show anxiety about it, maybe even foreboding, and some sense of loss. Co-editor Broersma (Ch 2) offers the most novel metaphor – of a journalistic paradigm 'continuously refractured,' whose repair has become 'more complicated, if not impossible,' and therefore can be said to suffer from 'a state of osteoporosis.' He suggests that journalism, its paradigm 'refractured over and over again,' has entered into 'a state of progressive degeneration in which the damage will not be curable any more.'

Professor Broersma invited me to contribute to this volume, anticipating that I might disagree with this, and he anticipated correctly. Of course, he knows that I am in some respects a completely typical American, unwilling to let go of optimism no matter how thin is the evidence by which I justify it. But in this case, my optimism is of a measured sort; it is not that I am convinced that the new journalistic environment is bound to produce great leaps forward in journalism – although, in truth, I think it has already done so – but that I do not think the 'journalistic paradigm' is of particularly long or lofty pedigree (as Broersma's own earlier paper helps establish), nor do I think we should expect it, or want it, to persist indefinitely into the future.

To return to my comparison to the novel, it would sadden me if I were convinced that the novel were a form of prose in a state of progressive degeneration. Novels past and present have enriched my life. Novels past and present have offered me a broad interpretive framework for thinking about character, about sensibility, about the subtleties of human encounters and emotions through which I have come directly or indirectly to understand myself and my own hopes for myself and my relationships with others. If the novel were dying, I think I would have to assume that my whole way of recognizing human experience were dying too. If I am told that the journalistic paradigm that has come to be regarded as traditional is dying, I would be losing a particular mode of quickly obtaining a sense of the flow of contemporary affairs, but I have already experienced at least three such transformations in my lifetime: from a more elite, establishment journalism to a more critical journalism in 1965–75; from a more homogeneous, middle-of-the-road, and deferential broadcast journalism to a more multi-channel, diverse, opinionated, and outspoken electronic journalism, with players as different as the conventional networks (National Public Radio, conservative talk radio, openly partisan Fox News and MSNBC on cable, CNN, and others) in the 1970s–1980s; and from a print- and television-focused journalism to a digital networked journalism, and not incidentally one all but continuous with a personal-computer-centred academic world, too. None of these developments have been without losses, but the gains have been very large and in the digital transformation, those gains are growing still. And with all of this, a commitment of serious journalists to independent truth-seeking, to verification, and to holding government accountable – the central value-orientations of the professional project in journalism – are upheld.

I think Hoyer was right to see a professionalizing trend over a century or so leading to a powerful and prevalent 'news paradigm.' Even if no news outlet ever fully subscribed to that paradigm, it *did* have pride of place in American journalism and, with certain variations, the journalism practices of Britain, Canada, northern Europe, and elsewhere. And Broersma (Ch 2) is right, too, to see that paradigm assaulted with the proliferation of alternative media outlets through satellite and cable television and the internet. What I do not see is osteoporosis. Osteoporosis suggests a brittle quality to journalism and what I think we are witnessing is – so far – just the opposite. The model should be not bones subject to repeated fracture but birch trees whose trunks in the storms of winter bend very far over without breaking.

I have no particular quarrel with the papers in this volume concerning 'public trust' but just about everything I have read about public trust has struck me for some years as dubious. The US data, at least, shows from the 1960s onwards a decline in trust in the President, the Congress, the medical profession, the military, the Supreme Court, business, unions, universities, and the news media. But most of the decline came in the first decade or so after the various 'trust' questions began to be asked. The era of the 1950s and early 1960s that is typically taken as the baseline came at a moment when American life was held together by Cold War fears, middle-class complacency, postwar affluence, and the denial of a voice in public life to women and minorities (Schudson, 1998: 302). When pollsters first asked the 'trust' questions, in other words, there was little social support for people who questioned authority. To question one's doctor or the President, the teacher of your ten-year-old child or the editor of your local newspaper was to announce oneself a troublemaker or a pest, not a discriminating consumer or appropriately sceptical citizen. That changed dramatically between 1965 and 1975 – and has not dipped very much further since then – the big drop came all at once. In these years dissent came to have social support not only from vocal and visible social movements but from rulings of the Supreme Court and the growing influence of an 'adversary culture' or a critical culture cultivated in universities and liberal arts colleges, a liberalizing trend in the churches and beyond. People did not lie to pollsters in the early 1960s – they simply were not in touch with their own doubts and worries about authoritative social institutions.

A second point is closely related: why assume that high levels of trust are good? College teachers, in my experience, are forever trying to decrease students' levels of trust! They should be more sceptical, more critical. They should learn that the authors of textbooks make mistakes and have points of view and they should learn to read critically enough to uncover the author's viewpoint and therefore be able to think through what might have been left out or slighted in the author's presentation. Yes, societies require people to have some basic level of trust in the good will and reliability of other people around them, to function at all – for traffic to flow, for strangers to congregate and behave in an orderly fashion on a train or in a queue at the supermarket checkout, or at a polling place on election day. But democracies also need people to have a level of distrust, too – to know that power tends to corrupt, that even our political favourites, once in office, grow too comfortable and absorb too quickly the insiders' viewpoint and quickly forget the constituents they represent (except, in the United States, those constituents with money who continue to 'vote' for their representatives with regular contributions even between elections). Democracies can erode from having levels of trust too high, as well as too low.

This notion is well developed here in Chris Peters' chapter on *The Daily Show*, suggesting that there are intimate relationships between the papers on public trust in Part I and the papers on 'emerging journalisms' in Part III. Peters (Ch 12) sees the data on decreasing levels of public trust in news not so much as a matter for alarm as an index of an epistemological shift – that people in recent years 'no longer view journalism just as an institutional provider of informational content, but as an epistemological performance or process of knowledge production as well (though probably not in these terms). As such, they increasingly learn to become critical consumers of the news they are provided.' And if they did not have that sense before becoming fans of *The Daily Show*, it does not take long for them to see that they are watching a show that is often far more scathing and exacting in its ridicule of the mainstream news media than of the politicians and other public figures that it takes on.

Political scientist John Hibbing argues that the decline in trust in Congress, among other institutions, has something to do with a general antipathy of ordinary people in this country to witnessing 'conflict, debate, deliberation, compromise, or any of the other features that are central to meaningful legislative activity in a polity that is open, democratic, heterogeneous, and technologically sophisticated' (Hibbing, 1999: 53). But democracies always have conflict. Why should Americans have become particularly frustrated with conflict in the mid-1960s to early 1970s? Because, Hibbing argues, 'it was only then that dissenting voices were heard and taken seriously – that people were made aware of the country's true diversity' (Hibbing, 1999: 60; see also Hibbing and Theiss-Morse, 2002). I think Hibbing has it about right, but we can go a little further. What the sixties taught many Americans and many others around the world was not just that the government cannot be trusted but that it is safe, perhaps admirable, and surely fashionable to say so. A question asked in 1966 about trust in government is not the same question, even if the words are identical, asked a decade later, or asked today in a more inclusive, more noisy, more irreverent society more comfortable with and more accustomed to open dissent – and therefore also more likely to offer an appreciative audience for 'fake news' shows and alternative journalisms of the sort Chris Atton (Ch 9) discusses in his contribution, and also a variety of user-generated content, as taken up in the papers in Part II of this work.

There is, in a sense, a tension between the anxiety about trust in the opening chapters of this volume and the measured but generally friendly embrace of new journalistic forms in a number of the papers in Parts II and III. My own sympathies, obviously, are with the more hopeful essays. Not that there are no grounds for scepticism, and one even longs for scepticism in the face of fashionable utopianisms that this volume stays free of.

Sometimes utopianism is hard to resist. I am struck over and over again by how good some bloggers are, simultaneously expert and entertaining. I am impressed, usually several times a week, with just how good Wikipedia is. One can point to 'crowd sourcing' efforts in gathering knowledge going back a century – in the United States, the field of ornithology has relied on an annual bird census that draws on thousands of bird watchers who volunteer to count birds in a given time and place and send their results on to the Audubon Society. Still, there is no getting around the fact that comparable activities are everywhere today – in social science, in the humanities, in journalism, in investigative reporting. It is hard to ignore the power of digital cameras and cell-phone cameras in documenting our world and occasionally changing it, or the influence of new communicative forms whose age is not yet in double digits – YouTube or Wikipedia, Craigslist or the mind-bogglingly efficient search engines. It is also hard to ignore the inventiveness of some traditional news organizations in blending new media and old, and in learning to enlist their audiences in research, as several of the chapters on participatory forms of journalism observe. Not only do reporters themselves blog on the websites of their own news organizations but they benefit from reading blogs – and they say so. As I am completing this essay, a front-page story in the *New York Times* on a federal judge's refusal to accept a settlement agreement between the Securities and Exchange Commission and Citigroup, cited expert opinion from a securities law professor whom the paper identified as a 'professor at the University of Cincinnati College of Law who edits the Securities Law Prof Blog' (Wyatt, 2011: 1, 4).

There is one example I have not stopped thinking about since learning of it. In 2008, I read an obituary in the *New York Times* for Doris Dungey. And what led the *Times* to devote some of its precious print space to a death notice for Ms Dungey? She was a middle-aged blogger in Ohio – there are millions of bloggers, so why her? Because this woman with a college degree in literature worked in the mortgage banking business for twenty years and began blogging (on the blog 'CalculatedRisk' run by Bill McBride) with such skill and verve that she attracted the attention of economists of considerable note, not least of them Nobel Prize economist and *New York Times* columnist Paul Krugman. He cited her in his column. Others, less expert, just liked reading her. One grateful reader wrote after her death, 'I didn't even care about mortgages when I stumbled across her writing, and to tell you the truth, the only reason I care now was because it gave me a chance to read her writing' (Calculated Risk Blog, 2008).

I am enough of a believer in the 'news paradigm' and in professional values and in the substantial financial investment it often requires to support time-consuming, painstaking, and possibly lawyered journalism (the lawyers either to assist in Freedom of Information Act requests and sometimes subsequent litigation or to help in vetting draft stories to prevent successful and damaging libel lawsuits against the news organization) to be wary of any presumption that user-generated content or independent blogs or news dissemination by social media or any of the growing number of other remarkable and absorbing new developments in journalism or all of them together can, will, or should displace the likes of the *New York Times* from its perch of prominence. But I find the blends and hybrids of journalistic coverage and commentary exciting and energizing, not the heralds of apocalypse.

One of Tamara Witschge's (Ch 11) articulate interviewees, a senior journalist at BBC online, worries that the site may 'lose that original journalism thing,' that is, that in the frenzy of the new multi-media newsroom, journalists may fail to hold foremost the work of providing 'original journalism,' doing the primary reporting on which all the rest of the chattersphere lives. Many of the papers here share that reporter's concern. Able and ambitious social theorists of our day encourage these concerns when they describe societies moving from one kind of world to another – Ansgard Heinrich (Ch 6) cites Ulrich Beck's claim that we have moved from a globe of territorial states to an interconnected 'world society', and cites also Manuel Castells' suggestion that the 'network' is the fundamental organizing principle of social life today, and not the forms of hierarchy that have dominated for such a long time. Heinrich then concludes that a new journalistic model – 'network journalism' – is a work paradigm for 'the global news exchange sphere that has superseded the traditional media system.' This rightly calls attention to the fact that, from the reporter's desk, where he or she has instant access to the output of nearly any news organization around the world that maintains a website, it is an absolutely earthshaking transformation of what resources can be assembled in putting a story together.

And yet. And yet 'supersede' is a bolder word than I would be prepared to use. Extended? Augmented? Challenged? Refigured? In 2011, most people in Europe and the United States, the primary sites of study in this volume, got their news from television. Much of television gets its news from wire services, newspapers, and online sources – most of them also produced by newspaper and news weekly organizations and television websites. Television in part 'superseded' print, but in large part lived off the intellectual capital and reportorial investment that print made available.

A great deal has happened in journalism in the past decade and a great deal is yet to happen. As these changes transpire, journalists who identify with 'the news paradigm' will inevitably feel under assault, both their livelihoods and their professional ideals at risk. But the news paradigm, for all of its importance, and professionalization, for all of its virtues, has never held the field by itself. In my own estimation, it is not yet an endangered species, and is not likely to be any time soon. But it now jousts with new and revived forms (Joseph Addison in *The Spectator* of 1710 was essentially a blogger) of commentary on contemporary life. And 'jousts' is not quite right. The original reporting that is at risk as newspapers lose readers and newsrooms shed jobs feeds the rest of the new forms of journalism, but it is also fed by them. WikiLeaks, for reasons of its own, brought together major news organizations for a cooperative publishing venture; rival news operations across the United States are in the throes of economic stress and the affordances of new technologies cooperating with one another when such behaviour would not long ago have been anathema. Online nonprofits like ProPublica, the best funded and best known, give away to traditional newspapers the products of their investigative reporting. There are now some more than 60 member organizations of the 'Investigative News Network' that was established in 2009 – they do not make up for the loss of some 20,000 newspaper newsroom jobs in the past decade. Still, these mostly small and scrappy organizations are dedicated primarily to investigative reporting or 'accountability journalism,' as most conventional newsrooms are not. They are finding ways to make the best of new technologies and new opportunities without giving up the professional dedication that has sometimes, over the long century of its emergence, made journalism worth our highest regard.

14

JOURNALISM, PARTICIPATIVE MEDIA AND TRUST IN A COMPARATIVE CONTEXT

Thomas Hanitzsch

Journalism is in transition, there is no question about it. The online environment has substantially shaken up long-held beliefs about the nature of news and over-pampered practices of journalism, even to the extent that the future of professional news-making has become a matter of concern. Crisis narratives are thriving in the literature, with some scholars already proclaiming the 'death' or 'end' of journalism (McChesney and Nichols, 2010; Charles and Stewart, 2011). Deuze (2006a: 2) has called journalism a 'zombie institution', and the University of Bedfordshire devoted an entire conference to 'The End of Journalism?' in 2008. In this volume, too, McNair (Ch 5) diagnoses an 'existential crisis' of journalism, while he concedes that new communication technologies do not necessarily reduce the need for professional journalism but actually enhance them. All these contributions clearly seem to suggest that journalism as we know it is in search of a redefinition of its purpose and social contract, as well as a reconstitution of its boundaries, which have become alarmingly fuzzy with the rise of participatory modes of communication.

At the same time, practitioners, observers and scholars have noted startling signs of declining public trust in the media. Brants (Ch 1) notes in this volume that trust in media is seen as the 'life blood of journalism's role in and contribution to people's sense making'. In a world of shrinking confidence in the media, it seems, journalism is pushing itself to the margins of public debate. After the evaporation of public trust in political actors, along with a growing sense of cynicism expressed by the larger public, we now seem to witness a collapse of public confidence in journalism's capacity to act in the public interest. This chapter aims to interrogate these observations from a cross-national and comparative perspective.

The institution of journalism

Cook (1998: 70), in his influential book *Governing with the News*, defines institutions as 'social patterns of behaviour identifiable across the organizations that are generally seen within a society to preside over a particular social sphere.' In this view, journalism may not be a full-fledged profession but can be considered a social institution. Cook further argues that the news media fulfil all three criteria that are essential to institutions in accordance to the new institutionalism approach he advocates: journalism's practices are based on distinctive roles, routines, rules, and procedures; these practices endured over time and extend across news organizations; and the news media are viewed by journalists, as well as by others, as presiding over a given part of social life. Sparrow (1999) has advanced similar ideas, conceptualizing the news media as an institution that stands for a public good and serves in the role of a guardian of a democratic political system.

People may disagree over their expectations on journalism, or on the media writ large, within and across societies. There is indeed bold comparative evidence attesting to the differential normative functions and performative roles of journalism in different national settings in accordance to journalism's social contract (Weaver, 1998; Hanitzsch et al., 2011). Clearly, the contingent contextual conditions in which the news media operate have produced a considerable variety of trajectories and traditions of journalistic cultures (Hallin and Mancini, 2004).

Yet one can identify a fundamental understanding of the social functions, professional worldviews, and everyday practices of journalism that is widely shared among the members of the profession around the world. At the core of this 'professional ideology' are many traditionally held values, sometimes also referred to as 'elements of journalism': Accordingly, journalism is primarily oriented toward the factual, provides timely and relevant information, and requires intellectual autonomy and independence. Furthermore, it is a professional service to the public that is usually carried out in organized contexts (Kovach and Rosenstiel, 2001; Deuze, 2005; Hanitzsch, 2007).

The various authors in this book have made similar observations. For one, despite the manifold challenges posed by participative modes of communication in the internet, it is remarkable that most contributors to this volume still adhere to the notion of journalism as a profession, or at least as some sort of professional undertaking. Bogaerts and Carpenter (Ch 4), for instance, point to a number of 'core nodal points' of journalism's professional ideology, including public service, ethics, management, autonomy, membership of a professional elite, immediacy and objectivity. Even though different journalistic traditions, communities and cultures will articulate these elements differently, they remain crucial building blocks for a professional identity. The journalists interviewed by Witschge (Ch 11) continually referred to the public-service ideal of journalism, regardless of whether they worked for online or offline media. Broersma (Ch 2) puts the news media's claim to truth at the core of the journalistic paradigm; and Porlezza and Russ-Mohl (Ch 3) emphasize the centrality of accuracy in reporting.

The cross-national *Worlds of Journalism Study* has provided comparative evidence in support of such claims. From the qualitative responses of 2,000 journalists from 20 countries, we found the concepts of objectivity, accuracy and truth to be at the core of a shared normative understanding of professional ethics among journalists from around the world (Hanitzsch, Plaisance and Skewes, 2012). It turned out that even though these norms may often be difficult to achieve in practice, they are important elements of the global imaginary of 'good' journalism. These tenets are thriving in journalism textbooks; they are taught in journalism schools; and they constitute key elements of many, if not most, professional codes of conduct. As such, these values clearly drive journalism's 'occupational ideology' (Golding and Elliott, 1979: 115) and 'instrumental myth' (Sigelman, 1973: 133); and as professional narratives about the past they populate the collectively shared memory of journalists.

Broersma is absolutely right when he argues that 'the journalistic paradigm is continuously refractured' (Ch 2). However, his claim that this puts journalism into 'a state of osteoporosis' is too much doomsaying. The institution of journalism is constantly under pressure to adjust to a changing environment, and considering its history makes us realize that it has always been this way. It goes without saying that such a transition does often necessitate a correction in journalism's formulae, but this does not necessarily herald the end of professional news media. In fact, it demonstrates journalism's flexibility to respond to its transforming social contexts. But even in a time of an ongoing and partly fundamental reconstitution of public and private communication, to which the internet has contributed in many substantial ways, the essence of journalism has remained remarkably robust over time.

This robustness is not a symptom of the news media's resistance to change, but it indicates that even in the age of the internet, journalism's social contract has not expired. There is still a widely shared consensus on the vital role that the institution of journalism plays in democratic societies, as McNair (Ch 5) and Heinrich (Ch 6) note. Journalists may not be the gatekeepers they once used to be, but resemble more a kind of public gatewatcher (Bruns, 2005). In a world where information is available in abundance to almost everyone, the institution of journalism may have lost its authority to act in the exclusive capacity of a producer of knowledge (Broersma, Ch 2). Instead, journalism of the postmodern has turned into an organizer and verifier of knowledge, as well as a provider of orientation in an increasingly multi-optional society. As a consequence, professional journalism remains an institution of vital importance to the fabric of society, as well as to the needs of individual citizens and consumers.

Journalism and user-generated content

The rise of participative modes of communication on the internet is seen, by practitioners and scholars alike, as constituting a major challenge to the news media in the twenty-first century. The boundaries of journalism have become fuzzier than ever with the emergence of participatory or citizen-based forms of information exchange in the web. The confusion often arises from the question of whether these communicative practices should be regarded as modes that are either complementary to or competing with traditional journalism – or whether they should be considered to be part of journalism.

Here, again, different contextual conditions have produced different outcomes and normative expectations. In the United States, the opportunities provided by interactive media – most notably by social networks – are much more extensively used for political campaigning and public discourse than in many other countries. This chapter is not the place to discuss the different political cultures in the US and Western Europe, but the point is this: the importance of social networks and other kinds of user-generated content has been considered by many American scholars as a potential, and perhaps even existential, threat to institutionalized journalism. This is not necessarily true for Western Europe. However, due to the US-centrism of much journalism and political-communication scholarship, American trends have triggered concern even in countries with different political cultures and media systems.

Does the rising quantity of user-generated content lead to a future in which the institution of journalism has lost its relevance to public conversation? There are several reasons why I think that posing the question this way can be misleading. And much of it has to do with an often imprecise or even confusing use of conceptual terminology. In the literature, participatory or citizen journalists, bloggers, amateurs, contributors to discussion forums and other producers of user-generated content are often lumped together with professional journalists. In Chapter 8 of this volume, for instance, Graham subsumes user commentary under the label of participatory journalism. User commentary without any doubt constitutes an increasingly important practice in the realm of user-generated content, but is it journalism? Would anyone seriously dare to call published letters to the editors 'participatory journalism'?

The problem, as Atton (Ch 9) notes, is that for some, it appears as if the differences between amateur contributors and professional journalists have been erased just because of the ubiquitous nature of online communication. Some time ago, Hargreaves (1999: 4) contended that '[i]n a democracy everyone is a journalist', and Hartley (2000: 45) seconded by arguing that '[e]veryone is a journalist, and journalism is everywhere'. Such broad definitions, however, essentially eliminate the difference between journalists and sources. In the vast majority of cases, participatory media practices generate material that is potentially used by journalists, and vice versa. In other words, journalists and amateur media producers consider each other sources, and not players in the same field. Both institutionalized journalism and alternative media make important contributions to public debate, but they do so in fundamentally different ways. Journalism draws on an institutional framework and a social contract geared towards public service, the organization and verification of knowledge, as well as the supply of social orientation in everyday life. Amateur media producers do not subscribe to such an institutional framework, and they mostly do not feel obliged to the ideal of public service. Sacrificing the distinction between journalism and alternative media may therefore have important ramifications even in the normative realm, as I will discuss further below.

Much of the debate on the relationship between traditional corporate journalism and participatory media is confined to the individual level of practices, ignoring their corresponding institutional contexts. Not every communicative practice on the internet that reproduces journalism's discursive techniques deserves the label of 'journalism'. Journalism is more than a mere collection of practices and routines – it is, again, essentially a social institution. It is true that people 'are increasingly publishing and sharing their stories, comments, news, photos, videos and podcasts, while chatting, debating, tagging, blogging and tweeting in online communities', as Graham (Ch 8) notes. However, users do so not necessarily in their roles as *citizens*. I would even argue that the overwhelming majority of content generated by individual users bears no relationship whatsoever with citizenship and membership of a political community that, again, according to social contract theory come with both rights and responsibilities. This seems to be one of the greatest misunderstandings in the debate. It is for this reason that Atton (Ch 9) questions the extent to which alternative media projects actually demonstrate active citizenship.

The potential of participative communication practices on the internet to 'democratize' public conversation may therefore be overly optimistic. Deuze and Fortunati (2011: 167) recently argue very forcefully for 'a democratization of media access, as an opening up of the conversation society has with itself, as a way to get more voices heard in an otherwise rather hierarchical and exclusive public sphere'. Bogaerts and Carpentier (Ch 4) chime in, maintaining that what Hartley (2000) describes as a 'redactional society' may challenge journalism's elitist position and the notion of public service by the practices of citizen journalism. The question, however, is: Who are these citizen journalists, and are they really in a position to challenge journalism's central position as a social institution?

It is of essential importance to recognize that even though the internet gives people the opportunity to make their voices heard, not every citizen has the desire to participate in public conversation. In fact, it is a fairly small elite of privileged, digitally literate, educated, politically interested and media-savvy individuals who can afford a sustained participation in political conversation. They constitute, using a term from Firdaus and Volkmer's contribution to this book (Ch 7), a 'digital bourgeoisie' of high-income, urban and younger members of middle and higher income countries. They are, in many respects, not much different from the profile of a typical journalist, yet they are expected to have the potential to 'destabilize' traditional journalism (Bogaerts and Carpentier, Ch 4).

The internet may potentially be open to everyone, but it is not a space devoid of power relations. The unequal distribution of power and intellectual resources on the internet is related to a number of factors, most notably to the possession of economic, social and cultural capital. It may be true that in most Western societies, everybody can be a journalist. However, not everyone *acts* in such a capacity. As a consequence, it is not 'society' as a whole that has a conversation with itself. It is a conversation among members of a distinguished digital information elite. Atton (Ch 9) therefore rightly questions the capacity of citizen journalists to transform professional journalism, especially as they seem to merely reproduce the discursive techniques of conventional journalism.

The internet does not by itself necessarily pose an existential threat to journalism. Witschge argues in Chapter 11 that the introduction of new media technologies has in fact not led to a profound change in journalism's practices and norms. The greatest peril of modern institutional journalism is its problem of funding. In what has turned out to be one of the most far-reaching collective failures of the media industries, audiences were allowed to get used to free-of-charge news on the web. Traditional business models of institutionalized journalism have thus come under a great deal of pressure, which has led to a serious downsizing of news organizations across the Western world. Peters, however, aptly concludes in Chapter 12 that journalism is recognized as a public good in many countries – 'a foundation it would be wise to reinforce'. Witschge (Ch 11) adds that we need to be creative and 'think of how we can inject new life into public service journalism'. Hence, if journalism has value for society and democracy, we – that is, journalists, media regulators, academics and civil society – should think about alternative types of business models and funding sources in order to help this important institution to fulfil its social contract.

One way of giving credit to the institution of journalism is by maintaining the analytical distinction between institutional, professional journalism on the one hand, and participative amateur media practices on the other. Such a distinction is in journalism's and the larger public's best interest. Contracts are usually concluded between contracting parties. Journalism's social contract, and the normative expectations that come with it, become meaningless if we dissolve the idea of what journalism essentially stands for. We cannot extend or blur the boundaries of journalism without essentially terminating its social contract.

Journalism is too important a social service to leave it in the hands of amateurs. We may therefore have to reconsider even one of the most fundamental privileges of journalism in most democratic countries: the formally unrestricted access to the occupation of news-making. There are many reasons why I think that journalism's social contract should be amended so that the institution of journalism is allowed – or forced – to claim authority over the profession. But one note of caution is in order: Any effort to demarcate professional journalism from amateur practices may become difficult to defend when we allow individuals such as those who tapped private phone lines of grieving parents for the *News of the World* to legally call themselves 'journalists'. In order to be protected from practices that seriously undermine journalism's legitimacy and social contract, the profession therefore needs legal authority to impose sanctions on those who crossed the line of professional and ethical behaviour.

Disdaining the media?

Several chapters in this book also argue that, perhaps as a consequence of journalism's failures and breaches, trust in the media has collapsed dramatically in most parts of the Western world. The public's disdain for the media, as Gronke and Cook (2007) aptly put it, has alarmed scholars, journalists and larger civil society. In 2001, Cook and Gronke noted that in the case of the United States, the drop in confidence from 1973 to 2000 is greatest for the news media out of all the public institutions they studied. The question, however, is whether these signs of eroding trust constitute a universal phenomenon around the world.

A brief look at the data series collected as part of the *World Values Survey* (WVS) can be illuminating in this respect.[1] In the large majority of countries for which time series are available, trust in the press has actually remained fairly stable over time. Confidence in the media has most substantially dropped in Australia, Brazil, Canada, Great Britain, Italy, Taiwan, Turkey and the United States. The drop in the US, however, was a fairly light one between 1995 and 2006. The number of those who said that they have 'a great deal' and 'quite a lot of confidence' in the press declined from 27.4 to 23.9 per cent, while there was indeed a sharp drop from 56.3 per cent in 1990. At the same time, trust in the press has in fact increased in a non-trivial number of countries, including Austria, China, Iceland, India, Japan, Morocco, Portugal, Romania and Switzerland, among others. In a recent comparison of Western media systems, Müller (2010) found declining levels of trust in the press especially for countries that belong to what Hallin and Mancini (2004) called the North Atlantic or Liberal Model of media systems. By contrast, trust levels remained mostly stable for countries in the Mediterranean or Polarized Pluralist Model and the Northern European or Democratic Corporatist Model.

Is trust in the media lower than confidence in political institutions? Again, inspecting the data from the 2005 – 2007 wave of the WVS may provide some useful answers. As it turned out, publics in the overwhelming majority of the 56 countries for which we have comparative data actually expressed more confidence in the press and television than in political parties. Only in China and Ethiopia did people express more trust in political parties than in the media. If we combine levels of trust in the government, parliament and political parties, the relationship remains largely unchanged. In most of the countries, the public turned out to have more trust in the media than in their major political institutions. The relationship was reversed only in Australia, China, Cyprus, Ethiopia, Vietnam, Switzerland and Great Britain (for trust in the press).

What can we conclude from these results? It seems that levels of public confidence in the media have developed quite differently depending on various contextual factors. Making generalizations based on specific, and sometimes perhaps even peculiar, countries may be misleading. In the United States, for instance, television tends to present the news in a more overtly opinionated style (Feldman, 2011). Audiences are increasingly polarized in terms of ideological views and selective exposure to media content. At the same time, there exists widespread evidence for a phenomenon that is commonly referred to as hostile media effect (Vallone, Ross, and Lepper, 1985). According to this phenomenon, partisans on opposing sides of an issue have a tendency to see identical news coverage of that issue as biased in favour of the other side (Feldman, 2011). In the context of a highly polarized audience, like in the US, the perception of media as being hostile to one's own point of view may contribute to a growing dismay with journalism. The United States may therefore constitute a fairly peculiar – and actually not quite representative – case when put in an international perspective.

Such evidence notwithstanding, claims about eroding trust in the media often go fairly unquestioned. How is this possible? One reason may be, again, a confusion of levels of analysis: between trust in journalists as individuals and trust in journalism as a social institution. In the United States, journalists belong to the least prestigious occupations, as indicated by the 2009 Harris Poll.[2] Only 17 per cent of the public found journalists to have 'very great prestige', which puts them in the range of bankers (16 per cent) and movie actors (15 per cent). On top of the list of the 'most prestigious occupations' rank firefighters (62 per cent), scientists (57 per cent) and doctors (56 per cent). The picture is not much different in Germany, where, according to the 2011 Allensbach Occupational Prestige Scale, only 17 per cent of the population listed journalists among the five most esteemed professions, and only 4 per cent mentioned television anchors.[3] Doctors, schoolteachers and professors, by comparison, were listed by 82, 42 and 33 per cent, respectively.

It seems that when we ask for confidence in journalists as individuals, we get even more negative assessments of the public image of the news media. One reason might be that the image of journalists, as carried by the media themselves, has radically shifted during the last 40 years. There was a time when movies presented a rather heroic image of reporters, in films such as *All The President's Men* (1976, Robert Redford and Dustin Hoffmann playing two relentless reporters uncovering the Watergate scandal) and *Under Fire* (1983, Nick Nolte playing a fearless reporter who sacrifices his life in Nicaragua). Today, journalists are often depicted as 'exploitative jackals' (Project for Excellence in Journalism, 2007) 'devoid of conscience' (Rowe, 1992: 27), and as paparazzi who capitalize on the private lives of celebrities (see the movie *Paparazzi*, produced in 2003 by Mel Gibson).

Nonetheless, even though claims about eroding trust in the media might therefore be overstated for most part of the globe, the *World Values Survey* data also indicate that the publics in most countries do indeed have – and I would add: always had – fairly little confidence in the institution of journalism. The problem therefore is not a more or less dramatic decline of trust in the media but the rather little confidence people have had in the media since the 1980s. This is also true, or perhaps especially so, for political actors. A number of recent studies have impressively shown that what was once considered a symbiotic relationship between politics, media and the public has now turned into one of mutual mistrust (Van Aelst et al., 2008; Brants et al., 2010), or into a 'Bermuda Triangle', as Brants (Ch 1) puts it. Data from the *Worlds of Journalism Study* also indicate a generally cynical attitude of journalists towards political actors, which turned out to be a strikingly consistent phenomenon in all of the investigated societies (Hanitzsch and Berganza, 2011).

Overall, I tend to think that the causal link between journalism's performance and the public's very limited esteem for the media is less straightforward than many of us believe. For one, the relationship between news performance and public trust in media may be not a linear one. There is no doubt that violations of journalism's social contract, such as the phone-hacking scandal at Murdoch's *News of the World*, can seriously undermine the public image of journalism. At the same time, however, publics can get frustrated exactly *because* journalism properly fulfils its social contract – a paradox that is indicated, for instance, by the widespread public discontent with the vigorous media disclosure of German President Christian Wulff's private loan and press censure affair in early 2012. The troubled nature of the relationship between news-media performance and trust in journalism might well have to do with our quite limited knowledge about the nature of trust and what it essentially means to have trust in an institution.

Furthermore, the publics' limited respect for the news media should also be situated within a general and all-embracing crisis of trust in public institutions. Political scientists and communication scholars have long noted alarming signs of widespread public discontent with political institutions (Moy, Pfau and Kahlor, 1999; Norris, 1999; Torcal and Montero, 2006). For Anshari (2008: 6), these developments mark a 'cross-national convergence of citizen and elite withdrawal from democratic processes.' Since journalism is in many ways regarded to be an essentially political institution (Cook, 1998; Sparrow, 1999), it may run the danger of getting caught in the maelstrom of evaporating trust in institutions. Ironically, and very unfortunately, parts of the media are contributing to such erosion of general trust in substantial ways. This situation might create a vicious circle by which the problem gets further aggravated: cynical journalists and the media's obsession for conflict produce negative coverage of political affairs; this coverage contributes to public distrust in political institutions and, in turn, fuels public discontent with the institution of journalism. Against this background it is not surprising that trust in the media is shrinking, primarily in highly adversarial journalistic cultures such as Great Britain and the United States.

Journalism's different routes

By picking up on some of the ideas presented in the previous sections of this book, this chapter has tried to modestly contribute to recent debates about a crisis of journalism partly brought about by new communication technologies and participative modes of communication, as well as declining public trust in the news media. This chapter interrogated these assumptions from the perspective of cross-national and comparative research.

One general conclusion is that making generalizations on the grounds of evidence from particular – if not peculiar – countries may be misleading and even dangerous. Communication researchers are often obsessed with developments occurring in the United States and Great Britain; and there is a tendency to extrapolate this experience to other parts of the world. As comparative research can impressively demonstrate, journalism has taken slightly but meaningfully different routes in different societies, generating some considerable variance in values, practices and relationships with the public.

Despite these differences, however, professional journalism is still a remarkably robust social institution. In an era of potentially unlimited access to and accelerated exchange of information, professional journalists, as sense-makers of the actualities of the day, are needed more than ever. Unfortunately, much journalism scholarship continues to paint the picture of a proclaimed end-time crisis of journalism – sometimes, it seems, even by writing it into being. And part of this problem, I should add, is the proliferative use of the category of 'journalism' for practices that may not deserve this label.

Notes

1 The data set is freely available from the project's website at http://www.worldva luessurvey.org.
2 http://www.harrisinteractive.com/vault/Harris-Interactive-Poll-Research-Pres-Occupa tions-2009–08.pdf.
3 http://www.ifd-allensbach.de/pdf/prd_1102.pdf.

15

'TRUST ME, I'M AN INNOVATIVE JOURNALIST,' AND OTHER FICTIONS

Kevin G. Barnhurst

Twenty-first century journalism is in crisis. Although less acute in Europe and other countries than in the United States, the predicament has squeezed journalism as the public attends to news tweets and aggregators and the boundaries blur between professional and amateur writers and profit and nonprofit news outlets (Schudson, 2011). The crisis seems to spring from declining trust from the public, growing technical pressures on journalists, and widening demand for citizen participation in news. But what if journalism practitioners and scholars have misdiagnosed the crisis? If so, then journalism must reconsider its relation to trust, innovation, and citizenship, concepts that may seem self-evident.

Opinion polls show the public has little confidence in the press as an institution, raising fears among journalists and media leaders. But should citizens be more trusting, and is seeking trust good for journalism? Scepticism toward the news media might instead be a valuable asset for public life. Rethinking journalism might require a different perspective on public trust. Critics object that the news media are lagging in technical innovation, and journalists fear the consequences. But should news media strive to be at the cutting edge of technology? Holding back might instead serve a wider public. Rethinking journalism might require a different perspective on innovation. The public performs poorly on measures of citizen involvement and political knowledge, leaving news leaders doubtful about 'citizen' journalism. But should citizenship require so much engagement and knowledge? Citizens may already be as involved and informed as they need to be. Rethinking journalism might require a different perspective on citizenship.

Declining trust

In 2008 the British Committee on Standards in Public Life reported that public trust in popular journalism languishes 'near the bottom, along with estate agents,' among institutions (www.public-standards.org.uk). In July 2010 *Forbes* magazine published a Special Report on 'The Trust Gap,' with articles from commentators in business, philosophy, and law and from new and old media across the political spectrum, asking whether US Americans can regain their faith in institutions (www.forbes.com). Trust seems essential for journalism to survive the 'bumpy ride to uncertainty': media markets changing, sensationalism growing, and technology and politics shifting (Brants, Ch 1). The fall from the high modern moment of journalism has led to the 'dwindling trust of audiences' (Bogaerts and Carpentier, Ch 4). Inaccuracies endanger trust (Porlezza and Russ-Mohl, Ch 3), and hoaxes like the fake Abu Ghraib story undermine public trust in media and demonstrate how 'the crisis of journalism is … vaporizing trust' (Broersma Ch 2).

Trust is central to the crisis, but what exactly is it? The Russell Sage Foundation asked social psychologists, sociologists, anthropologists, economists, political scientists, and others, only to find 'no clear consensus among them' about what *trust* means, despite agreement 'that trust plays a significant role' in how society functions (Cook, 2003: xxvii). One difficulty is that trust is a hybrid, growing out of interpersonal experience and extending into the complexity of institutional life (Luhmann, 1979). Trust also exists in a combination of passion and policy, as unthinking habit and as social rationality (Misztal, 1996).

Trust is subjective in character. The *Oxford English Dictionary* (*OED*) defines *trust* as 'confidence in or reliance … without investigation or evidence' and 'confident expectation of something; hope.' The American *Merriam-Webster* lists two main synonyms: confidence and credence. To examine trust, research asks respondents to rate institutions of government and media, yielding averages and trends that seem alarming. But the surveys hide as much as they reveal. One underlying assumption disparages the character of trust, which is first an emotion, a subjective response to felt qualities, not an objective, quantifiable descriptor. The assumption contrasts reason and emotion, turning the emotional into something irrational. Making emotion the opposite of enlightened reason introduces a contradiction in the definition of the term *trust*. Despite being subjective, trust is not outside the realm of rationality.

Trust is a quality of political relationships, with three poles: politicians rely on media to inform the public, journalists rely on politicians to provide news content, and citizens rely on media for sensible, skilful reports (Brants, Ch 1). The latter interaction is an 'imaginary contract between journalism and citizens,' so that journalism acts as 'a trustee of the public' (Broersma, Ch 2). Relations among the poles are complex, moving between but also through each other. Any agent in the triad mediates between the other two, an indirect flow that builds confidence in institutions. Trust flows a fourth way, through internal channels, so that journalism may for instance lose trust in itself (Bogaerts and Carpentier, Ch 4). Although common ideas about the politics of trust come from personal experiences, the political economy of trust involves multiple actors, collective memories, field characteristics, and magnitudes of power unavailable within personal relationships.

Merriam-Webster lists 'character, ability, strength, or truth' as the qualities that inspire the 'assured reliance' typical of trust, and the qualities have in common two dimensions, truth and skill. Recent media research identifies them as reliability—honesty, responsiveness—and competence: skilfulness, decisiveness, and perspicacity (Brants, Ch 1; Adriaansen, 2011). For reliability, journalists' honesty and responsiveness to the public deserve separate consideration. Journalists' competence, or *credibility,* involves offering believable interpretations and separating fact from opinion (Brants, Ch 1). In its history, media research has confirmed that truth and skill are dimensions of trust in media (Porlezza and Russ-Mohl, Ch 3), and has developed a multidimensional model of credibility (Matthes and Kohring, 2007). Skilled factors—journalists' *selectivity* (of topics and of facts), combined with their skill at *assessment*—produce accurate depictions, so that *accuracy* is the central product of journalists' skill. The qualities researchers identify for trust in media imagine media workers building trust much as individuals do in personal relations.

If trust is 'the cement and the precondition of every relationship,' then perhaps *cynicism* is its opposite on a continuum (Brants, Ch 1). That antonym causes alarm because it seems to be increasing along with *mistrust* (Bogaerts and Carpentier, Ch 4; Porlezza and Russ-Mohl, Ch 3; and Peters, Ch 12). Both terms go beyond *distrust,* the direct and more neutral antonym for trust. Mistrust is about *uncertainty,* a 'lack of sureness,' implying doubt that makes one unable to act 'based upon suspicion,' says *Merriam-Webster.* Cynicism, beyond its reference to historical philosophy, implies either an attitude 'contemptuously distrustful of human nature and motives' or 'a belief that human conduct is motivated primarily by self-interest.' Cynicism is 'deeply distrustful,' and being 'cynical implies having a sneering disbelief in sincerity or integrity.' To call the public cynical is extreme, but even *mistrust* is harsh. A misanthropic view of others in the political economy of trust seems unlikely, and suspicions driving the interactions among press, politics, and public may lead to political paralysis. But the terms mistrust and cynicism occur widely in political communication and journalism studies research (e.g., Cappella and Jamieson, 1997; Brants et al., 2010; Guggenheim, Kwak, and Campbell, 2011) and in the media trade (Kovach and Rosenstiel, 2001).

As their choices of antonyms suggest, media practitioners and social researchers tend to see trust in the media and in journalists as an asset and its loss as an evil (Brants, Ch 1; Meyer and Lund, 2008; cf. Barnhurst, 2011a). A climate of suspicion or pessimism is difficult at the personal level, and so journalism studies and media research focus on how to improve media performance by making journalism more responsive and transparent. Correcting errors quickly might reinforce accuracy but is complex because social media reproduce mistakes and make corrections more visible (Porlezza and Russ-Mohl, Ch 3). Expanding media responsiveness can lead to journalism based on social responsibility, strategic commercialism, empathic advocacy, or populist doubt (Brants, Ch 1). But journalism must adapt to the 'age of the database' by joining the new reality and reconsidering its reliance on truth claims (Broersma, Ch 2). In the encounter between old and new media, mainstream journalism employs coping strategies that marginalize rival media, absorb and normalize the environment online, and reassert journalists' authority by shifting focus from news dissemination to news judgment and knowledge conveyed in subjective tones that seem more authentic (Bogaerts and Carpentier, Ch 4).

Adaptations and coping strategies in journalism to remedy distrust make sense at the 'micro' level of interactions mainly between individual journalists on one hand and political elites and audience members on the other. But are the responses of journalism valid at the 'macro' or institutional level? A surprising lesson for the student of economics is that what serves the public in microeconomics might be harmful in macroeconomics. Reducing debt is smart for individuals, but for macroeconomics the supply and demand for debt seeks aggregate equilibrium. Savings are a microeconomic good, and more savings secure a stable life for one's dependants now or heirs later. But for a nation, more individuals saving produces a higher savings *rate* that can drag down the collective wealth.

From a 'macro' perspective, there are good reasons to wonder whether—and if so how much—trust is necessary. Economists find that more trust does not uniformly reduce volatility, because markets that require trust also work to *destroy* trust (Perelman, 1998; Sangnier, 2009). Trust may not be as important for democracy as political scientists think (Mishler and Rose, 2005). The imprecise and inconsistent questions in surveys that measure trust cast doubt on what is declining in the data (Gershtenson and Plane, 2007; Poletti and Brants, 2010). Political research suggests that distrust may not diminish political participation but may indicate that citizens are 'interested and critical' (De Vreese, 2005: 283). In economics and political science, trust does not distribute itself fairly in society, especially among the disenfranchised, and in communication research, how news coverage relates to trust remains unclear. For a public that needs to think, understand, learn, and 'make sense of the world,' choosing to follow news may be unrelated to increasing distrust in news (Tsfati and Cappella, 2005: 252).

An alternative is the term *scepticism,* which *Merriam-Webster* defines as an 'unwillingness to believe without conclusive evidence.' Unlike the alternatives, scepticism is a moderate way to describe the public. An intelligent citizenry *should* be sceptical of institutions, including government and media (Peters, Ch 12; Barnhurst, 2011a). And the public should not place faith in the press, as Jefferson insisted, because distrust is an indicator of healthy democracy (Wijfjes, 2004). News is always a secondary account, and an adept citizenry should question any information derived second hand, as it does in Spain (Barnhurst, 2000).

The ideas widely held in industry, and in some studies, seem nostalgic about the high modern era of journalism, which was no golden age. Regular glitches in accuracy and patterned misinformation span from the inventions of US correspondents during the First World War (Barnhurst, 2005) to the phone-hacking scandals in the British press. Inaccuracies and corrections are a normal feature of journalism, not the causes of declining trust.

As journalists' socioeconomic status and education levels improved over the past century, their stories shifted away from event-centred reporting to emphasize the interpretation of events (Salgado and Strömbäck, 2012). Explaining and placing what happens in context are part of the professional project of journalism (Barnhurst, 2012), which has enhanced the authority of journalists over the course of twentieth century. Professionalization of news work may have paradoxically reduced public trust in mainstream news, so that the more news stories implied, 'Trust me, I'm a professional journalist,' the more sceptical the audience became.

Innovation

A common view is that innovations in techniques have a direct and powerful influence on public life. Especially since the mid-twentieth century, technical innovation has appeared to determine the political lay of the land (Winner, 1978), and some innovations, such as the internet, stand out. The view is widespread—a web search on the terms 'technology changes politics' yields three hundred million hits—but also held among elites, who say that new technologies have always changed politics (Barnhurst, 2011a). Mobile devices are the latest opportunity to view innovation as a product of technological inventions that the mainstream blog *MediaShift* describes as a series of waves marking 'significant moments in political history' (www.pbs.org/mediashift).

If innovation drives politics, then news organizations must stay current. News is an up-to-date product, and journalists must use new technologies to disseminate what the public needs to know (Barnhurst, 2010). Industry leaders as early as the 1930s began predicting that journalists would soon junk the machinery employed to produce news, replacing each generation of tools with others not yet invented. Insiders have adopted an especially sharp tone in recent years, chastising fellow journalists for resisting change. In the mid-2000s, for example, a decade after news first went online, insiders noted that reporters and editors were still viewing technology with trepidation and news organizations were still arriving late to new techniques.

Critics have been even harsher on the news media for failing to innovate. As the internet changed the world, they said, its first casualty would be old media. Novelist Michael Crichton called them 'The Mediasaurus,' the title of his 1993 *Wired* magazine article predicting that they would 'vanish without a trace' within a decade, and a year later author Jon Katz called newspapers 'the biggest and saddest losers in the information revolution' (www.wired.com). By 2009 Arianna Huffington, founding editor of the online *Huffington Post*, criticized the legacy media for misinformation that led to the Iraq war and disparaged them for attacking search engines, hoarding content behind paywalls, and metering users to extract micropayments (commerce.senate.gov). The future of high-quality journalism did not depend on legacy media, she said, which were in crisis because they failed to innovate.

But what is innovation? The *OED* traces the current meaning for *innovation* to the 1930s, a period when businesses responded to the Great Depression by focusing on ways to push the market toward consumption (Schumpeter, 1939). Society may invent more ideas and things than it can absorb (Blaug, 1963), but innovation is the process of absorbing them—what society but especially business does to change the circulation of goods and ideas. Inventions such as the internet and mobile apps are not innovations until they disseminate. The distinction matters because the new sense of *innovation* depends especially on news, an important avenue for spreading novel ideas.

The 'diffusion of innovation' is a communication process connected to economic development and pushing consumption, not invention. 'It matters little whether' it is better than what 'it is replacing' but 'whether the individual perceives the relative advantage of the innovation' (Rogers, 1962: 124). Innovations spread from early to late adopters (Ryan and Gross, 1943), diffusing through mediated and interpersonal channels (Rogers, Singhal, and Quinlan, 2009). The earliest adopters of telephones gained little from their expensive devices because so few others were available to call. So innovators seem daft for not waiting until costs go down as the user-base grows. Products like hybrid corn seeds and medications follow a similar diffusion path, but journalism products spread faster. All 'products' involve invention, but research on diffusion tends to conflate *invention* with *innovation*.

The *OED Historical Thesaurus* shows how synonyms for *innovation* began emerging rapid-fire in the 1960s, from *product launch* in 1963 and *relaunch* in 1968 to just *launch* in 1969. The shortened terms seemed to match the pace of innovation as inventions poured from corporate research and development (Jewkes, Sawers, and Stillerman, 1969). In the ensuing decades, ideas about using electronic devices diffused widely, becoming synonymous with *innovation* in the period of high-tech start-ups. Invention and innovation fused in popular understanding, so that technology seemed to reshape politics, media struggled to keep pace, and critics predicted their demise. Then journalists faced layoffs as newspapers failed or abandoned print, and talk of crisis grew. Is there no other way to understand innovation in journalism?

Instead of thinking technology 'shapes what they do,' journalists might think less of inventions and innovate as an 'interpretive performer' in the face of cultural transformation (Allan, Ch 10). Improvisation could open journalism to organizations and individuals outside the mainstream media. Or journalism might innovate by shifting focus from concrete places to networked spaces where news flows faster and more openly from the push of journalists and the pull and push of empowered users (Heinrich, Ch 6; Volkmer, 2003). Journalism might innovate with narrative, sharing the internet platform with more alternative journalism (Atton, Ch 9). Improvisations, networks, and narratives are upbeat and hopeful ways of rethinking journalism.

Instead of assuming they must lead innovation, journalists might reconsider leadership. Social scientists began studying leaders by looking for personality traits (Lewin, Lippitt, and White, 1939). Autocrats lead by going out front of organizational life, but democrats lead from the middle, giving and taking guidance that produces the best input from members and the richest group life. Laissez-faire leaders delegate decisions to the group and follow behind, but members become less cooperative and productive. Leadership traits have two dimensions, concern for tasks and concern for people, but leave out the context (Warrick, 1981). Leading from the middle has advantages in organizations, but what about entire industries, like media, or occupations, like journalism?

Press history tells a different story about innovation. In their autobiographies, prominent editors and publishers claim they were early adopters of new techniques. But going back to the founding of newspapers in Europe and America, the press has imitated older forms (Barnhurst and Nerone, 2001), and publishers were slow to adopt technology (Mott, 1942). They waited until the commercial success of each technique was clear. They resisted methods of reproduction such as the stereotype, then followed the demands of advertisers. They argued against modes of representation such as the halftone image, which they, like their public, found inferior to engraving for clarity, narrative, and documentary. The television industry followed a similar pattern (Steele and Barnhurst, 1996). News media survived each wave of technical change by innovating, adopting new ideas for living, but not in the early or late phases of diffusion.

Earlier journalism could adapt at the opportune moment because it shared with a broad public the prevailing sense of time. In the modern era each generation has found the pace of change accelerating, but what has transformed is the understanding of time itself (Kern, 1983). Journalism aligned with time sensibilities that emerged with the twentieth century, but resisted as the latest time-shift occurred (Barnhurst, 2011b), remaining fixed in modernist time. Deadlines, scoops, exclusives, and competition encourage thinking of news as a time-value product with a short shelf life, but the new time regime involves a flow of change, along with ever-present access to the archived past, with processes and networks as products. Press history suggests the need for moderation, aligning journalism innovation with the public and its technical aspirations.

Early adopters, by living new ideas ahead of others, are out of touch and soon forgotten if their inventions do not diffuse widely. Leadership from the middle is more engaging and democratic, but implies equality and community. And innovation, the bringing of products to market, is of value only in its commercial domain and focuses on inventions, especially new technology, not on communication at the core of journalism. Rethinking journalism requires big-picture, historical, and inclusive ideas, because its predicament is only the latest in a long history of adjusting to change by riding the middle.

Citizenship

Citizens may not be interested in journalism or have much knowledge about politics, but news producers need their attention online. To help the media adjust, charitable foundations have created initiatives to connect citizens and journalists through digital media and interactive journalism (Barnhurst, 2011a). Along with research on 'the possibility for audience participation' (Bird, 2003: 183), media industries now look to foster collaboration with audiences in creating information. Interactivity has become one of the 'participatory expectations' for audiences, who may join with satirical news programs, for instance, in critiquing the hypocrisy, disingenuousness, and superficiality of cable newscasters, learning 'how to think about journalism' within the modernist definition of news and the justice aims of activism (Peters, Ch 12). One form of interactivity is user-generated content. The comment fields of news websites promise 'new ideas, perspectives, facts, and sources' and generate information along with adversarial content (Graham, Ch 8). A buzzword for interactivity is the 'citizen journalist,' perhaps an empty term when unpaid users may not see themselves as citizens but journalists, whom they might supplant (McNair, Ch 5). The citizen-journalist model seems to impinge on full-time journalists even in far-flung places (Volkmer and Firdaus, Ch 7). Discussions of citizen journalism assume that democracy needs rational citizens, whom journalism can inform about the main decisions of citizenship, such as voting (Witschge, Ch 11; Graham, Ch 8).

But what is citizenship? Besides an older definition simply contrasting permanent residence to conditional transience, the *OED Historical Thesaurus* indicates a new meaning emerged in nineteenth-century America. The Progressive Movement then expanded the definition of citizenship. A key proponent, John Dewey (1927), described three characteristics. *Responsibility* meant duties like voting and serving on juries. *Sociability* meant fully joining the community, from family life to civic associations. Tocqueville had found sociability a remarkable aspect of life in the United States. And *communication* was a prerequisite to the other two and possibly a root cause. Dewey quoted Carlyle's dictum that the invention of the printing press made democracy inevitable. Progressive citizenship required following political events through the media, forming and expressing opinions by writing to officials, debating the issues in community settings, helping solve community problems, participating in elections, and demonstrating when necessary against injustice. Fully engaged citizenship amounted to a full-time job. Thinkers in Europe of the era and elsewhere were not so sure (Weber, 1958), but the new definition spread.

Political scientists elaborated ideal citizenship by describing a pyramid of instrumental activity, with narrow legal duties like voting at the base and leadership in political office and activism at the pinnacle (Barnhurst, 2007). Theorists found themselves worrying that as society approached the ideal, active citizenship might destabilize the state. But the rise of polling statistics documented the opposite problem, a citizenry with low levels of political knowledge in different countries (Delli Carpini and Keeter, 1996; Mondak, 2006). Studies for a century seemed to show that citizens lack knowledge of how government works, what elected officials do, or which issues are current (Barnhurst, 2007). To fill the gap 'between the expectation of an informed citizenry' and their poor knowledge in surveys (Neuman, 1986: 3), researchers suggested citizens were relying on either pre-formed schemas of the world or the advice of 'opinion leaders' or institutions (Lupia and McCubbins, 1998). But political science was unable to resolve the dilemma (Barnhurst, 2007). Voters dedicate little time to the work of getting informed, rarely join actively in politics, and tend to avoid political conversations. Cultural analyses also characterize citizens as incompetent or infantile, and communication-studies research tracks how citizens have abandoned the press as a means for informing themselves.

The long debate over citizenship has focused on the news media (Entman, 1989). Progressive leaders who proposed the citizenship ideal were editors and journalists (Barnhurst, 2007). They suggested a remedy for the lack of public knowledge and involvement: citizens should emulate progressive activists by working at the grass roots, moving into leadership in organizations, parties, and perhaps government. The remedy reveals something fundamental about journalism: its tendency to identify its practitioners as a model of informed citizenship that others might imitate.

But journalists are unlike citizens, who aspire to nothing like full-time political work. So much involvement would keep them from other productive work, harming the economy and making politics chaotic. Only the rare exception can expect to earn a living in citizen journalism (Atton, Ch 9). The prospect of users practicing journalism in large numbers goes against sensible public engagement in political and economic life. Reimagining journalism means reconsidering citizenship (Luskin, 2003), along with the idea of audiences. Answering political surveys and relying on schemas, 'opinion leaders,' or institutions say little about what the public knows. But the share of citizens completing college may suggest that public knowledge is increasing (Whitney and Wartella, 1989), and citizens who join focus groups to discuss politics tend to employ sophisticated reasoning and an appropriate level of knowledge (Graber, 2001). Even youths who know the least about politics follow issues that matter to them without attending to the products of mainstream media news divisions (Barnhurst, 2000). Journalists' picture of citizenship obscures how the public manages to be shrewd and as knowledgeable as needed.

Social science until recently ignored the subjective lives of citizens. Progressive thinkers of a century ago acknowledged how political life occurred at the periphery of rational thought (Barnhurst, 2007), but attention to emotion in politics returned only recently. Instead of subjective phenomena, researchers focus on affect, the subset of feelings associated with functional action. In the late 1980s, studies began drawing on psychology, physiology, and later neuroscience to discover how passion works along with reason (Marcus, Neuman, and MacKuen, 2000). Rational needs trigger affect to shift attention away from a goal satisfactorily attained and toward higher priorities in the face of life's complex challenges. Political 'affective intelligence' sometimes lets politics take priority. Understood in the aggregate, emotion affects public life, especially in campaigns and elections (Neuman et al., 2007). But a broader view might return from the rational and instrumental side of citizenship to the sociology of emotion, looking through the lens of representation from critical and culture studies (Barnhurst, 2011a).

In the last century, social science and journalism grew around a kind of 'citizenship' that did not fare well. It imagined an unreachable ideal that ignored how people enact citizenship in daily life and devalued their political passions. It allowed journalists and political scientists to take a lofty stance toward the public but guaranteed that citizens would fail. The primarily US definition misunderstands citizenship in the era of online users and feeds fears about citizen journalism. But journalism can reconsider citizenship, a step that might make for better news and better politics.

Journalism lost and regained

Journalism is in crisis, especially in the United States. Despite their importance in political life, legacy media can no longer assemble the mass audiences of a century ago. Daily newspapers began declining before the mid-twentieth century and now reach a fraction of their former share of the US population. Broadcast network television news has also declined in audience share, and cable outlets make up a small share by comparison. The legacy media no longer have the advertising support they once commanded, and the lost revenue leads to reducing the staff for journalism. Having fewer full-time journalists results in less-robust content, further eroding audience attention. And as investors become aware of conditions, stock prices decline and publicly traded media companies have difficulty raising capital, leading to more cutbacks. The spiral continues downward with no end in sight (Barnhurst and Nerone, 2012).

But the vicious circle of old-media decline began long before the internet. Daily newspapers first lost interest in reaching working-class audiences (Nerone, 2009), and the move 'up market' cost readership. Only later did online services replace revenue streams once exclusive to the press, such as classified advertising that workers needed to seek jobs. While legacy media underestimated their vulnerability, the public continued spending more on media. Supposedly free content online is expensive for users, who buy a computer or mobile device and pay monthly for access. Instead of paying for news, users supply revenue for digital media: indirectly through advertising on search engines and web browsers, and directly to retail and auction sites, software producers, internet service providers, telecommunication companies, and equipment manufacturers.

As US journalism entered crisis, journalists already recognized the growing disconnection from citizens. A local senior housing project in Antrim, New Hampshire, was in turmoil because of mismanagement that the residents experienced as stress leading to illness. When I told the story to a former student, a reporter for the regional daily, he replied that a decade earlier the newspaper would have followed up on the tip, but there were no reporters to go out on local stories anymore. One resident, forced to move out, became a pedestrian fatality, reported directly from the police blotter in the local press, and then users posted comments blaming the victim. Other journalists were unable to see how news had lost its public. On another story of personal loss, the paper did follow up on a story about an Illinois student detained for twenty hours without food or a bed and then held for nine days in a ward for the criminally insane, all for writing the word *death* in an emailed poem. But the published story followed the official line, referring to shootings on other university campuses and quoting university representatives concerned with safety. The long-news style preferred big political contexts to private grief, and again the online comments blamed the victim (Barnhurst, 2009). The stories illustrate the combined issues of institutional trust, citizens being heard, and media innovation, made more pressing by economic difficulties.

In 2011 the Arab Spring was an international phenomenon 'brought to you' by social media. Reports called the uprising in Egypt the 'Facebook Revolution' and gave credit to online organizing for leading to regime change. But face-to-face interviews showed otherwise (Aouragh and Alexander, 2011). Activists on the ground said the reports lacked context and overplayed Western corporations like Facebook and Twitter. New media operated not in isolation but in concert with interpersonal communication, where most organizing took place, and with satellite television, mainly Al Jazeera newscasts despite the government shutdown of Egyptian internet and cellular networks. The activists distrusted technology and media and planned for when systems would fail. They knew that beliefs about new-tech politics added strength to their cause, but relied on old media and personal contacts. The Arab Spring demonstrates how Western journalists and researchers project their expectations about trust, innovation, and citizenship into their work, treating tweets and webpages as reality instead of shadows projected on cave walls.

The current predicament of journalism grows from a confusion of commercial metaphors with the public-service mission of the press. Trust in a consumer market is vital for brands and their manufacturers. Adopting technical inventions early is sensible for businesses to innovate and beat competitors. And ideal citizenship poses a kind of volunteerism leading to apprentice, journeyman, and master leadership that originated in medieval craft guilds when the fundamentals of commerce and trade emerged. In each case, thinking of journalism as participating in a 'market' for public information lets forces external to the common good drive industry practices, even in non-commercial or blended news systems. Questioning the crisis and unpacking its underlying definitions can lead to new ways of understanding, rethinking the trust relations of the press, its distance from the landscape of product innovation, and its position in the service of citizenship.

BIBLIOGRAPHY

Adriaansen, M. L. (2011) *The Versatile Citizens. Media Reporting, Political Cynicism and Voter Behavior*, Amsterdam: ASCoR.

Ali, S.M. (1990) 'Asian Journalism in the 1990s: And the Challenges Ahead', *The Journal of Development Communication*, 1(2): 52–56.

Allan, S. (ed.) (2010) *The Routledge Companion to News and Journalism*, London: Routledge.

Allan, S. (2012) *Citizen Witnessing*, Cambridge: Polity, in press.

Allan, S. and Thorsen, E. (eds) (2009) *Citizen Journalism: Global Perspectives*, New York: Peter Lang.

Allan, S. and Thorsen, E. (2011) 'Journalism, Public Service and BBC News Online', in G. Meikle and G. Redden (eds) *News Online: Transformation and Continuity*, London: Palgrave Macmillan: 20–37.

Althaus, S.L. and Tewksbury, D. (2002) 'Agenda Setting and the "New" News: Patterns of Issue Importance among Readers of the Paper and Online Versions of the *New York Times*', *Communication Research*, 29(2): 180–207.

Anderson, B. (1983) *Imagined Communities: Reflections on the Origin and Spread of Nationalism*, London: Verso.

Anshari, J.A. (2008) 'The Living Death of West European Democracy?', *Market Forces*, 4(1): 4–15.

Anuar, M.K. (2005) 'Politics and the Media in Malaysia', *Philippine Journal of Third World Studies*, 20(1): 25–47.

Aouragh, M. and Alexander, A. (2011) 'The Egyptian Experience: Sense and Nonsense of the Internet Revolution', The Arab Spring Issue, *International Journal of Communication*, 5: 1344–58.

Appadurai, A. (1990) 'Disjuncture and Difference in the Global Cultural Economy', in M. Featherstone (ed.) *Global Culture: Nationalism, Globalization and Modernity*, London: Sage: 295–310.

——(1996) *Modernity at Large: Cultural Dimensions of Globalization*, Minneapolis, MN: University of Minnesota Press.

Ashley, L. and Olson, B. (1998) 'Constructing Reality: Print Media's Framing of the Women's Movement, 1966–86', *Journalism and Mass Communication Quarterly*, 75(2): 263–77.

Assange, J. (2010a) 'Defending the Leaks: Q& a with WikiLeaks' Julian Assange', *Time.com*, 27 July, Available: http://www.time.com/time/world/article/0,8599,2006789,00.html (accessed 2 February 2012).

——(2010b) 'WikiLeaks Founder Julian Assange on the "War Logs"', *Spiegel Online*, 27 July, Available: http://www.spiegel.de/international/world/0,1518,708518,00.html (accessed 2 February 2012).

——(2010c) 'WikiLeaks Founder Julian Assange: "Transparent Government Tends to Produce Just Government"', *Democracy Now*, 28 July, Available: http://www.democracy-now.org/2010/7/28/wikileaks_founder_julian_assange_transparent_government (accessed 2 February 2012).

——(2010d) 'The Truth Will Always Win,' *The Australian*, 7 December.

——(2011) *Julian Assange: The Unauthorised Autobiography*, Edinburgh: Canongate.

Associated Press (2004) 'Young America's News Source', 2 March, Available: http://edition.cnn.com/2004/SHOWBIZ/TV/03/02/apontv.stewarts.stature.ap/ (accessed 28 May 2007).

Atton, C. (2004) *An Alternative Internet: Radical Media, Politics and Creativity*, Edinburgh: Edinburgh University Press.

——(2005) *Alternative Media*, London, Thousand Oaks, New Delhi: Sage.

——(2009) 'Why Alternative Journalism Matters', *Journalism: Theory, Practice and Criticism*, 10(3): 283–85.

Atton, C. and Hamilton, J.F. (2008) *Alternative Journalism*, London: Sage.

Avilés, J.A.G. and Carvajal, M. (2008) 'Integrated and Cross-media Newsroom Convergence: Two Models of Multimedia News Production – the Cases of Novotécnica and La Verdad Multimedia in Spain', *Convergence: The International Journal of Research into New Media Technologies*, 14(2): 221–39.

Baerns, B. (1999) 'Kommunikationsrisiken und Risikokommunikation: Das Nationale Risikoverfahren (Stufenplanverfahren) zur "Pille der dritten Generation"', in L. Rolke and V. Wolff (eds) *Wie Medien die Wirklichkeit steuern und selber gesteuert warden*, Opladen/Wiesbaden: Westdeutscher Verlag: 93–125.

Bakker, P. and Pantti, M. (2009) 'Beyond News: User-generated Content on Dutch Media Websites' Conference Paper, Future of Journalism conference, School of Journalism, Media and Cultural Studies, University of Cardiff, September 2009.

Banda, F. (2010) *Citizen Journalism and Democracy in Africa: An Exploratory Study*, Grahamstown: Highway Africa.

Bardoel, J. (1996) 'Beyond Journalism: A Profession Between Civil Society and Information Society', *European Journal Of Communication*, 11(3): 283–302.

Bardoel, J. and Deuze, M. (2001) '"Network Journalism": Converging Competencies of Old and New Media Professionals', *Australian Journalism Review*, 23(2): 91–103.

Barnett, S. (2008) 'On the Road to Self-Destruction', *British Journalism Review*, 19(2): 5–13.

Barnhurst, K.G. (2000) 'Political Engagement & the Audience for News: Lessons from Spain', *Journalism & Communication Monographs*, 2(1).

——(2002) 'News Geography & Monopoly: The Form of Reports on U.S. Newspaper Internet Sites', *Journalism Studies*, 3(4): 477–89.

——(2005) 'Declining Events and the "What" of News', Paper delivered to the Political Communication Division, International Communication Association, New York, May 29.

——(2007) 'A Phenomenology of Citizenship among Young Europeans', in S. Millar and J. Wilson (eds) *The Discourse of Europe: Talk and Text in Everyday Life*, Amsterdam: John Benjamins: 17–47.

——(2009) 'The Fate of Two Stories: How U.S. Journalism Is Forgetting the People', *Journalism: Theory, Practice & Criticism*, 10(3): 282–85.

——(2010) 'Technology and the Changing Idea of News: 2001 U.S. Newspaper Content at the Maturity of Internet 1.0', *International Journal of Communication*, 4: 1082–99.

——(2011a) 'The New "Media Affect" and the Crisis of Representation for Political Communication', *International Journal of Press/Politics*, 16(4): 573–93.

——(2011b) 'The Problem of Modern Time in American Journalism', *KronoScope*, 11(1–2): 98–123.

——(2012) 'The Rise of the Professional Communicator', in J. Nerone (ed.) *Media History and the Foundations of Media Studies*, London: Blackwell.

Barnhurst, K.G. and Nerone, J. (2001) *The Form of News, A History*, New York: Guilford.

——(2012) 'The Media in North America', in *Europa World*, London: Routledge.

Bauman, Z. (2000) *Liquid Modernity*, Cambridge: Polity.

Bauer, D. (2003) 'Jon Stewart and Comedy Central's "The Daily Show" at the Top of Political and Media Satire', Associated Press.

Bauman, Z. (2000) *Liquid Modernity*, Cambridge: Polity.

Baumgartner, J. and Morris, J. (2006) 'The Daily Show Effect', *American Political Research*, 34(3): 341–67.

Baym, G. (2005) 'The Daily Show: Discursive Integration and the Reinvention of Critical Journalism.' *Political Communication*, 22: 259–76.

Baym, G. and Jones, J. (2010) 'A Dialogue on Satire News and the Crisis of Truth in Postmodern Political Television', *Journal of Communication Inquiry*, 34(3): 278–94.

Beck, U. (2000) *What is Globalization?* Malden, MA: Polity.

Becker, H.S. (1967) 'Whose Side are We On', *Social Problems*, 14(3): 239–47.

Beckett, C. (2008) *SuperMedia: Saving Journalism So It Can Save the World*, Oxford: Blackwell.

Beckett, C. and Ball, J. (2012) *WikiLeaks: News in the Networked Era*, Cambridge: Polity.

Beckett, C. and Mansell, R. (2008) 'Crossing Boundaries: New Media and Networked Journalism', *Communication, Culture & Critique*, 1(1): 92–104.

Bell, A. (1991) *The Language of News Media*, Oxford: Blackwell.

Bell, D. (2007) *Cyberculture Theorists: Manuel Castells and Donna Haraway*, London, New York: Routledge.

Bell, M. (1998) 'The Journalism of Attachment', in M. Kieran (ed.) *Media Ethics*, New York: Routledge: 15–22.

Benkler, Y. (2006) *The Wealth of Networks: How Social Production Transforms Markets and Freedom*, New Haven, London: Yale University Press.

Bennett, S., et al. (1999) 'Video Malaise Revisited: Public Trust in the Media and Government', *International Journal of Press/Politics*, 4(4): 8–23.

Bennett, W.L. (2007) 'Relief in Hard Times: A Defense of Jon Stewart's Comedy in an Age of Cynicism', *Critical Studies in Media Communication*, 24(3): 278–83.

Bennett, W.L., Gressett, L.A. and Haltom, W. (1985) 'Repairing the News. A Case Study of the News Paradigm', *Journal of Communication*, 35(2): 50–68.

Bennett, W.L. et al. (2004) 'Managing the Public Sphere: Journalistic Construction of the Great Globalization Debate', *Journal of Communication*, 54(3): 437–55.

Benson, R. and Neveu, E. (eds) (2005) *Bourdieu and the Journalistic Field*, Cambridge: Polity.

Bentele, G. (1988) 'Der Faktor Glaubwürdigkeit. Forschungsergebnisse und Fragen für die Sozialisationsperspektive', *Publizistik*, 2(3): 406–26.

——(1994) 'Objektivitätsanspruch und Glaubwürdigkeit', in O. Jarren (ed.) *Medien und Journalismus 1. Eine Einführung*, Opladen/Wiesbaden: Westdeutscher Verlag: 295–312.

——(1998) 'Vertrauen/Glaubwürdigkeit', in O. Jarren, U. Sarcinelli and U. Saxer (eds) *Politische Kommunikation in der demokratischen Gesellschaft*, Opladen/Wiesbaden: Westdeutscher Verlag: 305–11.

Bergstrom, A. (2011) 'The Scope of User Generated Content: User Contributions within Online Journalism', in B. Franklin and M. Carlson (eds) *Journalism, Sources and Credibility: New Perspectives*, London: Routledge: 167–81.

Berkowitz, D. (2000) 'Doing Double Duty: Paradigm Repair and the Princess Diana What-a-Story', *Journalism*, 1(2): 125–44.

Berry, D. (2008) *Journalism, Ethics and Society*, Farnham: Ashgate Publishers.

Berry, F. (1967) 'A Study of Accuracy in Local News Stories of Three Dailies', *Journalism Quarterly*, 44(Autumn): 482–90.

Bird, S.E. (1992) *For Enquiring Minds: A Cultural Study of Supermarket Tabloids*, Knoxville: University of Tennessee Press.

——(2003) *The Audience in Everyday Life: Living in a Media World*, New York: Routledge.

Bishop, R. (1999) 'From Behind the Walls: Boundary Work by News Organizations in their Coverage of Princess Diana's Death', *Journal of Communication Inquiry*, 23(1): 90–112.

Blaug, M. (1963) 'A Survey of the Theory of Process-Innovation', *Economica*, 30(117): 13–32.

Blumler, J. and Kavanagh, D. (1999) 'The Third Age of Political Communication. Influences and Features', *Political Communication*, 16(3): 209–30.

Boczkowski, P.J. (2005) *Digitizing the News: Innovation in Online Newspapers*, Cambridge: MIT Press.

Bogaerts, J. (2011) 'On the Performativity of Journalistic Identity', *Journalism Practice*, 5(4): 399–413.

Borden, S. and Tew, C. (2007) 'The Role of Journalist and the Performance of Journalism: Ethical Lessons From "Fake" News (Seriously)', *Journal of Mass Media Ethics*, 22(4): 300–314.

Bourdieu, P. (2005) 'The Political Field, the Social Science Field and the Journalistic Field', in R.D. Benson and E. Neveu (eds) *Bourdieu and the Journalistic Field*, Oxford: Polity: 29–47.

Brants, K. (2007) 'Changing Media, Changing Journalism', in W. Meier and J. Trappel (eds) *Power, Performance and Politics. Media policy in Europe*, Baden-Baden: Nomos: 105–23.

——(2008) 'Media, Politiek en de Spiraal van Wantrouwen' [Media, Politics and the Spiral of Distrust], in B. Snels and N. Thijssen (eds) *De Grote Kloof. Verhitte Politiek in Tijden van Verwarring* [*The Great Gap. Heated Politics in Confusing Times*], Amsterdam: Boom: 163–91.

Brants, K., et al. (2010) 'The Real Spiral of Cynicism: Symbiosis and Mistrust between Politicians and Journalists', *The International Journal of Press/Politics*, 15(1): 25–40.

Brants, K. and De Haan, Y. (2010) 'Taking the Public Seriously: Three Models of Responsiveness in Media and Journalism', *Media, Culture & Society*, 32(3): 411–28.

Breiden, A. (2002) *Die Rolle der Nachrichtenagenturen im Zusammenspiel von Öffentlichkeitsarbeit und Journalismus*, Master's Thesis, Freie Universität Berlin.

Braun, J. and Gillespie, T. (2011) 'Hosting the Public Discourse, Hosting the Public: When Online News and Social Media Converge', *Journalism Practice*, 5(4): 383–98.

Brewer, P. and Marquardt, E. (2007) 'Mock News and Democracy: Analyzing The Daily Show', *Atlantic Journal of Communication*, 15(4): 249–67.

Briggs, M. (2008) 'The End of Journalism as Usual', *Nieman Reports*, Cambridge: Harvard University, Available: http://www.nieman.harvard.edu/reports/article/100689/The-End-of-Journalism-as-Usual.aspx (accessed 22 August 2010).

Broddason, T. (1994) 'The Sacred Side of Professional Journalism', *European Journal of Communication*, 9(3): 227–48.

Broersma, M. (2007a) 'Form, Style and Journalistic Strategies. An Introduction', in M. Broersma (ed.) *Form and Style in Journalism: European Newspapers and the Representation of News, 1880–2005*, Leuven: Peeters: ix–xxix.

——(2007b) 'Visual Strategies: Dutch Newspaper Design Between Text and Image 1900–2000' in M. Broersma (ed.) *Form and Style in Journalism: European Newspapers and the Representation of News, 1880–2005*, Leuven: Peeters: 177–98.

——(2010a) 'Journalism as Performative Discourse. The Importance of Form and Style in Journalism' in V. Rupar (ed.) *Journalism and Meaning-making: Reading the Newspaper*, Cresskill, N.J.: Hampton Press: 15–35.

——(2010b) 'The Unbearable Limitations of Journalism: On Press Critique and Journalism's Claim to Truth', The International Communication Gazette, 72(1): 21–33.

——(2010c) 'Transnational Journalism History: Balancing Global Universals and National Peculiarities', *Medien & Zeit*, 25(4): 10–15.

——(2011) 'A Daily Truth: The Persuasive Power of Early Modern Newspapers', in J.W. Koopmans and N.H. Petersen (eds) *Commonplace Culture in Western Europe in the*

Early Modern Period: Legitimation of Authority, Leuven, Paris and Walpole, MA: Peeters: 19–34.

Broesma, M. and Graham, T. (2012) 'Social Media as Beat: Tweets as a News Source during the 2010 British and Dutch Elections', *Journalism Practice*, 6(3): 403–19.

Brown, C.H. (1965) 'Majority of Readers Give Papers an A for Accuracy', *Editor & Publisher*, 13 February: 63.

Bruns, A. (2003) 'Gatewatching, Not Gatekeeping: Collaborative Online News', *Media International Australia*, 107: 31–44.

—— (2005) *Gatewatching: Collaborative Online News Production*, New York: Peter Lang.

—— (2006) 'Wikinews: The Next Generation of Alternative Online News?', *Scan* 3(1), Available: http://scan.net.au (accessed 6 January 2011).

—— (2011a) 'News Produsage in a Pro-Am Mediasphere: Why Citizen Journalism Matters', in G. Meikle and G. Redden (eds) *News Online: Transformation and Continuity*, London: Palgrave Macmillan: 132–47.

—— (2011b) 'Citizen Journalism and Everyday Life: A Case Study of Germany's *MyHeimat. de*', in B. Franklin and M. Carlson (eds) *Journalism, Sources and Credibility: New Perspectives*, London: Routledge: 182–94.

Burns, T. (1969) 'Public Service and Private World', in P. Halmos (ed.) *The Sociology of Mass Communications*, Sociological Review Monograph, 13: 53–73.

Calculated Risk Blog (2008) 'In Memoriam: Doris "Tanta" Dungey', Available: www. calculatedriskblog.com/2008/12/In-memoriam-doris-tanta-dungey.html (accessed 1 February 2012).

Cammaerts, B. and Carpentier, N. (2009) 'Blogging the 2003 Iraq War: Challenging the Ideological Model of War and Mainstream Journalism?', *Observatorio (OBS*) Journal*, 3(2): 1–23, Available: http://obs.obercom.pt/index.php/obs/article/view/276 (accessed 1 February 2012).

Campbell, W.J. (2010) *Getting it Wrong: Ten of the Greatest Misrepresented Stories in American Journalism*, Berkeley and Los Angeles: University of California Press.

Cappella, J. and Hall Jamieson, K. (1997) *The Spiral of Cynicism: The Press and the Political Good*, New York: Oxford University Press.

Carlson, M. (2007) 'Blogs and Journalistic Authority: The Role of Blogs in US Election Day 2004 Coverage', *Journalism Studies*, 8(2): 264–79.

—— (2009) 'The Reality of a Fake Image: News Norms, Photojournalistic Craft, and Brian Walski's Fabricated Photograph', *Journalism Practice*, 3(2): 25–139.

Carpentier, N. (2005) 'Identity, Contingency and Rigidity: The (Counter-)Hegemonic Constructions of the Identity of the Media Professional', *Journalism*, 6(2): 199–219.

Carpentier, N., Lie, R. and Servaes, J. (2003) 'Community Media: Muting the Democratic Media Discourse?', *Continuum*, 17(1): 51–68.

Carpentier, N. and Spinoy, E. (eds) (2008) *Discourse Theory and Cultural Analysis: Media, Arts, and Literature*, Cresskill: Hampton Press.

Carpentier, N. and Trioen, M. (2010) 'The Particularity Of Objectivity: A Post-Structuralist and Psychoanalytical Reading of the Gap Between Objectivity-as-a-Value and Objectivity-as-a-Practice in the 2003 Iraqi War Coverage', *Journalism*, 11(3): 311–28.

Carr, D. (2010) 'WikiLeaks Taps Power of the Press', *The New York Times*, 12 December.

Castells, M. (1996) *The Rise of the Network Society*, Oxford: Blackwell.

—— (2000) *The Rise of the Network Society*, 2nd edn, Oxford: Blackwell.

Castells, M. and Ince, M. (2003) *Conversations with Manuel Castells*, Cambridge: Polity.

Chalaby, J. (2000) '"Smiling Pictures Make People Smile". Northcliffe's Journalism', *Media History*, 6(1): 33–44.

Champagne, P. (2009) 'The "Double Dependency": The Journalistic Field Between Politics and Markets', in R. Benson and E. Neveu (eds) *Bourdieu and the Journalistic Field*, Cambridge: Polity: 29–47.

Charles, A. and Stewart, G. (2011) *The End of journalism: News in the Twenty-First Century*, Oxford: Peter Lang.

Charnley, M. (1936) 'Preliminary Notes on a Study of Newspaper Accuracy', *Journalism Quarterly*, 13(4): 394–401.

Chivers, C.J., et al. (2010) 'View is Bleaker than Official Portrayal of War in Afghanistan', *The New York Times*, 25 July.

Chung, D.S. (2007) 'Profits and Perils: News Producers' Perceptions of Interactivity and Uses of Interactive Features', *Convergence: The International Journal of Research into New Media Technologies*, 13(1): 43–61.

Clayman, S. (2002) 'Tribune of the People: Maintaining the Legitimacy of Aggressive Journalism', *Media, Culture and Society*, 24(2): 197–216.

Cohen, N. and Stelter, B. (2010) 'Iraq Video Brings Notice to a Web Site', *The New York Times*, 6 April.

Cohn, D. (2007) 'Network Journalism versus Citizen Journalism versus the Myriad of other Names for Social Media in the News World', *Newassignment*, 6 September, Available: http://www.newassignment. net/blog/david_cohn/sep2007/06/network_journali (accessed 24 July 2010).

Coleman, S. and Ross, K. (2010) *The Media and the Public. 'Them' and 'Us' in Media Discourse*, Malden, MA: Wiley-Blackwell.

Coleman, S., Scott, A. and Morrison, D. (2009) *Public Trust in the News: A Constructivist Study of the Social Life of the News*, Oxford: Reuters Institute for the Study of Journalism.

Comedia (1984) 'The Alternative Press: The Development of Underdevelopment', *Media, Culture & Society*, 6(2): 95–102.

Comedy Central (2007) *The Daily Show* [official website]. Available: http://www.thedaily show.com (accessed 25 March 2007).

Conboy, M. (2004) *Journalism: A Critical History*, London: Sage.

——(2011) *Journalism in Britain: A Historical Introduction*, London: Sage.

Cook, K.S. (ed.) (2003) *Trust in Society*, New York: Russell Sage Foundation Publications.

Cook, T.E. (1998) *Governing with the News: The News Media as a Political Institution*, Chicago: University of Chicago Press.

Cook, T.E. and Gronke, P. (2001) *The Dimensions of Institutional Trust: How Distinct Is Public Confidence in the Media?* Conference Paper, Annual Meeting of the Midwest Political Science Association, Chicago.

Corner, J. and Pels, D. (eds) (2003) *Media and the Restyling of Politics*, London: Sage.

Costera Meijer, I. (2007) 'The Paradox of Popularity', *Journalism Studies*, 8(1): 96–116.

Cottle, S. (2000) 'Rethinking News Access', *Journalism Studies*, 1(3): 427–48.

Couldry, N. (2003) *Media Rituals: A Critical Approach*, London: Routledge.

——(2010) 'New Online News Sources and Writer-Gatherers', in N. Fenton (ed.) *New Media, Old News: Journalism and Democracy in the Digital Age*, London: Sage: 138–52.

Couldry, N., Livingstone, S. and Markham, T. (2007) *Media Consumption and Public Engagement: Beyond the Presumption of Attention*, Houndmills: Palgrave Macmillan.

Croteau, D. and Hoynes, W. (2006) *The Business of Media: Corporate Media and the Public Interest*, 2nd edn, London: Pine Forge Press.

Curran, J. and Witschge, T. (2010) 'Liberal Dreams and the Internet', in N. Fenton (ed.) *New Media, Old News: Journalism and Democracy in the Digital Age*, London: Sage: 102–18.

Dahlgren, P. (1995) *Television and the Public Sphere: Citizenship, Democracy and the Media*, London: Sage.

——(2005) 'The Internet, Public Spheres, and Political Communication: Dispersion and Deliberation', *Political Communication*, 22(2): 147–62.

Davies, N. (2008) *Flat Earth News: An Award-Winning Reporter Exposes Falsehood, Distortion and Propaganda in the Global Media*, London: Chatto & Windus.

——(2010) 'Afghanistan War Logs: Story Behind Biggest Leak in Intelligence History', *Guardian*, 25 July.

Davis, S. (2000) 'Public Journalism: The Case Against', *Journalism Studies*, 1(4): 686–89.

Delli Carpini, M. and Keeter, S. (1996) *What Americans Know About Politics and Why It Matters*, New Haven, CT: Yale University Press.

Delli Carpini, M. and Williams, B. (2001) 'Let Us Infotain You: Politics in the New Media Environment', in W.L. Bennett and R. Entman (eds) *Mediated Politics: Communication in the Future of Democracy*, Cambridge: Cambridge University Press: 160–81.

Deuze, M. (2003) 'The Web and its Journalisms: Considering the Consequences of Different Types of News Media Online', *New Media & Society*, 5(2), 203–30.

——(2005) 'What is Journalism? Professional Identity and Ideology of Journalists Reconsidered', *Journalism*, 6(4): 442–64.

——(2006a) 'Liquid and Zombie Journalism Studies', *Journalism Studies Interest Group*, Available: http://www.icahdq.org/divisions/JournalismStudies/jsigweb4/newsletterS06/debatedeuzefull.html (accessed 8 November 2009).

——(2006b) 'Liquid Journalism', *International Communication Association & American Political Science Association*, 16(1), Available: http://frank.mtsu.edu/~pcr/1601_2005_winter/roundtable_Deuze.htm (accessed 8 November 2009).

——(2006c) 'Participation, Remediation, Bricolage: Considering Principal Components of a Digital Culture', *The Information Society*, 22(2): 63–75.

——(2006d) 'Global Journalism Education', *Journalism Studies*, 7(1): 19–34.

——(2007) *Media Work*, Cambridge: Polity.

——(2009a) 'Understanding Journalism as Newswork: How it Changes, and How it Remains the Same', *Westminster Papers in Communication and Culture*, 5(2): 4–23.

——(2009b) 'The People Formerly Known as the Employers', *Journalism*, 10(3): 315–18.

Deuze, M., Bruns, A. and Neuberger, C. (2007) 'Preparing for an Age of Participatory News', *Journalism Practice*, 1(3): 322–38.

Deuze, M. and Fortunati, L. (2011) 'Journalism without Journalists', in M. Graham and G. Redden (eds) *News Online: Transformations and Continuities*, Basingstoke, England: Palgrave Macmillan.

De Vreese, C.H. (2005) 'The Spiral of Cynicism Reconsidered', *European Journal of Communication*, 20(3): 283–301.

Dewey, J. (1927) *The Public and Its Problems*, New York: Henry Holt & Co.

Dickinson, R. (1997) *Imprinting the Sticks: The Alternative Press Outside London*, Aldershot: Arena.

Djerf-Pierre, M. and Weibull, L. (2008) 'From Public Educator to Interpreting Ombudsman' in J. Strombeck, M. Orsten and T. Aalberg (eds) *Communicating Politics: Political Communication in the Nordic Countries*, Goteborg: Nordicom: 195–214.

Domingo, D. (2008a) 'Inventing Online Journalism: A Constructivist Approach to the Development of Online News', in C. Paterson and D. Domingo (eds) *Making Online News: The Ethnography of New Media Production*, New York: Peter Lang: 15–19.

——(2008b) 'Interactivity in the Daily Routines of Online Newsrooms: Dealing with an Uncomfortable Myth', *Journal of Computer-Mediated Communication*, 13(3): 680–704.

Domingo, D. et al. (2008) 'Participatory Journalism Practices in the Media and Beyond: An International Comparative Study of Initiatives in Online Newspapers', *Journalism Practices*, 2(3): 326–42.

Domscheit-Berg, D. (2011) *Inside WikiLeaks: My Time with Julian Assange at the World's Most Dangerous Website*, London: Jonathan Cape.

Donsbach, W. and Klett, B. (1993) 'Subjective Objectivity. How Journalists in Four Countries Define a Key Term of their Profession', *The International Communication Gazette*, 51(1), 53–83.

Dovifat, E. (1931) *Zeitungswissenschaft, Band 1: Allgemeine Zeitungslehre*, Berlin/Leipzig: De Gruyter.

Downing, J. (2002) 'Independent Media Centers: A Multi-local, Multi-media Challenge to Global Neo-liberalism', in M. Raboy (ed.) *Global Media Policy in the New Millennium*, Luton: Luton University Press: 215–32.

——(2003) 'The IMC Movement beyond "The West"', in A. Opel and D. Pompper (eds) *Representing Resistance: Media, Civil Disobedience, and the Global Justice Movement*, Westport, CT: Praeger: 241–58.

Downing, J., et al. (2001) *Radical Media: Rebellious Communication and Social Movements*, Thousand Oaks: Sage.

Eason, D.L. (1986) 'On Journalistic Authority: The Janet Cooke Scandal', *Critical Studies in Mass Communication*, 3(4): 429–47.

EJO (2011) 'Transparency or Bluff?', *European Journalism Observatory*, June 12, Available: http://en.ejo.ch/3118/ethics/transparency-or-bluff-an-ejo-study (accessed 31 January 2012).

Ellsberg, D. (2011) 'Why the Pentagon Papers Matter Now', *Guardian*, 13 June.

Enli, G.S. and McNair, B. (2010) 'Trans-National Reality TV: A Comparative Study of the UK's and Norway's Wife Swap', in S. Van Bauwel and N. Carpenter (eds) *Trans-reality Television: The Transgression of Reality, Genre, Politics and Audience*, Maryland: Lexington Books: 205–23.

Entman, R.M. (1989) *Democracy Without Citizens: Media and the Decay of American Politics*, New York: Oxford University Press.

Epstein, E.J. (1975) *Between Fact and Fiction: The Problem of Journalism*, New York: Vintage Books.

Ettema, J.S. (2007) 'Journalism as Reason-giving: Deliberative Democracy, Institutional Accountability, and the News Media's Mission', *Political Communication*, 24(2): 143–60.

——(2009a) 'The Moment of Truthiness: The Right Moment to Consider the Meaning of Truthfulness', in B. Zelizer (ed.) *The Changing Faces of Journalism. Tabloidization, Technology and Truthiness*, London and New York: Routledge: 114–26.

——(2009b) 'New Media and New Mechanisms of Public Accountability', *Journalism*, 10(3): 319–21.

Eurobarometer 69 (2008) and 71 (2010) *Public Opinion in the European Union*, European Commission: TNS Opinion Social.

Evans, B. (1959) 'Improvisation in Jazz', Liner notes for *Kind of Blue*: Miles Davis, Produced by Irving Townsend, Columbia Records, CL 1355.

——(1963) 'Notes', Liner notes for *Soulmates*: Ben Webster and Joe Zawinul, Produced by Orrin Keepnews, Riverside Records, RLP 9476.

Feldman, L. (2007) 'The News about Comedy: Young Audiences, *The Daily Show* and Evolving Notions of Journalism', *Journalism*, 8(4): 406–27.

——(2011) 'Partisan Differences in Opinionated News Perceptions: A Test of the Hostile Media Effect', *Political Behavior*, 33(3): 407–32.

Fenton, N. (ed.) (2010) *New Media, Old News: Journalism and Democracy in the Digital Age*, London: Sage.

Fenton, N. and Witschge, T. (2010) 'Comment is Free, Facts are Sacred: Journalistic Ethics in a Changing Mediascape', in G. Meikle and G. Redden (eds) *News Online: Transformation and Continuity*, London: Palgrave Macmillan: 148–63.

Fishman, M. (1980) *Manufacturing the News*, Austin, TX: University of Texas Press.

Fitzgerald, T. (2006) 'Yes, America Does Turn to Jon Stewart', *Media Life*, 8 November, Available: http://www.medialifemagazine.com/cgi-bin/artman/exec/view.cgi (accessed: 27 March 2007).

Foucault, M. (1980) *Power/Knowledge: Selected Interviews and Other Writings*, New York: Pantheon Books.

Fox, C., et al. (2009) *Accuracy in Irish newspapers: Report for the Press Council of Ireland and the Office of the Press Ombudsman*, Dublin: Centre for Society Information and Media, Dublin City University.

Fox, J., et al. (2007) 'No Joke: A Comparison of Substance in The Daily Show with Jon Stewart and Broadcast Network Television', *Journal of Broadcast and Electronic Media*, 51(2): 213–27.

Fox News (2010) 'Administration Calls War Document Leak Illegal, Harmful Amid Calls for Probe', *FoxNews.com*, 26 July, Available: http://www.foxnews.com/politics/2010/07/26/administration-calls-war-document-leak-illegal-harmful-amid-probe/ (accessed 2 February 2012).

Franklin, B. (1997) *Newzak and the News Media*, London: Arnold.

——(ed.) (2008) *Pulling Newspapers Apart: Analysing Print Journalism*, London: Routledge.

Freedman, D. (2009) '"Smooth Operator?" The Propaganda Model and Moments of Crisis', *Westminster Papers in Communication and Culture*, 6(2): 59–72.

– —(2010) 'The Political Economy of the "New" News Environment', in N. Fenton (ed.) *New Media, Old News: Journalism and Democracy in the Digital Age*, London: Sage: 35–50.

Frost, C. (2007) *Journalism Ethics and Regulation*, Harlow: Pearson.

Galtung, J. and Ruge, M.H. (1965) 'The Structure of Foreign News', *Journal of Peace Research*, 2(1): 64–91.

Gans, H. (1980) *Deciding What's News: A Study of CBS Evening News, NBC Nightly News, Newsweek and Time*, London: Constable.

Garcelon, M. (2006) 'The "Indymedia" Experiment: The Internet as Movement Facilitator against Institutional Control', *Convergence The International Journal of Research into New Media Technologies*, 12(1): 55–82.

Gaziano, C. and McGrath, K. (1986) 'Measuring the Concept of Credibility', *Journalism Quarterly*, 63(3): 451–62.

Gebauer, M., et al. (2010) 'Explosive Leaks Provide Image of War from Those Fighting It', *Der Spiegel*, 25 July.

Gerlis, A. (2008) 'Who is a Journalist?', *Journalism Studies*, 9(1): 125–28.

Gershtenson, J. and Plane, D.L., (2007) 'Trust in Government', Pilot Report, April, Ann Arbor, MI: American National Election Studies.

Giddens, A. (1994) 'Living in a Post-Traditional Society', in U. Beck, A. Giddens and S. Lash (eds) *Reflexive Modernization: Politics, Tradition and Aesthetics in the Modern Social Order*, Oxford: Polity: 56–109.

Gillmor, D. (2004) *We the Media: Grassroots Journalism by the People, for the People*, Sebastopol, CA: O'Reilly Media.

– —(2006) *We the Media: Grassroots Journalism by the People, for the People*, 2nd edn, Sebastopol, CA: O'Reilly Media.

——(2010) *Mediactive*, Creative Commons.

Globalization and World Cities Research Network (2008) 'The World According to GaWC 2008', Available: http://www.lboro.ac.uk/gawc/world2008t.html (accessed 20 February, 2011).

Giroux, H. (2000) 'Public Pedagogy as Cultural Politics: Stuart Hall and the "Crisis" of Culture', *Cultural Studies*, 14(2): 341–60.

Gitlin, T. (1980) *The Whole World is Watching: Mass Media in the Making and Unmaking of the New Left*, Los Angeles and London: University of California Press.

Glasser, T.L. (2000) 'The Politics of Public Journalism', *Journalism Studies*, 1(4): 683–86.

Glynos, J. and Stavrakakis, Y. (2004) 'Encounters of the Real Kind. Sussing out the Limits of Laclau's Embrace of Lacan', in S. Critchley and O. Marchart (eds) *Laclau: A Critical Reader*, London: Routledge: 20–216.

Goetz, T. (2005) 'Reinventing Television', *Wired*, 13(9), Available: http://www.wired.com/wired/archive/13.09/stewart.html (accessed 8 July 2007).

Golding, P. and Elliott, E. (1979) *Making the News*, London: Longman.

Goldstein, T. (2007) *Journalism and Truth: Strange Bedfellows*, Evanston, Ill.: Northwestern University Press.

Good, H. (1993) *The Journalist as Autobiographer*, Metuchen, N.J: Scarecrow Press.

Graber, D.A. (2001) *Processing Politics: Learning from Television in the Internet Age*, Chicago: University of Chicago Press.

Graham, T. (2009) 'What's Wife Swap Got to do With It? Talking Politics in the Net-Based Public Sphere', PhD thesis, University of Amsterdam.

Graybeal, M. and Hayes, J.L. (2011) 'A Modified News Micropayment Model for Newspapers on the Social Web', *International Journal on Media Management*, 13(2): 129–48.

Greenfield, M. (2001) *Washington*, New York: Public Affairs Books.

Greenslade, R. (2010) '"Data Journalism" Scores a Massive Hit with WikiLeaks Revelations', *Greenslade Blog*, 26 July, Available: http://www.guardian.co.uk/media/greenslade/2010/jul/26/press-freedom-wikileaks (accessed 2 February 2012).

Greer, J. and Mensing, D. (2004) 'The Evolution of Online Newspapers: A Longitudinal Content Analysis', *Newspaper Research Journal*, 25(2): 98–112.

Gronke, P. and Cook, T.E. (2007) 'Disdaining the Media: The American Public's Changing Attitudes Toward the News', *Political Communication*, 24(3): 259–81.

Groshek, J. (2008) 'Homogenous Agendas, Disparate Frames: CNN and CNN International Coverage Online', *Journal of Broadcasting and Electronic Media*, 52(1): 52–68.

Guggenheim, L., Kwak, N. and Campbell, S.W. (2011) 'Nontraditional News Negativity: The Relationship of Entertaining Political News Use to Political Cynicism and Mistrust', *International Journal of Public Opinion Research*, 23(3): 287–314.

Haas, T. (2007) *The Pursuit of Public Journalism: Theory, Practice and Criticism*, London: Routledge.

Habermas, J. (1989) *The Structural Transformation of the Public Sphere: An Inquiry into a Category of Bourgeois Society*, translated from German by T. Burger with the assistance of F. Lawrence, Cambridge, MA: MIT Press.

——(1996) *Between Facts and Norms: Contributions to a Discourse Theory of Law and Democracy*, translated from German by W. Rehg, Cambridge, MA: MIT Press.

——(2006) 'Political Communication in Media Society: Does Democracy Still Enjoy an Epistemic Dimension? The Impact of Normative Theory on Empirical Research', *Communication Theory*, 16(4): 411–26.

Hafez, K. (2005) 'Globalization, Regionalization, and Democratization: The Interaction of Three Paradigms in the Field', in R.A. Hackett and Y. Zhao (eds), *Democratizing Global Media: One World, Many Struggles*, Lanham: Rowman and Littlefield: 145–63.

——(2007) *The Myth of Media Globalization*, Cambridge: Polity.

Hall, S. (1989) 'New Ethnicities', in Kobena Mercer (ed.) *Black Film, British Cinema*, London: BFI: 27–31.

Hall, S., et al. (1978) *Policing the Crisis: Mugging, the State, and Law and Order*, London: Macmillan.

Hallin, D. (1992) 'The Passing of the "High Modernism" of American Journalism', *Journal of Communication*, 42(3): 14–25.

——(1994) *We Keep America On Top of the World*, London: Routledge.

——(2006) 'The Passing of the "High Modernism" of American Journalism Revisited', *Political Communication Report*, *International Communication Association & American Political Science Association*, 16(1), Available: http://frank.mtsu.edu/~pcr/1601_2005_winter/commentary_hallin.htm (accessed 1 February 2012).

——(2009) 'Not the End of Journalism History', *Journalism*, 10(3): 332–34.

Hallin, D. and Mancini, P. (2004) *Comparing Media Systems*, Cambridge: Cambridge University Press.

Halloran, J., Elliott, P. and Murdock, G. (1970) *Demonstrations and Communication: A Case Study*, London: Penguin.

Hamdy, N. (2009) 'Arab Citizen Journalism in Action: Challenging Mainstream Media, Authorities, and Media Laws', *Westminster Papers in Communication and Culture*, 6(1): 92–112.

Hamilton, J.F. (2003) 'Remaking Media Participation in Early Modern England', *Journalism: Theory, Practice, Criticism*, 4(3): 293–313.

Hanitzsch, T. (2007) 'Deconstructing Journalism Culture: Towards a Universal Theory', *Communication Theory*, 17(4): 367–85.

Hanitzsch, T., et al. (2011) 'Mapping Journalism Cultures Across Nations,' *Journalism Studies*, 12 (3): 273–93.

Hanitzsch, T. and Berganza, R. (2011) *Trust in Public Institutions among Journalists: Comparative Evidence from 18 Countries*, Conference Paper, 61th Annual Conference of the International Communication Association, Boston.

Hanitzsch, T., Plaisance, P.L. and Skewes, E.A. (2012) 'Ethical Orientations of Journalists around the Globe: Implications from a Cross-National Survey', *Communication Research*, forthcoming.

Hannerz, U. (1996) *Transnational Connections: Culture, People, Places*, London, New York: Routledge.

——(2004) *Foreign News: Exploring the World of Foreign Correspondence*, Chicago: University of Chicago Press.

Hargreaves, I. (1999) 'The Ethical Boundaries of Reporting', in M. Ungersma (ed.) *Reporters and the Reported: The 1999 Vauxhall Lectures on Contemporary Issues in British Journalism*, Cardiff: Centre for Journalism Studies.

Hariman, R. (2007) 'In Defense of Jon Stewart', *Critical Studies in Mass Communication*, 24(3): 273–77.

Harold, C. (2007) *OurSpace: Resisting the Corporate Control of Culture*, Minneapolis: University of Minnesota Press.

Harrison, J. (2009) 'User-generated Content and Gatekeeping at the BBC Hub', *Journalism Studies*, 11(2): 243–56.

Hart, R. and Hartelius, E. (2007) 'The Political Sins of Jon Stewart', *Critical Studies in Media Communication*, 24(3): 263–72.

Hartley, J. (2000) 'Communicative Democracy in a Redactional Society: The Future of Journalism Studies', *Journalism: Theory, Practice and Criticism*, 1(1): 39–48.

——(2009) 'Journalism and Popular Culture', in K. Wahl-Jorgensen and T. Hanitzsch (eds) *Handbook of Journalism Studies*, New York and London: Routledge: 310–24.

Hassan, R. (2007) 'Network Time', in R. Hassan and R.E. Purser (eds) *24/7: Time and Temporality in the Network Society*, Stanford, CA: Stanford Business Books: 37–61.

Hauslohner, A. (2011) 'Is Egypt about to have a Facebook Revolution?', *Time.com*, 24 January, Available: http://www.time.com/time/world/article/0,8599,2044142,00.html (accessed 25 July 2011).

Heinrich, A. (2011) *Network Journalism: Journalistic Practice in Interactive Spheres*, New York: Routledge.

——(2012) 'Foreign Reporting in the Sphere of Network Journalism', *Journalism Practice*: 6(5), forthcoming.

Hendler, C. (2010) 'The Story Behind the Publication of WikiLeaks's Afghanistan Logs', *Columbia Journalism Review*, 28 July.

Henry, N. (2008) *American Carnival: Journalism Under Siege in an Age of New Media*, Los Angeles: University of California Press.

Herman, E.S. and Chomsky, N. (1988) *Manufacturing Consent: The Political Economy of the Mass Media*, New York: Pantheon Books.

Hermida, A. (2001) 'The BBC Goes Blogging: Is "Auntie" Finally Listening?', Conference paper, 9th International Online Journalism Symposium. Available: http://online.journalism. utexas.edu/2008/papers/Hermida.pdf (accessed 5 November 2009).

——(2009) 'The Blogging BBC: Journalism Blogs at "the World's Most Trusted News Organisation"', *Journalism Practice*, 3(3): 1–17.

Hermida, A. and Thurman, N. (2008) 'A Clash of Cultures: The Integration of User-generated Content within Professional Journalistic Frameworks at British Newspaper Websites', *Journalism Practice*, 2(3): 343–56.

Hibberd, M. (2010) 'Trans-professionalism Undone? The 2007 British TV Scandals', in S. Van Bauwel and N. Carpenter (eds) *Trans-reality Television: The Transgression of Reality, Genre, Politics and Audience*, Maryland: Lexington Books: 87–102.

Hibbing, J. (1999) 'Appreciating Congress' in J. Cooper (ed.) *Congress and the Decline of Public Trust*, Boulder, CO: Westview Press, 43–64.

Hibbing, J. and Theiss-Morse, E. (2002) *Stealth Democracy: Americans' Beliefs About How Government Should Work*, Cambridge: Cambridge University Press.

Hiler, J. (2001) 'Borg Journalism: We Are the Blogs. Journalism Will Be Assimilated', Microcontentent News, 1 April 2001, Available: http://www.microcontentnews.com/ articles/borgjournalism.htm (no longer available online).

Hill, A. (2007) *Restyling Factual TV: Audiences and News, Documentary and Reality Genres*, London: Routledge.

Hindman, E.B. (2005) 'Jayson Blair, the *New York Times*, and Paradigm Repair', *Journal of Communication*, 55(2): 225–41.

House of Lords (2008) *The Ownership of the News: Vol I: Report*, Norwich: Select Committee on Communications; The Stationery Office Limited, Available: http://www.publications. parliament.uk/pa/ld200708/ldselect/ldcomuni/122/122i.pdf (accessed January 2011).

Hoyer, S. (2005) 'The Idea of the Book: Introduction' in S. Hoyer and H. Pöttker (eds) *Diffusion of the News Paradigm 1850–2000*, Goteberg: Nordicom: 9–16.

Hoyer, S. and Nonseid, J. (2005) 'The Half-Hearted Modernisation of Norwegian Journalism 1908–40' in S. Hoyer and H. Pöttker (eds) *Diffusion of the News Paradigm 1850–2000*, Goteberg: Nordicom: 123–36.

Hovland, C., Janis, I. and Kelley, H.H. (1953) *Communication and Persuasion*, New Haven: Yale University Press.

Hovland, C. and Weiss, W. (1951) 'The Influence of Source Credibility on Communication Effectiveness', *Public Opinion Quarterly*, 15(4): 635–50.

Høyer, S. and Pöttker, H. (eds) (2005) *Diffusion of the News Paradigm 1850–2000*, Göteborg: Nordicom.

Huang, E. et al. (2004) 'Converged Journalism and Quality: A Case Study of the *Tampa Tribune* News Stories', *Convergence*, 10(4): 73–92.

Hume, E. (1999) 'Wired World, Wired Learning: the Serf Surfs', Conference paper, Net-Media Conference, London, 1 July, Available: http://www.ellenhume.com/articles/serfsurfs_printable.html (accessed 8 November 2009).

Hutchins, R. (1947) '*Commission on the Freedom of the Press*', *A Free and Responsible Press*, Chicago: University of Chicago Press.

Jacobs, S.P. (2010) 'New York Times Strikes Back at WikiLeaks Founder', *TheDailyBeast.com*, 28 July.

Jarvis, J. (2006) 'Networked Journalism', *BuzzMachine*, 5 July. Available: http://www.buzz machine.com/2006/07/05/networkedjournalism/ (accessed 21 January 2012).

——(2009) *What Would Google Do?* New York: Collins Business.

Jenkins, H. (2006) *Convergence Culture: Where Old and New Media Collide*, New York: New York University Press.

Jewkes, J., Sawers, D. and Stillerman, R. (1969) *The Sources of Invention*, 2nd edn, New York: Macmillan.

Jönsson, A.M. and Örnebring, H. (2011) 'User-generated Content and the News: Empowerment of Citizens or Interactive Illusion?' *Journalism Practice*, 5(2): 127–44.

Jones, James (2010) 'Statement of National Security Advisor General James Jones on Wiki-leaks', Office of the Press Secretary, 25 July, Available: http://www.whitehouse.gov/the-press-office/statement-national-security-advisor-general-james-jones-wikileaks (accessed 2 February 2012).

Jones, Jeffrey (2009) 'Believable Fictions: Redactional Culture and the Will to Truthiness', in B. Zelizer (ed.) *The Changing Faces of Journalism: Tabloidization, Technology and Truthi-ness*, London and New York: Routledge: 127–43.

——(2010) *Entertaining Politics: Satiric Television and Political Engagement*, New York: Rowman & Littlefield.

Jones, Julie and Himelboim, I. (2010) 'Just a Guy in Pajamas? Framing the Blogs in Main-stream US Newspaper Coverage (1999–2005)', *New Media & Society*, 12(2): 271–88.

Josephi, B. (2009) 'Journalism Education', in K. Wahl-Jorgensen and T. Hanitzsch (eds) *Handbook of Journalism Studies*, London: Routledge: 42–56.

Keen, A. (2007) *The Cult of the Amateur: How Today's Internet is Killing our Culture*, London: Currency.

Keller, B. (2010) 'The War Logs Articles', *The New York Times*, 25 July.

Kern, S. (1983) *The Culture of Time and Space, 1880–1918*, Cambridge: Harvard University Press.

Khatchadourian, R. (2010) 'No Secrets: Julian Assange's Mission for Total Transparency', *The New Yorker*, 7 June.

Kim, E.-G. and Hamilton, J.F. (2006) 'Capitulation to Capital? *OhmyNews* as Alternative Media', *Media, Culture & Society*, 28(4): 541–60.

Kocher, D.J. (1981) 'Measuring Mass Media Accuracy', *International Communication Gazette*, 28(3): 171–76.

Kocher, D.J. and Shaw, E.F. (1979) *Newspaper Errors and Perceived Bias: A New Direction for Accuracy Research*, Unpublished Discussion Paper, University of Tennessee, Knoxville.

Kovach, B. and Rosenstiel, T. (1999) *Warp Speed: America in the Age of Mixed Media*, New York: The Century Foundation Press.

——(2001) *The Elements of Journalism: What Newspeople Should Know and the Public Should Expect*, New York: Crown Publishing Group.

Kovacic, M.P. and Erjavec, K. (2008) 'Mobi Journalism in Slovenia: Is this Really Citizen Journalism?', *Journalism Studies*, 9(6): 874–90.

Kriesi, H., et al. (2008) *West European Politics in the Age of Globalization*, Cambridge: Cambridge University Press.

Krotz, F. (2007) 'The Meta-process of "Mediatization" as a Conceptual Frame', *Global Media and Communication*, 3(3): 256–60.

Kunelius, R. and Renvall, M. (2010) 'Stories of a Public: Journalism and the Validity of Citizens' Testimonies', *Journalism: Theory, Practice and Criticism*, 11(5): 515–29.

Kurtz, H. (2010) 'Air Leaks from the WikiLeaks Balloon', *The Washington Post*, 28 July.

Laclau, E. (1988) 'Metaphor and Social Antagonisms', in C. Nelson and L. Grossberg (eds) *Marxism and the Interpretation of Culture*, Urbana: University of Illinois: 249–57.

——(1990) *New Reflections on the Revolution of our Time*, London: Verso.

——(2000) 'Constructing Universality', in J. Butler, E. Laclau and S. Žižek (eds) *Contingency, Hegemony, Universality: Contemporary Dialogues on the Left*, London: Verso: 281–307

Laclau, E. and Mouffe, C. (1985) *Hegemony and Socialist Strategy: Towards a Radical Democratic Politics*, London: Verso.

Landry, C., et al. (1985) *What a Way to Run a Railroad: An Analysis of Radical Failure*, London: Comedia.

Lasica, J.D. (2001) 'A Scorecard for Net News Ethics', *Online Journalism Review*, 20 September, Available: http://www.ojr.org/ojr/ethics/1017782140.php (accessed 8 November 2009).

Lasswell, H. (1948) 'The Structure and Function of Communication in Society', in L. Bryson (ed.) *The Communication of Ideas*, New York: Institute for Religious and Social Studies: 37–51.

Latif, A. (1998) 'The Press in Asia: Taking a Stand', in A. Latif (ed.) *Walking the Tightrope: Press Freedom and Professional Standards in Asia*, Singapore: Asian Media Information Centre: 3–15.

Lawrence, G.C. and Grey, D.L. (1969) 'Subjective Inaccuracies in Local News Reporting', *Journalism Quarterly*, 46(Winter): 753–57.

Lee-Wright, P. and Phillips, A. (2011) 'Doing it all in the Multi-skilled Universe', in P. Lee-Wright, A. Phillips and T. Witschge (eds) *Changing Journalism*, London: Routledge: 63–80.

Lee-Wright, P., Phillips, A. and Witschge, T. (2012) *Changing Journalism*, London: Routledge.

Leigh, D. and Harding, L. (2011) *WikiLeaks: Inside Julian Assange's War on Secrecy*, London: Guardian Books.

Levey, N.N. and Martinez, J. (2010) 'WikiLeaks Reflects New Model for Muckraking', *Pittsburgh Post-Gazette*, 27 July.

Lévy, P. (1997) *Collective Intelligence*, Cambridge: Perseus.

Lewin, K., Lippitt, R. and White, R.K. (1939) 'Patterns of Aggressive Behavior in Experimentally Created Social Climates', *Journal of Social Psychology*, 10(2): 271–301.

Lewis, J., et al. (2008) *The Quality and Independence of British Journalism*, Cardiff, UK: School of Journalism, Media and Cultural Studies, Cardiff University.

Lieberman, J. (2010) 'Lieberman Condemns Leak of Afghan War Materials', 26 July, Available: http://lieberman.senate.gov/index.cfm/news-events/news/2010/7/lieberman-condemns-leak-of-afghan-war-materials (accessed 2 February 2012).

Lipset, S. and Schneider, W. (1987) *The Confidence Gap: Business, Labor, and Government in the Public Mind*, Baltimore: John Hopkins University Press.

Livingstone, S. (2004) 'The Challenge of Changing Audiences: Or, What is the Audience Researcher to Do in the Age of the Internet?', *European Journal of Communication*, 19(1): 75–86.

Livingstone, S., et al. (2008) 'Converging Traditions of Research on Media and Information Literacies: Disciplinary, Critical and Methodological Issues', in D.J. Leu et al. (eds) *Handbook of Research on New Literacies*, Mahwah, NJ: Lawrence Erlbaum: 103–32.

Lloyd, J. and Seaton, J. (2006) *What can be Done? Making the Media and Politics Better*, Malden, Mass., Oxford: Blackwell Pub.

Lowrey, W. (2006) 'Mapping the Journalism-Blogging Relationship', *Journalism*, 7(4): 477–500.

Luhmann, N. (1979) *Trust and Power*, New York: Wiley.

——(2000) *Vertrauen: Ein Mechanismus der Reduktion sozialer Komplexität*, 4th edn, Stuttgart: UTB.

Lule, J. (1992) 'Journalism and Criticism: The Philadelphia Inquirer Norplant Editorial', *Critical Studies in Mass Communication*, 9: 91–109.

Lupia, A. and McCubbins, M.D. (1998) *The Democratic Dilemma: Can Citizens Learn What They Need to Know?*, Cambridge: Cambridge University Press.

Luskin, R.C. (2003) 'The Heavenly Public: What Would a Fully Informed Citizenry Be Like?' in M.B. MacKuen, and G. Rabinowitz, *Electoral Democracy*, Ann Arbor, MI: University of Michigan Press: 238–61.

Lyotard, J. (1979) *La Condition Postmoderne: Rapport sur le Savoir*, Paris: Minuit.

Madrigal, A. (2010) 'Wikileaks May Have Just Changed the Media, Too', *The Atlantic*, 25 July.

Maier, S.R. (2003) 'How Sources, Reporters View Math Errors in News', *Newspaper Research Journal*, 24(4): 48–63.

——(2005) 'Accuracy Matters: A Cross-market Assessment of Newspaper Error and Credibility', *Journalism & Mass Communication Quarterly*, 82(3): 533–51.

——(2007) 'Setting the Record Straight: When the Press Errs, Do Corrections Follow?', *Journalism Practice*, 1(1): 33–43.

——(2009) 'Confessing Errors in a Digital Age', *Nieman Reports*, Cambridge: Harvard University. Available: http://www.nieman.harvard.edu/reports/article/101903/Confessing-Errors-in-a-Digital-Age.aspx (accessed 2 February 2011).

Manin, B. (1997) *The Principles of Representative Government*, Cambridge: Cambridge University Press.

Manning, P. (2001) *News and News Sources: A Critical Introduction*, London: Sage.

Manosevitch, E and Walker, D. (2009) 'Reader Comments to Online Opinion Journalism: A Space of Public Deliberation', Conference paper, 10th International Symposium on Online Journalism, Austin, TX, April 2009.

Marcus, G.E., Neuman, W.R. and MacKuen, M. (2000) *Affective Intelligence and Political Judgment*, Chicago: University of Chicago Press.

Matheson, D. (2000) 'The Birth of News Discourse: Changes in News Language in British Newspapers, 1880–1930,' *Media, Culture & Society*, 22(5): 557–73.

——(2003) 'Scowling at their Notebooks: How Journalists Understand their Writing', *Journalism*, 42(2): 165–83.

——(2004) 'Weblogs and the Epistemology of the News: Some Trends in Online Journalism', *New Media & Society*, 6(4): 443–68.

Matheson, D. and Allan, S. (2007) 'Truth in a War Zone: The Role of Warblogs in Iraq', in S. Maltby and R. Keeble (eds) *Communicating War: Memory, Media and Military*, Bury St. Edmunds: Arima: 75–89.

Mathiesen, T. (1997) 'The Viewer Society', *Theoretical Criminology*, 1(2): 215–34.

Matthes, J. and Kohring, M. (2007) 'Trust in News Media: Development and Validation of a Multidimensional Scale', *Communication Research*, 34(2): 231–52.

Manovich, L. (2001) *The Language of New Media*, Cambridge, MA: MIT Press.

Mayring, P. (2000) 'Qualitative Content Analysis', *Forum: Qualitative Social Research*, 1, Available: http://www.qualitative-research.net/index.php/fqs/article/view/1089 (accessed 5 July 2011).

McAthy, R. and Gunter, J. (2010) 'Wikileaks Editor Julian Assange Says There is "More to Come" After Afghanistan Leak', *Journalism.co.uk*, 26 July. Available: http://www.journalism. co.uk/news/wikileaks-editor-julian-assange-says-there-is-039-more-to-come-039-after-afghanistan-leak/s2/a539793/ (accessed 2 February 2012).

McChesney, R. and Nichols, J. (2010) *The Death and Life of American Journalism: The Media Revolution that Will Begin the World Again*, New York: Nation Books.

McChesney, R. and Pickard, V. (eds) (2011) *Will the Last Reporter Please Turn Out the Lights: The Collapse of Journalism and What Can be Done to Fix It*, New York: The New Press.

McCombs, M. (2004) *Setting the Agenda: The Mass Media and Public Opinion*, Oxford: Polity.

McIntyre, J. (2010) 'WikiLeaks: Whistleblowers or Info-Terrorists?', *LineOfDeparture.com*, 27 July. Available: http://www.lineofdeparture.com/2010/07/27/wikileaks-whistleblowers-or-anti-privacy-terrorists/ (accessed 2 February 2012).

McNair, B. (1998) *The Sociology of Journalism*, London, New York, Sydney, Auckland: Arnold.

——(2006) *Cultural Chaos: Journalism, News and Power in a Globalised World*, London, Routledge.

——(2008) 'I, Columnist', in Franklin B. (ed.) *Pulling Newspapers Apart: Analysing Print Journalism*, London: Routledge: 112–20.

——(2009a) 'Journalism in the 21st Century – Evolution, not Extinction', *Journalism: Theory, Practice and Criticism*, 10(3): 347–49.

——(2009b) *News and Journalism in the UK*, 5th edn, London: Routledge.

——(2011) 'Managing the Online News Revolution: The UK Experience', in G. Meikle and G. Redden (eds) *News Online: Transformations & Continuities*, London: Palgrave Macmillan: 38–53.

McNair, B., Dekavalla, M., Boyle, R. and Meikle, G. (2010) *Mapping Futures For News: Trends, Challenges and Opportunities for Scotland*, University of Strathclyde, Institute of Advanced Studies.

McQuail, D. (1994) *Mass Communication Theory: An Introduction*, London: Sage.

——(2003) *Media Accountability and the Freedom of Publication*, Oxford: Oxford University Press.

Meckel, M. (2010) 'Proudly Content Free', *Publizistik*, 55(3): 223–29.

——(2011) 'Journalisten an der Crowdsourcing-Front', *Focus Online*. Available: http://www.focus.de/digital/internet/dld-2011/debate/tid-20968/medienwandel-journalisten-an-der-crowdsourcing-front_aid_589439.html (accessed 14 January 2011).

Media Awareness Network (2011) 'Media Education in Canada: An Overview'. Available: http://www.media-awareness.ca/english/teachers/media_education/media_education_overview.cfm (accessed 10 October 2011).

Meikle, G. and Redden, G. (eds) (2011) *News Online: Transformations & Continuities*, London: Palgrave Macmillan.

Mensing, D. and Oliver, M. (2005) 'Editors at Small Newspapers say Error Problems Serious', *Newspaper Research Journal*, 26(4): 6–21.

Meyer, G. and Lund, A.B. (2008) 'Spiral of Cynicism: Are Media Researchers Mere Observers?' *Ethical Space: International Journal of Communication Ethics*, 5(3): 33–42.

Meyer, P. (1988) 'Defining and Measuring Credibility of Newspapers: Developing an Index', *Journalism Quarterly*, 65(3): 567–74.

Meyrowitz, J. (1998) 'Multiple Media Literacies', *Journal of Communication*, 48(1): 96–108.

Milioni, D.L. (2009) 'Probing the Online Counterpublic Sphere: The Case of Indymedia Athens', *Media, Culture & Society*, 31(3): 409–31.

Miller, D.T. and Ross, M. (1975) 'Self-serving Biases in the Attribution of Causality: Fact or Fiction?', *Psychological Bulletin*, 82(2): 213–25.

Mindich, D. (1998) *Just the Facts: How 'Objectivity' Came to Define American Journalism*, New York: New York University Press.

——(2005) *Tuned Out: Why Americans Under 40 Don't Follow the News*, New York: Oxford University Press.

Mishler, W. and Rose, R. (2005) 'What Are the Political Consequences of Trust? A Test of Cultural and Institutional Theories in Russia', *Comparative Political Studies*, 38(9): 1050–78.

Misztal, B.A. (1996) *Trust in Modern Societies*, Cambridge, UK: Polity.

Mitchelstein, E. and Boczkowski, P. (2009) 'Between Tradition and Change: A Review of Recent Research on Online News Production', *Journalism*, 10(5): 562–68.

Mnookin, S. (2004) *Hard News: The Scandals at The New York Times and Their Meaning for American Media*, New York: Random House.

Mondak, J.J. (2006) 'Political Knowledge and Cross-National Research on Support for Democracy', Paper delivered to the Latin American Public Opinion Project (LAPOP) and UN Development Programme (UNDP) Workshop on Candidate Indicators for the UNDP Democracy Support Index (DSI), Vanderbilt University, Nashville, Tennessee, May.

Morgan, P. (2005) *The Insider: The Private Diaries of a Scandalous Decade*, London: Ebury Press.

——(2008) 'Adventures of the Comeback Kid', *British Journalism Review*, 19(4): 17–29.

Morris, E. (2010) 'The Anosognosic's Dilemma: Something's Wrong but You'll Never Know What It Is', *New York Times*, 20 June. Available: http://opinionator.blogs.nytimes.com/2010/06/20/the-anosognosics-dilemma-1/ (accessed: 10 October 2011).

Mott, F.L. (1942) 'Trends in Newspaper Content', *Annals of the American Academy of Political and Social Science*, 219(1): 60–65.

Moy, P., Pfau, M. and Kahlor, L.A. (1999) 'Media Use and Public Confidence in Democratic Institutions', *Journal of Broadcasting & Electronic Media*, 43: 137–58.

Müller, J. (2010) 'The (Ir)relevance of Trust in the News Media: Dynamics, Causes, and Consequences of Trust in the News Media in Democratic and Authoritarian Regimes', Ph.D. thesis, Bremen: Jacobs University.

Mulder, R. (1980) 'Media Credibility: A Use-Gratifications Approach', *Journalism Quarterly*, 57(3): 474–77.

Muthukumaraswamy, K. (2010) 'When the Media Meet Crowds of Wisdom: How Journalists are Tapping into Audience Expertise and Manpower for the Processes of Newsgathering', *Journalism Practice*, 4(1): 48–65.

Myers, S. (2010) 'How WikiLeaks is Changing the News Power Structure', *www.poynter.org*, 27 July. Available: http://www.poynter.org/latest-news/top-stories/104595/how-wiki-leaks-is-changing-the-news-power-structure/ (accessed 2 February 2012).

Naït-Bouda, F. (2008) 'From Identity to Identity Strategies: The French Pigiste Group Identity as an Exemplary Case Study', in N. Carpentier et al. (eds) *Democracy, Journalism and Technology: New Developments in an Enlarged Europe*, Tartu: Tartu University Press. Available: http://www.researchingcommunication.eu/reco_book4.pdf (accessed 1 February 2012).

Negroponte, N. (1995) *Being Digital*, New York: Knopf.

Nemeth, N. and Sanders, C. (2009) 'Number of Corrections Increase at Two National Newspapers', *Newspaper Research Journal*, 30(3): 90–104.

Nerone, J. (2009) 'The Death (and Rebirth?) of Working-class Journalism', *Journalism: Theory, Practice & Criticism*, 10(3): 353–55.

Neuberger, C. and Nuernbergk, C. (2010) 'Competition, Complementarity or Integration?', *Journalism Practice*, 4(3): 319–32.

Neuman, W.R. (1986) *The Paradox of Mass Politics: Knowledge and Opinion in the American Electorate*, Cambridge: Harvard University Press.

Neuman, W.R., et al (eds) (2007) *The Affect Effect: Dynamics of Emotion in Political Thinking and Behavior*, Chicago: University of Chicago Press.

Nguyen, A. (2011) 'Marrying the Professional to the Amateur: Strategies and Implications of the OhmyNews Model', in G. Meikle and G. Redden (eds) *News Online: Transformations & Continuities*, London: Palgrave Macmillan: 195–209.

Norris, P. (1999) 'Introduction: The Growth of Critical Citizens?', in P. Norris (ed.) *Critical Citizens: Global Support for Democratic Governance*, Oxford: Oxford University Press.

——(2000) *A Virtuous Circle: Political Communication in Post-Industrial Democracies*, Cambridge: Cambridge University Press.

Nossek, H. (2009) 'On the Future of Journalism as a Professional Practice and the Case of Journalism in Israel', *Journalism*, 10(3): 358–61.

Nystedt, D. (2009) 'Wikileaks Plans to Make the Web a Leakier Place', *ComputerWorld.com*, 9 October. Available: http://www.computerworld.com/s/article/9139180/Wikileaks_plans_to_make_the_Web_a_leakier_place (accessed 2 February 2012).

Oblak, T. (2005) 'The Lack of Interactivity and Hypertextuality in Online Media', *Gazette: The International Journal for Communication Studies*, 67(1): 87–106.

Ofcom (2007) *New News, Future News: The Challenges for Television News after Digital Switch-over*. Available: http://stakeholders.ofcom.org.uk/binaries/research/tv-research/newnews.pdf (accessed 2 February 2012).

Örnebring, H. (2008) 'The Consumer as Producer – of What? User-generated Tabloid Content in *The Sun* (UK) and *Aftonbladet* (Sweden)', *Journalism Studies*, 9(5): 771–85.

Ognianova, E. and Endersby, J. (1996) 'Objectivity Revisited: A Spatial model of Political Ideology and Mass Communication', *Journalism and Mass Communication Monographs*, 159: 1–36.

Ordine dei Giornalisti (1993) 'Charter of Duties of the Journalists'. Available: http://www.odg.it/content/carta-dei-doveri-del-giornalista (accessed 20 January 2011).

Organisation for Economic Co-Operation and Development (2010) *The Evolution of News and the Internet*, Report of the OECD Working Party On the Information Economy.

Pan, Z., Chan, J.M. and Lo, V. (2008) 'Journalism Research in Greater China: Its Communities, Approaches, and Themes' in M. Loeffelholtz and D. Weaver (eds) *Global Journalism Research*, Malden: Blackwell: 197–210.

Pantti, M. and Bakker, P. (2009) 'Misfortunes, Memories and Sunsets: Non-professional Images in Dutch News Media', *International Journal of Cultural Studies*, 12(5): 471–89.

Paterson, C. (2005) 'News Agency Dominance in International News on the Internet', in D. Skinner, J.R. Compton and M. Gasher (eds) *Converging Media, Diverging Politics: A Political Economy of News Media in the United States and Canada*, Oxford: Lexington Books: 154–64.

Paterson, C.A. and Domingo, D. (eds) (2008) *Making Online News: The Ethnography of New Media Production*, New York: Peter Lang.

Patterson, M. and Urbanski, S. (2006). 'What Jayson Blair and Janet Cooke Say about the Press and the Erosion of Public Trust', *Journalism*, 7(6): 828–50.

Paulussen, S., et al. (2007) 'Doing it Together: Citizen Participation in the Professional News Making Process', *Observatorio (OBS*) Journal*, 1(3): 131–54.

Pavlik, J. (2000) 'The Impact of Technology on Journalism', *Journalism Studies*, 1(2): 229–37.

Perelman, M. (1998) 'The Neglected Economics of Trust: The Bentham Paradox and Its Implications', *American Journal of Economics & Sociology*, 57(4): 381–89.

Perlmutter, D.D. (2008) *Blogwars: The New Political Battleground*, Oxford: Oxford University Press.

Peters, C. (2009) *The Truthiness Factor: Blurring Boundaries and the Shifting Status of Objectivity and Emotion in Television News*, PhD thesis, Carleton University, National Library and Archives Canada.

——(2010) 'No Spin Zones: The Rise of the American Cable News Magazine and Bill O'Reilly', *Journalism Studies*, 11(6): 832–51.

——(2011) 'Emotion Aside or Emotional Side?: Crafting an "Experience of Involvement" in the News', *Journalism: Theory, Practice and Criticism* 12(3): 297–316.

——(2012) 'Journalism To Go: The Changing Spaces of News Consumption', *Journalism Studies*, 13(5) (forthcoming).

Pew Research Center (2004) 'Internet and Cable News Loom Large in Fragmented Political Universe'. Available: http://people-press.org/report/200/cable-and-internet-loom-large-in-fragmented-political-news-universe (accessed 10 October 2011).

——(2005) 'Trends 2005'. Available: http://pewresearch.org/assets/files/trends2005.pdf (accessed on 5 July 2011).

——(2008) 'The Daily Show: Journalism, Satire of Just Laughs?'. Available: http://pewresearch.org/pubs/829/the-daily-show-journalism-satire-or-just-laughs (accessed 10 October 2011).

——(2009) 'Press Accuracy Rating Hits Two Decade Low'. Available: http://www.people-press.org/2009/09/13/press-accuracy-rating-hits-two-decade-low (accessed 10 October 2011).

——(2010a) *Distrust, Discontent, Anger and Partisan Rancor: The People and Their Government*, Washington: The Pew Research Center for the People & the Press.

——(2010b) 'Understanding the Participatory News Consumer: How Internet and Cell Phone Users Have Turned News into Social Experience'. Available: http://www.pewinternet.org/Reports/2010/Online-News.aspx (accessed 5 July 2011).

Phelps, A. (2011) 'Why we Didn't Delete the Tweet', *HubBub The Buzz of Boston WBUR*, 10 January. Available: http://hubbub.wbur.org/2011/01/10/giffords-coverage-twitter (accessed 24 January 2011).

Phillips, A. (2005) 'New Sources, Old Bottles', in N. Fenton (ed.) *New Media, Old News: Journalism and Democracy in the Digital Age*, London: Sage: 87–101.

——(2010) 'Old Sources: New Bottles', in N. Fenton (ed.) *New Media, Old News: Journalism and Democracy in the Digital Age*, London: Sage: 87–101.

Phillips, A. and Witschge, T. (2011) 'The Changing Business of News: Sustainability of News Journalism', in P. Lee-Wright, A. Phillips and T. Witschge (eds) *Changing Journalism*, London: Routledge: 3–20.

Picard, R.G. (2005) 'Money, Media and the Public Interest', in G. Overholser and K. Hall Jamieson (eds) *The Press*, Oxford: Oxford University Press: 337–50.

Poletti, M. and Brants, K. (2010) 'Between Partisanship and Cynicism: Italian Journalism in a State of Flux', *Journalism: Theory Practice & Criticism*, 11(3): 329–46.

Pöttker, H. (2004) 'Objectivity as (Self-)Censorship: Against the Dogmatization of Professional Ethics in Journalism', *Javnost/The Public*, 11(2): 83–94.

Poulsen, K. and Zetter, K. (2010) 'US Intelligence Analyst Arrested in Wikileaks Video Probe', *Wired.com*, 6 June. Available: http://www.wired.com/threatlevel/2010/06/leak/ (accessed 2 February 2012).

Powers, S. and El-Nawawy, M. (2008) 'New Media and the Politics of Protest: A Case Study of Al Jazeera English in Malaysia', in M. Kugelman (ed.) *Kuala Lumpur Calling: Al Jazeera English in Asia*, Washington DC: Woodrow Wilson International Center for Scholars: 65–82.

Price, M.E. (2008) 'Governance, Globalism and Satellites', *Global Media and Communication*, 4: 245–59.

Project for Excellence in Journalism (PEJ) (2007) *State of the News Media 2007: An Annual Report on American Journalism*. Available: http://stateofthemedia.org/2007/overview/public-attitudes (accessed 9 December 2011).

——(2010) *State of the News Media 2010*. Available: http://www.stateofthemedia.org/2010 (accessed 10 October 2011).

Quandt, T., et al. (2006) 'American and German Online Journalists at the Beginning of the 21st Century: A Bi-National Survey', *Journalism Studies*, 7(2): 171–86.

Rally to Restore Sanity (2010a) Event Announcement [official website]. Available: http://www.rallytorestoresanity.com (accessed 10 October 2011).

——(2010b) 'Jon Stewart's Final Speech at Rally to Restore Sanity' [video]. Available: http://www.youtube.com/watch?v=6JzGOiBXeD4 (accessed 10 October 2011).

Redden, J. and Witschge, T. (2010) 'A New News Order? Online News Content Examined', in N. Fenton (ed.) *New Media, Old News: Journalism and Democracy in the Digital Age*, London: Sage: 171–87.

Reese, S.D. (1990) 'The News Paradigm and the Ideology of Objectivity: A Socialist at the Wall Street Journal', *Critical Studies in Mass Communication*, 7(4): 390–409.

Reger, J., Myers, D.J. and Einwohner, R.L. (eds) (2008) *Identity Work in Social Movements*, Minneapolis: University of Minnesota Press.

Reich, Z. (2008) 'How Citizens Create News Stories: The "News Access" Problem Reversed', *Journalism Studies*, 9(5): 739–58.

Reinardy, S. (2007) 'Newspaper Journalism in Crisis: Burnout On The Rise, Eroding Young Journalists' Career Commitment', *Journalism*, 12(1): 33–50.

Rice, X. (2007) 'The Looting of Kenya', *Guardian, 31 August.

Riegert, K. (ed.) (2007) *Politicotainment: Television's Take on the Real*, New York: Peter Lang.

Robinson, M. (1976) 'Public Affairs Television and the Growth of Public Malaise: The Case of "The Selling of the Pentagon"', *American Political Science Review*, 70(2): 409–32.

Robinson, P., et al. (2006) *Media Wars: News Media Performance and Media Management During the 2003 Iraq War*, ESRC Research Report No. RES-000-23-0551, Swindon: Economic and Social Research Council.

Robinson, S. (2006) 'The Mission of the J-Blog: Recapturing Journalistic Authority Online', *Journalism*, 64(7): 65–83.

Rodriguez, C. (2001) *Fissures in the Mediascape: An International Study of Citizens' Media*, Cresskill: Hampton Press

Rogers, E.M. (1962) *Diffusion of Innovations*, New York: Free Press.

Rogers, E.M., Singhal, A. and Quinlan, M.M. (2009) 'Diffusion of Innovations' in D.W. Stacks and M.B. Salwen (eds) *An Integrated Approach to Communication Theory and Research*, 2nd edn, New York: Routledge: 418–34.

Roper, B.W. (1985) *Public Attitudes Toward Television and Other Media in a Time of Change*, New York: Television Information Office.

Rose, N., O'Malley, P. and Valverde, M. (2009) 'Governmentality', Legal Studies Research Paper No. 09/94, Sydney Law School.

Rosen, J. (1991) 'Making Journalism More Public', *Communications*, 12(4): 267–84.

——(2010) 'The Afghanistan War Logs Released by Wikileaks, the World's First Stateless News Organization', Pressthink.org, 26 July.

Rosenberg, S. (2011) 'Correct, Don't Delete, that Erroneous Tweet', *Wordyard*. Available: http://www.wordyard.com/2011/01/10/correct-dont-delete-that-erroneous-tweet/ (accessed 24 January 2011).

Rowe, C. (1992) 'Hacks on Film', *Washington Journalism Review*, 14(11): 27–29.

Russial, J. (2009) 'Copy Editing not Great Priority for Online Stories', *Newspaper Research Journal*, 30(2): 6–15.

Ryan, B. and Gross, N.C. (1943) 'The Diffusion of Hybrid Seed Corn in Two Iowa Communities', *Rural Sociology*, 8(1): 15–24.

Salgado, S. and Strömbäck, J. (2012) 'Interpretive Journalism: A Review of Concepts, Operationalizations and Key Findings', *Journalism Theory Practice & Criticism*, 13: 144–61.

Sampedro Blanco, V.F. (ed.) (2005) *13-M: Multitudes On-line*, Madrid: Catarata.

Samuel-Azran, T. (2010) *Al-Jazeera and US War Coverage*, New York: Peter Lang.

Sangnier, M. (2009) 'Does Trust Favor Macroeconomic Instability?' PSE Working Papers 2009-40, PSE (Ecole Normale Supérieure), revised September 2010.

Sassen, S. (1994) *Cities in a World Economy*, Thousand Oaks: SAGE Publications.

Schlesinger, P. (1987) *Putting 'Reality' Together: BBC News*, London, New York: Methuen.

Schmidt, T.S. (2007) 'A Wiki for Whistle-Blowers', *Time*, 22 January.

Schoenbach, K., De Waal, E. and Lauf, E. (2005) 'Research Note: Online and Print Newspapers. Their Impact on the Extent of the Perceived Public Agenda', *European Journal of Communication*, 20(2): 245–58.

Schudson, M. (1978) *Discovering the News: A Social History of American Newspapers*, New York: Basic Books.

——(1998) *The Good Citizen*, New York: The Free Press.

——(1999) 'What Public Journalism Knows about Journalism but Doesn't Know About "Public"', in T. Glasser (ed.) *The Idea of Public Journalism*, New York: Guilford Press: 118–34.

——(2001) 'The Objectivity Norm in American Journalism', *Journalism*, 2(2): 149–70.

——(2009) 'Factual Knowledge in the Age of Truthiness', in B. Zelizer (ed.) *The Changing Faces of Journalism: Tabloidization, Technology and Truthiness*, London: Routledge: 104–13.

——(2011) 'The First News Revolution of the Twenty-first Century', in *The Sociology of News*, 2nd edn, New York: Norton: 205–30.

Schudson, M. and Anderson, C. (2009) 'Objectivity, Professionalism and Truth-seeking in Journalism', in K. Wahl-Jorgensen and T. Hanitzsch (eds) *The Handbook of Journalism Studies*, London: Routledge: 88–101.

Schumpeter, J.A. (1939) *Business Cycles: A Theoretical, Historical and Statistical Analysis of the Capitalist Process*, New York: McGraw-Hill.

Sennett, R. (1986) *The Fall of Public Man*, London: Faber and Faber.

——(2008) *The Craftsman*, London: Allen Lane.

Servaes, J. (2009) 'We Are All Journalists Now!', *Journalism*, 10(3): 371–74.

Shah, H. (1996) 'Modernization, Marginalization, and Emancipation: Toward a Normative Model of Journalism and National Development', *Communicative Theory*, 6(2): 143–66.

Shirky, C. (2008) *Here Comes Everybody: The Power of Organizing without Organizations*, New York: Penguin Press.

Shoemaker, P.J. and Cohen, A. (eds) (2006) *News Around the World: Content, Practitioners and Publics*, New York: Routledge.

Siebert, F., Peterson, T. and Schramm, W. (1956) *Four Theories of the Press*, Urbana, IL: University of Illinois Press.

Sifry, M.L. (2011) *WikiLeaks and the Age of Transparency*, Berkeley, CA: Counterpoint.

Sigelman, L. (1973) 'Reporting the News: An Organizational Analysis', *American Journal of Sociology*, 79(1): 132–51.

Silverman, C. (2007) *Regret the Error: How Media Mistakes Pollute the Press and Imperil Free Speech*, New York: Sterling Publishing Co.

——(2008) 'Scrubbing Away Their Sins: You Can't Disappear your Errors Online', *Columbia Journalism Review*. Available: http://www.cjr.org/regret_the_error/scrubbing_away_their_sins.php (accessed 22 August 2011).

——(2010) 'How WikiLeaks Outsourced the Burden of Verification', *Columbia Journalism Review*, 30 July.

——(2011) 'To Delete or Not to Delete', *Columbia Journalism Review*. Available: http://www.cjr.org/behind_the_news/to_delete_or_not_to_delete.php?page=all (accessed 24 January 2011).

Singer, J. (2003) 'Who Are These Guys? The Online Challenge to the Notion of Journalistic Professionalism', *Journalism*, 4(2): 139–63.

——(2004) 'Strange Bedfellows? The Diffusion of Convergence in Four News Organizations', *Journalism Studies*, 5(1): 3–18.

——(2005) 'The Political J-Blogger "Normalizing" a New Media Form to Fit Old Norms and Practices', *Journalism*, 6(2): 173–98.

——(2006) 'Stepping Back from the Gate: Online Newspaper Editors and the Co-Production of Content in Campaign 2004', *Journalism and Mass Communication Quarterly*, 83(2): 265–80.

——(2007) 'Contested Autonomy: Professional and Popular Claims on Journalistic Norms', *Journalism Studies*, 8(1): 79–95.

——(2009) 'Separation within a Shared Space: Perceived Effects of User-generated Content on Newsroom Norms, Values and Routines', conference paper, Future of Journalism conference, School of Journalism, Media and Cultural Studies, University of Cardiff, September 2009.

——(2010) 'Journalism in the Network', in Allan, S. (ed.) *The Routledge Companion to News and Journalism*, London: Routledge: 277–86.

Singer, J.B. and Ashman, I. (2009) '"Comment is Free, but Facts are Sacred": User-generated Content and Ethical Constructs at the *Guardian*', *Journal of Mass Media Ethics*, 24(1): 3–21.

Skinner, D., Gasher, M.J. and Compton, J. (2001) 'Putting Theory to Practice: A Critical Approach to Journalism Studies', *Journalism: Theory, Practice and Criticism*, 2(3): 34–60.

Soloski, J. (1990) 'News Reporting and Professionalism: Some Constraints on the Reporting of the News', *Media, Culture & Society*, 11(4): 207–28.

Sparrow, B.H. (1999) *Uncertain Guardians: The News Media as a Political Institution*, Baltimore: Johns Hopkins University Press.

Sreedharan, C., Thorsen, E. and Allan, S. (2012) 'WikiLeaks and the Changing Forms of Information Politics in the Network Society', in E. Downey and M. Jones (eds) *Public Service, Governance and Web 2.0 Technologies: Future Trends in Social Media*, Hershey PA: IGI Global: 167–80.

Standage, T. (2011) 'Bulletins from the Future', *The Economist*, 11 July.

Stanton, R.C. (2007) *All News is Local: The Failure of the Media to Reflect World Events in a Globalized Age*, Jefferson, North Carolina: McFarland and Company.

Stanyer, J. (2007) *Modern Political Communication: Mediated Politics in Uncertain Times*, Cambridge: Polity.

Steele, C.A. and Barnhurst, K.G. (1996) 'The Journalism of Opinion: Network Coverage in U.S. Presidential Campaigns, 1968–1988', *Critical Studies in Mass Communication*, 13(3): 187–209.

Steele, J. (2009) 'Professionalism Online: How Malaysiakini Challenges Authoritarianism', *The International Journal of Press/Politics*, 14(1): 91–111.

Steiner, L. (2009) 'Disambiguating the "Media" and the "Media Plot"', *Journalism*, 10(3): 381–83.

Stewart, J. (2004) *America (The Book): A Citizen's Guide to Democracy Inaction*, New York: Warner Books.

Stohl, C. (2011) 'Paradoxes of Global Connectivity: Boundary Permeability, Technological Variability and Organisational Durability', keynote address, Annual Conference of the Australia and New Zealand Communication Association, University of Waikato, Hamilton, New Zealand, 6–8 July 2011. Available: http://coursecast.its.waikato.ac.nz/Panopto/Pages/Viewer/Default.aspx?id=08585dd2–40b3–4755-a852–54ed23b3e98da (accessed 1 February 2012).

Straubhaar, J.D. (2007) *World Television: From Global to Local*, Los Angeles, London, New Delhi, Singapore: Sage.

Stray, J. (2010) 'Is This the Future of Journalism?', *Foreign Policy*, 7 April.

Strom, S. (2010) 'Pentagon Sees a Threat from Online Muckrakers', *The New York Times*, 17 March.

Swiss Press Council (2008) 'Erklärung der Rechte und Pflichten der Journalistinnen und Journalisten'. Available: http://www.presserat.ch/24350.htm (accessed 22 August 2011).

Tapscott, D. and Williams, A.D. (2008) *Wikinomics. How Mass Collaboration Changes Everything*, expanded edn, London: Atlantic Books.

Taylor, C. (2011) 'Why Not Call it a Facebook Revolution?', *CNN.com*, 24 February. Available: http://articles.cnn.com/2011-02-24/tech/facebook.revolution_1_facebook-wael-ghonim-social-media?_s=PM:TECH (accessed 25 July 2011).

Television Critics Association (TCA) (2007) 'Award Winners'. Available: http://www.tvcriticsassociation.com/tca/node/154 (accessed 25 January 2008).

Tenore, M.J. (2011) 'Conflicting Reports of Gifford's Death were Understandable, but not Excusable', *Poynter*. Available: http://www.poynter.org/latest-news/top-stories/113876/conflicting-reports-of-giffords-death-were-understandable-but-not-excusable/ (accessed 24 January 2011).

The New York Times (2011) *Open Secrets: WikiLeaks, War and American Diplomacy*, e-book, ISBN: 978-0-615-43957-0.

Thiessen, M. (2010) 'WikiLeaks Must be Stopped', *The Washington Post*, 3 August.

Thomassen, J. (2010) *De Permanente Crisis van de Democratie [The Permanent Crisis of Democracy]*, Enschede: Universiteit Twente.

Thompson, B. (2003) 'Is Google Too Powerful?', BBC News website, February 21. Available: http://news.bbc.co.uk/1/hi/technology/2786761.stm (accessed 1 February 2012).

Thurman, N. (2008) 'Forums for Citizen Journalists? Adoption of User Generated Content Initiatives by Online News Media', *New Media & Society*, 10(1): 139–57.

Thussu, D.K. (2007) *News As Entertainment: The Rise of Global Infotainment*, London: Sage.

Tillinghast, W.A. (1982) 'Newspaper Errors: Reporters Dispute most Source Claims', *Newspaper Research Journal*, 3(Fall): 14–23.

Tong, Y.S. (2004) 'Malaysiakini: Threading a Tightrope of Political Pressure and Market Factors', in S. Gan, J. Gomez and U. Johannen (eds) *Asian Cyberactivism: Freedom of Expression and Media Censorship*, Bangkok: Friedrich Naumann Foundation: 270–317.

Torcal, M. and Montero, J.R. (2006) 'Political Disaffection in Comparative Perspective', in M. Torcal and J.R. Montero (eds) *Political Disaffection in Contemporary Democracies: Social Capital, Institutions, and Politics*, Abingdon: Routledge.

Torfing, J. (1999) *New Theories of Discourse. Laclau, Mouffe and Žižek*, Oxford: Blackwell.

Townend, J. (2009) 'Difficult to Get Western Media Attention on Kenyan Killings and Disappearances, says WikiLeaks Editor', *Journalism.co.uk*, 5 June. Available: http://www.journalism.co.uk/news/difficult-to-get-western-media-attention-on-kenyan-killings-and-disappearances-says-wikileaks-editor-/s2/a534659/ (accessed 2 February 2012).

Trice, M. (2010) 'Comment Fields and Content Analysis: A Means to Study Interaction on News Sites', Conference paper, Fourth International Conference on Online Deliberation, Leeds, England, July 2010.

Tsfati, Y. and Cappella, J. (2003) 'Do People Watch What They do not Trust? Exploring the Association between News Media Scepticism and Exposure', *Communication Research*, 30(5): 504–29.

——(2005) 'Why Do People Watch News They Do Not Trust? The Need for Cognition as a Moderator in the Association Between News Media Skepticism and Exposure', *Media Psychology*, 7(3): 251–71.

Tuchman, G. (1972) 'Objectivity as Strategic Ritual: An Examination of Newsmen's Notions of Objectivity', *American Journal of Sociology*, 77(4): 660–79.

——(1978) *Making News: A Study in the Construction of Reality*, New York: The Free Press.

Tulloch, J. (2007) 'Tabloid Citizenship: The *Daily Mirror* and the Invasions of Egypt (1956) and Iraq (2003)', *Journalism Studies*, 8(1): 42–60.

Turner, G. (2009) *Ordinary People and the Media: The Demotic Turn*, London: Sage.

UNESCO (1982) *Grunwald Declaration on Media Literacy*. Available: http://www.unesco.org/education/pdf/MEDIA_E.PDF (accessed 10 October 2011).

——(2011) *Media and Information Literacy: Curriculum for Teachers*. Available: http://unesdoc.unesco.org/images/0019/001929/192971e.pdf (accessed 10 October 2011).

Urban, C. (1999) *Why Credibility has been Dropping: A Study for the American Society of News Editors*, American Society of News Editors. Available: http://asne.org/kiosk/reports/99reports/1999examiningourcredibility/index.html (accessed 2 August 2011).

Vallone, R.P., Ross, L., and Lepper, M.R. (1985) 'The Hostile Media Phenomenon: Biased Perception and Perceptions of Media Bias in Coverage of the Beirut Massacre', *Journal of Personality and Social Psychology*, 49(3): 577–85.

Van Aelst, P., et al. (2008) 'The Fourth Estate as Superpower? An Empirical Study of Perceptions of Media Power in Belgium and the Netherlands', *Journalism Studies*, 9(4): 494–511.

Van Bauwel, S. and Carpentier, N. (eds) (2010) *Trans-reality Television: The Transgression of Reality, Genre, Politics and Audience*, Maryland: Lexington Books.

Van Cuilenburg, J., Neijens, P. and Scholten, O. (eds) (1999) *Media in Overvloed [Media in Abundance]*, Amsterdam: Amsterdam University Press.

Van Drom, A. (2010) '"Perhaps this is not Fiction": The Discursive Construction of National and Regional Identities in Belgium's Public Television Broadcast Hoax on Flemish Independence.' *European Journal of Cultural Studies*, 13(1): 81–97.

Van Zoonen, L. (2005) *Entertaining the Citizen*, Lanham, MD: Rowman & Littlefield.
——(2012) '"I"-Pistemology: Changing Truth Claims in Popular and Political Culture', *European Journal of Communication*, 27(1), forthcoming.
Vobič, I. (2007) 'The Normalization of the Blog in Journalism: Online Newspapers of Slovene Traditional Media', *Medij. Istraž*, 13(2): 59–83.
Volkmer, I. (2003) 'The Global Network Society and the Global Public Sphere', *Development*, 46(1): 9–16.
Wahl-Jorgensen, K. (2001) 'Letters to the Editor as a Forum for Public Deliberation: Modes of Publicity and Democratic Debate', *Critical Studies in Media Communication*, 18(3): 303–20.
——(2006) 'Letters to the Editor in Local and Regional Newspapers: Giving Voice to the Readers', in B. Franklin (ed.) *Local Journalism and Local Media: Making the Local News*, London: Routledge: 221–31.
Wahl-Jorgensen, K. and Hanitzsch, T. (eds) (2009) *The Handbook of Journalism Studies*, London: Routledge.
Walker, R. (2001) 'The News According to Blogs', *Slate*, 7 March. Available: http://www. slate.com/id/102057/ (accessed 1 February 2012).
Wall, M.A. (2003) 'Social Movements and the Net: Activist Journalism Goes Digital', in K. Kawamoto (ed.) *Digital Journalism. Emerging Media and the Changing Horizons of Journalism*, Lanham, MD: Rowman & Littlefield: 113–22.
Ward, S. (2004) *The Invention of Journalism Ethics: The Path to Objectivity and Beyond*, Montreal: McGill-Queen's University Press.
Wardle, C. and Williams, A. (2008) *ugc@thebbc: Understanding its Impact upon Contributors, Non-contributors and BBC News*, Cardiff University Report to the BBC Knowledge Exchange Programme and the Arts and Humanities Research Council. Available: www. bbc.co.uk/blogs/knowledgeexchange/cardiffone.pdf (accessed 20 January 2011).
——(2010) 'Beyond User-generated Content: A Production Study Examining the Ways in which UGC is Used at the BBC', *Media, Culture & Society*, 32(5): 781–99.
Warrick, D.D. (1981) 'Leadership Styles and their Consequences', *Journal of Experiential Learning and Simulation*, 3(3–4): 155–72.
Weaver, D.H. (1998) 'Journalists Around the World: Commonalities and Differences', in D.H. Weaver (ed.) *The Global Journalist: News People around the World*, Cresskill, NJ: Hampton.
Weaver, D.H. and Wilhoit, G.C. (1996) *The American Journalist in the 1990s: US News People at the End of an Era*, Mahwah, NJ: Erlbaum.
Weaver, D.H. et al. (2007) *The American Journalist in the 21st Century: U.S. News People at the Dawn of a New Millennium*, London: Lawrence Erlbaum Associates.
Weber, M. (1958) *From Max Weber: Essays in Sociology*, New York: Oxford University Press.
Westerståhl, J. (1983) 'Objective News Reporting', *Communication Research*, 10: 403–24.
Wetzenbacher, B. (1998) *So Stimmt's: Die Korrekturspalte – Teil eines Innerredaktionellen Qualitätsmanagementsystems?*, Graduate Thesis, Freie Universität Berlin.
Whitaker, B. (1981) *News Limited: Why You Can't Read All About It*, London: Minority Press Group.
Whitney, D.C. and Wartella, E. (1988) 'The Public as Dummies', *Knowledge: Creation, Diffusion, Utilization*, 10(2): 99–110.
Wijfjes, H. (2004) 'Getting Truth or Getting Pizzas: A Historical Perspective on the Debate on Journalism and Public Trust in Politics', in F.R. Ankersmit and H. te Velde (eds) *Trust: Cement of Democracy?*, Leuven: Peeters: 125–43.
Williams, R. (1983) *Towards 2000*, London: Chatto and Windus.
Winkler, R. (2002) 'Deliberation on the Internet: Talkboard Discussions on the UK Parliamentarian Elections 2001', *Medien Journal*, 4: 1–20.
Winner, L. (1978) *Autonomous Technology: Technics-out-of-control as a Theme in Political Thought*, Cambridge: MIT Press.
Witschge, T. (2011a) 'Changing Audiences, Changing Journalism?', in P. Lee-Wright, A. Phillips and T. Witschge (eds) *Changing Journalism*, London: Routledge: 117–34.

——(2011b) 'The "Tyranny" of Technology', in P. Lee-Wright, A. Phillips and T. Witschge (eds) *Changing Journalism*, London: Routledge: 99–114.

Witschge, T., Fenton, N. and Freedman, D. (2010) *Protecting the News: Civil Society and the Media*, London: Carnegie UK. Available: http://www.carnegietrust.co.uk/publications/protecting_the_news– civil_society_and_the_media (accessed December 2010).

Witschge, T. and Nygren, G. (2009) 'Journalism: A Profession under Pressure?', *Journal of Media Business Studies*, 6(1): 37–59.

Wolff, M. (2010) 'Can WikiLeaks Save Journalism?', *Newser.com*, 27 July, Available: http://www.newser.com/off-the-grid/post/511/can-wikileaks-save-journalism.html (accessed 2 February 2012).

Woodstock, L. (2002) 'Public Journalism's Talking Cure: An Analysis of the Movement's "Problem" and "Solution" Narratives', *Journalism: Theory, Practice and Criticism*, 3(1): 37–55.

Wyatt, E. (2011) 'Judge Rejects an S.E.C. Deal With CitiGroup', *New York Times*, November 29, 1, 4.

Xin, X. (2010) 'The Impact of "Citizen Journalism" on Chinese Media and Society', *Journalism Practice*, 4(3): 333–44.

Young, D. and Tisinger, R. (2006) 'Dispelling Late-Night Myths', *Press/Politics*, 11(3): 113–34.

Zelizer, B. (1993a) 'Has Communication Explained Journalism?', *Journal of Communication*, 43(4): 80–88.

——(1993b) 'Journalists as Interpretive Communities', *Critical Studies in Mass Communication*, 10(3): 219–37.

——(2004a) 'When Facts, Truth and Reality are God-Terms: On Journalism's Uneasy Place in Cultural Studies', *Communication and Critical/Cultural Studies*, 1(1): 100–119.

——(2004b) *Taking Journalism Seriously: News and the Academy*, Thousand Oaks, CA, London: Sage.

——(ed.) (2009) *The Changing Faces of Journalism: Tabloidization, Technology and Truthiness*, London: Routledge.

——(2010) 'Journalists as Interpretive Communities, Revisited', in S. Allan (ed.) *The Routledge Companion to News and Journalism*, London and New York: Routledge.

INDEX

60 Minutes 28, 180

Aargauer Zeitung 50
accountability 21–2, 27, 39, 41
accuracy 45–6, 48–58, 213
Adbusters 142
adversary culture 196
advertising 4–6, 76–7, 219
Afghanistan war logs 149–55
Al Jazeera 103–4, 219
alternative journalism 131–2, 136–9, 141, 158; as separate from professional journalism 68, 80–1, 132–8, 141, 203–5; interaction with professional journalism 69, 91–2, 105, 136–42
Arab Spring 97–8, 219–20
Assange, Julian 83, 147, 153–7, 159
The Atlantic 151
audiences 1, 3–5, 8–10, 18–19, 25, 29, 80, 92–3, 116, 134–5, 175–6, 187, 218–19; *see also* participatory journalism

Basler Zeitung 50
BBC 24, 64, 68, 80, 82, 84, 86, 94–5, 98, 104, 116, 133–5, 163–4, 166, 168, 170
Beck, Ulrich 91
Becker, Howard 111
Bernama TV 104
Berner Zeitung 50
Bild 24
Blair, Jayson 30
blogging 19, 20, 23, 26, 55, 66, 68–9, 98, 104–6, 108–11, 123, 147–8, 166–7, 197–8

Breekijzer (Crowbar) 25
Broersma, Marcel 192

cable news 173, 184–6
Castells, Manuel 89, 92, 94–5
CBS Evening News 185
Channel News Asia 104
Charnley, Mitchell 48–50
citizen journalism; *see* alternative journalism
citizenship; *see* democracy
civic journalism; *see* public journalism
climate change 3, 120, 122
CNBC 183–4, 186
CNN 56, 95, 104, 183–4, 186, 195
The Colbert Report 185, 188
Columbia Journalism Review 157
Comedia 132, 136
comment fields 114, 117, 125–6, 134–5; different functions 19, 118–24
commercialization 22–3, 142, 168–71
convergence 78, 116, 160, 162–4, 170
Cooke, Janet 30
craftsmanship 167
Craigslist 5, 197
credibility 18, 29, 44–8, 50, 52–4, 57, 109–10
Crossfire 173, 186
crowd–sourcing 58, 83, 197
cynicism 15–17, 212–13

The Daily Beast 157
Daily Express 37–8
Daily Mirror 28, 30–1, 34–5, 37–8, 40, 42
Daily Record/Sunday Mail 76

The Daily Show 26, 173–5, 179–82, 188, 196
Daily Star 37–8
database logic 42–3
Davies, Nick 1, 6, 149–50, 159
De Standard 24
de-industrialization 3–8
democracy 2–4, 9–11, 15, 19–20, 25–6,
    43, 66, 105, 126, 196–7; deliberative
    democracy 115, 118–19, 125, 218;
    citizenship 204, 216–18
Democracy Now! 156
democratization of media 115, 134, 204
demotic turn 132–5
Der Spiegel 149–50, 154–5, 157, 159
de-ritualization 8–11, 176
Dewey, John 217
dislocation 65–7, 70

economic downfall, 1–2, 4–6, 135,
    168–71, 204–5, 219
The Economist 147
Elsevier 40
emotion 7, 174, 218
ethics 11, 38, 46, 63, 85, 112, 148, 185, 205

Forbes 211
Foreign Policy 148
form 19, 44, 77, 192–3
Foucault, Michel 10
Fox News 56, 183–4, 186–7, 195
Frontline 180

gatekeeping 63, 69–70, 134
gatewatching 10, 86, 202
GeenStijl 26
Glass, Stephen 30, 86
Glasser, Theodore 32
Good Night, and Good Luck 175
Greenslade, Roy 38
Guardian 38, 58, 79, 80, 82–3, 117–19,
    121–4, 147, 149–50, 152, 155, 157, 159,
    169, 175

Habermas, Jürgen 114, 125; *see also* public
    sphere
Hallin, Daniel 60
high modernism 60–1, 193
hoaxes 28–31, 85–6
hostile media effect 206
Hoyer, Svennik 191–2
Huffington Post 6, 188, 214

Il Giornale di Brescia 50
Il Giornale di Sicilia 50

Il Resto del Carlino 50
Il Secolo XIX 50
industrial logic 4–7
Indymedia 139–40
infotainment 79–80, 176, 184–5
innovation 214–16
Investigative News Network 199

jazz 144–5
journalism education and training 138,
    143, 162, 177, 179
journalism routines 162, 168–70
Journalism.co.uk 147
journalistic paradigm 7, 29, 31–4, 42–4,
    174, 191–5, 199

Keller, Bill 150–1, 155, 157

leadership 215–16
L'Eco di Bergamo 50
Liquid Modernity 61, 65–7, 70–1

Manchester Evening News (MEN Group)
    162–3, 165, 168
Manovich, Lev 42–3
Matheson, Donald 192–3
McCombs, Maxwell 110–11
McIntyre, Jamie 154
Media Awareness Network 177
media literacy 174–5, 177–9, 184–7
Media Matters for America 175
media rituals; *see* de-ritualization
MediaShift 214
metanarratives of journalism 175, 181
Mill, John Stuart 21
Morgan, Piers 35, 37, 40
MSNBC 183–4, 186–7, 195
Multimedia newsrooms; *see* convergence

National Public Radio (NPR), 56,
    98, 195
network journalism 90–100, 112–13, 198
networked communication 5–7, 43, 90,
    101–3
Neue Luzerner Zeitung 24
new media 2, 4–5, 8–9, 19, 46, 54–7,
    65–6, 75–6, 89, 101–2, 160–2, 214
New Republic 86
New York Times 56, 86, 148–50, 153–7,
    159, 179, 197–8
The New Yorker 28, 158
News of the World 25, 76, 176, 205, 207
Newswipe 175
Nightline 180

norms 7, 23, 26, 29, 32, 62–3, 107–9,
   137–9, 145–6, 158, 161, 164–6, 171,
   183–6, 201–2
novels 193, 195

objectivity 7, 32–3, 41–2, 44, 61, 64–6,
   84–5, 186
Observer 117
OhmyNews 138

paradigm repair 29–31, 42, 62; *see also*
   journalistic paradigm
participatory journalism 82–3, 96–7,
   115–16, 120, 124–6, 165–6, 197–8, 203,
   205, 216–17
Pentagon Papers 153
performativity 11, 31, 33, 35, 42, 84, 145,
   157–8
personalization 1, 5, 7–8, 10
Pew Research Center 16, 45, 76–7, 115,
   181
Pittsburgh Post-Gazette 155
political economy 137
Politico.com 159
popular culture and journalism 86, 175, 207
PowNed 26
Poynter.org 155
PR 49, 168–9
Press Association (PA), 168–9
PressThink; *see* Rosen, Jay
professional identity 2–3, 7–9, 60–70,
   77–8, 81–2, 201–2, 207
professionalization 166–7, 194, 205, 213
ProPublica 199
public good 4, 11, 27, 63, 66, 82, 158,
   165, 167–71, 188, 203–5
public journalism 135–6, 142
public pedagogy 175–9, 185–7
public service ideal; *see* public good
public sphere 114–15, 118–19, 120, 124, 126

Rally to Restore Sanity 173
redactional journalism 66, 140, 184
reflexive modernization 10, 176, 183
responsiveness 18, 22–7
Reuters 148
Rolling Stone 179
Rosen, Jay 152, 175
RTE 24

Schudson, Michael 4, 7, 32–3
Scoop (website) 138

Scotland On Sunday 76
Sennett, Richard 70, 167
sensationalism 19, 173
Sesame Street 175
Singer, Jane 68
social institution 201, 203–4
social media 10, 54–7, 90, 97–9, 115, 125,
   197, 203, 219
social responsibility 20–1, 23–4, 63
sources 30, 47–8, 51–3, 107–12, 121–3,
   155–6
The Spectator 199
Steffens, Lincoln 7
Stewart, Jon 173–4, 183
Südostschweiz 50
Sunday Herald 76
The Sunday Times 77

Tages-Anzeiger 50
Telegraaf 39
The Telegraph 82
Time 146, 153, 179
The Times 77, 79
transparency 27, 33, 56
trust 11, 16–18, 27, 42–8, 85–7, 175–6,
   180, 186, 195–6, 200, 205–8, 210–14; in
   politics 16–17, 27; *see also* cynicism,
   credibility
truth 7, 31–4, 42, 61, 84, 183; truthiness
   19, 26, 44, 69–70, 80, 186
Tuchman, Gaye 32, 110–12
Turner, Graeme 132–3

UNESCO 178–9
user-generated content 78–80, 99, 104–13,
   115–17, 133–5, 203–4; amateur
   photography 34–5, 37, 98, 134

values; *see* norms
Volkskrant 28, 30–1, 35–9, 41–2

Walski Brian, 30
Washington Post 58, 152, 158, 194
weblogs; *see* blogging
whistle-blowing 146–7, 150, 155
WikiLeaks 145–9, 151, 158, 199;
   interaction with traditional news outlets
   83, 150–7
Williams, Raymond 131–2, 139
Wired 150, 214
World Values Survey 205–7
Worlds of Journalism Study 201–2, 207

THE GLOBAL JOURNALIST
in the 21st Century

Edited by David H. Weaver & Lars Willnat

R

The Global Journalist in the 21st Century

Edited by **David H. Weaver**, Indiana University, USA and **Lars Willnat**, Indiana University, USA

Series: *Routledge Communication*

The Global Journalist in the 21st Century systematically assesses the demographics, education, socialization, professional attitudes and working conditions of journalists in various countries around the world. This book updates the original *Global Journalist* (1998) volume with new data, adding more than a dozen countries, and provides material on comparative research about journalists that will be useful to those interested in doing their own studies.

The editors put together this collection working under the assumption that journalists' backgrounds, working conditions and ideas are related to what is reported (and how it is covered) in the various news media round the world, in spite of societal and organizational constraints, and that this news coverage matters in terms of world public opinion and policies.

May 2012: 254 x 178: 596pp
Hb: 978-0-415-88576-8: £140.00
Ebk: 978-0-203-14867-9